No. 2897
$26.95

HARD DISK MANAGE-MENT

with MS-DOS® and PC-DOS®

DAN GOOKIN AND ANDY TOWNSEND

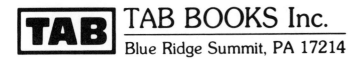

TAB BOOKS Inc.

Blue Ridge Summit, PA 17214

FIRST EDITION
FIRST PRINTING

Copyright © 1987 by Dan Gookin and Andy Townsend
Printed in the United States of America

Library of Congress Cataloging in Publication Data

Gookin, Dan.
Hard disk management with MS-DOS and PC-DOS.

Includes index.
1. File organization (Computer science) 2. MS-DOS
(Computer operating system) 3. PC DOS (Computer
operating system) 4. Magnetic disks. I. Townsend,
Andy. II. Title.
QA76.9.F5G66   1987   005.74   87-7097
ISBN 0-8306-0697-1
ISBN 0-8306-2897-5 (pbk.)

Questions regarding the content of this book
should be addressed to:

Reader Inquiry Branch
Editorial Department
TAB BOOKS Inc.
P.O. Box 40
Blue Ridge Summit, PA 17214

Contents

Introduction   vi

Part 1
Hard Disk Organization

1 The Basics of Disk Storage   3

Data Representation—Magnetic versus Electronic Storage—Hard Disks versus Floppy Diskettes—
Disk Formats—Disk Access—Random versus Sequential File Storage

2 Preparing Hard Disks   17

Logical versus Physical Formatting—Preparing a Hard Disk—Altering the Structure of the Hard Disk—
Installing New Versions of DOS—Performing a Low-Level Format

3 Filenames and Directories   34

Filenames and Wild Cards—Disk Directories and File Allocation Tables—The Directory Command—
Find, More and Sort—Redirecting Directory Output

4 Other Essential DOS Commands   48

The Role of the Command Processor—Resident Commands—External Commands

5 Subdirectories and Paths   72

Hard Disk Organization Strategies — Subdirectory Commands — Using DOS Commands with
Subdirectories—The PATH and TREE Commands

6 Batch File Programming 97

DOS Macros—Automatic Startup Batch Files—Messages, Prompts and Variables—Replaceable Parameters

7 Batch File Menus 111

Programming Techniques—Menu Systems—Developing a Simple Menu System—Submenus and Help Screens

8 Fancy Menus 137

Improving Your Menu Screens—Working with EDLIN—A Summary of EDLIN Commands—Adding Borders to Your Menu with EDLIN—Fancy Menu Screens with WordPerfect—Controlling the Screen Characteristics

9 DOS Shells 166

Menu Generators—Automenu—Password Security and File Encryption—DOS Shells and Front Ends—DOS-A-MATIC—Coming Up

**Part 2
Hard Disk Security**

10 Backing Up Data and Programs 185

Preventative Maintenance—The BACKUP Command—The RESTORE Command—Some Final Notes on BACKUP & RESTORE—The XCOPY Program—The REPLACE Program—Commercially Available Backup Programs—Extra Hard Disk Precaution: PARK—A Daily BACKUP Batch File

11 Tape, Removable Disk, and Fault-Tolerant Systems 202

Streaming Tape Systems—Fault Tolerant Systems—Removable Hard Disks

12 Password Security 211

A Batch File to Test for Passwords—Other Ways of Protecting the Hard Disk

13 Hidden Files and Data Encryption 222

How DOS Hides Files—What Is Data Encryption?

14 Tracking Computer Usage 239

A Batch File Program for Tracking Usage

**Part 3
Hard Disk Optimization**

15 Storage Optimization 249

Review of Disk Formats and Random Storage—Formatting Techniques for Increasing and Optimizing Storage—Cleaning Up the Directory—Archiving Programs—Hardware Solutions

16 Disk Access Optimization 266

Overlay Files—EMS Memory—RAM Disks and How They Work—Disk Caching—Commercially Available Disk Caches

17 Shareware Programs 279

Supplemental Program Contents—Installing the Programs—The MANUAL and .DOC Files—PKX34A20.COM—AUTOMENU.ARC—DISKTOOL.ARC—PACKDISK.ARC—TOOLS1.ARC

Appendix A: Summary of DOS Commands   **290**

Appendix B: Summary of EDLIN Commands   **296**

Appendix C: Extended ASCII Chart   **299**

Appendix D: Product Names and Addresses   **304**

Index   **306**

Introduction

There is a revolution taking place in the personal computer industry. While this revolution is driven by technology, it is affecting the type and range of applications for which personal computers are being used. At the heart of this revolution is the declining cost in computer power. Dramatic cost reductions have taken place in processing power, random access memory, and data storage. For example, in 1980, the cost of one megabyte of storage was over $100. Now, a megabyte costs around $30. At the same time, personal computers have become increasingly powerful and sophisticated. The typical 8-bit, 64K, dual drive IBM PC that used to be the desktop standard has been replaced by the 16-bit, 512K, AT with a 30-megabyte hard drive and a 1.2 megabyte floppy drive. And even more powerful machines are just around the corner.

Until recently, personal computers with hard disk drives were too expensive for home and small business use. A ten megabyte hard drive unit alone used to cost over $1,000. PC's equipped with hard drives were mainly used for applications involving large amounts of data. After all, that's what hard disks are for—storing lots of data, right? But times have changed.

The latest generation of personal computers, with faster microprocessors and increased memory capacities, are changing the applications programs used with microcomputers. Word-processing programs, spreadsheets, and database programs are all getting faster, fancier, and bigger. Another trend in software is the move to integrated programs which incorporate the functions of a word processor, spreadsheet, database, graphics and more into a single package. Such programs tend to be massive, consuming floppy diskettes like bagels at a bar mitzvah.

While many of these programs can still be run on floppy drive computers, most recommend the use of a hard disk, and some actually require one. Even if it is possible to run large applications on a floppy-drive system, the amount of disk swapping involved makes their use tedious at best. In fact, floppy diskettes have been dubbed "swappy" diskettes by disgruntled users who face the constant task of replacing diskettes every time their software needs to access a different portion of the program. For this reason alone, many personal and small business computer users are switching to hard-disk systems.

Paralleling the trend toward larger application programs is the continuing decline in the cost of data storage. The same ten-megabyte hard drive, which cost over $1,000 several years ago, can be purchased today for under $350. Also, the storage capacities of personal computer hard drives are increasing. Today, the *de facto* standard hard drive is 20 megabytes, with the 30 megabyte drive edging this standard out even as this book is being printed. Hard drives capable of storing over a gigabyte, or one billion characters of information, are presently available for use with personal computers.

Finally, small business and departmental computing is on the rise. Where manual systems, time-sharing, and centralized data processing once accounted for much of the data handling of small businesses and individual departments, today most small businesses and departments within large organizations are opting for on-site and distributed data processing.

Clearly, the increasing need for hard-disk computer systems to run larger applications and manage more data, coupled with the decreasing cost of hard disk technology, has led to an expanding number of hard disk personal computer systems in operation. Most of these systems are based on the MS-DOS operating system. (PC-DOS is IBM's own version of this widely adopted microcomputer operating system.) In fact, the latest generation of MS-DOS computers, those based on the 80×86 microprocessor, are designed to be configured with some form of hard disk. Even their floppy diskette drives store more data.

This book is about taming your hard disk. The subject of hard disks is a bewildering one. Even experienced computer users can become lost in the maze of megabytes and special commands associated with hard disks. The differences in technology, data storage capacities, and commands separate hard disk computer systems from those employing floppy diskette drives.

On the one hand, it can be said that hard disks are nothing more than rigid floppy diskettes. There is nothing conceptually different in the way they store data. It is only their rigidity that allows them to store higher quantities, or *densities,* of data. On the other hand, hard disk technology, and the increased data handling capacity that goes with it, engender an entirely new set of problems not encountered with floppy drives.

The special problems associated with hard disks can be broken down into three major areas of concern. The first, and most obvious, is the need for some means of organizing the massive storage capacity of a hard disk. Unless the drive is being used to maintain a single, enormous database, it is likely that there will be hundreds, if not thousands, of different program and data files stored on it. Keeping track of programs and data can be a daunting proposition, especially to someone who is unfamiliar with computers in the first place.

The first section of this book describes several methods for organizing your hard disk into manageable units. You will learn how to divide your hard disk into partitions and subdirectories. You will also learn how to create professional looking menus and programs for accessing your programs and data. These techniques will take the hassle out or your hard disk and leave the power readily available at your fingertips.

A second concern to hard disk owners is the problem of security. The issue of security includes both data and program security. First, of course, you want to make sure your data is secure from accidental loss resulting from a hard disk failure. Hard disks do occasionally fail, and when they do, the data stored on them is usually lost. Also, people sometimes forget and reformat their hard disks by mistake. Again, data may be lost. The second section of this book describes methods for duplicating the data stored on your hard disk to prevent the permanent loss of valuable data.

Hard disk security extends beyond protecting data from accidental loss. If your computer system will be shared by others, or if your computer is accessible to unauthorized use, you have a different type of security problem. On the one hand, you need to ensure that multiple users do not accidentally destroy each others' data. On the other, you need to be sure that confidential data is secure from prying and tampering. Password security and data cryption are two features which can be added to your system to protect confidential data. This book describes a variety of techniques and programs which can be employed to insure your data against security violations.

A third concern of hard disk users is performance. When you first begin using a hard disk, the contrast between the hard disk system and floppy systems is striking. This is due to the reduced time required by the disk drive to read in data and programs from the hard disk. Once you get used to this increased performance, you take it for granted. However, for reasons discussed in this book, a hard disk's performance deteriorates as more files are added to it. This deterioration can significantly slow down your computer system. The final section of this book describes a number of techniques and tricks for enhancing the performance of your hard disk.

Personal computer users are often categorized according to their experience and the amount of time they spend working with computers into novices, advanced, and power users. Of course, as with any such scheme, there is actually a continuum, and you may fall anywhere between the rankest rookie and the most hardened "tech weenie." The authors have made every effort to make this book accessible to all readers, including those at both ends of the computer-user spectrum.

If you are new to computers, or if this is your first hard drive system, you will find a wealth of information describing the technology and terminology involved. You will also find step-by-step instructions for formatting your hard disk and storing programs onto it. You will probably find these instructions easier to follow than those provided with your Disk Operating System manual.

Novice users will also appreciate the information on subdirectories and the various commands associated with multiple directories. The information covered in the first five chapters of this book is devoted to discussions of hard-disk technology, preparing hard disks for use, and commands associated with subdirectories and paths. As the novice user becomes comfortable working with files and programs stored in different subdirectories, he or she will want to move onto the more advanced subjects covered in the later chapters.

Advanced users will find the information on menu systems and batch file programming particularly useful. Using the information and programs provided with this book and the optional supplemental programs diskette, they will be able to design and create professional-looking menu systems for use by themselves and less experienced users.

The topics of data security and improved performance, covered in Part 2 and Part 3 of this book, will also be of interest to advanced users.

Power users will find the utilities provided on the supplemental programs diskette to be worth the price of the book. These utilities provide sophisticated file management; a fast, professional menu generator; file encryption and attribute manipulation; and disk storage optimization. Power users will also find some of the tricks for providing security and logging computer usage of interest. Some of these tricks are not documented in the DOS technical reference manual.

While many of the techniques described in this book may be implemented directly from the text, some of the most powerful and useful applications require special utility programs.

A diskette is offered by PC-SIG that contains special purpose programs for creating menus, locating files, hiding and encrypting files, enhancing the performance of your hard disk, and much more. The programs contained on the programs diskette have been compiled by authors in cooperation with the PC-SIG Library. Most of the programs are in the *public domain*. That is, they have been made available to anyone who wishes to use them, and they may be freely duplicated and passed on to others.

Other programs contained on the programs diskette are made available to you on a shareware basis. These shareware programs are copyrighted and are provided to you for trial use. If you find that you like a particular program and plan to use it on a regular basis, you are asked to send the owner of the copyright a fee. Shareware fees are quite reasonable and are well worth the investment. Once you send in your fee, you become a registered user of the shareware program. As improvements are made to the program, you will receive updates automatically. Also, you may call the shareware company directly if you need telephone support.

Remember, shareware programmers are in business just like anyone else. They usually offer excellent products for a fraction of what you would pay for commercial software with similar features. Each of the shareware programs contained on the supplemental programs diskette has been tested by the authors and found to be of high quality. Shareware programs are identified as such either with an initial sign-on message or in a special documentation file. Instructions for registering and the amount of the registration fee are included in the sign-on message or the documentation file.

In addition to public domain and shareware programs, there is a host of commercial programs available for performing special functions associated with hard disks. Such special-purpose programs are referred to as *utilities*. There are utilities for backing up the data stored on your hard disk, utilities for managing files and data, utilities for creating menus, and still other utilities for improving the performance of your hard disk. Some of these programs are well worth their purchase price in terms of the time and effort they will save you in the long run.

There is also a large market in special-purpose hardware devices for use with hard-disk computer systems. Most of these are designed to perform high-speed backup of the data stored on your hard disk. These products include streaming tape units, removable *Bernoulli* drives, and on fault-tolerant systems. Other units are designed to improve the hardware performance of your hard disk.

A number of commercially available programs and hardware components are reviewed in this book. The authors are not making any recommendations regarding any of these products, nor do they receive any financial remuneration from the publishers of these programs. Information has been provided solely for your convenience in determining if you should purchase any of these products for your own use.

Part of the purpose of this book is to educate you about hard disk technology. While the authors have done their best to avoid overly technical discussions, it is in your own interest to understand the terminology associated with this technology. When a new term is introduced, it appears in italics. The term is defined in the paragraph in which it is introduced. The primary reference in the index refers to this initial definition.

Throughout the text of this book, you will be shown new commands. Most of these will be from the PC-DOS or MS-DOS operating system, or from one of the utility programs associated with these operating systems. The authors have followed the format of the MS-DOS users manual in listing the syntax of commands. Commands are shown in uppercase, with user supplied information, such as drive designators and file specification, in lowercase. Optional information is displayed in brackets. Optional command parameters are displayed in uppercase within brackets. For example, the syntax of the FORMAT command is shown as:

FORMAT [d:] [/S]

The authors have adopted the convention of displaying commands in uppercase, although DOS does not require this. When referring to disk drives in the text, only the letter corresponding to the drive is used. However, in commands, the full-drive designator, including the colon, is included. When you are instructed to enter commands, they will appear according to the following format: The computer display will be shown in regular typeface, and the keystrokes you are to enter will be shown in boldface. It is assumed that you are to press the Enter key at the conclusion of each command. For example, suppose you are to enter the command to format the hard disk, including the option to place the system files on the hard disk. Assume that the A drive is the floppy drive. The command would be displayed as follows:

A>FORMAT C:/S

Every attempt has been made to ensure that the information contained within this book is as easy to follow as possible. While the subject matter is at times difficult and technical, the style of the book is friendly and unintimidating. The authors hope that you find this book interesting and useful in helping you tame your own hard disk.

Part 1
Hard Disk Organization

Chapter 1

The Basics of Disk Storage

To many people hard disks, with their massive storage capabilities and "black box" appearance, may seem a bit mysterious. This is especially true for novice computer users, who often find the thought of all that storage space intimidating. If you feel this way about your hard disk, don't worry. This book will help dispel the mysteries of megabytes, paths, and partitions and put you firmly in command of your hard disk.

Remember, the computer is just a tool, albeit a very powerful one, which you ultimately control. As tools go, your computer is really quite simple to learn and use. However, computers represent a different type of tool than you may be used to working with. Computers have been referred to as "mind tools" which is an apt description.

Although computers consist of various hardware components, such as keyboards, screens, CPU's, and storage devices, what causes them to run the way we want them to is software. You can't see software; you can't touch it (although you can see and hold the floppy diskette that contains the software).

Software is the ultimate "mind tool" because you control it by understanding how it works. As you have probably learned by now, an excellent computer program which is not adequately explained through documentation is a pretty useless tool. The software itself is just as good whether it is well-documented or not, but its value as a tool is limited by the user's lack of understanding.

This same concept applies to your hard disk. Whether you have recently upgraded your computer to add some type of hard disk storage device or just purchased an XT or AT compatible computer, you must gain some basic understanding of how it operates before you can use it successfully. Of course, this is true of any powerful tool. How useful would your automobile be if you didn't know how to turn it on, drive it, and maintain it? The automobile analogy is quite helpful in explaining why you need some elementary knowledge about your hard disk and how it operates.

Consider the two types of knowledge you need in order to use your automobile effectively. First, you need "how to" knowledge—commonly called "know how." You need to "know how" to turn it on, operate the various switches and pedals, steer, brake, and so on. But you also need some "why" knowledge as well. At a minimum, you need to know "why" the car goes when you press on the accelerator pedal. What would happen if your car ran out of gas on the freeway and you hadn't a clue as to why it stopped running?

Your basic understanding of how your automobile works helps you maintain it in proper working order and diagnose what's wrong when it isn't. This type of knowledge is frequently referred to as "practical theory." While you don't have to know all the technical details about how your automobile works, a little practical theory can go a long way.

This chapter provides some practical theory relating to hard disk technology. Although there is no "how to" information involved, the concepts and terms presented here serve as the foundation for the remainder of the book. If terms like sector, recording density, and access time are unfamiliar to you, you should definitely read this chapter before proceeding any further. If you already have some understanding of magnetic storage and how hard disks differ from their floppy cousins, you can skim this material and go on to Chapter 2.

DATA REPRESENTATION

The first step in understanding how computer storage works is to master the concept of *bits* and *bytes*. You've probably heard these two terms used before, and you may know that bytes are made out of bits. Bits are the basic units of data storage. A bit can have one of two values: zero or one. For this reason, computer data is often referred to as *binary*.

A single zero or one does not contain much information, however. For this reason bits are grouped together in clusters called "bytes." The most common grouping size for bytes is eight bits, although seven-bit and ten-bit bytes are frequently used as well. It takes at least one byte to represent any useful data, such as a character or a number.

Computers generally process whole bytes, or groups of bytes, when manipulating data. The number of bytes of data a computer can work with at one time is called its *word length* and depends upon the type of microprocessor it contains. The early microcomputers employed 8-bit microprocessors, while the IBM AT utilizes a 16-bit microprocessor. In practical terms, this means that a PC can process and manipulate two bytes of data at a time. Some personal computers, such as the Apple Macintosh, have 32 bit word lengths.

When working with data, your computer is able to distinguish between *alphanumeric* and *numeric* data. Alphanumeric data include text and digits (0 through 9), as long as the digits have no arithmetic value. A street address, such as "123 Any St." is an example of alphanumeric data.

To represent alphanumeric data, your computer uses a coding scheme known as the *ASCII code*. Every character on the keyboard, including both upper and lowercase letters, is given its own code value in terms of zeroes and ones. For example, the capital letter "A" has the ASCII value 01000001 and the digit "9" has the value 00111001.

Whenever you strike the capital letter "A", the ASCII byte "01000001" is transmitted up the keyboard cable to your computer for input.

Numeric data is coded differently. With numeric data, the bit values actually represent the arithmetic value of the data. This is accomplished using the binary place values of the individual bits within a byte. Figure 1-1 shows the binary place values for the first eight bit positions.

Using this binary arithmetic approach, the number nine has the binary code value 00001001. There is a 1 in the eight's place and another 1 in the one's place; all the other bit positions contain 0's. Since eight and one add up to nine, this specific sequence of bits represents the number nine. Notice that the binary coded number nine differs from the ASCII digit nine. Don't worry if binary arithmetic is not one of your stronger subjects; you won't need to convert decimal numbers to their binary equivalents. The computer will do it for you.

Your computer is able to differentiate between numeric and alphanumeric data according to the instructions of the software you are using. This means that you, the user, do not have to worry about data representation. Instead, you merely key in the data from the keyboard, or load it from a disk, and leave it to the software and the computer to wrestle with the bits and bytes while you concentrate on the job at hand.

In order for the computer to process any data, or even load a program, the data or program must be converted into binary values. The instructions in a computer program can be considered a special type of data. While we normally distinguish between programs and data, to the computer it's all just 0's and 1's. When these instructions are converted into binary values, they are said to be in "machine" code, or "native" code. Machine code is not humanly readable. (You've already discovered this if you've ever used the DOS TYPE command on a .COM or .EXE file.)

Kilobytes, Megabytes, and Gigabytes

Since the binary number system is the basis for data representation, people who work with computers often measure things in binary. However, so as not to totally confuse the rest of us, the computer types usually stick to binary numbers that have a close decimal equivalent. Three common binary values that are used in computer terminology, especially when referring to computer storage, are K, M, and G.

The letter *K* stands for kilo which comes from the metric system and means one thousand. A K is not strictly 1,000; it is actually 2 raised to the tenth power, which equals 1,024. Since this is so close to 1,000, most people are willing to neglect the difference and consider a K to be 1,000. "Close enough for government work" is one way of looking at it.

The letter *M*, for *megabyte*, means a K of K's or 1,048,576. You can compute this

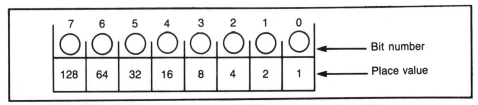

Fig. 1-1. Binary place values for the first eight bit positions of a binary number.

for yourself by multiplying 1,024 times 1,024. One megabyte is roughly a million bytes of storage. This may seem like a lot of storage until you start thinking in terms of gigabytes. As you probably guessed, a *gigabyte* is a K of M's, which is a whopping 1,073,741,844. Again using round numbers, this is roughly equivalent to a billion. We use these large numbers because bytes of data are really quite small compared to the large volumes of data which frequently are processed by computers.

MAGNETIC VERSUS ELECTRONIC STORAGE

How does your computer keep track of all the bytes of programs and data you use? To do so it must rely on various storage devices. Computers use two different types of storage: electronic and magnetic.

Electronic storage, usually in the form of *RAM* (random access memory), is used by the computer while it is in operation. The computer needs some place to store the program instructions which tell it what to do, and it also must keep track of what it has done. In addition, it may need to remember the results of computations temporarily so it can use those results in yet other computations. These three types of electronic storage are called program memory, data memory, and scratch pad memory.

Consider a simple example involving a word processing program. Before you can execute the word processing program, it must first be loaded into your computer's RAM (in an area referred to as the TPA, or transient program area). The program instructions will be retained in RAM throughout your word processing session. When you begin typing a new document, the processed words are retained in your computer's RAM in a data area designated by the word processing program.

As the word processing program accepts the characters you type at the keyboard and displays them on the screen, it also keeps track of how many characters it is placing on the current line. When the number of characters reaches a specified value (the right margin setting) the word processing program commands your computer to move the cursor down to the next line automatically. This is how word wrap works. In order to keep track of the number of characters you have typed, the program uses some more RAM in the form of scratch pad memory.

Without getting technical, most forms of electronic storage operate through the use of microscopic gates or switches which can be opened or closed according to the instructions of the program operating the computer. (How the first switches get set to hold the initial, or "bootstrap", program is beyond the scope of this book.) These switch settings remain in effect through the force of electricity. If the power to the computer were interrupted, as in the case of a power outage, the switch settings would return to their original state.

In terms of the word processing example, this means that the program, the document under construction, and the scratch pad memory would all be lost. It is for this reason that most types of electronic storage, including RAM, are considered to be *volatile.* If you have ever lost important data because you inadvertently turned off your computer before saving (or the power company did it for you) you know the true definition of volatility.

There are some types of computer storage which do not need an external supply of electricity in order to retain data. One such type of storage is CMOS RAM. *CMOS* circuits have very low power requirements and can retain their switch settings by receiving a tiny amount of current supplied by an internal battery. Another form of computer memory which requires no electricity at all to retain data is bubble memory. *Bubble memory* does not use gates as RAM does but relies instead upon the positioning of tiny magnetic bubbles. These bubbles are moved around by tiny electric charges, but once in place, they remain where they are without further force.

Since neither CMOS nor bubble memories require external power supplies, they are frequently used in laptop and portable computers. Unfortunately, these memory devices are still fairly expensive and are not commonly found in desktop computers. This leaves the problem of RAM volatility. Unless you plan to leave your computer on all the time, you will have to find some way of storing your data from one session to the next.

Another problem with electronic storage is its limited capacity. You are limited in the amount of RAM available to you by two factors: space and DOS. Space is a physical limitation- RAM chips may be small, but they do occupy space in your computer. RAM chips are categorized according to the number of gates they contain. Some common RAM chips contain 64K or 256K bits, or gates. Note that, when referring to RAM chips, the K stands for bits, not bytes.

While 256K may seem like a lot of switches to squeeze onto a single chip, it takes nine 256K-bit chips to make up 256K of data or program. Today, many programs require much more than this amount of RAM in order to run. In addition, you need room to store your data. A single-spaced page of text contains approximately 4K of data. This converts to roughly 64 pages per 256K of storage. Considering that the 1986 edition of the *Encyclopedia Britanica* contains over 20000 pages (of course, it's not all text, but pictures require even more storage than words), you quickly see that 256K is a rather puny amount of storage. In order to hold a database of any real size, you would need more RAM chips than you could fit into the case of your computer. And to think that the original Apple had only 16K of RAM!

The second limitation is one imposed by your DOS. Current versions of PC or MS-DOS limit access to 640K of RAM. Although there are a number of methods for overcoming this limitation, they require either additional hardware, software, or both. Future versions of DOS will certainly expand the limits of RAM into the gigabyte range and even beyond. Even with such advances, unless the bit densities of RAM chips can be significantly increased, the space limitation will continue to restrict the amount of data that can be held in RAM.

For these two reasons, volatility and storage limitations, computers usually come equipped with a second type of storage, called *magnetic storage*. Magnetic storage usually involves placing a magnetic imprint of the data to be stored on some medium, such as disk or tape. Magnetic storage enjoys several advantages over electronic storage. For one thing, magnetic storage media require no power at all since they don't rely on electronic switch settings to represent data. For another, magnetic media are very space efficient. On an AT computer's high-capacity drive, a single 5 1/4" diskette can hold 1.2M (megabytes, or a thousand kilobytes) of storage. Considering how compactly floppy disks can be stored, it is possible to store over a gigabyte of data on a single shelf of a bookcase.

The basic principles of magnetic storage are the same whether the medium used is tape, floppy diskette, or hard disk. A surface (usually mylar for tape and floppy diskette and aluminum for hard disks) is coated with a thin film containing molecules of ferric

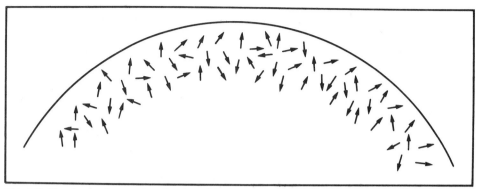

Fig. 1-2. Randomly dispersed molecules of ferric oxide on the surface of a disk.

oxide (FeO_2) or a similar metallic oxide. The molecules exhibit a property known as *polarity,* which means that they have tiny magnetic poles just as a magnet does.

Initially, these polarized molecules are randomly dispersed across the surface of the medium, so that their individual magnetic fields cancel each other. Figure 1-2 illustrates this random situation. However, by subjecting localized areas of the surface to a strong magnetic force, it is possible to align the poles of clusters of these molecules so that they exert a magnetic field of their own. When such a cluster has been created, a bit of data can be represented in that location on the surface. In the case of computer magnetic storage, it is the action of the read/write head in the disk drive or tape unit that aligns the clusters of ferric oxide molecules on the surface of the medium as shown in Fig. 1-3.

Once the data has been stored in this fashion, it can be read later by passing the surface of the medium under the read/write head, which can detect the magnetic fields of the aligned clusters of molecules. The data will remain on the surface of the storage medium until it is either intentionally changed or the medium becomes damaged.

Magnetic storage media can become damaged in a variety of ways, many of which you were warned about when you first learned how to use your computer. Fingerprints, soft drinks, dirt, dust, and exposure to electromagnetic fields can all cause data to disappear. How the data is lost depends upon the cause. The thin film containing the ferric oxide

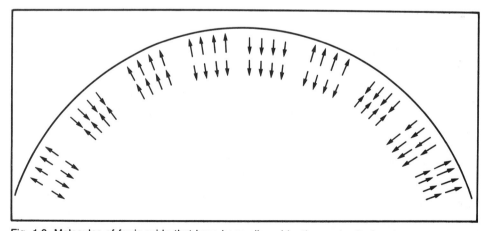

Fig. 1-3. Molecules of ferric oxide that have been aligned by the read-write head.

molecules can be scratched or corroded away. In these cases, the oxide molecules are literally lost.

It is also possible for the molecules to become "scrambled" through exposure to errant electromagnetic fields. Even the most innocent-looking appliances, such as telephones and answering machines which tend to congregate with computers on desktops, can be the source of electromagnetic radiation. The mere ringing of a telephone can be enough to scramble data on a nearby floppy disk. Since data stored on magnetic media can be lost, it is important to create multiple copies, or backups, of your data. You will learn more about creating backups in Chapter 11, "Backing Up Data And Programs."

HARD DISKS VERSUS FLOPPY DISKETTES

In the microcomputer world, the two most common magnetic storage media are floppy diskettes and hard disks. This was not always the case. The earliest microcomputers used cassette tapes to record programs and data. You can still see evidence of this in the IBM Cassette BASIC that is stored in ROM in the IBM PC. This is the version of BASIC that appears if you start up an IBM PC without first mounting a system disk in the A drive. Although you can successfully enter and run a BASIC program from the keyboard, just try to save the program to disk. You can't. You would need a cassette tape connected to your computer. You may have noticed this connection, which is located next to the keyboard cable input at the back of the IBM PC.

Unless you were involved in the pioneering days of the microcomputer revolution, though, you are probably more familiar with floppy diskettes. This is currently the most prevalent storage medium for home and small business computers. However, as advances in technology and increased production bring prices down, more and more microcomputers are being equipped with hard disks. The major advantages of hard disks over their floppy cousins are: increased storage capacity, faster access time, and greater convenience. If you have recently switched from a floppy system to one sporting a hard disk, you are well aware of these advantages.

Interestingly enough, hard disk technology actually preceded floppy diskette technology. Hard disks evolved from magnetic drum storage. In fact, a drum symbol is still used to represent auxiliary storage in systems design flowcharts. Magnetic drums were hard metallic cylinders with an oxide coating. The drum rotated under a read/write head which recorded and read data on its surface. There were many disadvantages to drum storage, not the least of which was the physical size of the drums.

One of the earliest forms of hard disk was developed by IBM in the early 1970's. These disks were capable of storing 30 megabytes of data per side. This characteristic quickly gained them the code name "Winchester disks" after the famed 30/30 rifle. The first Winchester disks were a whopping 14 inches in diameter and today survive only in the form of coffee tables. Contemporary Winchester disks are typically 5 1/4 or 3 1/2 inches in diameter. However, the basic design concepts of Winchester disks are still employed in most hard disk drive units used with microcomputers.

Fixed Hard Disks

Winchester disks are fixed disks. This means that the disk drive motor, the read/write head, and the disk itself are all enclosed within a sealed unit. In fact, the IBM XT and

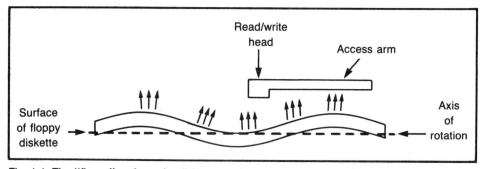

Fig. 1-4. The "floppy" surface of a diskette requires stronger magnetic fields to represent data.

AT User's Manuals refer to these computers' hard disks as fixed disks. For reasons that will become apparent in a moment, hard disk units need to operate in a vacuum. This is one of the reasons that hard disk drives are more expensive than floppy drives. The disk must either be sealed in a vacuum at the time of manufacture, as is the case with Winchester drives, or some method must be employed to create a vacuum when the drive is in operation.

The reason hard disks can store so much more data than floppy diskettes involves the rigidity of the disk itself. Floppy diskettes are exactly that—floppy. When they revolve in their jacket, they actually wobble. This wobbling effect means that, at any given point in time, the surface of the diskette may be fairly far away from the read/write head. This in turn requires that the magnetic fields recorded on the diskettes be relatively strong in order to be sensed by the read/write head. Due to the strength of the magnetic fields on the diskette's surface, each localized, magnetically recorded bit must be separated from its neighbors. Otherwise, the magnetic fields would interfere with each other, resulting in unreliable data. Figure 1-4 illustrates this situation.

Hard disks, on the other hand, are rigid. They do not wobble, even at high revolutions. For this reason, the read/write head in a hard disk drive can be placed very close to the surface of the disk. Head clearances in hard disk drives are typically on the order of 1 millionth of an inch. As a consequence, the magnetic fields recorded on the disk can be much weaker and can be placed much closer together. Compare Fig. 1-4 with Fig. 1-5, which represents data stored on a hard disk. The overall result is far greater storage capacity on hard disks than floppy diskettes.

Of course, there is a price to pay for this increased storage capacity. Because the head clearance is so microscopically small, the hard drive must operate in a vacuum

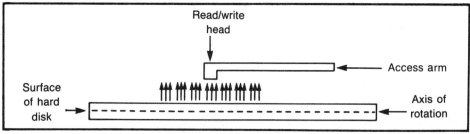

Fig. 1-5. The rigid surface of a hard disk allows the heads to "float" very close to the disk surface permitting the use of weak magnetic fields to represent data.

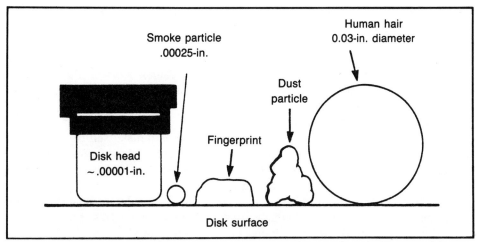

Fig. 1-6. Head tolerances on the order of 1 micron compared to a variety of air-born particles.

as was mentioned earlier. Figure 1-6 shows the relative size of some common airborne particles in comparison to the head clearance of a typical Winchester disk drive. Note that even a fingerprint exceeds this clearance.

Due in part to their rigidity, hard disks can revolve very rapidly in their drives, often as fast as 3,600 rpm. The read/write heads used in these drives are aerodynamically designed so that they float, or fly, on the cushion of air created by the rapidly revolving disk. At such high speeds and with such low tolerances, any particulate matter that got in the way would cause the head to literally crash into the surface of the disk. The resulting collision would scratch the surface of the disk, rendering it unusable. Since the disk is an integral part of the Winchester drive unit, the entire drive would have to be replaced. Such head crashes are by no means unheard of and are one of the primary reasons for performing hard disk backups.

One way of comparing the amount of data that can be stored on different media is to measure the number of bits that can be recorded in a given area. This measurement is given in terms of bits per inch, abbreviated bpi. (The inch component actually refers to a one inch segment of the innermost track of the disk—see the following section entitled "Disk Formats".) Because different manufacturers of Winchester disk drives employ different techniques for writing data to disk, there is a wide variety of bit densities to choose from. Some common recording densities are 6,270 bpi, 7,900 bpi, and 9,300 bpi. Recent advances in recording media have lead to recording densities in excess of 20,000 bpi. Floppy diskette recording densities typically fall in the 5,000 bpi range.

Fixed Disks Versus Removable Disks

The Winchester fixed disk is currently the most commonly used type of hard disk. Almost all internally mounted hard disk drives are of this type. In fact, in the operations manual that accompanies both the XT and AT computers, IBM uses the term *fixed disk* to refer to the internal hard disk. As mentioned previously, fixed disk drives include the read/write head, the drive mechanism and the disk itself in a single, integrated, vacuum-sealed unit. Fixed disk technology is well-established, and costs for 20-megabyte drives have fallen dramatically so that such drives are affordable for even modest computing budgets.

There are limitations to fixed disk technology, however. Because the hard disk is physically fixed inside the drive unit, it cannot be removed if it becomes damaged or completely filled with data. A damaged disk means a damaged drive, which must be returned to the factory for repair. And, while you may not be believe it right now, someday all those megabytes of storage are going to be used up. Then what?

To overcome these limitations, several different alternative technologies have been developed. All involve some method of separating the hard disk itself from the drive and read/write mechanism. These hard drive units are referred to as removable disks or Bernoulli disks, depending upon the technology employed. These removable disk devices will be reviewed and discussed along with tape backup units in Chapter 11, Tape, Removable Disk, Bernoulli, and Fault Tolerant Systems. The techniques for hard disk management are the same whether you are working with a fixed disk or a removable disk. For this reason, the term *hard disk* will be used throughout this book to refer to either a fixed or a removable disk.

DISK FORMATS

As was mentioned earlier, the recording surface of the disk consists of a thin layer of randomly dispersed molecules of ferric oxide. Data is magnetically imprinted on the disk by aligning the poles of these molecules. Once a byte of data has been stored on the disk, the disk drive must have some method of retrieving that byte. If the surface of the disk were truly uniform, it would be impossible for your computer to locate data once it had been recorded. To overcome this problem, your computer uses an addressing scheme when storing and retrieving data from a disk. This addressing scheme utilizes a series of magnetic markers on the surface of the disk. These markings constitute the disk's *format*.

Disk formats differ from one brand of computer to another and even from one version of DOS to another. Despite the seemingly bewildering array of disk formats, certain key elements remain the same from one format to another. All disk formats employ tracks and sectors to accomplish their particular addressing schemes.

Tracks consist of concentric rings, which start from the outer edge of the disk and continue inward. Each track is assigned a number, or address, starting with 0 for the outermost track. The tracks are further divided into segments called sectors. The *sectors* within each track are also assigned a number. In Fig. 1-7 you see a simplified representation of a formatted disk. The number of actual tracks and sectors varies depending upon the disk format.

Disks typically do not come with the tracks and sectors imprinted on their surface. Instead, they are sold blank, or unformatted. This is so they can be used in a variety of computers. It is up to the user to format the blank disks using a special formatting program. (Note: many hard disks are pre-formatted; more on this in Chapter 2, Preparing Hard Disks.)IBM PC and XT floppy diskettes are formatted 40 tracks to a side, while both the 5 1/4 inch high-capacity diskettes and the 3 1/2 inch microfloppies used with AT computers utilize a more sophisticated format and employ 80 tracks per side. Hard disks usually have hundreds of tracks. For example, the 10 megabyte hard disks used in the IBM XT have 306 tracks, while the AT's 20 megabyte hard drives contain 612.

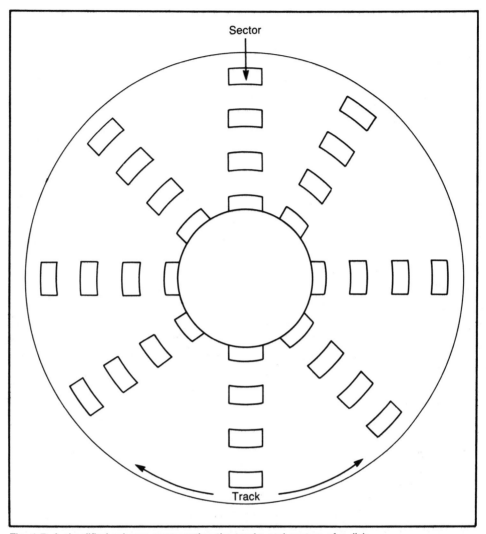

Fig. 1-7. A simplified scheme representing the tracks and sectors of a disk.

Surprisingly, the tracks do not cover the entire surface of the disk. In fact, the distance between the outermost and innermost tracks is just about 2 centimeters (roughly three-quarters of an inch). The number of tracks per inch (abbreviated *tpi*) depends on the disk density. (Note: disk density is related to recording density, or bpi, but is used in reference to tracks rather than bits.) IBM PC's and XT's use double-density diskettes; AT's use quad-density diskettes. Double-density diskettes, which record 48 tpi, are physically different from quad-density diskettes, which record 96 tpi. Although double-density diskettes may be used in AT drives, they can only be formatted at 48 tpi. In order to format at the higher 96 tpi, you must purchase special quad-density diskettes.

The number of sectors per track also differs depending upon the format. The original DOS version 1.1 used a format with 8 sectors per track. Subsequent versions of DOS (2.xx and above) employ a 9-sector format. The AT uses 15 sectors per track on its

1.2MB diskettes. Hard disk drives are normally formatted with 17 sectors per track. Each sector contains the same number of bytes, regardless of its location on the disk. The most common sector size is 512 bytes, although some hard disks have 1,024-byte sectors.

Since the width of the sectors remains constant across all tracks, you might think that there should be more sectors in the outer tracks than in the inner ones. However, this would interfere with the addressing scheme, which depends upon a constant number of sectors from track to track. Instead, there are unused gaps between the sectors in the outer tracks. In fact, much of the surface of the disk goes unused.

The problem of unused space is exemplified in DOS 1.1, which can only format one side of a floppy diskette. This is because when this version of DOS originated most floppy drives contained only one read/write head and could only record data on one side of the diskette. Following the old adage that two heads are better than one, later drives contained heads for both sides of the diskette. Thus, DOS versions 2.xx and higher are capable of formatting both sides of the diskette.

Unfortunately, this situation has given rise to some misleading terminology. Diskettes manufactured for use in drives with only one head are called *single-sided,* while diskettes intended for use in dual-headed drives are referred to as *double-sided* or *dual-sided* and are marketed as such.

Actually, there's no such thing as a single-sided diskette. Every disk has two sides just as every coin has two sides. During manufacturing, each disk is coated on both sides with an oxide emulsion. However, during quality control inspection, single-sided diskettes are tested on only one side. Double-sided diskettes, on the other hand, get the deluxe treatment and are tested on both sides. Since double-sided diskettes usually cost more than single-sided diskettes, knowledgeable computer users frequently buy single-sided diskettes for use in their double-sided drives. Of course, whether you choose to do so is up to you.

Hard drive units usually contain a number of disks, or *platters* as they are sometimes called. The sides of these platters are referred to as *surfaces.* Both the XT and the AT come with hard drives that contain two platters. It is possible, though, to purchase disk drives containing many platters. The number of platters contained in a drive unit in part determines the amount of storage it provides. Although a hard disk drive may contain several platters, it is common to refer to these enclosed platters as a single hard disk. Thus, individuals often say, "My hard disk holds 30 megabytes of data," when, in fact, the drive they are referring to contains two physical disks.

When discussing hard disks, track locations are described in terms of *cylinders.* This is because the same-numbered track on multiple surfaces essentially constitutes a cylinder in space. Instead of describing the location of data by surface, track, and sector, you use the surface, cylinder, and sector. Using the information provided for a given disk drive, you can determine the amount of formatted storage it can hold. Consider, for example, a disk drive containing two platters, with a recording density of 345 tpi (resulting in 306 usable tracks per surface). If the disk is formatted with 17 sectors per track, 512 bytes per sector, that creates 2,663,424 bytes of storage per surface, or 10,653,696 bytes in all (remember, the drive contains 4 recording surfaces).

DISK ACCESS

In addition to their increased storage capacity, hard disk drives have the advantage of providing much faster access to the data they contain. *Access time* is a measure of the time required to locate and retrieve a sector of data. Although data may not come in nice, neat 512 byte blocks, the disk drive always reads and writes a sector at a time. (Technically, this is incorrect. See the section entitled Directories and File Access Tables in Chapter 3 for a more accurate description.) Access times for hard disks are typically around 40 milliseconds (1 millisecond equals 1/1000 second) compared to floppy disk drive access times, which fall in the range of 175 to 300 milliseconds. Some of the newest drives have access times under 25 milliseconds.

The reason for the striking differences in access times between hard and floppy drives is due to the mechanical differences between the two types of drives. In order to appreciate these differences, you need to have a basic understanding of how disk drives operate. Certain components are common to every drive, whether it is designed to hold floppies or hard disks, single-sided or double-sided disks, or multiple platters. The disk is held by a spindle much like a phonograph record. This spindle is rotated by the drive motor. There is a separate read/write head for each recording surface. Since the read/write head must be able to access data on any of the tracks, it must be movable, so it is placed on an *access arm* similar to the arm of a phonograph turntable. The access arm can be directed to move in or out according to the location of the track containing the sector to be accessed.

The difference in rotation speed between hard and floppy drives is one reason hard drives have faster access times. Hard drives revolve at 3,600 rpm as opposed to 360 rpm for floppy drives. Even though hard drives have twice the number of sectors per track, it takes only one tenth as long to position the read/write head over a given sector in a hard drive. This time lag is known as *latency*.

Another element of access time is the amount of time it takes the access arm to move over the appropriate track. This is referred to as *seek time*. In floppy drives, the read/write head is usually mounted on a pair of rails, and track seeking is accomplished by moving the head in and out through the action of a stepper motor. With most hard disk drives, each read/write head is mounted on its own access arm, and the access arms swing in or out as a single unit. Due to the mechanics involved, seek times tend to be faster for hard drives than for floppy drives.

RANDOM VERSUS SEQUENTIAL FILE STORAGE

Hard disk devices are designed to hold large volumes of data and programs. Although the disk is divided into tracks (or cylinders) and sectors, it is not very helpful to know that the data you are looking for is stored on surface 2, cylinder 7, sectors 15, 16, 17, and 18. Instead, you want to assign some easy-to-remember name to the data. For this reason, data and programs are given filenames, which are assigned by the individual writing the program or entering the data. In Chapter 3, Filenames and Directories, the rules for filenames will be described in detail. For now, all you need to know is that both programs and data are considered as files by the operating system and are saved accordingly.

There are two methods for storing and retrieving files from disk: sequential storage and random storage. With *sequential storage,* the entire contents of the file is written to the disk onto adjacent sectors within a given track. If one track is insufficient for all the data in the file, the head moves onto the next track and continues writing data.

Sequential storage requires that there be enough empty consecutive tracks and sectors to hold the entire file. Since this is not always likely, sequential file storage is not performed during normal operation of your computer. Instead, files are stored randomly. *Random storage,* as its name implies, means that files are stored randomly on the disk according to the availability of sectors. For reasons that will be explained in Chapter 3, sectors are grouped together into clusters.

Consider the following example. Assume you are using an AT to create a marketing proposal using your favorite word processor. By the time you're done, the document is around 27K in length. When you issue the Save command, your word processor hands the job of saving the file over to DOS.

At that moment, the read/write head happens to be positioned over cylinder 6, sector 9. DOS investigates surface 0 and finds data stored in this sector, so it moves on to surface 1. On this surface, sector 9 is empty, so DOS places the first 2K of the file into this and the subsequent adjacent sectors. However, the next available cluster on surface 1, cylinder 6, is full, so DOS moves down to surface 2. If this cluster and the corresponding cluster on surface 3 are both full, then DOS will move the access arm over the next cylinder looking for an empty cluster, where it stores the next 2K of data. This process continues until all 27K of the file have found a home.

Obviously, all this searching for empty sectors takes time. As you might expect, random storage and retrieval is slower than sequential storage and retrieval. Retrieval times are typically twice as fast for sequential files as for random files. Unfortunately, random storage is dictated by the random sizes of the files stored on a disk. If you think about it, you will realize that sequential storage can only be employed when copying the entire contents of one disk onto another. Then the operating system has a chance to work with a fresh disk and can write the files sequentially, one after another, onto the new disk.

One final note on random and sequential storage—these terms refer to the file storage method, not the contents of the files themselves. In programming, it is possible to create either sequential access or random access data files. Random and sequential access refer to the way individual records are stored within the data file itself. A *sequential access data file* will normally be stored randomly on the disk, although it may be stored sequentially if it is copied onto a new disk.

This chapter is an overview of disk storage. Most experienced computer users are familiar with the concepts and terms included in this chapter. However, there are many more technical details pertaining to disk formats and file storage that you must be aware of when working with hard disks. Chapters 2 and 3 cover these two subjects in greater depth. Unless you are quite familiar with hard disk formats and the use of the directory command, you should read the next two chapters carefully.

Chapter 2

Preparing Hard Disks

Preparing hard disks for use involves three separate procedures: partitioning, formatting, and sysgening. Usually, one or more of these steps are performed by the hard disk manufacturer or the computer dealer prior to sale. If you have been using your hard disk for some time and these three terms are still unfamiliar to you, the chances are that your hard disk was prepared for you. In this case, you may wonder why you should bother reading this chapter.

Nothing in the world of microcomputers is static. Both technology and the needs of the individual user change, often more rapidly than we would like. Because of changing software needs, or through the addition of a network, or merely as a result of your increased sophistication, you may find that the original setup of your hard disk is no longer appropriate.

In this chapter, you will learn how to partition, format, and install the operating system on your hard disk for initial use. You will also learn how to repartition and reformat your hard disk, as well as install different versions of DOS on your hard disk, to accommodate your changing software and computing needs. Each of these operations will be explained in detail. However, before proceeding with specific instructions, the difference between logical and physical disk formats needs to be explained.

LOGICAL VERSUS PHYSICAL FORMATTING

As you read in Chapter 1, disks must be formatted prior to use. This is true regardless of the size or type of disk; even hard disks must be formatted. DOS disk formats actually consist of more than just the tracks and sectors which are laid down on the surface of the disk. In addition to these *physical* data addresses, a DOS disk format includes what may be considered to be logical information. This *logical information* includes technical details regarding the disk format, as well as two work areas, called the directory and the File Allocation Table. You will learn more about these two logical features of a disk's format in Chapter 3, Filenames and Directories.

With hard disks, the processes of physical and logical formatting are often performed independently. These two formats are sometimes referred to as the disk's low-level format and high-level format. Before discussing these two components of a hard disk's format, it might be helpful to follow the process of formatting a floppy diskette, in which the processes of physical formatting and logical formatting occur during the same operation.

The basic command to format a diskette in drive B on a two-drive system is:

A>FORMAT B:

You have probably used this command dozens of times to format floppy diskettes. If so, you realize that the diskette in drive A must contain a copy of the DOS format utility program. You may also recall that it is possible to format a diskette so that it may be used as a *system* diskette by including the /S formatting option:

A>FORMAT B:/S

This and other formatting options will be explained in greater detail later in this chapter.

The Physical Format

When you enter the above command, DOS prompts you to insert a diskette in the B drive and press any key when ready. Once you have given the go-ahead, DOS proceeds to format the diskette. For floppy diskettes, the formatting process consists of several steps. First, DOS lays down the magnetic tracks and sectors on the diskette's surface, starting with the outermost track. As each track is formatted, the individual sectors within the track are established. The number of tracks per surface and the number of sectors per track are dictated by the version of DOS you are using. The tracks and sectors constitute the diskette's physical format.

In the case of floppy diskettes, DOS *initializes* each sector as it is created by filling in the individual bytes with dummy data. The actual value used by DOS is the decimal number 246, or F6 in hexadecimal. This initialization process is intrinsic to the process of physical formatting and cannot be circumvented. It is possible to reuse a diskette that has been used in a different type of computer or which has been used with the same computer but for a different purpose. However, any data stored on the diskette will be overwritten.

Initializing the diskette ensures that no prior data or machine code remain from the diskette's former life. This can be both beneficial and destructive. It is beneficial if you really want to reuse the diskette for some new purpose. However, it can be devastating if you mistakenly format a diskette containing important information or a valuable program.

Unfortunately, formatting a floppy diskette physically replaces the old data with new, dummy data, and the process is irreversible.

The Logical Format

Once the physical formatting is complete, DOS proceeds with the logical formatting of the diskette. Logical formatting establishes the work areas on the diskette. These work areas are used to control how and where files will be stored. The logical format of a disk, be it hard or floppy, consists of three separate work areas. The first of these is the boot record. The *boot record* is stored in the first sector on the diskette and is quite brief. In fact, it occupies less than the full 512 bytes allocated to it.

The primary function of the boot record is to assist DOS in booting, or loading, the operating system on computer startup. This function of the boot record will be discussed further later in this chapter. Another purpose of the boot record is to serve as an ID record of the diskette's characteristics. These include the version of DOS used to format the disk and details of the disk's physical format, such as the number of tracks per side and sectors per track. Additional information pertains to the diskette's other work areas: the directory and the File Allocation Table. Finally, the boot record contains a special two-byte ID code which DOS uses to indicate the type of disk format employed on the diskette.

The special information contained in the boot record assists DOS in determining the diskette's physical format and in locating and reading files stored on the diskette. You can think of the boot record as the diskette's "dog tags."

Immediately following the boot record is the diskette's *File Allocation Table* (there are two of them, actually). This table is a special work area reserved for keeping track of the physical location of the various files stored on the disk. This work area is established and initialized during the second, or logical, phase of the formatting procedure.

Adjacent to the File Allocation Table is the diskette's root directory. The *root directory* is a special file that contains entries for each individual file stored on the disk. As with the File Allocation Table, the directory is initially full of dummy data. The actual entries in the diskette's directory occur as files are added to the diskette.

Although the boot record is always located in the first sector, the size and resulting locations of the File Allocation Table and the directory vary according to the type of format employed on the diskette. These two size characteristics are part of the diskette's format information and are recorded in the boot record. Using this information, DOS can determine where the data portion of the diskette is located. The data portion of the diskette is the area allocated for actual file storage.

Floppy Versus Hard Disk Formatting Procedures

When formatting floppy diskettes, DOS performs both physical and logical formatting. This is not the case with hard disks. Instead, most hard disks come pre-formatted. This means that the physical format (i.e., the tracks and sectors) is already established on the disk by technicians at the factory which produced it. The physical format, or *low-level format* as it is sometimes called when referring to hard disks, is usually a permanent feature of the disk. However, it is possible for the format of the hard disk to become damaged, just as it is possible to damage a floppy diskette's format. For this reason, you should be familiar with the process of re-establishing the physical format of your hard disk. A procedure for low-level formatting of a hard disk is included at the end of this chapter.

Drive Designators

Normally, you will only be required to establish a hard disk's logical, or *high-level*, format. Surprisingly, you use the same FORMAT command to perform this high-level formatting procedure. DOS is able to distinguish between your computer's hard disk and floppy drive(s). To understand how DOS recognizes a disk drive as either hard or floppy, you need to be familiar with drive designators.

Most microcomputers have at least two disk drives, although the original IBM PC came stocked with only one floppy drive. Many users add additional hard and floppy drives to their computers for various reasons. Each physical drive is assigned a *logical device designator*, which consists of a letter followed by a colon. These logical drive designators enable DOS to identify which drive a specific command is intended for. The number of logical device designators is determined by the version of DOS you are using. For example, DOS 3.2 allows up to 16 logical devices.

Usually, the designators A: and B: are employed for floppy drives, with the remaining alphabetical designators assigned to hard drives or other storage devices. You can even assign a drive designator to a portion of your RAM and treat your memory like a disk drive. You'll learn how to create RAM disks, as they're called, in Chapter 16, Disk Access Optimization. On an XT or AT with one hard drive and one floppy drive, the floppy drive may be referred to as either A: or B:. The hard drive is assigned the C: drive designator.

When you enter the FORMAT command, you normally include the designator for the drive containing the disk to be formatted. (In fact, DOS 3.2 *requires* a drive designator with the FORMAT command.) DOS then checks a table of drive designators for the specific computer you are working on. This table is stored in the computer's ROM BIOS, which is a special read-only memory chip installed in the computer by the manufacturer. This table determines the type of disk to be formatted, and DOS is instructed to proceed accordingly.

On a hard disk, the DOS FORMAT command dispenses with the physical formatting process and only performs the logical, or high-level, formatting tasks. These include writing the boot record, establishing the File Allocation Table, and installing the empty directory. Contrary to floppy diskette formatting, DOS does *not* initialize the data area of a hard disk during formatting. This means that data stored on the hard disk is not actually destroyed during reformatting, although access to the data is removed because the directory and File Allocation Tables are rewritten. However, there are special utility programs that can help you reconstruct the original directory and File Allocation Tables.

PREPARING A HARD DISK

Once you understand the difference between physical and logical formats, you can put the process of hard disk preparation into a sequence of individual operations. The first step in preparing the hard disk is physically formatting the surface of the disk (remember from Chapter 1 that there may be several platters involved). The physical format is usually written to the disk at the factory, and the disk is said to be *pre-formatted*, or low-level formatted.

The next step in hard disk preparation is to divide the hard disk into separate partitions. *Partitions* separate different file storage areas on the disk. One use of hard disk partitions is to create individual environments for different operating systems. Another is to separate networking files from an individual user's files on a hard disk that is acting as a network file server. Most hard disks are prepared with a single partition in which all files are stored. This is probably the way your hard disk is currently set up if it is already in use.

Once the hard disk is partitioned, each individual partition must receive its high-level format. The details of high-level formats vary from one operating system to another. This book deals only with MS/PC-DOS. If you plan to utilize one or more partitions on your hard disk to run other operating systems, such as the p-System or CP/M 86, you will need to follow the specific instructions for formatting hard disks included with those systems' user's manuals. Just remember that these format routines will only perform logical formatting within the hard disk partition allocated to them.

The final step in preparing a hard disk is transferring a copy of the operating system to the disk. This procedure is sometimes called *sysgening* because it "generates" a copy of the operating "system" on the disk. As you will see, DOS consists of three separate system files, two of which are hidden from view. Once the operating system has been installed, the computer can be booted from the hard disk. This means that the computer will start up and load the operating system directly from the hard disk without requiring a system disk in the A drive.

Partitioning a Hard Disk

Assuming that the hard disk has been physically formatted, the first thing you need to do when preparing a new hard disk is perform the task of partitioning it. Even if you only intend to operate your computer as a stand-alone DOS computer, you will still need to perform this operation. However, you might want to check with your computer dealer, who may have performed this step as a service to you before delivering your computer. If so, you can skip this section and proceed to the section labeled Formatting A Hard Disk.

Hard disk partitions are created using the DOS FDISK command. This command invokes a special program that prompts you for certain information and then uses this information to create a partition table on the disk. This *partition table* is written to the first sector of the hard disk and contains information on the number, size, and location of all the partitions.

Although the partition table is created with the DOS FDISK command, the information contained in the table is accessible to other operating systems as well. This enables you to format separate partitions under different operating systems. You can think of partitioning as dividing your hard disk into several smaller hard disks, each with its own operating system and format. Without the partition table created by FDISK, programs or data from one operating system might attempt to read or write over programs and data from another operating system. The result would be chaos, a condition in computing we assiduously try to avoid.

For whatever purpose you have in mind, the DOS FDISK command allows you to establish up to four partitions on your hard disk. One of the partitions established is considered to be the *active* partition. This is the partition which DOS looks to when booting the computer, and it is the partition where programs and data will be stored and retrieved. Any one of the partitions can be made active, and you can change the active partition at any time.

The instructions for the FDISK command are included in your DOS manual under the chapter on preparing your fixed disk; however they will be summarized here. To use the FDISK command, you will need to place your DOS diskette in the floppy drive of your computer and turn it on. Once you reach the A prompt, enter:

A>FDISK

After DOS loads the FDISK program, the FDISK Options menu will appear on your screen (see Fig. 2-1). This menu displays the ID number of the current fixed drive and a set of enumerated options. In Fig. 2-1 there are five options. Your screen will probably only display the first four. This is because the fifth option, Select Next Fixed Disk Drive only appears if you have more than one hard disk in your computer. If you do have multiple hard drives, they will be numbered in correspondence to the letters "C", "D", etc., with drive C identified as drive number 1. You can use option 5 to change the current drive correspondingly.

```
IBM Personal Computer
Fixed Disk Setup Program Version 3.20
(C)Copyright IBM Corp. 1983,1985

FDISK Options

Current Fixed Disk Drive: 1

Choose one of the following:

        1.   Create DOS Partition
        2.   Change Active Partition
        3.   Delete DOS Partition
        4.   Display Partition Data
        5.   Select Next Fixed Drive

Enter choice: [1]



Press ESC to return to DOS
```

Fig. 2-1. The FDISK Options menu.

```
Create DOS Partition

Current Fixed Disk Drive: 1



Do you wish to use the entire fixed disk
for DOS (Y/N).....................? [Y]
```

Fig. 2-2. The "Create DOS Partition" entry screen.

As you can see from the Options menu, you can only create and delete DOS partitions. Partitions for other operating systems must be created with their own programs. However, you can make a non-DOS partition active with the FDISK program. Choice 3, Delete DOS Partition, will be described later in the chapter in the section labeled Changing The Hard Disk Setup.

To create a new DOS partition, you would use choice 1, Create DOS Partition (Fig. 2-2). A new screen asks if you want to use the entire hard disk for a single DOS partition. Your first response might be to answer "Y" to this question as suggested by the prompt. However, you might want to consider your future computing needs before doing so.

Your hard disk probably contains more storage space than you can use initially. If you allocate it all to a single partition, you will be faced with a major task if you decide later to install one or more additional partitions. FDISK does not require that you utilize the entire disk in a single partition or even multiple partitions. Instead, you can leave some disk space unallocated.

This strategy enables you to create additional partitions later without having to resize the original DOS partition. If you have any uncertainty as to the type of programs you will be using in the future, or if your current requirements for disk storage are modest, you might be well-advised to leave up to half your hard drive unallocated. Remember, you can always increase the size of the DOS partition later (although this involves as much work as reducing the size).

On the other hand, if you're fairly sure that you will only be using DOS programs in a stand-alone situation, you might as well get the most out of your hard disk and allocate the whole 20 megabytes (or however much you've purchased) to a single DOS partition. To do so, merely accept the "Y" response to the question, "Do you wish to use the entire fixed disk for DOS?" DOS will then display a confirming message instructing you to insert your DOS diskette and press any key when ready. Following this instruction will cause DOS to write the partition information to the partition table and reboot the computer from drive A.

In case you answered "N" to the "use entire fixed disk" prompt, you will be prompted to supply some additional information about the size and location of the partition you wish to create. To assist you in making this decision, the FDISK program will display a message describing the size of your hard disk in cylinders. Figure 2-3 is a sample display from an unpartitioned 20-megabyte hard drive. To determine cylinder size in bytes, you can divide the total number of cylinders into the total byte size of your disk.

```
Total fixed disk space is 609 cyclinders
Maximum available space is 609
cylinders at 000
```

Fig. 2-3. Sample status display provided by the DOS FDISK utility.

In this example, each cylinder contains roughly 34K of formatted storage.

You can use this information to determine the partition size. If you know accurately the number of bytes required for the partition, you can convert back to cylinders. Usually, though, you will work in terms of percentages. For example, you might decide to devote two thirds of the hard disk to the DOS partition. To determine the number of cylinders involved, you would simply multiply the total cylinders by .66.

Once you know the size of the partition you wish to create, you enter that value at the "Enter partition size" prompt. Note that the total cylinder space is recommended for you. Of course, you can accept this value—but that's the same thing as using the entire fixed disk for a single partition, and you've already opted against that choice.

Having entered the partition size, you will be asked to "Enter the starting cylinder number". The next available cylinder will be suggested to you. Unless you have some specific reason for skipping a group of cylinders (to leave room for another partition at some later time), you should accept this recommendation. FDISK will then write the information you entered into the partition table and return you to the FDISK Options menu.

Before leaving the FDISK Options menu, you might want to view the Display Partition Data option by selecting number 4. This will give you information about all the partitions on your hard disk. At this point, you should have only one partition, which, by default, becomes the active partition. Options 2 and 3 from the FDISK Options menu are used in modifying the structure of the hard disk and will be discussed in a later section of this chapter.

Since it is possible to have more than one partition on the hard disk, each partition must have its own boot record, which gets created when the partition is high-level formatted. In addition, there is a special boot record for the entire hard disk. This boot record uses the information contained within the partition table to determine which partition is active. It then transfers control to the boot record stored in the first sector of that partition.

Ordinarily, there should only be one DOS partition on a hard disk. However, you may find two or more DOS partitions when you investigate the Display Partition Data option. These additional DOS partitions are usually associated with hard disks in excess of 30 or so megabytes. The reason for this is a quirk of DOS. DOS versions 3.xx and earlier impose an arbitrary limit of 32 megabytes on the size of any disk drive. At the time the original DOS was written, this seemed more than adequate. However, it is now possible to purchase hard disk drives with a hundred or more megabytes of storage.

In order to get around the 32-megabyte limit, manufacturers of these large disk drives include special installation files which create multiple 32-megabyte DOS partitions on the disk. These partitions are then linked together by special *device drivers* which are called into play through the system configuration file, CONFIG.SYS. If you have such a disk, your owner's manual should describe the step-by-step procedure for installing your disk drive. You may want to refer to Chapter 12 for more information on device drivers and the CONFIG.SYS file.

Formatting a DOS Partition

As was mentioned earlier, each partition on the hard disk must receive a high-level format. You may recall that the high- level format is only a logical format, not a physical format. As such, it does not alter the sector data already stored on the disk. Instead, the high-level format writes the DOS records and tables onto the partition which enables the partition to act as a separate DOS disk. These include the boot record, the File Allocation Table, and the root directory. The logical formatting of a hard disk is done using the same FORMAT command you use to format floppy diskettes. Remember that DOS is able to distinguish between hard drives and floppy drives and will perform the appropriate formatting tasks accordingly.

Ordinarily when you format a hard disk partition, you want to transfer the operating system files onto the hard disk as well. This is accomplished by including the system option, /S, with the FORMAT command. There are three files you need to include on any *bootable* system disk: COMMAND.COM, IBMBIO.COM, and IBMDOS.COM (note: for MS DOS the files are COMMAND.COM, IO.SYS and MSDOS.SYS). Two of these files, IBMBIO.COM and IBMDOS.COM are *hidden* files. That means that you can't see them in a disk's directory. All three files are required for both floppy and hard disks if they are to be used as boot disks.

A *boot disk* is a disk that can load the disk operating system into memory on computer startup, thus enabling the computer to function as a DOS computer. You've probably seen the message:

> Non-System disk or disk error . . .
> Replace and strike any key when ready . . .

This message appears when you attempt to start up your computer with a non-bootable disk in the system drive.

It's worth investigating how a DOS computer locates these three files. The process is essentially the same whether the computer is set up to boot off a floppy or a hard drive. In this case, assume the computer has one floppy and one hard drive, with the system files installed in a DOS partition on the hard drive. When the power is turned on, a special program stored in the computer's BIOS ROM is activated. This program directs the computer to check the floppy, or A drive for a disk. If a disk is present, the boot record is checked for the presence of the two system files, IBMBIO.COM and IBMDOS.COM. If these files are present, they are loaded into the computer's RAM and control is passed to them.

If there is no disk in drive A, the computer next checks the hard drive. The master boot record is checked to see where the active partition is located. Then the boot record in this active partition is investigated to locate the two system files. Again, if these files are present they are loaded into RAM. The end result is that you are presented with a system prompt, which will be either an A prompt or a C prompt, depending upon which disk the computer booted from.

Most hard disk drives are set up to boot off the hard disk, but not all. This is because

DOS itself only recognizes certain device configurations, and not all manufacturers conform to them. If a hard drive cannot boot off the hard disk, then a system disk must be initially inserted in the floppy drive on startup. Once the computer has booted, the hard drive can be made the current drive. Changing the current drive is described in more detail in Chapter 3. Hard disks that require a floppy boot should not be formatted with the system option.

To format a DOS partition, you will need to load the FORMAT program off your DOS diskette. If you have just completed establishing the DOS partition with the FDISK program, this diskette will still be in the A drive. The command to format the active DOS partition and transfer the system files is:

A > FORMAT C:/S

After entering this command, you will be presented with the following message:

> WARNING, ALL DATA ON NON-REMOVABLE DISK
> DRIVE C: WILL BE LOST!
> Proceed with Format (Y/N)?

To this ominous message you should answer "Y". DOS then proceeds to format the disk cylinder by cylinder, surface by surface. You can follow the progress of the formatting as the cylinders and heads (surfaces) are clocked off on the screen. Note that some versions of DOS merely record the tracks as they are formatted. This is because early versions of DOS were designed to format mainly floppy diskettes, for which cylinders and heads have no meaning. In any case, once the entire disk has been formatted, the message

> Format complete
> System transferred

will be displayed along with information about your disk, such as the following:

> xxxxxx   bytes total disk space
> xxxxx   bytes used by system
> xxxxxx   bytes available on disk

You will also be asked if you want to format another disk, to which you should respond "N".

Format Options and the LABEL Command

The FORMAT command includes several options in addition to the system option. There are several options that allow you to control the number of sides a diskette should be formatted on and the number of sectors that should be formatted per track. These options are used when formatting floppy diskettes and are not employed when formatting hard disks. The FORMAT command defaults to 15 sectors per track for hard disk formats, so you don't have to worry about the sectors option.

One very useful FORMAT option is the volume option. This option allows you to specify an identifying volume label which will be written to the disk at the conclusion of the formatting process. *Volume labels* are especially useful in identifying floppy diskettes, of which you are likely to have quite a few. However, volume labels are also a handy way of keeping track of multiple partitions. For this reason, most users add a volume label when formatting DOS partitions on their hard disks as well as when formatting floppy diskettes.

The volume option is invoked by adding a /V to the FORMAT command as follows:

A>FORMAT C:/V

With the addition of this option, you will be prompted to enter a volume label at the conclusion of formatting. Volume labels follow most of the rules for filenames, with the difference that they may contain up to eleven characters.

The LABEL command may be used to add a label to an unlabeled disk, or to change or delete an existing label. To use the LABEL command to affect your hard disk, you will need to have your DOS diskette in drive A. When using the LABEL command, you must specify the drive you wish to label, in this case drive C; otherwise drive A will be labeled by default. To append a label to a previously unlabeled disk, you would enter the LABEL command followed by a C: and the volume label you wish to use. For example, to add the label DOSPART1 to your hard disk, you would enter:

A>LABEL C:DOSPART1

To change or delete an existing volume label, you enter the label command followed by the drive letter and a colon. DOS will respond with the disk's current label and prompt you for a new one. You can either enter a new volume label to change the label or press Enter to delete the existing label. In case you do not really want to delete the old label, DOS prompts you with a confirmation message, to which you would respond "Y" to delete the label or "N" if you pressed Enter by mistake.

Volume labels in DOS versions 3.xx serve an additional function beyond merely identifying a DOS partition. They can help prevent unintentional formatting of a previously formatted hard disk partition. If you give the command to format a previously formatted partition, DOS will request that you enter the disk's current volume label. This forces you to think about the disk you are formatting. Unfortunately, it is all too easy to leave off the disk drive designator when entering the FORMAT command. Under previous versions of DOS, if you entered the command:

C>FORMAT /S

instead of:

C>FORMAT A:/S

DOS would have merrily gone about the task of reformatting your hard disk without giving you an opportunity to retract the erroneous command.

Preparing a Hard Disk Under DOS 3.2

DOS 3.2 has provided a special command, SELECT which you can use to format your DOS partition and copy the DOS system files onto the newly formatted disk. The SELECT command differs from the FORMAT/S command in that it allows you to specify a keyboard routine and a country code. The keyboard routines and country codes provided in DOS version 3.2 enable you to configure your computer's keyboard to represent foreign characters, such as the "~" over the "n" in Spanish, and to alter the date, time and currency formats to conform to different national standards. The SELECT command is described in detail in the Disk Operating System manual which accompanies DOS 3.2. Unless you have a special need for foreign characters or alternate date, time and currency formats, you can use the FORMAT/S command in 3.2 with no problems.

ALTERING THE STRUCTURE OF THE HARD DISK

The number and location of disk partitions, the format of these partitions, and the type and version of the operating system installed on the partitions all constitute what may be referred to as the disk's *structure*. This structure is not immutable, and may be changed in a variety of ways. Probably the most common change required involves updating DOS as new versions are released. However, it is possible to reallocate the space on the hard disk using the FDISK command.

Repartitioning the Hard Disk

Normally, once you have partitioned and formatted your hard disk, you can forget about the FDISK and FORMAT C: commands. But the FDISK command can also be used to add additional partitions or remove unwanted ones from your hard disk. Refer back to the FDISK Options menu in Fig. 2-1. Note that the Create DOS Partition option can be used to add an additional DOS partition. While this is not normally done, such action may be required to accommodate disks with more than 32 megabytes of storage.

It is also possible to add other, non-DOS partitions to your hard disk. Such partitions are required if you intend to run programs written for other operating systems from your hard disk. For example, several of the software packages marketed through Dow-Jones Software are written in UCSD Pascal. These programs can only run under the control of the UCSD p-System. To install these programs on your hard disk, you must first create a p-System partition for them to reside in. The specific instructions for establishing and formatting non-DOS partitions should be provided by the software company providing the program and operating system you plan to use.

Whether you are adding a DOS or a non-DOS partition, you still must remove the existing partition(s) from the disk before proceeding to add new ones. Unfortunately, the process of removing old partitions can be quite time consuming, as it involves backing up the files stored on the old partition onto floppy diskettes or some other medium. The techniques for backing up data stored on a hard disk are covered in Chapters 10 and 11. For now, just be aware that deleting an existing partition will cause the data stored there to be lost.

Assuming you have only a single, DOS partition on your disk and you want to add another, non-DOS partition, you would follow these steps:

1. Back up all files on the disk.

2. Use FDISK Option 3 to delete the existing DOS partition.
3. Install a new, smaller DOS partition, leaving space for the additional partition.
4. Reformat the DOS partition.
5. Restore the files into the recreated DOS partition.
6. Create the non-DOS partition and format it according to the instructions provided with by the software company.
7. Install the software into the non-DOS partition.

Adding additional DOS partitions involves some finagling with the DOS CONFIG.SYS file to get around the DOS restriction permitting only one DOS partition per disk. Most manufacturers of large-volume hard disk drives provide special installation files which handle the job of partitioning and modifying CONFIG.SYS for you. When working with multiple partitions on a hard disk, you will need to identify which partition you wish to work with. This can be done using FDISK Option 2, Change Active Partition. Selecting this option will cause a screen such as Fig. 2-4 to be displayed. Note that the DOS partition is listed as "A" under the Status column. This means that the DOS partition is currently the active partition. You can change to another partition by entering the desired partition number at the prompt. The selected partition will become the new active partition, and this status will be written to the partition table. When the computer is booted, control will be passed to the operating system stored in that partition.

If you do repartition the hard disk, you will be required to reformat the DOS partition. To do so, just follow the instructions indicated in the section on Preparing A Hard Disk. Be sure to include the /S option; otherwise the system files won't be transferred to the hard disk, and you will have to boot off the floppy drive. An optional volume label is also highly recommended.

An important point to keep in mind when using the FDISK command is that, if the active partition is a non-DOS partition, you will need to boot up your computer with a DOS system diskette in drive A if you want to use FDISK to change back to the DOS partition. Once a non-DOS partition has been made active, the only way you can have access to DOS is to boot on a DOS system diskette in the floppy drive.

You should also be aware that, although FDISK can be used to select an established non-DOS partition, it cannot be used to create or delete non-DOS partitions. The only way to remove non-DOS partitions is either through the non-DOS operating system itself or through re-establishing the low-level format on the disk. Before accepting any hard disk, especially one which has had previous data stored on it, it is a good idea

```
Change Active Partition

Current Fixed Disk Drive: 1

Partition Status      Type    Start   End    Size
     1         A        DOS     000    399    400
     2         N      non-DOS   400    608    209
```

Fig. 2-4. The "Change Active Partition" entry screen.

to use FDISK Option 4 to view the partitions stored on the disk. If there are any unwanted non-DOS partitions, be sure to have them removed for you. Otherwise you will be stuck with partitions that you can't remove short of physically reformatting the entire disk.

INSTALLING NEW VERSIONS OF DOS

Nothing is static in the world of personal computers, not even operating systems. The authors of DOS are continually adding enhancements and refinements to the basic operating system of your computer. While this can result in increased ease of use and greater utility, it often means extra work and greater confusion when new versions of DOS are released. To date, there have been three generations of PC/MS DOS. Unfortunately, confusion is created by the fact that corresponding versions of PC and MS DOS are not always numbered the same. Added to this is the fact of multiple minor revisions within a major version. Such is currently the case with DOS versions 3.0, 3.1, and 3.2.

The original DOS version 1.1 was superseded fairly quickly by version 2.xx and is not often used today. However, there are still quite a few DOS 2.xx versions floating around. As of the publication date of this book, DOS versions 3.xx are the most current, with slight variations between 3.0, 3.1, and 3.2. Where will it all end?

The presence of multiple versions of DOS has important ramifications for hard disk users. One important consideration is that, as new versions of DOS are released, you may want to upgrade the version of DOS installed on your hard disk.

Transferring the System Files

The MS-DOS operating system consists of three files: 10.SYS, MSDOS.SYS, and COMMAND.COM. The first two files are *hidden* files, and do not show up on your directory. (For more on these hidden files, see Chapter 3). In PC-DOS, the hidden files are called IBMBIO.COM and IBMDOS.COM. Since hidden files cannot be copied with the COPY command, DOS provides a SYS command which copies these hidden files from the original DOS diskette onto the target disk. Note: you must still use the COPY command to transfer a copy of COMMAND.COM onto the target disk. Normally, you shouldn't have to use the SYS command, because the /S option of the FORMAT command accomplishes the same thing.

The SYS command will work only if there is room at the beginning of the root directory to hold the system files. That is, the SYS command only works if a disk has recently been formatted, or if room has been reserved on the disk to accommodate the system files. In fact, one function of the SYS command is to transfer the system files onto applications programs diskettes which are sold without the operating system installed.

To use the SYS command to update the DOS system files on your hard disk, start your system with the new DOS system diskette into your floppy drive and enter the following:

A>SYS C:

The completion of this operation will be indicated by the message:

System transferred

After this command has been executed, make sure to copy a version of the updated COMMAND.COM onto your hard disk as well. To accomplish this, enter the command:

A>COPY COMMAND.COM C:

The SYS command cannot always be used to update your hard disk whenever a new version of DOS is released. The problem is that the size of the system files may change with new versions of DOS. For example if you attempt to use the SYS command to update version 1.1 of DOS from a 2.xx or 3.xx DOS system diskette, you will likely see a message such as the following:

Incompatible system size

In such cases, the only way to update your hard disk is to reformat and begin from scratch with the new DOS system diskette. Make sure you backup your files before performing this operation! Note that BACKUP and RESTORE won't serve you for this purpose. Instead, you will need to use the COPY command to transfer all needed files onto floppies and then recopy these files back onto your newly formatted hard disk.

PERFORMING A LOW-LEVEL FORMAT

Performing a low-level format on a hard disk drive is a fairly drastic action. All the data contained on the hard disk will be irrevocably lost. Remember, the low-level formatting process overwrites every data byte on the disk with dummy data. You normally don't need to perform a low-level format on your hard disk, which is why you won't find the instructions for low-level formatting in your DOS Operations Manual. The DOS FORMAT command will usually be sufficient for reformatting your hard disk should the need arise.

When to Perform a Low-Level Format

There are certain instances in which a high-level format will not suffice, and you will need to low-level format the hard drive. One situation which requires a low-level format is removing non-DOS partitions. Suppose you have inherited a hard drive and the former user had established one or more non-DOS partitions on this drive. Unless you have access to the operating system software used to establish these partitions, the only way you can remove them and recover the storage areas they isolated is to perform a low-level format.

Another reason for performing a low-level format is if magnetic or physical damage has occurred to your hard disk and this damage is affecting the use of the boot record, File Allocation Table, or the root directory. If you get many "Boot Failure" error messages when you attempt to start your computer from your hard disk, or if you get messages like:

Directory not found

when you try to read your root directory, then you may need to perform a low-level format. Of course, you should always try performing a high-level format first in hopes that this will correct the problem.

Since low-level formatting permanently overwrites any data stored on your hard drive, this procedure should only be used as a last resort. Of course, if you need to remove non-DOS partitions, or if your hard drive is not booting properly, you really have nothing to loose. If at all possible, be sure you backup all the data stored on your hard disk before proceeding!

Using DEBUG to Perform a Low-Level Format

The process of low-level formatting is actually performed by your *hard disk controller*. This is a special set of circuits, or chips, which are either located on the hard disk itself, or, more likely, on a special circuit board known as the *hard disk controller card*. The instructions for operating the hard disk controller are normally stored in the hard disk controller ROM chip. The address of this ROM chip is located in bank C of DOS memory. (Note: DOS can actually access memory above the 640K limit, but this memory is normally reserved for video display, special ROM memory such as the hard disk controller ROM, and the ROM BIOS.)

To access the instructions stored in the hard disk controller ROM, you need to use the special DOS tool, DEBUG. A copy of DEBUG.COM is located on your DOS Supplemental Programs diskette. To use DEBUG, you will need to place a working copy of this diskette into your A drive. Enter the DEBUG program by typing the following at the system prompt:

A>DEBUG

DEBUG will load and display its own prompt, which is a hyphen (-). To view the contents of the hard disk controller ROM, which is located at hexadecimal address 800 in bank C of memory, type the following command:

-dc800:0

About half a screen of data is displayed. Off on the right hand of the screen you may see a description of your hard disk controller or the manufacturer's name. (See Fig. 2-5.)

From DEBUG, you can instruct your hard disk controller to perform a low-level

```
-dc800:0
C800:0000   55 AA 10 EB 7C E9 28 05-28 43 29 20 43 6F 70 79   U...¦.(.(C) Copy
C800:0010   72 69 67 68 74 20 31 39-38 34 20 57 65 73 74 65   right 1984 Weste
C800:0020   72 6E 20 44 69 67 69 74-61 6C 20 43 6F 72 70 6F   rn Digital Corpo
C800:0030   72 61 74 69 6F 6E CF 02-25 02 08 2A FF 50 F6 19   ration..%..*.P..
C800:0040   04 64 02 04 65 02 65 02-0B 05 00 00 00 00 00 00   .d..e.e.........
C800:0050   00 64 02 02 80 00 80 00-0B 05 00 00 00 00 00 00   .d.............
C800:0060   00 64 02 04 65 02 80 00-0B 05 00 00 00 00 00 00   .d..e..........
C800:0070   00 32 01 04 32 01 00 00-0B 05 00 00 00 00 00 00   .2..2..........
```

Fig. 2-5. Sample screen displaying information pertaining to a hard disk as a result of the DEBUG command dc800:0.

format. The machine instructions to do this are located at offset 5 from address C800. To tell the hard disk controller to proceed, or go, you enter the following DEBUG command:

-g = c800:5

Entering this command will produce one of two results: The hard disk controller may go right ahead and reformat your hard disk. Or it may display a menu offering you a variety of options. The action taken by the hard disk controller depends upon the manufacturer. Actually, a third possible result is that the hard disk controller will do nothing at all. This will only occur if you have a non-standard hard disk controller which does not conform to the normal DOS memory assignments.

If your hard disk controller displays a menu or prompts you for input as to the relative disk head number, head count, number of platters, interleave factor, etc., you will have to refer to your hard disk drive owner's manual. These numbers might need to be entered by setting specific microprocessor registers with DEBUG. If this is too daunting a task for you to face, you may want to take your computer into the shop and have a professional perform this task for you. Otherwise, between the manual and the instructions on the screen, you should be able to proceed with no problem. Typically, the choices already offered (if there are default values) will be fine.

Remember, the worst you can do at this point is reformat your hard disk, which is exactly what you want to do. You can't do any physical damage to your drive.

If the above procedure doesn't work, you may need to use a special program provided on a diskette which came with the hard drive unit. Typical names for programs which perform a low-level format are HSECT, DTCFMT, LFORMAT, etc. These programs perform the low-level format either as a convenience to the user or on certain brands of hard drives which require non-standard controllers. In most cases, however, you can use the DEBUG command, g = c800:5 to perform a low-level format.

You are ready to begin using your hard disk system. The first thing you will need to do is install your application software onto your hard disk. To do so, you will need to understand the concepts of filenames and directories. The following chapter provides a thorough treatment of these two subjects and teaches you the DOS commands you will need to know to set up work areas on your hard disk to store your programs and data.

Chapter 3

Filenames and Directories

By far the most frequently used DOS command is the directory command, DIR. This command provides you with a list of the files stored on a disk as well as other useful information about the disk. You are probably already familiar with this command. There is more to the directory command than meets the eye, however, as this chapter will reveal. You can use the directory command to obtain an alphabetically sorted listing of the files on your disk, or to obtain a partial listing of just your Lotus spreadsheets. You can also print out your directory listings for reference purposes. These and other handy techniques will be explained in this chapter.

FILENAMES AND WILD CARDS

To use the directory command to its fullest, you need to understand the rules for filenames and wild cards. DOS filenames consist of two components. The first part of the filename is used to describe the file's contents and is often referred to as the *descriptive* name. DOS limits descriptive filenames to eight characters, although you may use fewer than eight characters if you wish. In addition, a filename may include an optional extension. *Extensions* are used to classify files according to the type of data or programs they contain. File extensions are separated from the descriptive component of the filename by a period and may consist of from one to three characters. Certain application programs automatically assign file extensions to the files they create. For example, Lotus 1-2-3 releases 1.x add the extension .WKS to worksheet files. DOS itself recognizes the following reserved file extensions:

.COM   A command file (program file)

.EXE	An executable file (program file)
.BAT	A batch file
.BAS	A BASIC program

Rules for Filenames

Not all keyboard characters are allowable in filenames. Acceptable characters include the letters and the digits (0 through 9) as well as the following characters:

! @ # $ % & ( ) - _ { }

Characters that are not permissible include:

? / | * . , < > ^ + " [ ] ~

Filenames must begin with a character and may not include any spaces. Including spaces in filenames is probably the most common mistake made by novice computer users. Filenames may be entered in either upper or lower case, although DOS (and most programs) displays filenames in upper case. To avoid confusing filenames with text, filenames will appear in upper case throughout this book. If you use any of the disallowed characters in a filename, or if you do not correctly follow the rules for filenames, DOS will display the following message on the screen:

Invalid character in filename or file not found.

Some valid filenames include:

LETTER
LETTER1
LETTER.NEW
LETTER.OLD
MY_FILE
YOUR-FIL.84

The following represent examples of invalid filenames. See if you can spot the error in each of them:

YOUR_FILE
LONG.FILE
01/86.DAT
LETR 2.MOM
86+87.DAT

Wild Cards

Wild cards are special characters that may be substituted for one or more characters in a filename. The use of wild cards allows you to specify multiple files by making filenames generic. The two DOS wild cards are the "?" and the "*" characters. You can think of these two characters as variables.

The ? wild card is a variable that stands for any single character. For example, the filename LESSON? may be used to refer to LESSON1, LESSON2, or LESSON3. In fact, the filename actually refers to all three lesson files at once. In this case, the use of the ? saves you from typing three separate filenames. You may include more than one ? in a filename. For example, suppose you had more than nine lesson files. In order to include all lesson files, you would need two ?'s - LESSON??. This would encompass filenames like LESSON12 as well as single digit lesson files.

The ? wild card may be used in file extensions as well. Suppose you had a series of financial statements that were labeled P&L.78 through P&L.87. Imagine that you wanted to refer jointly to all the P&L files from 1980 on. What generic filename would you use? If your answer is P&L.8?, you are correct. (Your gold star is in the mail.)

The * wild card is more versatile. It can take the place of multiple ? wild cards. In the descriptive filename, an * replaces all characters up to the period. In file extensions, the * replaces the remaining characters in the extension. To refer to all the lesson files in the previous example, you could use a single *: LESSON*. In fact, you could have used LES*. In this case, it is unlikely that any non-lesson files will begin with the three letters LES. One use for the * is to save unnecessary keystrokes. Be careful, though; it probably would not be a good idea to use L* to refer to the lesson files. Why not?

As with the ? wild card, the * wild card can be used in file extensions. The most common usage of the * in extensions is to refer to "any extension." For instance, if you weren't sure what file extension you used, if any, when naming the lesson files, you could refer to them by LESSON*.*. In this example, there are two *'s, one before and one following the period. Although the * wild card can stand for multiple characters, you must use a separate * in the descriptive filename and the extension.

Another common usage of the * wild card is to represent any file with a given extension. To include all .COM files, you would use *.COM. From this example, it's a simple extension to using two *'s to refer to all files as *.*. This special filename, pronounced "star dot star," is very powerful. As you will learn in Chapter 4, one important use of this combination is copying files from one disk to another.

DISK DIRECTORIES AND FILE ALLOCATION TABLES

A disk directory is itself a file containing information about the other files stored on the disk. Although disks may contain more than one directory, every disk contains at least one directory, the root directory. The *root directory* is stored in a specific location on the disk, so DOS always knows where to find it. DOS then uses the information contained in the root directory to locate other files stored on the disk.

The root directory may be linked to other directories, called subdirectories. *Subdirectories* are not usually used with floppy diskettes but are commonly found on hard disks. The subject of subdirectories will be covered in detail in Chapter 5, Subdirectories And Paths. Disk directories consist of file entries containing important information about the files stored on the disk, such as filenames and where files are located.

Directory Entries

Each file has its own directory entry, which consists of 32 bytes of data. You can think of the individual file entries as consisting of records in the directory file. These records contain specific fields of information pertaining to each file recorded in the directory. Of course, the file entry includes the file's eight-character descriptive name as well as its three character-extension. These constitute the first two fields of file information. A file's directory entry also includes the location of the beginning of the file, called the *starting cluster address.* This tells DOS where the first segment of the file is stored on the disk.

The next field contains a four-byte integer which records the file's physical size in bytes. Although no file can be as large as the largest four-byte binary integer, this is the amount of room set aside in the file entry. Following the file size field are two two-byte fields used to record the file's DATE and TIME stamp. These two fields contain the date and time the file was created or last updated. You will learn more about the DOS DATE and TIME commands in Chapter 4, Other Essential DOS Commands.

In addition, each directory entry includes certain technical information about the file recorded in a single-byte field called the *file attribute.* Among other things, the file attribute is used to denote whether the file is hidden or read-only. You'll learn more about these special file characteristics in Chapter 13, Hidden Files and Data Encryption.

The number of file entries a directory can hold depends upon the size of the directory file itself. Sixteen file entries can fit into a single sector (512 / 32 = 16). In DOS 1.1, four sectors are allocated for the disk directory, which may contain up to 64 file entries. A double-sided diskette formatted under DOS 2.xx or later has seven sectors set aside for the disk directory, resulting in a maximum of 112 file entries. The size of the directory on a hard disk varies. In the case of the AT's 20 megabyte hard disk, the root directory is 32 sectors, allowing up to 512 directory entries.

File Allocation Tables

Files are not actually stored on a disk sector by sector. Instead they are stored in *clusters* of 512-byte sectors. The cluster size varies from one disk format to another. On double-sided diskettes, clusters are only two sectors, but on the original IBM XT's 10-megabyte hard disk, the cluster size is normally eight sectors, or 4096 bytes. This is why you don't see any files smaller than 4K when you call for a file directory on an XT. On the IBM AT, the cluster size has been reduced to four sectors, or 2048 bytes, to accommodate smaller files without wasting space.

Large files are stored in multiple clusters. For example, a 100K file requires 25 clusters on an XT. If a file does not fit exactly into some multiple of the cluster size, an additional cluster is used. Although the cluster may only be partially full, the remaining empty sectors cannot be used by another file. In the preceding example, if the file were only 97K, it would still require 25 clusters.

Chapter 1 discussed the differences between random and sequential file storage. Whether random or sequential storage is used to write a file to disk, unless the file is smaller than the cluster size, it will occupy multiple clusters on the disk. Piecing this file together again would be extremely difficult without the aid of the File Allocation Table.

The *File Allocation Table,* or FAT as it is known in DOS circles, works in conjunction with the disk directory to keep track of where files are located on the disk. Like the directory, the FAT is another file on the disk. In it are a series of two-byte addresses, one for each cluster on the disk. (Actually, the first two entries are used by DOS to record information about the disk—the first real cluster reference is found in entry 2.) As was mentioned earlier, the directory stores the address of the starting cluster for each file. To find the next cluster, DOS looks up the entry in the FAT for the starting cluster. This entry gives the location for the next cluster. (see Fig. 3-1.)

Following this procedure, DOS is able to locate the subsequent clusters that contain the complete file. When DOS checks the FAT for the reference value of the final cluster, it encounters a special control character which indicates that the end of the file has been encountered and there are no more clusters to be retrieved. Essentially, the FAT contains a series of pointers which DOS uses to chain together the various clusters into a complete file. Initially, all entries in the FAT are set to zero. The actual pointer values get entered into the FAT as files are written to the disk. A non-zero entry for a given cluster means that the cluster is occupied.

The FAT can also be used to record the fact that a cluster contains one or more bad sectors. Bad sectors are either physically or magnetically damaged and cannot be used to store data. If a cluster has been identified as containing bad sectors, a special code value will be recorded for it in the FAT.

As you might imagine, a file's FAT is very important. Without it, the data stored in files on the disk would be unrecoverable. In fact, even if the disk directory becomes damaged, it is possible to rebuild it from the information contained in the FAT. In Chapter 10, Backing Up Data and Programs, you will learn how to reconstruct disk directories using the DOS RECOVER command. Because the information in the FAT is so important, DOS actually stores a duplicate copy of it on the disk. If the original FAT becomes damaged, it is possible to use this backup copy to recover the data stored on the disk.

THE DIRECTORY COMMAND

As you probably know, the directory command is entered at the DOS prompt as follows:

A>DIR

When this command is entered, DOS retrieves the filenames of all files stored in the root directory and displays them on the screen. In Chapter 5 you will learn about subdirectories and how to obtain directory listings for them as well. For the sake of

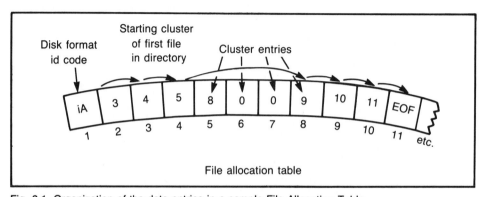

Fig. 3-1. Organization of the data entries in a sample File Allocation Table.

Table 3-1. A Sample Directory Listing.

```
Volume in drive A has no label
Directory of  A:\

COMMAND   COM      17792    10-20-83    12:00p
WSOVLY1   OVR      41216     1-01-80    12:18a
WSMSGS    OVR      29056     1-01-80    12:18a
WS        INS      48512     6-12-85    10:19a
WS        COM      21376     1-01-80    12:17a
LETTER1   DOC      48187     1-01-80    12:48a
LETTER2   DOC      39902     1-01-80     2:11a
LETTER3   DOC      37750     1-01-80     2:05a
LETTER4   DOC      33267     1-01-80     1:08a
LETTER6   DOC       1408     1-01-80    12:20a
LETTER5   DOC        343     1-01-80    12:13a
      11 File(s)       15360 bytes free
```

simplicity, however, all examples in this chapter assume that the root directory is the only directory on the disk.

A sample directory listing is shown above. The filenames are listed vertically down the screen in the order they were retrieved from the root directory. Notice that the period between the descriptive filename and the file's extension is not displayed. In its place is a space. Also, the file extensions are aligned in a separate column, beginning at column nine on the screen.

Next to each filename is the size of the file in bytes, along with the date and time the file was created or updated. Note that the date and time information for a given file are only correct if the proper date and time were entered at the DOS DATE and TIME prompts when the system disk was loaded. If you are unfamiliar with these two prompts, you can refer to the section on the DATE and TIME commands in Chapter 4.

In addition to information about individual files, the directory command provides you with two lines of information at the top of the listing. The first gives the volume name for the disk if any has been assigned. The next line gives the drive designator. In this case, the letter "A" followed by the colon refers to the A drive of the computer. The backslash character, "\," refers to the root directory. At the bottom of the listing DOS indicates the number of files contained in the directory and the amount of space that is still available for storage.

This bottom line of information can be used as a quick check to determine how much room is left on the disk. Remember, you are limited not only by the amount of physical storage space available on the disk but also by the amount of file entries in the root directory. In the case of the sample listing, there is plenty of physical space on the disk, and there is room for up to 51 more files.

No, this is not a mistake in arithmetic. If you came up with 53 files (64 - 11), you were correct in your assumption that the root directory of this double-sided disk can hold 64 file entries. However, what you did not take into account were the two hidden files, IBMBIOS.COM and IBMDOS.COM (IO.SYS and MSDOS.SYS in MS-DOS), stored in the directory as well as the 11 files that are displayed in the directory listing. As you remember from the preceding chapter, these two files are placed on any disk that is formatted using the /S option.

Changing the Current Drive

The directory command will display a listing of the *working directory* (for now, this means the root directory) on the currently logged disk drive. Most computers containing hard drives are set up to boot off the hard disk. This means that, when the power is turned on, the computer's boot ROM tells the CPU to check the A drive (floppy drive) for the presence of a diskette. If no diskette is in the drive, the CPU will next check the C drive (hard drive) to see if it can find the system files. If these files are present, they will be loaded and the C drive will become the current drive. This is communicated by the fact that the DOS prompt is displayed as a C prompt (C>).

As was mentioned previously, the directory command lists the current directory of the current drive. There are two ways to obtain a directory listing of a drive other than the current drive. The simplest way is to include the drive's designator as part of the directory command. For example, if the C drive were the current drive, and you wanted a listing of the files on the diskette in drive A, you would enter:

C>DIR A:

Note that with an XT or AT with a single floppy drive, you could also have entered:

C>DIR B:

since both drive designators are assigned to the floppy drive.

A second method for obtaining a directory listing of a non-current drive is to make that drive the current drive. This is just about as easy as the first method, but it requires two separate DOS operations. Following the same example, you would first make the floppy drive current by simply entering its drive designator at the C prompt:

C>A:

DOS would respond by displaying an A prompt instead of the former C prompt. You would then enter the directory command:

A>DIR

Directory Command Options

The standard directory command is fine when working with disks containing limited numbers of files. However, even with floppy diskettes, the number of files can quickly grow beyond the number that can be displayed on the screen at one time. With hard disks, the problem can become even more severe as the number of files in the root directory expands into the hundreds. If there are more files in the directory than can be displayed on a single screen, the directory command scrolls the screen as it continues to list the files in vertical sequence. Unless you are particularly sharp, you are apt to miss a filename that appears in the early part of the listing as it scrolls by.

There are two ways of getting around this problem. The first is to use the *wide display* option when entering the directory command. The wide display option is employed by adding a slash and the letter "W" to the standard directory command as follows:

A > DIR /W

The space between the DIR and the /W is optional.

The directory listing shown below was obtained using the wide display option to obtain a listing of the same diskette as the preceding directory listing. In this listing, the filenames are displayed across the screen in five columns, allowing up to five times as many files to be displayed on a single screen. Of course, there's no such thing as a free lunch. In this case, DOS sacrifices the file size information as well as the DATE and TIME stamps for each file in favor of additional filenames.

If you need to view the file size or DATE and TIME stamps, or if you have even more files than can be displayed with the wide display option, you can use the Ctrl NumLock key sequence to temporarily interrupt the scrolling process. Pressing this key sequence again will cause the scrolling to resume. Ctrl NumLock is a kind of freeze-frame key. You have to press it at just the right moment in order to capture the information you are interested in. If you are like most computer users and are not possessed of Rambo-like reflexes, you may prefer to use the pause option.

The *pause* option follows the directory command and can be used as a single option or in combination with the wide option. The following are two ways of using the pause option:

C > DIR /P

C > DIR /W/P

Whenever you add the pause option to the directory command, DOS displays as many files as will fit on the screen and then displays the message:

Strike a key when ready . . .

at the bottom of the screen. You can view the contents of the screen as long as you

Table 3-2. Directory Listing Obtained Using the / W Option.

```
 Volume in drive A has no label
 Directory of  A:\

COMMAND   COM     WSOVLY1   OVR     WSMSGS    OVR     WS        INS     WS        COM
LETTER1   DOC     LETTER2   DOC     LETTER3   DOC     LETTER4   DOC     LETTER6   DOC
LETTER5   DOC
        11 File(s)      15360 bytes free
```

41

like. When you wish to see the next screenful, just press any key. This screen-by-screen display will continue, with you controlling the pace, until the entire directory has been displayed.

Printing Directory Listings

It is often helpful to have a printed listing of the files stored on a disk. There are many specialized directory utilities which allow you to obtain a printed directory listing. A number of these are available as public domain programs. See Chapter 17, More Handy Utilities, for a description of one such program. However, you don't need any utilities at all to print a simple listing of your directories. Instead, you can make use of the DOS screen dump feature.

The IBM family of computers, and most compatibles, have a special key labeled PrtSc. On the PC and XT keyboards, this key is located immediately adjacent to the right Shift key. On compatibles the location varies with the manufacturer. Note that the PrtSc label appears as the upper key label. You have to hold the Shift key down in conjunction with this key. This is to prevent you from inadvertently hitting this key by mistake.

Striking the PrtSc key causes DOS to send a copy of the screen's contents to the printer. (Actually, a copy of the video RAM is sent to the printer, but who wants to get technical?) PrtSc will only give you a copy of what's currently displayed on the screen. For example, the PrtSc key will only work if your printer is on, on line, and connected to your computer. (You would be amazed at how often people forget this simple fact.)

If your directory listings take up multiple screens, there is an alternative to using the PrtSc key to print each screenful of information. Using the Ctrl PrtSc key combination will cause everything that is displayed on the screen to be sent to the printer until a second Ctrl PrtSc is entered. You can think of Ctrl PrtSc as a toggle switch. Pressing this key combination once enables the printer; pressing it again disables the printer.

Partial Directories

The directory command can also be used to determine if a given file is actually on the disk you are working with. Although you could issue the basic DIR command, which would show you all the files on the disk, you would then have to scan the list to see if the specific file you are interested in is present. This can be quite tedious, particularly if the listing runs to multiple screens. A simpler approach is to use the directory command in conjunction with the name of the file you are looking for. For example, if you want to see if LESSON1 is stored on drive A, you would enter:

C > DIR A:LESSON1

If the file is on the disk, DOS will display the filename and the size of the file, etc. If the file is not present, DOS will respond with the message:

File not found

The directory command can be used with filenames containing wild cards as well. Sometimes you may only want a partial listing of the files on your disk. Usually you will want to view all files satisfying a certain condition, such as all Lotus worksheets, or all .COM files. To obtain a listing of all .COM files on the hard disk, you would enter:

C > DIR *.COM

DOS would display a directory listing which included only those files with a .COM extension. If there weren't any files satisfying this condition, the "File not found" message would be displayed instead.

Partial directory listings are a handy way of limiting the time required to determine the name, size, existence, etc. of a given file when you don't know its exact spelling. Imagine that you are looking for a file you created last week using Lotus 1-2-3. You're sure you called it something beginning with "INS" because it was an analysis of insurance policies held by your company. Rather than searching through the entire directory, you could enter:

C > DIR A:INS*.WKS

This would give you a listing of all worksheet files beginning with "INS." Chances are there will only be a few of them. One word of advice—if several filenames are displayed and you still can't remember which one you want, jot all of them down on a piece of scratch paper (or use the PrtSc key to get a printed listing). It's amazingly difficult to remember more than two similar filenames without getting them confused.

FIND, MORE, AND SORT

As you have already noticed either from the examples presented in this book, or, more likely, from previous experience, the filenames in a directory listing are displayed in random order. This contributes to the difficulty you encounter when searching for a specific file in a long directory listing.

It is possible to have DOS sort the filenames for you before displaying them on the screen. To do so you employ two DOS tools: filters and pipes. DOS *filters* are separate utility programs that alter the output of other DOS commands. There are three DOS filters, FIND, SORT, and MORE. A DOS *pipe* simply passes, or pipes, the output of one DOS command or filter on to another DOS command or filter.

The SORT Filter

As its name implies, the SORT filter is used to arrange data into either ascending or descending order. When used with the directory command, the normally unsorted directory listing will be sorted alphabetically. To obtain a sorted directory listing, you must pipe the output of the directory command to the SORT filter.

The DOS pipe consists of the vertical bar character, "|". This character hides in different locations on the keyboard depending on the model of computer you have, but some diligent searching will reveal its whereabouts. On the IBM XT, it is located in the upper right-hand corner (on the backslash key). The complete command is entered as shown below:

C > DIR | SORT

As with the /P and /W directory options, the spacing between the DIR, the |, and the SORT is optional. Using the SORT filter on the sample diskette would result in the following directory listing.

The SORT filter includes two options. The /R option is used to reverse the order of the sort, resulting in listings from "Z" to "A." While you are unlikely to need a reverse alphabetical listing, you may want to sort files numerically in descending order according to their file size. To do this, you will use both the /R and the /+ options. The /+ option allows you to specify which column of data in a given file is to be used for organizing the sorted output. This corresponds to the sorting key used with spreadsheet or database programs such as Lotus 1-2-3 or dBASE III.

As you may remember from the discussion at the beginning of this chapter, the root directory is actually a file containing individual file entries, or records. The information about each file is contained in various columns, with the descriptive filename occupying columns 1 through 8. It turns out that the file size information begins at column 14. You can use this fact to sort your directory listings according to file size by entering the following command:

C>DIR | SORT /R/+14

The MORE Filter

The SORT filter may be used in conjunction with the MORE filter when directory listings are long. The MORE filter works much like the /P directory command option. Information is filtered through the MORE filter a screenful at a time, pausing after each new screen and displaying the message:

—MORE—

at the bottom of the screen. Pressing the Return key causes the next screenful of information

Table 3-3. Directory Listing Obtained Using the SORT Filter.

```
        11 File(s)      15360 bytes free
     Directory of  A:\
     Volume in drive A has no label
     COMMAND  COM    17792   10-20-83   12:00p
     LETTER1  DOC    48187    1-01-80   12:48a
     LETTER2  DOC    39902    1-01-80    2:11a
     LETTER3  DOC    37750    1-01-80    2:05a
     LETTER4  DOC    33267    1-01-80    1:08a
     LETTER5  DOC      343    1-01-80   12:13a
     LETTER6  DOC     1408    1-01-80   12:20a
     WS       COM    21376    1-01-80   12:17a
     WS       INS    48512    6-12-85   10:19a
     WSMSGS   OVR    29056    1-01-80   12:18a
     WSOVLY1  OVR    41216    1-01-80   12:18a
```

to be displayed. Since the MORE filter controls the screen display, it is always the last filter to be included in a sequence of DOS commands and filters. To use the MORE filter with SORT and DIR you would enter:

C > DIR | SORT | MORE

The FIND Filter

The FIND filter is usually used to locate the occurrence of a word, phrase, or group of characters within a specified file. A group of characters are referred to as *string* in computer terminology. Strings are indicated by appearing in quotes. To be designated as a string, as opposed to a command or filename, the phrase "HELLO THERE" would be entered as:

C > "HELLO THERE"

Since the directory is a file, it is possible to verify the existence of a given filename within the directory by piping the output from the DIR command through the FIND filter. Note that the FIND filter searches for strings, so the filename should be enclosed in quotes. To verify that the LESSON1 file is located on the diskette in drive A, you would enter:

C > DIR A: | FIND "LESSON1"

The FIND filter can also check for partial strings. This concept is similar to the use of wild cards. For instance, you could use the FIND command to list all the lesson files on the diskette by entering:

C > DIR A: | FIND "LESSON"

Most people find wild cards simpler to work with and easier to enter than the FIND filter. However, the FIND filter can do some tricks that wild cards can't. For one thing, the FIND filter can be used to filter out unwanted filenames by adding the /V option. Consider the case where you want to view all data files on a disk without including the program files. Entering the following command sequence would produce this result:

C > DIR A: | FIND/V ".COM"

The FIND filter can also be employed to determine which files were created or updated on a certain date:

C > DIR A: | FIND "3-15-87"

The SORT, FIND, and MORE filters are external utilities. *External utilities* are actually program files with the utility name as their descriptive filename and a .COM extension. Just because you have a copy of DOS on your disk does not automatically ensure that you have access to all DOS commands. The next chapter on DOS commands will explain the difference between internal and external commands, but for now you need to know that you must have copies of the SORT.EXE, FIND.EXE and MORE.COM files in your root directory before you can use them in DOS commands. These files come with your copy of DOS and are usually found on your DOS Systems disk.

Whenever you use a pipe to pass the output of one command or filter on to another, DOS creates a temporary file on the root directory of the current disk. This scratch pad file may show up in directory listings that are displayed during the piping process. Such files begin with "%PIPE" followed by some number and include the special DOS file extension $$$, such as %PIPE3.$$$. This extension is used to indicate a temporary file. These temporary pipe files will be removed from the root directory at the conclusion of the piping process, so don't worry if they appear in your directories.

REDIRECTING DIRECTORY OUTPUT

Normally, the output of a directory listing is sent to the screen. This seems only reasonable, right? After all, where else would you want the directory listing to go? In fact, it is sometimes useful to store a listing of a disk's directory in a data file for later reference. This will become more apparent after you have read Chapter 5, which describes subdirectories and paths.

Even excluding subdirectories, there is at least one valid reason for storing directory listings in a data file. This technique enables you to combine multiple disk directories into a single listing. For example, suppose you have five floppy diskettes worth of Word Perfect documents. You would like to have a single listing of all the files on these five diskettes. This can be accomplished by storing a copy of each diskette's directory into a data file. This data file can then be sorted or printed as needed.

First, consider the problem of transferring a single directory listing into a data file. It's really quite simple. You merely redirect the output of the directory command to a disk file of your choosing. This is done using the " > " key and supplying a filename when entering the directory command. Suppose you wanted to save a copy of the directory listing in a data file named DIRLIST.DAT. You would enter:

C>DIR > DIRLIST.DAT

More to the point, assume that you wanted to transfer a copy of the directory listings for each of the five Word Perfect data disks mentioned earlier. In this example, the diskettes will be placed in the A drive and the file DIRLIST.DAT will be stored on drive C. You would place the first diskette into the A drive and issue the command:

C>DIR A: > DIRLIST.DAT

This would place a copy of the first diskette's directory listing in the DIRLIST.DAT file. If you were to repeat this process with the second disk, what do you think would happen? You're right! The second directory listing would replace the first. This is not what you want. To avoid this, you would use two > 's in all subsequent commands as follows:

C>DIR A: > > DIRLIST.DAT

The double > causes the additional directory listings to be appended to the original listing instead of overwriting it (and each other).

Once the combined directory file has been compiled, it can be passed through the SORT filter to create a single, sorted listing of all the filenames. For this command, the DIRLIST.DAT file becomes the input, rather than the output, file. To indicate this, you would use the "<" character. The following command will use the DIRLIST.DAT file as the input for the SORT filter and place the sorted listing into the output file DIRSORT.DAT:

C>SORT < DIRLIST.DAT > DIRSORT.DAT

The contents of the DIRSORT.DAT file can be viewed on the screen with the TYPE command or sent to the printer with the PRINT command.

Chapter 4

Other Essential
DOS Commands

Using a personal computer, especially one equipped with a hard disk, requires a number of different skills. Certainly, you need to know how to run the applications programs that enable you to do useful work. Before you know it, you've added a word processing program, spreadsheet, database management, and maybe graphics or communications software to your repertoire. It's hard enough keeping track of all these programs and their commands. But besides the role of computer user, you wear another hat as well—that of computer operator.

As your system's operator, it is your responsibility to maintain the program and data files stored on your hard disk and to uphold the security of the system by creating duplicate copies of these files on floppy diskettes. File maintenance is an ongoing chore associated with using a personal computer, and the magnitude of this chore is directly proportional to the amount of disk storage on your system and the volume of data that you process on a regular basis.

There are a number of DOS commands which enable you to perform the task of file management on your computer. These include commands to copy files from one disk to another, delete and rename files, and view and compare the contents of files. There are also commands that allow you to check the status of your storage media. Still other DOS commands facilitate working with the operating system.

The information in this chapter includes some tricks and suggestions you won't find in your DOS manual, so you might want to skim the sections on the commands you already know in search of these special gems. There is nothing quite so gratifying in the field of personal computing as knowing and using some clever little short-cut that the rest of the world hasn't heard of yet.

THE ROLE OF THE COMMAND PROCESSOR

In Chapter 2, you read about the three system files, IBMDOS.COM, IBMBIO.COM, and COMMAND.COM. (Note: in MS-DOS, the first two files are named IO.SYS and MSDOS.SYS.) COMMAND.COM is the one system file that you can see in a disk's directory. This file is known as the *command processor*. What this term refers to is the file's function as an interpreter and performer of the DOS commands that you enter from the keyboard. COMMAND.COM intercepts anything you type at the system prompt and attempts to process your command. This results in one of three possible outcomes.

If the command you enter is a DOS command recognized by the command processor, it will execute that command directly. If your entry is not one of the basic DOS commands, the command processor will assume it is the name of a program file you wish to run. The command processor will then search the disk directory for the presence of that program and execute it for you. As you've probably discovered by now, there is another possible outcome. If the command processor doesn't recognize your entry as a DOS command and can't find a program file on your disk by that name, it replies with the following error message:

Bad command or file name

Resident Versus External Commands

There are two types of commands in DOS, resident and external. *Resident commands* are commands that are directly executable by the command processor. These include COPY, RENAME, ERASE, and TYPE, for example. Whenever you are working at the system prompt, you have access to these commands. You can think of these commands as coming free with COMMAND.COM. Resident commands really are commands in the true sense of the word.

On the other hand, many so-called DOS commands are actually special programs designed to perform a DOS-related function. These short programs are usually referred to as *utilities*. The FORMAT utility is an example of one such program. Since these commands cannot be executed unless the program file with the command filename is present on the disk, they are said to be *external*. This means that they are outside the command processor. External commands include FORMAT, FDISK, DISKCOPY, and CHKDSK, as well as many others. Your DOS manual identifies commands as either Internal (i.e. resident) or External.

The most commonly used external commands are stored on your DOS System diskette. These utilities were all copied to your hard disk if you followed the instructions in Chapter 2 for transferring the system files. To review, this was accomplished with the command:

A>COPY *.* C:

Your copy of DOS also includes a second supplemental programs diskette. This diskette contains files of interest to programmers and should not normally be copied to the hard disk. (Note: if you already have copied these files onto your hard disk, you will learn how to remove them in this chapter.)

RESIDENT COMMANDS

The resident commands you will use most frequently are COPY, RENAME, and

ERASE. These commands are used with individual files, although COPY and ERASE can be made to work with multiple files through the use of the wildcard characters, "?" and "*". These commands are entered at the system prompt and are executed directly by the command processor. They may be used to affect files stored on the current disk, or on an alternate disk with the addition of a drive designator. Each of these commands will be discussed in turn.

This book follows the conventions of your DOS manual in listing the format of DOS commands. A word about command formats is in order here. Computer programmers need to know a lot of information about how a computer works or how a programming language is organized. The rules for languages and operating systems are often specified in terms of *format*. A command's format is a shorthand notation describing the rules, or syntax, for the command's use. The format for DOS command is somewhat cryptic if you are a computer novice. Here is a simplified description of what all those symbols in your DOS manual actually mean.

All words in capital letters pertain to the DOS command itself. This includes any command options (called *parameters* in your DOS manual). Words or letters in italics refer to the file or device on which the command is operating. A set of square brackets ([ ]) imply that the word or characters within the brackets are optional. These DOS command format conventions should become more comprehensible as you read the descriptions of each of the commands included in this chapter.

The COPY Command

The COPY command primarily is used to transfer files from one disk to another. The basic format of this command is:

COPY [d:]filename[.ext] [d:] [filename] [.ext]

According to this format, the first filename (with optional extension) refers to the *source* file, while the second filename designates the *destination* file. Notice that the destination filename is optional. This means that, when copying a file from one disk to another, it is not necessary to include the filename a second time unless you wish the file to have an alternate name when stored on the destination disk. Normally this is not the case. Note also that drive designators are optional with the COPY command. If a drive designator is not provided, the current drive is used by default. If the file is present on the designated source disk, the file will be copied to the destination disk and a confirming message:

1 File(s) copied

will appear on the screen.

A note of caution here. Unlike some applications that warn you if the destination file is already present on the target disk, COPY will blithely copy over an existing file, destroying its contents and replacing it with the version on the source disk. While this is often what you want to accomplish, as when transferring altered files to a backup disk, it can occasionally result in the loss of important data. Know what is on your target disk before using the COPY command.

As an example, suppose you wanted to transfer a copy of the file FILE1.DOC from your hard disk to a diskette in drive A. You would enter:

C>COPY FILE1.DOC A:

No drive designator is used in front of FILE1.DOC because this file is stored on the current drive (i.e. C). Also, no filename is specified after the A: because the file is to retain the same name on the destination diskette.

Now reverse the example. In this case, you want to transfer a copy of FILE1.DOC from the floppy drive to the hard drive. The command is now:

C>COPY A:FILE1.DOC

In this case, the drive designator precedes the source file. There is no need for a second drive designator, or even a second filename, because the hard disk is the current drive and the file is to retain its name when it is copied.

It would be possible to copy the FILE1.DOC file from C to A with a new name, such as FILE2.DOC. The command to accomplish this would be:

C>COPY FILE1.DOC A:FILE2.DOC

One unobvious application of the COPY command is creating a backup of a file on the same disk. This can be handy if you are planning to modify a data file but you are not sure you will like the results and you're also not sure if you'll be able to return the data to its original form. Such might be the case if you were planning to sort the data in a spreadsheet file. To make a duplicate copy of the FILE1.DOC file with the name FILE2.DOC, both stored on the hard disk, you would enter:

C>COPY FILE1.DOC FILE2.DOC

You will notice that no drive designators are included in this command. While it is not necessary to include drive designators with the COPY command, forgetting to include them can lead to the error message:

File cannot be copied onto itself

This error message would be displayed with either of the following commands:

C>COPY FILE1.DOC FILE1.DOC
C>COPY FILE1.DOC

In the first command, the file is being copied from the C drive onto the C drive because no drive designators were specified. Since the source and destination filenames are identical, the command is impossible to execute. Because both the optional drive designator and destination filename are absent in the second command, DOS is being told to copy the file onto itself. This is akin to a popular, though vulgar, epithet, and DOS justifiably takes offense.

Using Wildcards With The COPY Command

In Chapter 3 you learned how to use DOS wildcard characters with the directory command to specify subsets of files stored on the disk. The wildcard characters can also be used with the COPY command to specify groups of files to be copied. For example, you could copy all the files with a .DOC extension from drive C to drive A with the following command:

C>COPY *.DOC A:

The "*" wildcard can also be used on both sides of the period to copy all files on a diskette onto either another diskette or the hard disk. The following command was employed in Chapter 2 to transfer the DOS system files onto the hard disk:

C>COPY A:*.* C:

The "?" wildcard may also be used in combination with the COPY command to substitute for individual characters in source filenames.

Wildcards can be used in destination filenames as well. One practical application of this is for creating backup files. Although some programs make backup files for you automatically, not all do. It is often convenient to keep an extra copy of a file on the same disk but under a different name. This provides you with quick access to the data in case the original file is damaged or destroyed due to program (or, more likely pilot) error. For example, you could periodically create backups of all your Lotus 1-2-3 worksheets with the following command:

C>COPY *.WKS *.BAK

Each worksheet file would be copied into a resultant file with the same descriptive filename but with a .BAK extension.

One thing to watch out for when including wildcards in the COPY command is the possibility that you may be biting off more than you can chew. For example, consider what would happen if you entered the command:

C>COPY *.* A:

DOS would proceed diligently transferring all files on the hard disk onto the floppy diskette. At some point, the diskette would become full, and DOS would abort the operation. The message:

Insufficient disk space

will be displayed and you will be returned to the system prompt.

Sometimes this happens when copying files even without the global wildcards, *.*. If the source file is larger than the remaining space on the destination disk, you will see this message displayed. When DOS has to abort copying a file in the middle because it has run out of room, there may be a strange filename left over in the directory on the source diskette. The filename will have an extension .??? and a file size of 0K. This indicates a file that was unsuccessfully copied. Although .??? files take up no room on the disk, their filenames do occupy file entries in the directory. Since directory entries are limited in number, you should remove these filenames with the ERASE command.

The * wildcard can also be used as a shortcut when you want to copy single files. Suppose you wanted to copy the file FILE1.DOC from drive A to drive C. If you know there is only one file on the diskette beginning with the letter "F," you can use wildcards as follows:

C>COPY A:F*.*

This will get any file beginning with "F" and having any extension. Referring to the file as F*.* is much easier than entering FILE1.DOC. Of course, there is always the risk of copying more files than you bargained for if there is more than one file beginning with "F" on the diskette.

The Verify Option

There are three options available with the COPY command. The first of these is the /V (for verify) parameter. This parameter may be added to the COPY command whenever you want to ensure that the target medium is undamaged. The /V parameter causes DOS to check the integrity of each sector into which the source file is copied prior to transferring the data. This gives you extra assurance that the file is transferred correctly. Of course, additional time is required to check each sector, which slows down the copying process. An alternative to using the verify option with the COPY command is to check the integrity of the entire destination disk in advance with the CHKDSK command. This command will be described later in this chapter.

Combining Files With The COPY Command

Two other options, /A and /B, are used when combining files using the COPY command. As the term implies, combining files allows you to place the contents of several files into a single file. The most common reason for combining files is to create a large print file. For example, you might want to combine CHAPT1, CHAPT2, CHAPT3, CHAPT4, and CHAPT5 into a file named PART1.PRN. This single file could then be printed out using only one print command from your word processing program rather than printing each file separately. This technique can result in significant time savings. If you have a reliable tractor feed printer, you can submit the print job and take a coffee break instead of sticking around to print each file individually.

A word of warning here if you plan to use this technique with your word processor: Make sure that each file concludes with a page break command. Otherwise, the chapters will all run together. To copy the five chapters into the single PART1.PRN file, you would enter:

C>COPY CHAPT1 + CHAPT2 + CHAPT3 + CHAPT4 + CHAPT5 PART1.PRN

The use of the " + " character causes the contents of each source file to be added to those of the preceding file, with the combined results stored in the destination file. This requires quite a lot of typing. Assuming that you only have the first five chapters on your disk, you could use the ? wildcard to accomplish the same thing with far fewer keystrokes using the following command:

C>COPY CHAPT? PART1.PRN

Think about what this command will do. Because of the ? wildcard, there are multiple source files specified, but only one destination file. Thus, all the chapter files will be copied into the single PART1.PRN file. In fact, it is possible to combine all the chapter files into the CHAPT1 file by eliminating the destination filename altogether. This process is known as *appending* and would be accomplished as follows:

C>COPY CHAPT1 + CHAPT2 + CHAPT3 + CHAPT4 + CHAPT5

Again, this command can be simplified through the use of the ? wildcard. In this case, you have only to enter the brief command:

C>COPY CHAPT1 + CHAPT?

to accomplish the same thing. Note: the command:

C>COPY CHAPT?

will *not* work as expected, but will result in a damaged CHAPT1 file and an error message such as:

Content of destination lost before copy

The /A and /B COPY parameters are used when working with binary files. These are usually either .COM or .EXE files containing machine code, or source program files in assembly language or BASIC which will appear with .BAS or .ASM extensions. Files normally include a special control code, called *end-of-file*, which indicates that the file has concluded. When combining regular data files, as above, each file's end-of-file marker is included, so the data are separated from each other in the resultant file. However, it is possible to combine several binary files into a single file with only one end-of-file marker by including the /B parameter.

In effect, the /B parameter indicates to DOS that the file is to be copied without the inclusion of its end-of-file marker, while the /A parameter indicates that an end-of-file marker is to be included. The /B parameter affects all files following the file it is attached to, as does the /A parameter. The standard format for combining binary files is to use the /B parameter with the first file and to include the /A parameter after the last file in the list (thus including an end-of-file marker in the resultant file). For example, to combine files PROG1.BAS, PROG2.BAS, and PROG3.BAS into a single file PROGRAM.BAS with only one end-of-file marker, you would enter:

C>COPY PROG1.BAS/B + PROG2.BAS + PROG3.BAS/A PROGRAM.BAS

Copying Files Between Devices

When copying files from one disk to another, you are actually copying files between devices. Each disk drive is considered to be a device by your computer. There are a number of different devices in your computer system. These include the disk drives, the screen and keyboard, the printer outputs (called ports), and any communications ports. Each of these devices has a special *device name* which is recognized by DOS.

The disk drives are named A:, B:, C:, etc. The combination of the keyboard and screen is known as the *console* and has the device name CON:. Parallel printer ports are given the device names LPT1:, LPT2:, and LPT3:. If you have a printer hooked up to your computer system, it will most likely be a parallel printer attached to LPT1:. This printer output has another commonly used device name, PRN:. Communications ports use the device names COM1:, and COM2:. (Note:, it is not necessary to include the colon (:) with the CON, LPTx, PRN, or COMx device names, but they have been included in this text for consistency.)

It is possible to copy files to or from any of these devices following the standard COPY command format and substituting the device name you wish for the optional drive designator, [d:]. The most frequent application of copying between devices is to create short text files directly from the keyboard without entering a word processing program. It is also possible to copy files directly to the printer for output, but a better technique is to use the TYPE command to accomplish this as you will see later.

To create a text file from the console using the COPY command, you specify the CON: device as the source device and the filename you want as the destination. You then proceed to type in the text you wish to store in the file, ending each line with a Return (sorry, no word wrap here). When you are done, you must conclude with the special end-of-file marker, which is a Ctrl Z character. You may either enter a Ctrl Z directly, or press the F6 key. The end-of-file marker must also be ended with a Return.

To see how easy this really is, try creating a simple text file following these directions:

1. C>COPY CON: A:FLATTERY <Return>
2. HELLO THERE, <Return>
3. YOU HANDSOME DEVIL <Return>
4. F6 <Return>

If you followed these instructions, when you hit the final Return you should have seen your A drive light go on and the confirming message:

1 file(s) copied

appear on your screen. You have just successfully created a text file.

To view the results of your handiwork, simply reverse the sequence of the COPY command as follows:

C>COPY A:FLATTERY CON:

You will see the text appear on the screen followed again by the confirmation message telling you that one file has been copied.

While the preceding exercise may seem trivial, this technique provides a quick-and-dirty method for creating special text files called *batch files* that can be used to automate certain repetitive sequences of DOS commands. You will learn more about batch files in Chapter 6, Batch File Programming.

The ERASE Command

From time to time, it becomes necessary to remove files from storage media. This is especially true for fixed disks. Although 10 or 20 megabytes may seem like a lot of storage, you may one day encounter the dreaded *Insufficient disk space* message relating to your hard disk. Normally, you wouldn't wait for this message to occur before removing files from your disk. Both the directory and the CHKDSK commands allow you to determine the amount of storage space left on your disk. This allows you to plan ahead.

The ERASE command may be used to remove single files from a disk, or it may be used in combination with wildcards to remove multiple files from disk. Be careful when using wildcards with the ERASE command. You may accidentally remove files you didn't intend to erase. The format for this command is:

ERASE [d:]filename[.ext]

The rules for using wildcards with the ERASE command are the same as for the COPY command with one exception. If you use the global wildcards, *.*, you will be prompted with the following message:

Are you sure (Y/N)?

The purpose of this confirmation message is to insure against inadvertently erasing all the files on a disk. Unfortunately, this message cannot protect you against forgetting to include the floppy drive designator and deleting all files on the hard disk by mistake. This will occur if you enter the following command from the C drive:

C>ERASE *.*

Fortunately, you will learn how to unerase files later in Chapter 17, More Handy Utilities.

There is another version of the ERASE command that may be familiar to old hands in the microcomputer world. It is the DEL command, which is a hold-over from the days of CP/M. The DEL command works just like the ERASE command; the only difference is that it is easier to type. For this reason, DEL will be used from now on in any examples that require files to be removed.

When you erase a file, the file is not actually removed from the disk. This would require physically rewriting zeroes in all the sectors which used to contain the file's data as well as rewriting the directory entry. This would entail quite a lot of DOS overhead, which is really unnecessary. Instead, the directory entry for the file receives a special marker which indicates that the file has been erased. This is somewhat like banishment. The file is still physically on the disk, but you can't see it in a directory listing, nor can you read the data stored in it. It is possible to remove this file marker and so recover the file. There is a special unerase utility provided on the diskette which accompanies this book. Its use is described in Chapter 17.

The DEL and ERASE commands cannot be used to remove hidden or read only files from a disk. Hidden files were discussed in Chapter 2. Two hidden files are IBMDOS.COM and IBMBIO.COM. Read-only files have a special file attribute that denotes them as available for use, but not for copying or deleting. In Chapter 13 you will learn how to alter file attributes. This will allow you to create your own read-only files and also to change read-only files into read-write files, which may be erased or copied.

The RENAME Command

The RENAME command is used to change the name of a file. You may wonder why you would ever want to change a file's name. After all, what's in a name, right? "A rose by any other name . . ." and all that. Actually, there are several reasons for changing a file's name. One compelling reason is that you may have made an error in typing the filename the first time it was created.

Another reason for changing filenames is dictated by the popular word processing program, WordStar. This program makes a backup copy of document files each time you change them. WordStar uses the .BAK extension to denote backup files. However, only one backup file is available for each filename. This means that the second time you change a file, the original version is lost because the first altered version assumes the role of the backup file and the latest version gets the original file name. Suppose you want to keep copies of all three versions. To do so, you would need to rename the original version to some new name. Although WordStar includes a rename command of its own, you could use the RENAME command to change the filename before accessing WordStar.

You can also use the RENAME command to rename .COM files. There is nothing sacred about .COM filenames. For example, you can rename the dBASE III program file DBASE.COM to DB.COM. This will save you three keystrokes each time you enter the dBASE program. Another instance where the RENAME command is useful is in the case of duplicate filenames. For example, two leading word processing programs, WordPerfect and MultiMate, both use the filename WP.COM for their program files. Since both files cannot be stored in the same location at the same time as long as they use the same filename, something's got to give. "This disk just ain't big enough for the both of us," is one way of looking at it. You can use the RENAME command to resolve this conflict by renaming one of the program files to some other handy name— MM.COM, for instance.

The format of the RENAME command is quite simple:

$$\text{RENAME [d:]filename[.ext] [d:]filename[.ext]}$$

Using the preceding example to illustrate the use of the RENAME command, to rename WP.COM to MM.COM, you would enter:

$$\text{C}>\text{RENAME WP.COM MM.COM}$$

You may recall that the COPY command can also be used to rename files. The difference between the preceding command and the following one:

C>COPY WP.COM MM.COM

is that the RENAME command leaves only one version of the file on the disk, whereas the COPY command leaves two copies of the file, one with the original name and one with the new one. However, the COPY command can be used to rename files as they are copied from one disk to another. If you wanted to copy the WP.COM file from the original program diskette to the hard disk with the new filename MM.COM, the following COPY command would be faster than copying the file and then renaming it:

C>COPY A:WP.COM MM.COM

The TYPE Command

The TYPE command is used to view the contents of a file. The TYPE command only displays legible information when used with text files. Using the TYPE command with .COM or .EXE files will result in funny-looking characters showing up on the screen, as well as perhaps bells and whistles going off in your computer. Using TYPE with such files has even been known to lock up the computer entirely, requiring restarting.

In addition, the TYPE command will only legibly display the contents of ASCII files. Some word processing programs store their documents in non-standard formats, including special control characters and even using the eighth data bit. WordStar is one such program. The results of using the TYPE command to view the contents of WordStar files are disappointing at best. Nonetheless, the TYPE command can give you some idea of the contents of text files, even non-ASCII files. This is one application of the TYPE command.

Another use for the TYPE command is to print out the contents of text files without resorting the print command of a word processing program. The format of the TYPE command is:

TYPE [d:]filename[.ext]

The contents of the file will be output to the screen in a continuously scrolling fashion until the entire file is displayed. You can also use the TYPE command to view the contents of a file a screenful at a time by piping the output through the MORE filter. (See Chapter 3 for more on pipes and filters.) To view the contents of a file on drive A with the filename LETTER.DOC, you would enter:

C>TYPE A:LETTER.DOC

The output of the TYPE command is normally sent to the screen. However, it is possible to redirect this output to the printer in a number of ways. You can use either the PrtSc key to print a single screenful or the Ctrl PrtSc key to print output that requires more than one screen. The use of these keys is described in Chapter 3.

To redirect the output to the printer without the PrtSc key, you can use the device name of the printer, LPT1: or PRN: in conjunction with the TYPE command. To do so, you would enter the following command:

C>TYPE A:LETTER.DOC > LPT1:

This command will send the output of the TYPE command to the device named LPT1:, which is the parallel printer port on most computers. If this doesn't work, check to make sure that the printer is connected to the computer, the printer's power is on, and Select is enabled. If these checks fail to reveal the problem, try using LPT2: as the device name instead.

If you are having trouble reading the output from the TYPE command because it is scrolling too quickly, you can pipe the output through the MORE filter. This will cause each screenful to remain on the screen until you press any character for the next screen. For example, to view the file LETTER.DOC on drive A one screen at a time, you would enter:

C>TYPE A:LETTER.DOC | MORE

Remember, though, that MORE is an external utility and must be on your hard disk before you can use it with the TYPE or any other command.

In the preceding section on the COPY command, you learned how to create and view simple text files by designating the CON: device as either the source or the destination for the copy. Ordinarily, you would use the TYPE command to view the contents of such text files rather than the COPY command, as it is both easier to enter and faster to execute. To view the contents of your FLATTERY file, just enter:

C>TYPE A:FLATTERY

The DATE And TIME Commands

The DATE and TIME commands are used to reset the system date and time. The DATE and TIME prompts appear at the beginning of any DOS session, allowing you to enter the current date and time from the keyboard. Most novice computer users don't pay much attention to the date and time, considering these prompts at system startup to be more of a nuisance than a convenience. However, the system date and time can be used quite effectively with a number of database programs to automatically place the current date into data records such as invoices, statements, etc.

The system date and time are also used to stamp the directory entry of a file when it is created or updated. You can see these dates and times whenever you view the directory in the long form. This information can be quite helpful in determining which version of a file is the most current. However, the system date and time are only useful if they are correct. If you bypass these prompts on startup by pressing the Return key, you are stuck with the default value for the date and time. These will usually be the date and time when your version of DOS was created. It is definitely worth your while to take the extra time required to enter the current date and time at system startup.

Some personal computers come with a special, battery-driven clock which will keep time for you. Even if your computer did not come with such a clock, it is possible to purchase an expansion card that includes a clock. Clocks keep track of the date and time even when the computer is turned off, and will set the system date and time for you automatically on startup. If you have a clock, you will have to set it originally with the DATE and TIME commands.

The DATE command allows you to enter the current date in one of several formats. The mm-dd-yy format is the default. (For more on alternate formats, see your DOS manual under COUNTRY and DATE.) When you enter the DATE command, as follows:

C>DATE

you will be presented with the current date and prompted to enter the new date with a display such as this:

Current date is Mon 1-01-1987
Enter new date (mm-dd-yy)

You can enter the current date separated by hyphens (-), slashes (/), or periods. Single digit months don't have to be preceded by zeroes. If you make a mistake in entering the date you will receive the message:

Invalid date
Enter new date (mm-dd-yy)

The TIME command works much like the DATE command. You are given the current time and asked to provide the new time:

Current time is 2400:01:00:00
Enter new time:

The time is kept in military time, up to one hundredth of a second, which doesn't mean that you have to enter the time to this level of accuracy. Normally all you will do is enter the hours and minutes. The seconds and hundredths of seconds will be set to zero by default. After all, you're not interested in using your computer as a stopwatch. All units of time are separated by colons (:).

Once the date and time have been set, either at system startup or through the use of the DATE and TIME prompts, the system will increment the time (and date if you work long hours) for you automatically until the computer is shut off. Again, if you have an internal, battery-powered clock, this incrementation will even continue when the computer is off.

The CLS and PROMPT Commands

The DOS command processor appears to be quite limited in its user interface. All you see is a simple letter prompt. Also, past commands, and worse, error messages, remain on the screen after a command has been executed. The sterile system prompt and cluttered screen can be somewhat annoying, especially to novice computer users. Fortunately, there are ways to alter the appearance of the DOS interface.

One simple yet underutilized command is CLS. If you enter this internal command at the system prompt, DOS will obligingly clear the screen for you. This is especially nice if you have just made an error and you don't want your boss looking over your shoulder and reading some DOS error message like:

File destroyed due to operator incompetence

A more powerful command for altering the appearance of the screen is the DOS PROMPT command. Basically, this command lets you determine what the system prompt will look like. For example, you could alter the system prompt so that it displayed the following:

> Today is Mon 1-01-86
> The time is 09:00:00.00
> Your wish is my command . . .

instead of the standard C>.

The PROMPT command allows you to insert your own text messages at the system prompt, as well as include the date, time, and the current drive. Once you enter the PROMPT information, it remains in effect until you restart your computer. It is simple to alter the standard system prompt. All you do is enter the PROMPT command followed by the text message you wish displayed. As an example, suppose you wanted the system prompt to read "Enter your command:". You could create this prompt by entering the following:

C>PROMPT Enter your command:

For the remainder of your working session, this would be the new system prompt.

Besides giving you control over text messages, PROMPT also lets you include date and time information, skip lines, and display the current drive letter. You can even include the familiar ">" symbol if you like. There are a number of parameters which may be included with the PROMPT command to embellish your customized system prompts. They are summarized below:

t	Displays the time.
d	Displays the date.
v	Displays the current DOS version number.
n	Displays the current drive letter.
g	Displays the ">" character.
l	Displays the "<" character.
b	Displays the "|" character.
q	Displays the "=" character.
_	(Underline) Creates a new line.

To use any of these parameters with the PROMPT command, they must be preceded by a "$" character. PROMPT parameters may be included with text. For instance, if you wanted the message:

Today is Mon 1/01/86

to appear in the prompt, you would enter:

C>PROMPT Today is $d

Even the underline character must be preceded by a $, otherwise it will be displayed as an underline character in the prompt. To display the entire prompt:

Today is Mon 1-01-86
The time is 09:00:00.00
Your wish is my command . . .

you would enter:

C>PROMPT Today is d__The time is t__Your wish is my command . . .

You can even include the current drive letter with the $n parameter. In fact, you could recreate the basic DOS prompt by entering:

C>PROMPT ng

Of course, you can always return to the boring letter prompt by simply entering:

C>PROMPT

Due to DOS incompatibilities, it is often helpful to have the booted version of DOS displayed as part of the system prompt. This can be accomplished with the $v parameter. For example, you might want to have the following prompt displayed on your screen:

IBM Personal Computer DOS Version 3.2
C>

This prompt would be created with the command:

C>PROMPT v__ng

Creating your own customized system prompts is both fun and helpful. It can also be a great source of entertainment as you sneak around changing the prompts behind your co-workers' backs.

The VER Command

As you have probably gathered by now, there are a number of different DOS versions in existence. In addition to the two distinct versions, MS-DOS and PC-DOS, there are major releases, such as 2.0 and 3.0, plus minor revisions, as in 3.1 versus 3.2. This can be rather confusing, especially as certain DOS commands occur in some versions but not others. Other problems involving differing DOS versions include incompatibilities in disk formats and command processors.

One especially aggravating problem is that DOS versions 2.xx cannot recognize disks formatted with DOS versions 3.xx. The maxim here is that newer DOS's can read older DOS's, but not vice-versa. You will also find that if you boot the computer with one version of DOS and then replace that disk with another containing a different version of DOS, you will run into problems whenever you try to execute any DOS commands from the system prompt. Instead you will receive the message:

Incorrect DOS version

The best way to avoid this is to keep all your program and data files on diskettes formatted with the same version as your hard disk. However, you may have collected programs and data over time. As new versions of DOS are released, you probably failed to copy your old programs and data onto newly formatted diskettes. That's understandable. At least you can tell which DOS version the diskettes were formatted with because you wrote the version number on the bottom of the disk label as a reminder. What, you mean you *forgot?* So now what?

Luckily for you, the DOS command processor includes the VER command. This command will report on the version of DOS used to create the current disk or diskette. To obtain this information, all you enter is:

C > VER

DOS will respond with the version number as follows:

IBM Personal Computer DOS version *x.xx*

where *x.xx* is the version number of the current disk or diskette, depending upon the drive currently serving as the system drive.

EXTERNAL COMMANDS

While the command processor contains many useful DOS commands, there are some DOS commands which require additional utility files. These utilities are actually separate programs and must be available on the current disk before you can employ them. You might wonder why DOS puts some commands in the command processor and makes others external. The reason has to do with the limited amount of memory available on many personal computers. If all the DOS utilities were placed into the command processor, it would take up much more memory than it already does. Since many of the DOS utilities, such as DISKCOPY, are only used infrequently, it makes more sense to place them into separate program files. These programs are loaded into memory as needed. This limits the resident size of DOS, freeing your computer's memory for applications and data.

There are a number of external DOS utilities. In the remainder of this chapter, you will learn about four very useful ones: DISKCOPY, DISKCOMP, COMP, and CHKDSK. In order to use any of these utilities, you must first have access to them. This means that the file with the utility name and either a .COM or .EXE extension must be present on the hard disk (or a diskette in the floppy drive). If you followed the instructions in Chapter 2 for copying the system files onto your hard disk, then you already have access to these utilities.

The DISKCOPY Utilities

The DISKCOPY utility is used to copy the entire contents of one diskette onto another. It should really only be used to copy floppy diskettes. To copy the contents of a hard disk, you will use another DOS utility, BACKUP, which is described in Chapter 10, Backing Up Data And Programs.

The general format of the DISKCOPY command is:

DISKCOPY [d:] [d:]

DISKCOPY is usually used to copy files from one disk drive to another, which is why there are two drive designators in the command format. The reason both designators are indicated as optional (enclosed within square brackets) is that it is possible to use the DISKCOPY command with a single floppy drive. When copying diskettes on a single floppy system, you only specify the designator of the one floppy drive. Unless you have an optional second floppy drive with your system, this is how you will have to copy diskettes. To illustrate, if you have a computer with a hard drive and one floppy drive, you would enter:

C > DISKCOPY A:

The A: indicates the drive you want to use to copy diskettes. In a one-drive disk copy operation, you will be prompted first to insert the source diskette in drive A, then to insert the target diskette into drive A, then the source diskette again, then the target diskette, etc. until the entire process is concluded. The number of swaps you have to make will depend upon the amount of RAM available and the version of DOS you are using.

If you have two floppy drives with your system, you would enter:

C > DISKCOPY A: B:

You would then be prompted to insert your source diskette in drive A and your target diskette in drive B. The two-drive disk copy operation will proceed without requiring disk swapping.

Once the disk copy operation is completed, you will be asked if you want to:

Copy another (Y/N)?

Responding with a "Y" will allow you to repeat the process with a different set of diskettes. An "N" response will terminate the DISKCOPY program and return you to the system prompt.

One nice feature of the DISKCOPY utility is that, if the target diskette has not been formatted previously, DISKCOPY will automatically format it for you. DISKCOPY assumes the format of the source diskette is to be used in this case. In fact, DISKCOPY can only transfer between diskettes of like format. If you tried to use DISKCOPY with a 1.2MB source diskette and a 360KB target diskette, you would be shown the following error message:

**Drive types or
diskette types not compatible**

To transfer files between diskettes of different formats, you need to use the COPY command. In particular, when copying between 360KB and 1.2MB diskettes, you will need to include the /4 parameter.

Many computer users routinely rely upon the DISKCOPY command to transfer files between floppy diskettes. Although this method works in the sense that all files are transferred, it is inefficient in the way files are stored on the target disk. What these users fail to realize is that the DISKCOPY command is not equivalent to the COPY *.* command.

The DISKCOPY command transfers an exact duplicate of the source diskette onto the target diskette. During its use, the files stored on the source diskette may have become fragmented. As you may recall from Chapter 3, the clusters in which a file is stored are not necessarily contiguous due to the nature of the random storage process. What this means is that disk access times when reading or loading fragmented files is increased. However, when files are copied to a freshly formatted diskette with the COPY *.*, they are copied one by one into contiguous clusters. The result is that the files are stored more efficiently, thus decreasing disk access time to these files.

For this reason, it is a good idea to periodically recopy data files onto newly formatted diskettes to reorganize them. This technique and others for improving the storage efficiency of your hard disk is explored in Chapter 16, Storage Optimization.

The COMP and DISKCOMP Utilities

The COMP and DISKCOMP commands let you compare files and diskettes to see if they are identical. The COMP command is used to compare single files or sets of files. The DISKCOMP command is used to compare entire diskettes. It is important to understand this distinction between these two utilities. The DISKCOMP utility cannot be used to compare hard disks. To compare files stored on hard disks with those stored on floppies, you must use the COMP command. The format of the DISKCOMP command is similar to that of the DISKCOPY command:

DISKCOMP [d:] [d:] [/1] [/8]

Again, the drive designator(s) you use will depend upon the number of floppy drives you have. For a single drive disk comparison operation, you would use the A drive designator and swap floppies as with a one-drive disk copy operation. With dual floppy systems, you can specify A as the source drive and B as the target drive.

The DISKCOMP command compares both the diskette formats and the contents of the two diskettes. If either the formats or the contents differ, you will get a message informing you that an error occurred on a given side and a given track, such as:

Compare error on side 0, track 23

DISKCOMP compares disks on a track-by-track basis. It bases its format comparison on the format of the source diskette unless you include the single-sided parameter, "/1", or the 8 sectors only parameter, "/8".

If two diskettes are identical, DISKCOPY issues the message:

Compare OK

After completing the comparison process, DISKCOMP asks if you want to:

Compare more diskettes (Y/N)?

You would respond to this question the same way you would to the prompt to copy more diskettes with the DISKCOPY command.

Since there is no verify option with the DISKCOPY utility, using DISKCOMP is a handy way to ensure that a target diskette was copied to accurately after a disk copy operation. Note, however, that just because two diskettes contain the same files does not necessarily mean that DISKCOPY will return a Compare OK message. This is because the files may be fragmented and stored in different clusters. If this is the case, the track-by-track comparison will indicate that the two diskettes are not identical.

Because DISKCOMP is really designed to compare diskettes rather than individual files, and because DISKCOMP cannot be used with hard disks, you must use the COMP utility when comparing files stored on your hard disk. This utility has the format:

COMP [d:]filename[.ext] [d:] [filename] [.ext]

The first filename is required and is called the primary filename. The second filename, referred to as the secondary filename, is optional. If a second filename is not provided, COMP will prompt you for it. However, if you provide a drive designator but no secondary filename, COMP assumes you want to compare two files with the same name but on different drives. If there is no file on either the source or the target drive matching the specified filename for that drive, COMP will inform you of this and prompt you again for the primary and secondary filenames.

The COMP command employs two techniques to determine if files are unequal. It first checks the lengths of the two files. If the file lengths differ, then the files are not identical, and COMP returns the message:

Files are different sizes

If the files are of the same length, then COMP proceeds with a byte-by-byte comparison of the two files. COMP will report the location of any mismatched bytes in terms of their location within their respective files. The offset values (how far into the files the error occurred) are given in hexadecimal. Normally you would not be concerned with the location of the mismatch. The mere fact that a mismatch is encountered is sufficient. COMP reports on the mismatched bytes encountered up to a maximum of ten. If ten mismatches are encountered, COMP concludes the comparison and issues the message:

10 Mismatches—ending compare

If the files are equal in length and identical in content, COMP displays the message:

Files compare OK

To illustrate the use of the COMP command, suppose you had two letter files, both named LETTER1.DOC, one of which was stored on your hard disk and another stored on a floppy. You could check to see if they were identical by entering:

C>COMP LETTER1.DOC A:

The COMP command may be used in combination with wildcards to check groups of files. For example, to compare all DOC files on drive A with those on drive C, you would enter:

C>COMP A:*.DOC C:

Note the sequence of the drives. A is the source drive in this case because there are likely to be .DOC files on C that are not on A. If you specified C as the source drive, you would be asking COMP to look for a lot of non-existent files on drive A.

When using wildcards, COMP compares files in the order they occur in the source directory with the corresponding files on the target disk. If there is no secondary file matching a given primary file, COMP displays the names of the two files plus the fact that the secondary file was not found as in the following instance:

A:LETTER2.DOC and C:LETTER2.DOC
C:LETTER2.DOC—File not found

The status of each comparison is reported until all files matching the wildcard file specification in the primary filename have been checked. At the conclusion of a COMP command, the message:

Compare more files (Y/N)?

is displayed.

It is possible to compare all files on one disk with those on another using the *.* global wildcards. However, simply specifying the drive designators with no filenames will accomplish the same thing:

C>COMP A: C:

It is possible for two files to be equal in content without being physically identical. Some programs always store their data files in multiples of 128 bytes. Thus, the last few characters of two files may not be identical because of the extraneous characters stored in the final sectors of the two files. Since COMP compares all bytes included in a file, it will consider these two files to be unequal. However, since COMP also looks for the end-of-file marker as the last character in a file, it will display the message:

EOF not found

If you see this message, it is possible that the two files may in fact be equal.

The CHKDSK Utility

The CHKDSK utility is one of the most useful of the external DOS commands. You are probably aware that this command can be used to find out how much storage space remains on a disk. However, the command can also be used with several optional parameters to reveal important information about the way files are stored or to recover lost sectors. These features are especially valuable when managing hard disks. As the owner of a hard disk system, you should familiarize yourself with this utility and use it frequently to improve the performance of your system.

The general format of the CHKDSK command is:

CHKDSK [d:] [filename] [.ext] [/f] [/v]

As you can see, only the command itself is required. All other elements of the command are optional. With floppy drive systems, most DOS users only employ the basic command itself and never learn the purpose or application of the filename, "/f" and "/v" options.

In its simplest form, the CHKDSK command will reveal the following helpful information: the disk volume name, the total storage space on the disk, the number and amount of storage used up by hidden files, the number and amount of storage taken up by user files, the amount of storage required by the directory, the amount of available storage remaining on the disk, the total amount of RAM, and the amount of RAM available after the system files and any RAM-resident programs are loaded. (Note: versions of DOS preceding 3.2 do not report on the directory size.) To obtain a listing of these statistics, you would simply enter the CHKDSK command followed by the drive designator of the disk you wish to investigate. If you want to check the status of the current disk, you can omit the drive designator. For example, to check the status of your hard disk you would enter:

C>CHKDSK

which would result in the following status report:

```
10378654  bytes total disk space
   45056  bytes in 3 hidden files
  297984  bytes in 42 user files
10046504  bytes available on disk

  655360  bytes in memory
  610768  bytes free
```

Table 4-1. Sample Status Display of a Hard Disk Produced by the DOS CHKDSK Utility.

68

If you wanted to check the status of one of your floppy diskettes, you would use the CHKDSK command with the optional drive designator of the floppy drive:

C > CHKDSK A:

You may have noticed that much of this information can be obtained by simply asking for a directory. You are correct. In fact, the only additional information provided by the above report is the information on the hidden files and the RAM allocation. CHKDSK all by itself is not particularly useful. However, when used with the optional filename or the "/f" and "/v" features, this utility can provide important information about your hard disk.

One important service which CHKDSK performs is informing you of the condition of your files. As you will recall from Chapter 2, files can either be stored in contiguous clusters or in fragmented clusters. File fragmentation occurs as more and more files are added to a disk. After a disk has been in use for some time, it becomes less likely that there will be just the right number of contiguous clusters available to store a new file (or one which has been revised). This new file must then be stored wherever empty clusters happen to be located on the disk. Of course, the addition of each new, fragmented file further exacerbates the problem, up to the point where any new files will be scattered all over the disk.

The problem with file fragmentation is that it reduces the performance of your system. In order to read data or access program instructions from a fragmented file, the access arm must move back and forth over the disk surface searching out the various tracks where the various clusters are located. This additional access time slows down the apparent operation of your computer. While CHKDSK cannot remedy this situation, it can at least report on it for you. You can then use the techniques described in Chapter 15, Storage Optimization, to reorganize your files into contiguous clusters.

To obtain a report on a particular file, you would include its filename in the CHKDSK command. For example, to check the file, LETTER1.DOC, on drive A for fragmentation, you would enter:

C > CHKDSK A:LETTER1.DOC

If the specified file is stored in contiguous clusters, the following message will be returned:

All specified file(s) are contiguous

However, if the file is stored in two or more non-contiguous clusters, this fact will be reported to you instead as follows:

A: \ LETTER1.DOC
Contains $\underline{n}$ non-contiguous blocks

where the value of $\underline{n}$ is the number of non-contiguous clusters involved. Note the backslash character, " \ ", included in the filename. This character refers to the file's path. If there is nothing between this character and the filename, then the file is stored in the disk's root directory and may be ignored. Paths become important when you have more than one directory on a disk. These additional directories are called subdirectories. Paths and subdirectories are the topic of the next chapter.

You may use wildcards in filenames with the CHKDSK command. If you do include wildcards, the status of all the files specified by the wildcard filename will be reported. One way to check on the overall degradation of your hard disk is to use the global wildcard combination *.*. This would be accomplished by the following command:

C>CHKDSK *.*

If you have recently formatted your hard disk and copied the DOS system files onto it, you should see the All specified file(s) are contiguous message. However, if your hard disk has been in use for some time, you probably will be surprised by the extent of file fragmentation that has taken place. If you are really concerned, you can skip ahead to Chapter 15 to learn how to correct the situation.

Two optional parameters, "/v" and "/f", may be included with the CHKDSK command as well. The first of these, "/v", displays all the files on the disk (regardless of whether they are stored in non-contiguous clusters) along with their paths. The purpose of this option will become apparent in the following chapter.

The "/f" option causes CHKDSK to check the File Allocation Table for missing sectors. (You may want to read the section on Directories And File Allocation Tables in Chapter 3 if you have not already done so.) Normally, all sectors are recorded in the FAT. However, sometimes the pointers from one sector to another get lost. If this happens, any data contained in these sectors will be unavailable to you. To recover this data, you must fix the FAT with the CHKDSK /f command.

When you include this option, CHKDSK first checks the FAT to see if there are any lost sectors. Usually there won't be any, as this is a fairly uncommon occurrence. If CHKDSK does discover any lost sectors, it will then ask if you want to recover the data which is stored in the clusters containing these sectors. The message looks something like this:

008 lost clusters found in 002 chains
Convert lost chains to files (Y/N)?

Unfortunately, CHKDSK cannot replace these lost clusters into their original files. Actually this could prove to be devastating. However, what CHKDSK will do is place the rediscovered clusters into individual files so you can look at them. Each cluster which is restored by CHKDSK is placed into a file beginning with the filename FILExxxx.CHK. The first cluster is named FILE0000.CHK, the second cluster is named FILE0001.CHK, etc. If the data is important, you can use whatever application program created it to restore it to the appropriate file.

As you can see, CHKDSK is a powerful and versatile utility. Not only can it be used to improve the performance of your system, it can also help you recover lost data. It is a good idea to perform periodic disk and file checks using CHKDSK. A good time to do this is just prior to your weekly system backup. You will learn how to backup your hard disk in Chapter 10, Backing Up Data And Programs.

The ASSIGN Command

While the use of a hard disk can greatly facilitate the use of most applications, there are some programs which do not run well from a hard disk. Such programs were usually written in the days before hard disk drives for personal computers became commonplace. The most common problem encountered with software designed to run on floppy drive computers is the default drive problem.

This problem arises due to the software assuming that the A drive is the default drive. Such programs include built-in commands to load certain .OVR, .DAT, or other auxiliary files from the A drive. When you copy the program onto your hard disk and try to run it, the auxiliary files can't be found when the software calls for them. You usually get some error message informing that the required file is not available, and the program ceases to continue.

This is the case when attempting to run the Lotus 1-2-3 PrintGraphs utility. The PrintGraphs utility trys to read the FONT1 and FONT2 files from the A drive, and, when it cannot find them, it responds with an error message and refuses to print the specified graph.

Fortunately, DOS provides a way to get around this software limitation. With the ASSIGN command you can reassign any drive letter to a user-supplied letter. The general format of the ASSIGN command is:

ASSIGN [d1 = d2] [d3 = d4] [etc.]

Once the ASSIGN command has been entered, any reference to drive letter d1 will result in the driver letter d2 being used in its place. For example, to reassign the A drive to drive C, the command would be:

C > ASSIGN A = C

This command does not alter the application software in any way. The program you are running will still ask for files from drive A. However, the DOS will interpret this request as drive C and will search drive C for the required file accordingly.

Other DOS Commands and Utilities

This chapter has described some of the most frequently used DOS commands and utilities. You will probably use these utilities on a daily or weekly basis. However, there are a number of other DOS commands and utilities you will need to be familiar with in order to manage your hard disk system effectively. These commands and utilities will be introduced throughout the remainder of the book.

In addition, there are numerous utility programs developed by independent programmers to make working with DOS and hard disks easier for the average computer user. Many of these utility programs have generously been placed into the public domain so that anyone is free to use them. They are described in Chapter 17.

In the next chapter you will learn how to create subdirectories to segregate the various program and data files which you will store on your hard disk. The techniques and commands introduced in this chapter will enable you to organize your files into an orderly, structured system for ease of use and retrieval.

Chapter 5

Subdirectories and Paths

There are two major managerial tasks involved with hard disks. One is the repetitive chore of backing up the data which accumulates on the hard disk. The need to perform periodic backups can be addressed in one of several ways (see Chapters 10 and 11). The other managerial task involves the creation and maintenance of an organized system for storing and retrieving data and program files on the hard disk. The first step in creating such a system is to segregate the hard disk into separate work areas according to user and/or application.

HARD DISK ORGANIZATION STRATEGIES

File organization becomes crucial when working with hard disk systems because the sheer number of files involved can prove overwhelming, especially to novice computer users. When you consider that hard disks provide enough storage to accommodate ten or more different users, each with their own programs and data files, you begin to realize the complexity of the problem.

The simple techniques for displaying directory listings described in Chapter 3 are unsuitable for use with fully-populated hard disks. The directory listing for a fully-utilized 20MB hard disk could easily run to twenty or more screens. Even with the use of the FIND and MORE filters, locating a given file under such circumstances can be a daunting task. Imagine the plight of the beginning computer user who must first locate her application program, execute it, and then locate and retrieve her data file from several hundred such files stored by herself and nine other coworkers. Scenarios such as this occur far too frequently in the world of personal computing.

There are a number of techniques used to organize files into a workable arrangement on the hard disk. The simplest of these is the use of segregated work areas on the hard disk. Segregated work areas allow each computer user to keep track of his or her own files without having to worry, or even know about, the files of the other users.

There are several advantages to using work areas. One obvious advantage is that directory listings for each work area will only show those files relevant to the user of that area. Another advantage is that separate users can employ the same filenames for different files. This avoids collisions which would occur when more than one user creates a file with the same name but different contents. In certain application programs, such collisions can cause the original file to be altered or deleted entirely. A third advantage involves data security. When data files are segregated into separate work areas, access to confidential data can be limited through the use of passwords. Specific techniques for ensuring data security through the use of passwords will be described in Chapter 12, Password Security. One final advantage is that the employment of individual work areas, each with its own directory, enables you to extend the number of file entries beyond the limit imposed by the use of a single directory.

Even if you are the only user of your hard disk, you will find the use of separate work areas to be advantageous. For one thing, you can separate your application programs into individual work areas. You will then find it easier to locate data files created with the various programs you use. You will also find that the DOS limitation of eight characters for filenames leads to unanticipated duplications. These are less likely to be a problem when data files are segregated by application.

Subdirectories

The segregation of a hard disk into separate work areas entails the creation of *subdirectories*. Subdirectories are just what the term implies: subgroups of file entries within the disk's root directory. Each subdirectory acts like a separate directory, containing all the file information for each of the files it contains. You may have as many subdirectories as you wish, and each subdirectory may contain its own subdirectories.

There is no limit to the number of files you can place into a subdirectory. Once created, a subdirectory serves as the organizing structure for a separate work area. All the files stored in the subdirectory can be viewed with the directory command, and files can be created or deleted without concern for files stored in other subdirectories. The subdirectory effectively separates those files contained within it from files contained within other subdirectories. However, it is possible to transfer files from one subdirectory to another and even to obtain access to files stored in other subdirectories if you need them. The power of subdirectories is that they provide separation without isolation.

While there is no limit to the number of subdirectories you may have, nor to the number of files within a subdirectory, it is still a good idea to give some thought to the location and organization of your programs and data files within your subdirectory scheme. For instance, if you have several users all working with Lotus 1-2-3, you need not have three separate Lotus subdirectories. Instead, you can create one Lotus subdirectory with separate subdirectories for each user. On the other hand, a single user may require more than one subdirectory depending upon the number of applications he uses.

To see how subdirectories can be employed to segregate a hard disk system both by user and application, consider this scenario: A small business, CompuCards, Inc., which creates and markets computer-generated greeting cards, employs an XT with a 20MB hard disk. The secretary, Sue, uses the computer to do word processing and to enter data into the customer database. The bookkeeper, Bob, runs a computerized accounting program off the hard disk. Jack, the sales manager, uses the data entered by Sue to produce sales reports and to plan marketing strategy. Mary, the graphics artist, works with a graphics program. Being the creative type, Mary also likes to play computer games while awaiting inspiration. Finally, Linda, the owner, uses the computer for financial management and to organize her annual and five-year business plans. A simple organization chart for this company is shown in Fig. 5-1.

Continuing with this scenario, consider the individual work areas that would be needed to accommodate all these users. There would need to be separate work areas for Bob's accounting program, Mary's art work, Jack's customer database, and Sue's word processing files. In addition, Linda, Jack, and Bob all use Lotus 1-2-3 to maintain various spreadsheet files, which they wish to keep segregated. Also, both Linda and Jack use WordStar to write business plans, marketing proposals and memos. Linda also uses an outline processor to help organize her thoughts. She wants to keep these brainstorming files separate from her actual written documents. Within the customer database work area, Jack, being somewhat of a swinger, wants to maintain his own private records of personal contacts and unlisted phone numbers. Finally, Linda suspects that Mary may be spending too much time blasting zeroids from Xenon and not enough time pumping out greeting cards. She wants to keep track of Mary's time by segregating the games from the graphics program and using a time-keeping utility to log Mary's time in each work area.

One way of organizing all these work areas would be to create three main subdirectories,

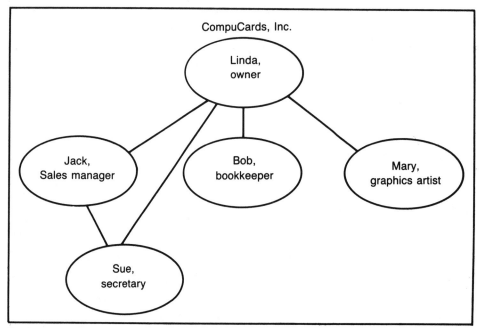

Fig. 5-1. Organizational chart for CompuCard, Inc.

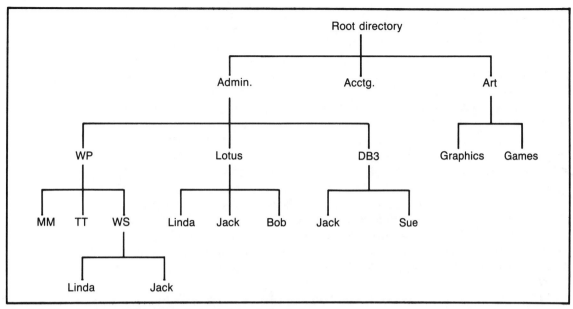

Fig. 5-2. The structure of CompuCard's hard disk subdirectories.

named ADMIN, ACCT, and ART. The ADMIN subdirectory would be further divided into three subdirectories, WP, LOTUS, and DB3. Each of these subdirectories would be divided by application and user. For example, the WP subdirectory would contain separate subdirectories for the three word processing applications, MM for MultiMate, WS for WordStar, and TT for ThinkTank. Under the WS subdirectory would be two user areas, LINDA and JACK. Similar user subdirectories would exist under the LOTUS and DB3 subdirectories. Finally, Mary's ART subdirectory would be subdivided into GAMES and GRAPHICS. The structure of the subdirectory system under this scheme is shown in Fig. 5-2.

While this structure seems to be quite comprehensive, one very important aspect of the overall system has been neglected—the system files and utilities. As you will see later, these files should be separated from the rest of the application programs for convenience and simplicity. This requires the addition of a fourth main subdirectory, which could be labeled DOS. Figure 5-3 illustrates the revised top level of the subdirectory structure.

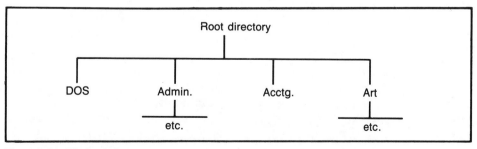

Fig. 5-3. Modified subdirectory system including a separate DOS subdirectory.

Trees and Paths

Notice how the appearance of this subdirectory structure resembles an inverted tree, with the root at the top. For this reason, the system of the root directory and subdirectories is often referred to as the *tree* structure of the disk. In fact, there is even a DOS TREE utility which you can use to display the various subdirectories and their relationships.

To access a subdirectory, you must follow the appropriate *path* to get to it. This path may lead through several preceding subdirectories before arriving at the subdirectory you wish to work in. The subdirectory path is established when the subdirectory is created. When working with subdirectories, it's a good idea to think in terms of levels. For the system outlined in Fig. 5-3, the root directory represents level 0, with the four subdirectories, ADMIN, ACCTG, ART, and DOS constituting level 1, and so on.

Each level is preceded by the level prior to it. The root directory is indicated by a single backslash (\ ). Level 1 subdirectories are indicated by a backslash followed by the subdirectory name, such as \ ADMIN, and so on. The path to a given subdirectory consists of all the subdirectory names required to enter that subdirectory. For instance, to access files in Linda's Lotus work area you would follow this path:

\ ADMIN \ LOTUS \ LINDA

The use of paths allows you to specify any subdirectory or file within a subdirectory from any other location within the tree structure of your hard disk. For example, even if Linda were working in her Lotus file subdirectory, she could still call for a file named LETTER.DOC located in her WordStar file subdirectory by specifying the appropriate path to this file:

\ ADMIN \ WP \ WS \ LINDA \ LETTER.DOC

The inclusion of a file's path along with its drive designator and filename completes the description of the location of that file. These three components, drive designator, path, and filename are called a file's specification, or *filespec* for short. You will see this term in your DOS manual, and it will be used in the remainder of the book.

Unless a subdirectory is protected through the use of passwords or some other form of security, you can have access to the files contained within that subdirectory by including the path to those files in any DOS command you enter. Note, however, that not all application programs are as liberated as DOS. Some programs do not recognize paths as part of a file's specification. If you include a path as part of a filename with such programs, you will receive some form of Invalid filename error message.

SUBDIRECTORY COMMANDS

The root directory of the disk is created for you automatically during the formatting process. Subdirectories, on the other hand, must be created by using the DOS MKDIR command. Once a subdirectory has been created, it can be further subdivided into additional subdirectories. After all the subdirectories have been created, you can move between them by employing the CHDIR command. Both MKDIR and CHDIR are internal commands.

Creating Subdirectories with MKDIR

The MKDIR command is used to establish a new subdirectory from within either the root directory or another subdirectory. This command may be abbreviated as MD. The general form of the MKDIR command is:

MKDIR [d:] [path] subdirectory

Note that the drive designator and path are optional. If you omit the drive designator, the subdirectory will be created on the currently logged drive. If you omit the path, the subdirectory will be created under the current directory or subdirectory. In this case, the current directory or subdirectory is said to be the *parent* of the new subdirectory. All level 1 subdirectories have the root directory as their parent. If you include the optional path, then the subdirectory will be created under the appropriate parent directory or subdirectory according to the specified path.

To see how this works, suppose you are currently located in the LOTUS subdirectory. If you entered the command:

C>MD LINDA

you would be creating the LINDA subdirectory under the LOTUS parent subdirectory. However, you could have reached the LINDA subdirectory under the WS parent subdirectory by entering the command:

C>MD \ADMIN\WP\WS\LINDA

One thing you have to watch out for is creating subdirectories with the wrong parent. This is easy enough to do if you do not specify the correct path. Many hard disk users misunderstand the meaning of the " \ " character and assume it must be included before each subdirectory. If you were to include the backslash when attempting to create the LINDA subdirectory under the LOTUS subdirectory:

C>MD \LINDA

you would actually be creating a level 1 subdirectory under the root directory. Later in this chapter, you will learn how to remove unwanted subdirectories, so don't worry if you have created one or more subdirectories with the wrong path.

It is possible to have more than one subdirectory on a hard disk with the same subdirectory name. For example, in Fig. 5-3, there are three separate subdirectories named JACK. However, such subdirectories must have different parents. This makes intuitive sense. You wouldn't expect to find two children named Jack living in the same family, but you might find them living next door to each other. By the same logic, you cannot have files and subdirectories with the same name under the same parent subdirectory. If you attempt to create a subdirectory under parent subdirectory that already contains a file or subdirectory with the same name, you will receive the message

Cannot create subdirectory

Moving Between Subdirectories with CHDIR

The CHDIR command is used to move from either the root directory or another subdirectory into a specified subdirectory. This command may be abbreviated as well by using CD. The general form of the CHDIR command is:

CHDIR [d:] [path]

Although the path is indicated as optional, you ordinarily include the path because that is how you let DOS know where you want to go. Suppose you wanted to move into the MM subdirectory. You would enter:

C > CD \ ADMIN \ WP \ MM

The full path to a subdirectory is not always required. For example, if you are in a parent subdirectory, you do not need to include the parent's name in the path. In the preceding example, if you were already in the WP subdirectory, all you would have to enter is:

C > CD MM

The reason the path is considered optional with the CHDIR command is that you can enter this command without any optional parameters to determine the current subdirectory. In the preceding example, if you were in the WP subdirectory, but weren't sure of this, you could enter:

C > CD

DOS interprets this command as a request for help, "Where am I?" and responds with the current subdirectory, in this case C: \ ADMIN \ WP. Once you know where you are, you can determine the appropriate path to where you want to go.

Removing Subdirectories with RMDIR

You can remove unwanted subdirectories just like you can delete unwanted files. The command to accomplish this is RMDIR, abbreviated RD. The general format of this command is:

RMDIR [d:] path

The path is not optional with the RMDIR command. This is because you cannot remove the current subdirectory or the root directory. Also, the subdirectory to be removed must be empty before it can be removed. There can be no files or subdirectories under the subdirectory to be removed. This includes hidden files. If you attempt to remove a non-empty subdirectory, you will be greeted with the message.

Invalid path, not directory,
or directory not empty

If this occurs, you will need to delete any files and subdirectories contained in the subdirectory you wish to remove. You can delete files with the global wildcard combination, *.*. Any subdirectories must be removed with the RD command.

For now, assume that the LINDA subdirectory under the LOTUS parent subdirectory is empty. If you are currently in the root directory, you could remove this subdirectory by entering:

CD>RD \ADMIN\LOTUS\LINDA

Consider another example. In this case, the LOTUS subdirectory is to be removed. Assume in this instance that the remaining subdirectories, JACK and BOB, contain files. To remove the LOTUS subdirectory, you must first remove the non-empty JACK and BOB subdirectories. To do so, you would have to delete all the files contained within these two subdirectories. Then you could remove them from the LOTUS subdirectory. Finally, you would be able to remove the LOTUS subdirectory itself. To accomplish all this from the root directory would require the following sequence of commands:

```
C>DEL \ADMIN\LOTUS\JACK *.*
C>DEL \ADMIN\LOTUS\BOB *.*
C>RD \ADMIN\LOTUS\JACK
C>RD \ADMIN\LOTUS\BOB
C>RD \ADMIN\LOTUS
```

USING DOS COMMANDS WITH SUBDIRECTORIES

The presence of subdirectories on your hard disk alters the way you use and enter certain DOS commands. Specifically, those commands which affect files must include the path to the file as well as the filename and disk drive designator. For instance, the complete format for the ERASE command is:

ERASE filespec

where the filespec is expressed as:

[d:] [path]filename[.ext]

While the inclusion of paths allows you to enter DOS commands from any subdirectory to affect files in any other subdirectory, it is incumbent upon you to include the appropriate path. Otherwise, DOS assumes that you omitted the path on purpose. When no path is specified, DOS executes the command within the current subdirectory, just as it executes commands on the currently logged drive unless another drive is specified.

Copying Files Between Subdirectories

Copying files into and between subdirectories requires that you pay particular attention to the paths of both the source and target files. The general format of the COPY command when copying files from or to subdirectories is:

COPY filespec filespec

With the COPY command, the drive designator or path for either the source or the target file, or both, are optional. This allows you to be in either the source or the target subdirectory when copying files between two subdirectories on the same disk. You can also be in the root directory of the hard disk when copying files from floppy diskettes into subdirectories on the hard disk. Finally, you can be logged onto the floppy disk drive directly and still copy files into a subdirectory on the hard disk.

When working with several subdirectories on the hard disk, you may find that you want to transfer files from one subdirectory to another. In such cases, the paths of both the source and the target files need to be considered. However, it is not always necessary to include both paths in the actual COPY command. If you are already located in the subdirectory which you want to copy the file from, you don't need to specify the path to this file. Similarly, if you are already in the subdirectory that you want to copy the file to, you don't need to include its path in the COPY command.

Consider the following three instances. In each case, Linda wants to transfer a file, LETTER.DOC from her WordStar subdirectory into her Lotus subdirectory. You might want to refer to the diagram illustrated in Fig. 5-3 to refresh your memory of CompuCard's hard disk tree structure.

In the first instance, assume that Linda is already in the LINDA work area of the WS subdirectory. To transfer the LETTER.DOC file into her Lotus work area, she would enter:

C > COPY LETTER.DOC \ ADMIN \ LOTUS \ LINDA

This command would copy the LETTER.DOC file from the current subdirectory, \ ADMIN \ WP \ WS \ LINDA, into the specified target subdirectory.

In the second instance, assume instead that Linda is in her Lotus work area. In this case, the target subdirectory is the current subdirectory, and it is the source subdirectory path which must be specified in the COPY command:

C > COPY \ ADMIN \ WP \ WS \ LINDA \ LETTER.DOC

Note that, since the target subdirectory is the current subdirectory and the filename does not change in the transfer process the complete filespec for the target file is omitted.

A final circumstance might be that Linda is not currently in either of the subdirectories involved in the COPY command. Suppose she is in the root directory instead. She could still transfer the LETTER.DOC file from her WordStar work area into her Lotus work area by entering:

C > COPY \ ADMIN \ WP \ WS \ LINDA \ LETTER.DOC ADMIN \ LOTUS \ LINDA

Notice that in this command the initial backslash is omitted from both the source and target paths. This is because the first backslash refers to the root directory, which in this case is the current directory.

These three examples should have led you to the following conclusion: The current subdirectory path does not have to be included in the COPY command. With this in mind, what command do you think Linda would enter to transfer a copy of the BUDGET.WKS file from Jack's Lotus work area into her own is she is already located in the LOTUS subdirectory? If you answered:

C > COPY JACK\BUDGET LINDA

then you've got the right idea and should have no problem copying files between subdirectories.

It is also possible to copy files from floppy diskettes directory into subdirectories on the hard disk. In this type of copy process, it is usually unnecessary to specify any path for the source files. You rarely find diskettes that have been segregated into subdirectories. While DOS allows you to use the MKDIR and CHDIR command with floppy diskettes, there is really little call for subdirectories on floppies because the amount of storage space is so small. You can copy files from a floppy diskette using the hard disk as the current drive, or you can log onto the floppy drive to perform the copy process. Both options will be illustrated later in this chapter in the section describing the procedure for setting up a separate DOS subdirectory on your hard disk.

Using the Directory Command with Subdirectories

When you create a subdirectory with the MKDIR command, you are actually creating a special file entry in the parent directory. The parent directory can be either the root directory or another subdirectory. Subdirectories act like the root directory in that they include entries for each of the files they contain. These file entries record the filename, date and time stamp, file size, and beginning cluster number in the File Allocation Table.

There is one difference between subdirectories and the root directory, however. The root directory is physically stored in a specific location on the disk, immediately following the FAT, and is fixed in length. The size of a root directory limits the number of file entries it can hold. For example, on a 20MB hard disk, the size of the root directory is 32 sectors, which allows up to 512 file entries. Subdirectories, on the other hand, are stored in the data section of the hard disk and may be any length. As a result, they can hold as many file entries as there is room on the disk.

If you have subdirectories created from the root directory, these will show up in a directory listing with the notation <DIR> next to them instead of a file size. The following is the listing for the root directory of CompuCard's hard disk.

Table 5-1. Directory Listing of CompuCard's Root Directory.

```
   Volume in drive C is COMPUCARD
   Directory of C:\

COMMAND    COM       23791        12-30-85     12:00p
ADMIN                <DIR>         1-01-87      1:00p
DOS                  <DIR>         1-01-87      1:00p
ART                  <DIR>         1-01-87      1:00p
ACCT                 <DIR>         1-01-87      1:00p
                5 file(s)       10387638 bytes free
```

Table 5-2. Directory Listing of CompuCard's DOS Subdirectory

```
Volume in drive C is COMPUCARD
Directory of C:\DOS

BACKUP   COM     BASIC    COM     BASICA   COM     CHKDSK   COM     COMMAND  COM
COMP     COM     DISKCOMP COM     DISKCOPY COM     DRIVER   SYS     EDLIN    COM
FDISK    COM     FIND     COM     FORMAT   COM     GRAFTABL COM     GRAPHICS COM
JOIN     EXE     KEYBFR   COM     KEYBGR   COM     KEYBIT   COM     KEYBSP   COM
KEYBUK   COM     LABEL    COM     MODE     COM     MORE     COM     PRINT    COM
RECOVER  COM     REPLACE  EXE     RESTORE  COM     SELECT   COM     SHARE    EXE
SORT     EXE     SUBST    EXE     SYS      COM     TREE     COM     VDISK    SYS
        40 File(s)         10386640 bytes free
```

Here the four level 1 subdirectories are indicated with the <DIR> notation. Notice that COMMAND.COM is the only other file displayed in the directory. It is best to keep individual files out of the root directory and place them in subdirectories instead. This keeps the root directory simple and easy to view, allowing the user to focus on the overall structure of the subdirectory system rather than getting muddled by a lot of file entries.

The DIR command works within subdirectories just as it does with the root directory. You can use any of the directory options or filters described in Chapter 3. However, when you view a directory listing of a subdirectory, you will see two additional entries at the top of the listing, "." and "..". For example, the above directory listing (Table 5-2) was obtained from the DOS subdirectory of CompuCard's hard disk.

The first two entries in this listing are followed by the <DIR> notation, so you know they refer to subdirectories. The . and .. are sometimes referred to as subdirectory *markers*. The . marker indicates that you are in a subdirectory. The name of the current subdirectory will be displayed at the beginning of the directory listing. The .. marker refers to the parent directory, that is, the directory that contains the current subdirectory's file entry. For the DOS subdirectory, the parent directory is the root directory, \. Although the name of the parent directory is not displayed, the .. notation can be used to represent the parent directory without having to enter its name. The utility of this abbreviation will become apparent later in this chapter in the discussion of subdirectory paths and tree structures.

The directory command can be used with the FIND filter to display only the actual files contained in a subdirectory without including the . and .. or other subdirectory entries. To accomplish this, you would pipe the output of the directory command through the FIND filter and request that all entries including the notation <DIR> be suppressed:

C>DIR | FIND / V "<"

In this command, the optional parameter, /v, suppresses any entry including the character "<". Since this character only occurs in the <DIR> notation, all subdirectories, including the . and .. markers will be suppressed.

On the other hand, it is also useful to be able to pick out the subdirectory entries from within a directory listing. You can also use the FIND filter to perform this task. In this case, you want to see all the entries with the <DIR> notation except the two subdirectory marker entries. The following command:

C > DIR | FIND "<" / V "."

will produce the desired output. In this case, all entries including the "<" character are displayed except for those entries which also include a period. Since the only entries that include a period are the two subdirectory markers, these two entries are suppressed.

Transferring the System Utilities into the DOS Subdirectory

To see how easy it is to work with subdirectories, consider the task of creating a DOS subdirectory and copying the system utilities into it. In Chapter 2, you learned how to format your hard disk and copy the DOS system files onto it. If you followed the instructions included in that chapter, the three DOS system files COMMAND.COM, IBMDOS.COM, and IBMBIO.COM, as well as a host of utility files, are currently residing in the root directory of your hard disk.

The only files that are required to be in the root directory are the three system files. The remaining DOS utility files are infrequently used and would be better stored in a special subdirectory set aside for that purpose. That way they won't clutter up the root directory.

The first step in establishing the DOS utilities in their own subdirectory is to create a subdirectory file entry in the root directory. You would create this subdirectory with the MKDIR command followed by the subdirectory name, in this case DOS. The abbreviated command would be entered as follows:

C > MD DOS

You can see the result of this command by asking for a directory listing of your root directory. In this listing you will see the subdirectory DOS listed with the characters < DIR > alongside it. On a well-organized hard disk, the root directory will consist of nothing but subdirectory listings along with COMMAND.COM and the two hidden system files, IBMDOS.COM and IBMBIO.COM.

Once the DOS subdirectory has been created you can move into the subdirectory with the CHDIR command followed by the subdirectory name. This command, abbreviated with CD, would be entered as:

C > CD DOS

Note that creating a subdirectory does not automatically place you into that subdirectory. You must always enter a subdirectory through the CHDIR command prior to working in it.

If you give the DIR command after entering this subdirectory, all you will see are the two subdirectory markers. This is because the newly-created DOS subdirectory is currently empty. Your next job is to copy the DOS utility files into it. There are several ways to copy the DOS utility files into this subdirectory. One method would be to enter the subdirectory and copy the files from the DOS System diskette. A second approach would be to log onto the A drive and copy the files to the subdirectory. This distinction will be made clear by the current example.

Since you are already in the DOS subdirectory, you will use the former technique. In this case, you simply place the DOS System diskette in the floppy drive and use the COPY command as if you were in the root directory:

C>COPY A:*.*

This command will copy the DOS system files from the floppy diskette in drive A into the DOS subdirectory on drive C.

This process could also have been accomplished directly from the root directory. In this instance, you would not have had to move into the DOS subdirectory with the CHDIR command. Instead, you would have specified the subdirectory you wanted the files to be copied into by including its path from the root directory:

C>COPY A:*.* \DOS

Alternatively, you could copy the DOS system files into the DOS subdirectory by logging onto the floppy drive with the following commands:

C>A:
A>COPY *.* C:\DOS

If the only files presently contained in the root directory of your hard disk are the DOS system files, you could have transferred them into the DOS subdirectory without resorting to the DOS System diskette at all. If you were in the root directory, you would enter:

C>COPY *.* \DOS

To accomplish the same thing from within the DOS subdirectory, you would copy the files from the source directory, which in this case is the root directory, with the command:

C>COPY *.*

If you have followed one of these methods for copying the DOS system files into the DOS subdirectory, you can now move into this subdirectory if you have not already done so and obtain a directory listing of the files stored in it. Notice that the DOS subdirectory contains the COMMAND.COM file. This file is not needed since it is already in the root directory. You can use the ERASE or DEL commands to remove this file. Whenever copying files into subdirectories, be sure to use the directory command when you are finished to check the results of the COPY command. Always remove unnecessary files, such as COMMAND.COM, which hitched along for the ride.

Speaking of unnecessary files, what about all those DOS utility files that are still in the root directory. Now that you have copied them into the DOS subdirectory, they are just taking up space in the root directory. You need to remove them with the DEL command. For example, you need to remove the FORMAT.COM file from the root directory. you would think you could do this with the command:

C>DEL FORMAT.COM

Be careful! If you enter the above command, which copy of FORMAT.COM do you think will be deleted? That's right, the one in the DOS subdirectory. Always check to see which subdirectory you are in before deleting files. You may be deleting them from the wrong place. If you are unsure as to which subdirectory you are in, you can always enter the CHDIR command without the optional path specification to find out.

To remove the DOS utility files from the root directory, you should return to the root directory. While this is not strictly necessary, it is a good practice to be in the directory or subdirectory where files are stored before deleting them. This ensures that the files are removed from the proper location. To return to the root directory from the DOS subdirectory, you would enter:

C > CD \

From here you could delete the utility files individually as demonstrated above for the FORMAT.COM file. However, deleting the utility files one by one would take quite some time. A more efficient approach would be to delete all the files from the root directory with the *.* global wildcard combination:

C > DEL *.*

Now if you ask for a directory listing, the only entry will be the DOS subdirectory listing. But what about COMMAND.COM and the two hidden system files? Don't worry, the two hidden files are still in the root directory. Remember, hidden files can't be deleted with DEL unless they are revealed. To get COMMAND.COM back, all you have to do is recopy it into the root directory from the DOS System disk as follows:

C > COPY A:COMMAND.COM

You now have the beginning of an organized subdirectory system. Your root directory consists of the three DOS system files and a single subdirectory containing all the DOS utility files. From here, you can proceed to create other subdirectories and copy the appropriate files into them as needed. Make sure you change to the correct directory before copying files, though, or you may end up copying files into the wrong subdirectory.

Using CHKDSK with Subdirectories

Recall from Chapter 4, the CHKDSK command provides you with information regarding the status of the specified disk and any files stored on it. If you simply enter the CHKDSK command without including any optional parameters or filenames, you will just get a display of the disk's status. With versions of DOS 3.2 and higher, this display includes the number of subdirectories included on the disk. For example, the result of running CHKDSK on CompuCard's hard disk results in this display:

The CHKDSK command can be used with the optional /v parameter to reveal a much more detailed picture of the subdirectory and file structure of a hard disk, however. When entered with this parameter, CHKDSK examines the disk and displays a listing of all the files in the level 0 directory (the root directory), then all the subdirectories in this directory. It then steps down one level and displays all the files in each of the

Table 5-3. Status of CompuCard's Hard Disk Produced by CHKDSK.

```
21204992 bytes total disk space
   45056 bytes in 2 hidden files
   20480 bytes in 19 directories
  277504 bytes in 30 user files
20861952 bytes available on disk

  655360 bytes total memory
  609184 bytes free
```

level 1 subdirectories and all of the subdirectories under each of the level 1 subdirectories. CHKDSK proceeds through each of the levels of the disk's tree structure, displaying the files and subdirectories at each level, until the final level has been reached. The following is the output obtained by running CHKDSK with the /v option on CompuCard's hard disk. At this point the complete tree structure has been established and the DOS utility files have been copied into the DOS subdirectory, but no user files have been created.

As you can see, the output from the CHKDSK command can be quite lengthy. Imagine how long the output would be if all the user files were included. If you just want to get an overview of a hard disk's tree structure, you will be better off using the TREE command described later in this chapter.

Including Subdirectory Paths in the System Prompt

In Chapter 4 you learned how to alter the system prompt using the PROMPT command. This command allows you to include special messages and other optional information, such as the system date and time. One of the options available with the PROMPT command is the $p parameter. You can include this parameter in combination with any of the other parameters or text messages to include the current drive and subdirectory path in the system prompt.

For example, you could create a customized prompt that displayed the date, time, logged drive, and current subdirectory, such as is listed at the top of page 88.

Table 5-4. Additional Information Provided by the CHKDSK / V Option.

```
Directory C:\
      C:\IBMBIO.COM
      C:\IBMDOS.COM
      C:\COMMAND.COM
Directory C:\DOS
      C:\DOS\ASSIGN.COM
      C:\DOS\ATTRIB.EXE
      C:\DOS\BACKUP.COM
      C:\DOS\CHKDSK.COM
```

```
                C:\DOS\COMMAND.COM
                C:\DOS\COMP.COM
                C:\DOS\DISKCOMP.COM
                C:\DOS\DISKCOPY.COM
                C:\DOS\EDLIN.COM
                C:\DOS\FDISK.COM
                C:\DOS\LABEL.COM
                C:\DOS\MODE.COM
                C:\DOS\MORE.COM
                C:\DOS\PRINT.COM
                C:\DOS\RECOVER.COM
                C:\DOS\REPLACE.EXE
                C:\DOS\RESTORE.COM
                C:\DOS\SELECT.COM
                C:\DOS\SHARE.EXE
                C:\DOS\SORT.EXE
                C:\DOS\TREE.COM
                C:\DOS\XCOPY.EXE
        Directory C:\ADMIN
        Directory C:\ADMIN\WP
        Directory C:\ADMIN\WP\MM
        Directory C:\ADMIN\WP\TT
        Directory C:\ADMIN\WP\WS
        Directory C:\ADMIN\WP\WS\LINDA
        Directory C:\ADMIN\WP\WS\JACK
        Directory C:\ADMIN\LOTUS
        Directory C:\ADMIN\LOTUS\LINDA
        Directory C:\ADMIN\LOTUS\JACK
        Directory C:\ADMIN\DB3
        Directory C:\ADMIN\DB3\JACK
        Directory C:\ADMIN\DB3\SUE
        Directory C:\ACCTG
        Directory C:\ART
        Directory C:\ART\GRAPHICS
        Directory C:\ART\GAMES
        Directory C:\BOB

  21204992 bytes total disk space
     45056 bytes in 2 hidden files
     20480 bytes in 19 directories
    277504 bytes in 30 user files
  20861952 bytes available on disk

    655360 bytes total memory
    609184 bytes free
```

```
Today is Wed 01-01-1987
Time is 09:01:30.50
Current disk is C
Current subdirectory is C: \ ADMIN \ LOTUS \ LINDA
```

While it does reveal quite a lot of information, the above prompt is rather wordy and takes up four lines on the screen to boot. A simpler but useful prompt might be:

C: \ ADMIN \ LOTUS \ LINDA >

To create this prompt you would enter:

C > PROMPT PG

Customizing the system prompt to include the current subdirectory is a simple yet powerful technique to facilitate working with your hard disk. You should definitely include it in your bag of tricks.

THE PATH AND TREE COMMANDS

The advantage of subdirectories is that they allow you to segregate user files and application programs into separate work areas. The numerous advantages to this approach have already been mentioned. There are disadvantages to segregated work areas as well as advantages, however. One critical limitation of subdirectories is that you cannot directly execute programs stored in a subdirectory unless you are in that subdirectory. While this is not usually a problem, as you will normally move into the appropriate subdirectory before using the desired program, there may be times when you will want to run programs stored in one subdirectory from some other subdirectory.

This is analogous to a household with several rooms, each with a different function. Suppose you are in the den watching a football game, and you decide you want to make a Dagwood sandwich. Unfortunately for you, the sandwich makings are in the kitchen. To make the sandwich, you will have to leave the football game and go to the kitchen. This is, to say the least, inconvenient, if not outright aggravating. On the other hand, would you want to live in a house with all the appliances and furniture, not to mention kids, in a single, large room? Not likely.

A similar situation arises when working with subdirectories on a hard disk. For example, if you were in the LOTUS subdirectory and you wanted to run the CHKDSK program which is in the DOS subdirectory, the command:

C > CHKDSK

would result in the error message:

Bad command or filename

You might think you could get around this problem by telling DOS where the program is located. You could do this by including the path to the program in the command:

Unfortunately, DOS isn't as obliging as you would like, and will ignore this command entirely (you won't even get an error message).

If there really were no way to circumvent this limitation, this single disadvantage might be enough to discourage many users from working with subdirectories. Fortunately there is a convenient solution to the apparent restriction imposed by DOS on running programs only from the current subdirectory. The DOS PATH command permits you to stipulate in advance the allowable subdirectories from which programs may be run. PATH is an internal command and may be entered from any subdirectory. Once the PATH command is in effect, programs from any of the specified subdirectories may be executed from any other subdirectory.

The general format of the PATH command is:

PATH [d:] [path] [;path] [;path] [;etc.]

The PATH command may be followed by one or more subdirectory paths. The individual paths are separated by semicolons; if only one path is indicated, the semicolon is omitted. Each path specified in the PATH command identifies a valid subdirectory to be searched whenever a program filename is entered at the system prompt. In fact, the PATH command is referred to in the DOS User's Manual as the "Set Search Directory Command."

The PATH command functions as follows. The individual paths specified when the command is entered are retained in memory. Whenever a filename is entered at the system prompt, DOS first checks the current subdirectory for a file with that filename and a .COM or .EXE extension. If none is found, DOS next checks the first subdirectory specified by the PATH command. If the file is not located in this subdirectory, DOS proceeds to check each subsequent subdirectory specified by the PATH command until the program is located or all the subdirectories have been investigated. If the program is found, it is executed as if it were in the current subdirectory. If the program is not located in either the current subdirectory or in any of the subdirectories specified in the PATH command, the Bad command or filename message is displayed.

To see how multiple paths can be established using the PATH command, consider the following scenario: Linda wants to use WordStar to write her annual report. She wants to be able to access ThinkTank though, to help her outline her ideas. Also, she wants to have access to the DOS utilities in case she needs to format a floppy diskette to store a backup copy of the finished document. In order to have access to the TT and DOS subdirectories from the WS subdirectory, she would enter the following command:

C > PATH \ ADMIN \ WP \ TT; \ DOS

The PATH command remains in effect until the computer is turned off or rebooted. Although your computer will remember the paths you established at the beginning of a long session, you yourself may forget. To refresh your memory, you can enter the PATH command with no parameters. For example, if Linda were to enter the command:

C > PATH

she would see the following displayed on the screen:

PATH = C: \ ADMIN \ WP \ TT;C: \ DOS

If any of the specified paths do not exist, DOS will simply ignore them when it searches the specified paths looking for a program file. This means it is incumbent upon you to specify subdirectory paths correctly as DOS will not catch your errors for you. To reset the previously established paths so that only the current subdirectory is searched, you would enter the PATH command with no paths but include a semicolon:

C > PATH;

Using PATH with Application Programs

One problem with the PATH command is that it only searches the specified subdirectories for .COM and .EXE files. Some programs, though, use additional files called *overlays*. These files commonly have the extension .OVR or .OVL. Overlay files are used to reduce the amount of RAM utilized by the active portion of the program. For example, WordStar stores most of its prompts and menu screens in a file called WSMSGS.OVR. These prompts and menus are not held in memory. Instead, WordStar recalls them from the overlay file as needed.

If a program relies on overlay files, you will have problems running it from another subdirectory using the path command. Although the PATH command will locate the .COM or .EXE portion of the program, it will not access the attendant overlay files. When the program tries to find its overlay files, DOS will only look for them in the current subdirectory. Since the overlay files are stored in the same subdirectory as the executable portion of the program, they won't be available through the PATH command, and the program will fail to run properly.

WordStar and dBASE

This limitation will be made clear by the following example. Assume Linda is currently in the LOTUS subdirectory and she has established a path to the WS subdirectory with the command:

C > PATH \ ADMIN \ WP \ WS

Located in the WordStar subdirectory are the files WS.COM, WSMSGS.OVR, and WSOVL.OVR. If Linda were to call for this program from the LOTUS subdirectory with the command:

C > WS

DOS would first look for the WS.COM file in the LOTUS subdirectory. Failing to find WS.COM in the current subdirectory, DOS would next try the WS subdirectory indicated in the PATH command. Since the file is located in this subdirectory, DOS would proceed to load this file into memory.

Up to this point, everything would be fine. However, one of the first things WS.COM does is to check to see if the WSMSGS.OVR file is present. How does it do this? By asking DOS to search the directory. DOS obligingly would search the current subdirectory, which in this case is the LOTUS subdirectory, and come up empty. Since the WSMSGS.OVR file is not a .COM or .EXE file, the search for this file would conclude with the current directory and DOS would report back to WS.COM that the WSMSGS.OVR file is not present. Without the WSMSGS.OVR file, WordStar cannot function properly, and so Linda would receive an error message.

WordStar also needs to have access to another overlay file, WSOVLY1.OVR. If you want to run WordStar from a subdirectory other than the one that contains the WS.COM, WSMSGS.OVR, and WSOVLY1.OVR files, the PATH command all by itself will not be enough. The .OVR files must be present in the current subdirectory. In order for Linda to run WordStar from her LINDA word processing work area, she would have to copy these two overlay files into the \ADMIN\WP\WS\LINDA subdirectory. So would Jack. This can be accomplished by the following sequence of steps:

```
C>CD ADMIN\WP\WS
C>COPY *.OVR LINDA
C>CD LINDA
```

Notice that the COPY command transfers both overlay files through the use of the * wildcard. Also, there is no need to specify the full path to the \ADMIN\WP\WS\LINDA subdirectory because the previous command has already established \ADMIN\WP\WS as the current subdirectory. If no backslash precedes the target subdirectory, DOS will assume that it is one level lower than the current subdirectory.

WordStar is by no means the only program to utilize overlay files. Many popular application programs fall into this category. Another popular family of programs which employ overlay files are the dBASE programs from Ashton/Tate. The actual names of the overlay files vary from version to version, but the technique for dealing with them is the same as for WordStar. The attendant overlay files must first be copied into the current subdirectory before dBASE will function properly.

For instance, in the case of CompuCard's hard disk tree structure, both Jack and Sue have work areas under the \ADMIN\DB3 subdirectory. In order for Jack to run dBASE III from his own subdirectory, \ADMIN\DB3\JACK, he must first copy the overlay files, DBASE.OVL and DBASE.MSG, into this subdirectory. Since the two overlay files have different extensions, this will require two separate COPY commands:

```
C>CD ADMIN\DB3
C>COPY DBASE.OVL JACK
C>COPY DBASE.MSG JACK
C>CD JACK
```

At this point you might be wondering why Jack shouldn't copy the DBASE.EXE file into his subdirectory as well. If Sue did the same, there wouldn't be any need for the parent subdirectory, \ADMIN\DB3. The reason this is not done in practice is that there would then be unnecessary duplication of files on the hard disk, thus taking up extra storage space. It is necessary to transfer the overlay files because the program won't function properly without them. However, the PATH command permits both Jack and Sue to use the single copy of the DBASE.EXE file stored in the \ADMIN\DB3 subdirectory.

Some users carry their concern for storage as far as to delete the overlay files from their work area at the conclusion of each work session. Although this necessitates recopying these files at the beginning of every session and deleting them at the end, these users believe it is important to avoid cluttering up their hard disks with duplicate overlay files. While you may feel that this is a bit extreme, in the next chapter you will discover that the entire process can be automated through the use of special batch files.

Lotus and WordPerfect

Some programs, such as Lotus 1-2-3, Symphony, and WordPerfect, must be run from the current subdirectory. You can still use multiple work areas with these programs, however, because they allow you to specify a different directory for data files. For example, Lotus 1-2-3 uses the command sequence:

\Worksheet Global Default Directory

to change the current directory for locating and storing data files. This command is entered after loading the Lotus 1-2-3 program from its own subdirectory. At this point you can use the Backspace key to delete the current subdirectory (in the case of CompuCard, this would be C:\ADMIN\LOTUS) and enter the path to the desired work area (such as C:\ADMIN\LOTUS\BOB).

WordPerfect has a special List Files key (F5) which can be used to accomplish the same thing. Pressing this key will reveal the current subdirectory at the bottom of the screen. In order to change the current subdirectory you press Return. This will display a set of options as follows:

1 Retrieve; 2 Delete; 3 Rename; 4 Print; 5 Text In;
6 Look; 7 Change Directory; 8 Copy; 9 Word Search; 0

To select a different subdirectory for storing and retrieving data files, enter option 7. You will be presented with a prompt asking you for the new directory and suggesting the current one. For example:

New Directory = C:\ADMIN\WP\WRDP

At this point you would simply enter the new subdirectory path (including the drive designator) and press Return.

You can also use this option to create new subdirectories, but you are better off performing this task from DOS. It is always a good idea to wear separate hats for different functions. When you want to work with an application program, use the application program. When you want to perform a system operator's task, do so from the system prompt.

The TREE Command

Unless the tree structure of your hard disk is very simple, you may find yourself forgetting how the various subdirectories were created and where files are stored. Also, a new user won't be familiar with the organization of subdirectories and files on a hard disk. One way to determine where files are stored would be to ask for a listing of the root directory to determine which subdirectories are stored there. With this information, you could then move into each subdirectory and obtain a listing of each one, and so on through each level of subdirectories stored on the disk.

As you might imagine, such a procedure could require quite a lot of time. It would be nice if there were a simple command which would produce a listing of all the subdirectories on the hard disk and the paths to each one. Fortunately, the DOS TREE command performs just this service. The general format of the TREE command is:

TREE [d:] [/F]

The TREE command has a single, optional files parameter, /f, which will be explained shortly. Without the files parameter, TREE simply lists all the subdirectories on the disk according to levels, with the level 1 subdirectories listed first. The following is the output TREE command:

C > TREE

applied to the CompuCard tree structure:

Table 5-5. TREE Command as Applied to CompuCard's Tree Structure.

```
DIRECTORY PATH LISTING
Path: \DOS
Sub-directories:   None

Path: \ADMIN
Sub-directories:   WP
                   LOTUS
                   DB3

Path: \ADMIN\WP
Sub-directories:   MM
                   TT
                   WS
Path: \ADMIN\WP\MM
Sub-directories:   None
Path: \ADMIN\WP\TT
Sub-directories:   None
Path: \ADMIN\WP\WS
Sub-directories:   LINDA
                   JACK
Path: \ADMIN\WP\WS\LINDA
Sub-directories:   None
```

```
Path: \ADMIN\WP\WS\JACK
Sub-directories:   None

Path: \ADMIN\LOTUS
Sub-directories:   LINDA
                   JACK
Path: \ADMIN\LOTUS\LINDA
Sub-directories:   None
Path: \ADMIN\LOTUS\JACK
Sub-directories:   None

Path: \ADMIN\DB3
Sub-directories:   JACK
                   SUE
Path: \ADMIN\DB3\JACK
Sub-directories:   None
Path: \ADMIN\DB3\SUE
Sub-directories:   None

Path: \ACCTG
Sub-directories:   None

Path: \ART
Sub-directories:   GRAPHICS
                   GAMES
Path: \ART\GRAPHICS
Sub-directories:   None
Path: \ART\GAMES
Sub-directories:   None
```

The optional files parameter, /f, may be appended to include all the files stored in the subdirectories as well. In this case, the output will be substantially longer. For example, a partial TREE listing for CompuCard's hard disk including the DOS subdirectory files is shown below:

Table 5-6. A Partial TREE Listing.

```
DIRECTORY PATH LISTING
Files:             COMMAND .COM
Path: \DOS
Sub-directories:   None
Files:             ASSIGN  .COM
                   ATTRIB  .EXE
                   BACKUP  .COM
                   BASIC   .COM
```

```
                                    BASICA   .COM
                                    CHKDSK   .COM
                                    COMMAND  .COM
                                    COMP     .COM
                                    DISKCOMP.COM
                                    DISKCOPY.COM
                                    EDLIN    .COM
                                    FDISK    .COM
                                    FIND     .EXE
                                    FORMAT   .COM
                                    GRAFTABL.COM
                                    GRAPHICS.COM
                                    JOIN     .EXE
                                    LABEL    .COM
                                    MODE     .COM
                                    MORE     .COM
                                    PRINT    .COM
                                    RECOVER  .COM
                                    REPLACE  .EXE
                                    RESTORE  .COM
                                    SELECT   .COM
                                    SHARE    .EXE
                                    SORT     .EXE
                                    TREE     .COM
                                    XCOPY    .EXE
```

Path: \ADMIN
Sub-directories: WP
                    LOTUS
                    DB3
Files: None

Path: \ADMIN\WP
Sub-directories: MM
                    TT
                    WS
Files: None

Path: \ADMIN\WP\MM
Sub-directories: None
Files: None

Path: \ADMIN\WP\TT
Sub-directories: None
Files: None

If your tree structure is fairly complex, the resulting output will scroll by quite quickly. You can freeze the scrolling with Ctrl NumLock, but a better alternative is to pipe the output through the MORE filter, as in:

C>TREE \F | MORE

Another option would be to redirect the output to the printer with the command:

C>TREE \F >PRN

You can then keep this printout as a reference to the tree structure and file location of your hard disk. Remember to print out a new copy whenever you revise the structure of your hard disk.

In this chapter, you have learned how to create and work with subdirectories on your hard disk. This involves a new set of DOS commands and special techniques. Some of these commands, such as MKDIR and TREE will only be used periodically. However, other commands, such as CHDIR, PROMPT, and PATH must be used every time you operate your computer. Since these commands can be quite lengthy to enter, especially on a repetitive basis, it would be nice if there were some way to retain them for reuse each time the computer is turned on. In fact, there is a technique for entering repetitive commands through the command processor without having to key them in each time you need them. This technique involves creating special DOS command files called batch files. You will learn how to develop and enter your own customized batch files in the next chapter.

Chapter 6

Batch File Programming

In the last chapter, you learned how to place program and data files into separate subdirectories and how to move into these subdirectories to access these files when needed. You also learned how to customize the DOS system prompt to include the current subdirectory. While useful, these and other DOS-related activities require you, the system operator, to enter a series of simple, yet repetitive, commands every time you start up your computer. DOS provides you with a way to automate these repetitive command sequences by placing them into special command files called *batch* files.

Batch files contain readable, ASCII text and are identified by the special extension, .BAT. Each line of text in a batch file represents a DOS command or a program call. When the command processor sees a file with this extension, it knows that it should execute the individual lines included in the file as DOS commands or requests to execute a program.

Batch files can be either quite simple or very elaborate. Most simple batch files are employed to automate repetitive processes such as setting the system prompt or changing the current subdirectory and starting a program. On the other hand, large, powerful batch files can be used to drive complete, menu-driven hard disk management systems. Such files can display specially designed menu screens, accept user input, and perform complex system-related tasks involving decision-making and looping. These sophisticated batch files are literally computer programs, and the techniques for creating them rightly deserve to be considered under the heading Batch File Programming.

In Chapter 4 you read that the command processor accepts user entries from the system prompt and determines whether each entry is a command or an executable program. Executable programs are indicated by either a .COM or a .EXE file extension. You also were told that if the entry were neither an internal command nor a .COM or .EXE file, the error message:

Bad command or filename

would be displayed. In fact, files with .BAT extensions can also be executed from the system prompt.

When you make an entry at the system prompt, the command processor first determines whether the entry is actually an internal command. If not, it next checks the current directory to see if there is a .COM or a .EXE file with a descriptive filename corresponding to the first word in the entry. If this is not the case, the command processor then checks the current directory to see if there is a .BAT file with a descriptive name that corresponds to the entry. If such a batch file is found, the commands stored in the file are then executed in turn by the command processor.

Because of the sequence the command processor follows in attempting to execute commands entered from the system prompt, it is important to adopt different names for batch files than for the commands they include. For example, a batch file to set the system prompt should not be called PROMPT.BAT because there is a DOS command by that name. Similarly, a batch file to load the WordStar program should not be named WS.BAT because the WS.COM file has the same descriptive filename.

DOS MACROS

To begin with, you will learn how to create and execute fairly simple batch files. For example, you might want to set up a special batch file to change the system prompt to save you from entering the PROMPT command every time you start up your computer. This batch file would include the PROMPT command plus the specialized text and parameters needed to customize your system prompt. You could assign a short, easily entered filename to this batch file. By entering this filename at the original C prompt, you would cause DOS to execute this file and change the system prompt for you automatically.

Batch files such as this serve a useful though limited function. They allow the user to store either single or multiple DOS commands into a file for execution at a later time. To execute the stored command(s), all the user has to do is enter the name of the batch file. Because a number of commands can be stored in a single batch file, the result of entering a single batch filename at the system prompt is greater than a single command entry. For this reason, such batch files are commonly called DOS *macros*.

You may have heard of macros in a slightly different context. Many application programs include macro capabilities among their features. Perhaps the most popular application programs to include macros are Lotus 1-2-3 and Symphony. When used in reference to application programs, the term macro means a stored sequence of program commands. For example, a Lotus user could create and employ a macro to automatically load and update a summary spreadsheet from each of several detail spreadsheets on a regular basis. Some word processing programs include macro capabilities in the form of *glossaries*.

Creating and Running Batch Files

For example, assume that you want your system prompt to display the current subdirectory as well as the current drive as described in Chapter 5. To refresh your memory, such a system prompt might look like this:

C:\ADMIN\LOTUS\LINDA>

To change the standard system prompt to display the current subdirectory, you would enter the following command:

C>PROMPT PG

Suppose you wanted to create a batch file containing this command for reuse. To remind you of its purpose, you might decide to name the file PRMPT.BAT. One way to create this file would be to place this command into an ASCII text file using your word processor. Be careful, though. Many word processors, such as WordStar and WordPerfect, do not automatically create ASCII text files, though documents created with these programs can be converted to ASCII files.

An easier and faster way to create the PRMPT.BAT file would be to enter it directly from the console at the system prompt following these simple steps (make sure you are in the root directory before starting):

C>COPY CON: PRMPT.BAT <Return>
PROMPT PG <Return>
^Z <Return>

Remember, "^ Z" is entered either by pressing the F6 function key or the Ctrl Z key sequence. When you press the final Return, you should see the confirming message:

1 file(s) copied

(If not, re-read the instructions and try again.)

You now have a simple batch file which you can use to change the system prompt each time you start up your computer. To execute this batch file, all you need to do is enter its descriptive filename at the C prompt:

C>PRMPT

The command processor will search the current subdirectory, which will be the root directory since the computer has just been booted, and will find and execute the command contained within the PRMPT.BAT file for you.

Another routine operation that is often performed at system startup is to set the path to certain commonly used subdirectories. In the CompuCard hard disk tree structure, all the DOS utilities are stored in the DOS subdirectory. In order to run any of these utilities, the path to this subdirectory must first be established. The PRMPT.BAT file could be modified to include this step as well. In this case, PRMPT.BAT would include two commands as shown below:

PROMPT.BAT

PROMPT PG
PATH \DOS

To modify an existing batch file, you could use either your word processor (if it can work with straight ASCII files) or use the DOS text processor, EDLIN. EDLIN is described in Chapter 8 however, for simple batch files such as PRMPT.BAT, it is just as easy to delete them and start over. For example, to delete the old PRMPT.BAT file and recreate the new one, you would move to the root directory and follow these steps (pressing Return to conclude each step):

```
C>DEL PRMPT.BAT
C>COPY CON: PRMPT.BAT
   PROMPT $P$G
   PATH \DOS
   ^Z
```

Batch Files that Load Application Programs

Batch files used as DOS macros may include either DOS commands or program calls. To see how program calls can be combined with DOS commands in a single macro, consider the recurring need to move into a subdirectory and run an application program. For instance, every time Linda wants to use WordStar to create a document, she must execute the following sequence of commands:

```
C>CD \ADMIN\WP\WS
C>COPY *.OVR LINDA
C>CD LINDA
C>PATH \ADMIN\WP\WS
C>WS
```

Assuming that Linda might also want to have access to the ThinkTank program, she would need to include a second path, \ADMIN\WP\TT. Any new PATH command destroys any previously established paths, such as the \DOS path created by the PRMPT.BAT file. This means that the \DOS path must be added as well.

All this involves quite a lot of keyboarding just for Linda to get into her work area and load the WordStar program. Clearly, it would be simpler to place this sequence of commands into a batch file named WSLINDA.BAT. This file could be created by entering (from the root directory):

```
C>COPY CON: WSLINDA.BAT
   CD \ADMIN\WP\WS
   COPY *.OVR LINDA
   CD \LINDA
   PATH \ADMIN\WP\WS;\ADMIN\WP\TT;\DOS
   WS
   ^Z
```

Once the file, WSLINDA.BAT, has been saved into the root directory, all Linda has to do to access her work area and begin using WordStar is to enter the batch filename, WSLINDA, from the root directory:

Similar batch files could be created for each of the users and their specific applications.

One limitation of the current WSLINDA batch file is that it leaves Linda in her WordStar work area after she exits from WordStar. Also, there are now copies of the two overlay files in her work area. An improved version of the WSLINDA.BAT file is shown below:

```
WSLINDA.BAT

CD \ ADMIN \ WP \ WS
COPY *.OVR LINDA
CD LINDA
PATH  \ ADMIN \ WP \ WS; \ ADMIN \ WP \ TT; \ DOS
WS
DEL *.OVR
CD \
PATH  \ DOS
```

This version will delete the overlay files from Linda's work area, change the current subdirectory back to the root directory, and reset the path to \ DOS after the WordStar program is exited. An important aspect of batch files is illustrated by this example. To quote a common expression, "It's not over until it's over." A batch file that contains subsequent commands after a program call will continue to execute even after the program is concluded.

When a batch file is called from the system prompt, the command processor retains a copy of the complete file in memory. It then executes each command or program call in turn. After each command or program has been executed, the command processor returns to the copy of the batch file in memory to see if the file has been concluded.

The conclusion of the batch file is indicated by the special end-of-file marker, ^Z. For this reason, it is important to include an end-of-file marker when creating batch files from the console. Word processors and text editors automatically place an end-of-file marker at the end of their files, so you don't have to worry about this step if you are using such a program to create your batch files.

Batch Files to Simplify DOS Commands

Many people want to use their computers without having to learn much about them. To such users, the computer is a productivity tool and nothing more. While they may be willing to learn the commands necessary to create documents with their word processing program or build worksheets with their spreadsheet program, they are not interested in learning the details of DOS. Unfortunately, such users do have to put on the system operator's hat from time to time, if only to perform such necessary tasks as formatting diskettes and copying files.

As the old saying goes, "A little knowledge is a dangerous thing." A computer user who knows a little DOS is potentially more harmful than one who knows nothing about DOS at all. The classic blunder made by such DOS dilettantes is formatting the hard disk when attempting to format a floppy. Perhaps this has even happened to you.

One application of batch files is to facilitate the use of DOS commands. In the remainder of this chapter, you will learn various techniques that will enable you to create special batch files to simplify such DOS commands as COPY, ERASE, FORMAT, etc. In fact, you've already learned how to create a batch file which simplifies the PROMPT command.

Consider the problem of inadvertently formatting the hard disk when attempting to format a diskette. One way to prevent this from occurring would be to create a special batch file called FORMAT.BAT which would format a floppy diskette by including the A: drive designator in the FORMAT command. Then, whenever a user entered FORMAT at the system prompt, the batch file would ensure that the floppy drive was used instead of the hard drive.

You are probably wondering how there can be a batch file, FORMAT.BAT, with the same descriptive filename as FORMAT.COM. As long as FORMAT.COM is not in the current subdirectory, the batch file will be executed. In the case of CompuCard's tree structure, FORMAT.COM is located in the DOS subdirectory. If the FORMAT.BAT file is stored in the root directory, then it will have precedence whenever the root directory is the current directory. You can ensure that this will be the case by entering all application programs through the use of batch files like WSLINDA, which return you to the root directory when you are through.

Before creating the FORMAT.BAT file, you might want to determine the necessary commands you would need to include. When planning a DOS macro, pretend you are entering each of the commands in the macro individually from the system prompt. First, you would have to move into the DOS subdirectory. Next, you would enter the FORMAT A: command. (You could include the optional /s parameter if you wanted to copy the DOS system files after formatting.) Finally, you would change back to the root directory.

The complete FORMAT.BAT file should look like this:

FORMAT.BAT

```
CD \ DOS
FORMAT A:
CD \
```

To execute this batch file from the root directory, you would enter its descriptive filename at the system prompt:

C>FORMAT

Now DOS will respond with the message:

Insert new diskette in drive A
and strike any key to continue

even though the drive designator, A:, was not included in the command. If the drive designator is included, it will be ignored. This means that the user could even enter:

C>FORMAT C:

with no adverse effects.

Terminating a Batch File

It may have occurred to you to employ the PATH command to gain access to the FORMAT.COM utility. You may think that the commands:

PATH \ DOS
FORMAT A:

will accomplish the same thing as the preceding batch file. However, if you enter the above commands into a file called FORMAT.BAT and try to run it, you will be surprised at the result.

Instead of following the \ DOS path to run the FORMAT.COM file, the FORMAT A: command will execute the FORMAT.BAT file located in the current directory. This is a case of a batch file running itself. Each time the FORMAT.BAT file encounters the command FORMAT A: it will run itself again. This is an example of an *infinite loop*. The only way to break out of this loop is to use the key sequence Ctrl Break (or Ctrl C). Infinite loops are a common occurrence in batch file programming. You will learn more about infinite loops and how to avoid them later in this chapter.

For whatever reason, you can terminate a batch file in the middle of execution by entering Ctrl Break. If your computer keyboard does not have a Break key, you can use the Ctrl C key sequence instead. Pressing Ctrl Break will cause the following message to appear on the screen:

Terminate batch file (Y/N)?

You must respond with either a "Y" or an "N" with obvious results.

While Ctrl Break can be used to terminate an unwanted batch file, you should be aware that Ctrl Break will not abort a DOS command once it has started. If, for example, the formatting process has started before pressing Ctrl Break, the batch file will not be terminated until this process has completed.

AUTOMATIC STARTUP BATCH FILES

Even though the PRMPT.BAT file simplifies setting the system prompt and establishing the path to the DOS utilities, it still must be entered from the C> each time the computer is turned on. Think about how many times your computer is turned on in a month and then multiply this number times five (the number of characters in PRMPT). In some sense, these keystrokes represent wasted effort. The PRMPT entry really belongs under the heading of an operating system entry. You, on the other hand, are more interested in working with the computer as a tool.

One of the functions of batch files is to limit or even eliminate the need for the computer user to deal with the operating system. For this reason, DOS has established a special batch filename, AUTOEXEC.BAT, which is recognized and executed automatically at system startup. You can assign this name to any batch file you wish. Once a batch file has been created in the root directory and given the filename AUTOEXEC.BAT, this file will be executed on startup without having to enter it by name.

Note that the AUTOEXEC.BAT file must be present in the root directory. DOS will not look elsewhere for it. If no file by the name AUTOEXEC.BAT is present, DOS proceeds with the standard startup procedure, which consists of prompting for the system date and time.

Automatic Date and Time Stamping

On the topic of the date and time prompts, if you do not include the commands DATE and TIME in your AUTOEXEC batch file, these prompts will not be displayed on startup. Without an opportunity to enter the date and time, any new or modified files will be stamped with the system's original date and time. For computers that don't have an internal clock, this means that the former PRMPT.BAT file should be amended and renamed as follows:

AUTOEXEC.BAT

DATE
TIME
PROMPT PG
PATH \ DOS

You can either delete the old PRMPT.BAT file and recreate a new file under the name AUTOEXEC.BAT or use your word processing program to edit and rename it.

In the above example, the AUTOEXEC batch file includes the DATE and TIME commands because the computer that uses this file doesn't have an internal clock. However, if your system does have a battery-driven clock installed, the last thing you want is to have to enter the date and time every time your computer is turned on. After all, that's why you installed the clock in the first place—to eliminate these extra steps. If this is the case, you would leave out the DATE and TIME commands from your AUTOEXEC.BAT file.

Automatic System Modification

Your system may have other special hardware features, such as a special video adapter or a serial printer. In such cases, you may need to set certain system parameters at system startup using the DOS MODE utility. This utility lets you change the system defaults. For example, programs ordinarily send output to the printer via the LPT1: logical device. This logical device is assigned to the parallel printer port. If you have a serial printer, though, you want the output to go to the serial port instead. This port is usually identified as COM1: (it may be COM2: if you have more than one serial port). To reassign the printer output to the serial port, you would use the command:

C > MODE LPT1: = COM1:

Rather than entering this command every time you start up your computer, you could place it into your AUTOEXEC.BAT file. The MODE command can also be used to change the character pitch and line spacing on your printer as well as set the video parameters of your monitor. For more on this command, see your DOS manual.

If you have added any special hardware components to your system, such as an internal clock or a RAMDISK, the chances are good that your hard disk already has an AUTOEXEC.BAT file located in the root directory. This AUTOEXEC file was either placed on your disk by the technician who installed the add-on device, or you were told to run an installation program which placed this file into your root directory for you. Before creating an AUTOEXEC file of your own, you should take the precaution of checking for an existing one.

If there is already an AUTOEXEC.BAT file present in your root directory, you have two options. You can print out a copy of the existing AUTOEXEC file with the following command:

C>TYPE AUTOEXEC.BAT >PRN

Once you have a hard copy of the commands contained in the original AUTOEXEC file, you can delete it and create a new one that contains all the original commands plus any extra commands you wish to include.

A second option is to use your word processing program or EDLIN to edit the original AUTOEXEC.BAT file. This may necessitate copying the AUTOEXEC.BAT file into the subdirectory containing your word processor or EDLIN. Don't forget to copy it back to the root directory when you are finished.

MESSAGES, PROMPTS, AND VARIABLES

Simple DOS macros such as PRMPT.BAT or FORMAT.BAT are useful for automating repetitive tasks and facilitating the use of DOS. However, batch files such as these are quite limited. All they can do is perform a series of pre-determined DOS commands, which could have been entered directly from the system prompt. It is possible to create batch files which can accomplish far more than the simple examples illustrated so far.

By including messages and prompts to the user, you can develop batch files which guide the user through a series of steps. Further, with the inclusion of variables, you can devise general purpose batch files to perform a variety of tasks. These generic batch files can be made to perform specific functions by replacing the variables with actual values at the time of execution.

Including Messages in Batch Files

If you have executed any of the batch files described so far in this chapter, you have probably noticed that DOS echoes each of the commands in the batch file as it is executed. For example, consider the screen display as the PRMPT.BAT file is executed:

```
C>DATE
    Current date is: Tue 1-01-1980
    Enter new date: 1-08-87

C>TIME
    Current time is: 0:01:56.00
    Enter new time: 9:00

C>PROMPT $P$G
```

```
C:\ >PATH \DOS
C:\ >
```

As you can see, each of the commands in the file are displayed next to the system prompt as if you had entered them yourself. This echo feature can be used to display messages on the screen during the execution of a batch file.

The REM Subcommand

DOS allows you to place remarks into your batch files with the REM batch file subcommand. (The DOS manual uses the term subcommand to refer to commands which are only used in batch files.) A remark is a batch file entry which is ignored by DOS during the execution of the batch file. The REM subcommand was initially intended to provide batch file programmers with a way to document their batch files. However, since every entry in a batch file is echoed to the screen, REM entries can be used to convey messages to the user during execution of a batch file.

Consider the FORMAT.BAT file. This batch file will only format floppy diskettes due to the inclusion of the A: drive designator in the FORMAT command which is imbedded in the file. To format the hard disk (a fairly rare situation), the user would have to insert the DOS System diskette in the A drive and follow the instructions for formatting the hard disk. A message to this effect could be included in the FORMAT.BAT file using a series of remarks which would be echoed to the screen when the FORMAT.BAT file was executed. The revised FORMAT.BAT file would look like this:

```
FORMAT.BAT

REM This batch file only formats floppy diskettes.
REM To format the hard disk,
REM place the DOS System diskette in drive A
REM and follow the instructions in the DOS manual
REM for formatting the hard disk.
REM To abort this batch file
REM press Ctrl Break.
FORMAT A:
```

The ECHO Subcommand

While the batch file echo feature is beneficial in echoing REM entries to the user, the echoing of other commands can be confusing. For this reason, echoing can be turned off with the ECHO OFF subcommand. If this command is placed at the top of a batch file, the remaining commands will not be echoed to the screen. Unfortunately, the ECHO OFF command itself is still echoed. However, this can be taken care of by including a CLS command immediately after the ECHO OFF command. Echoing can be turned back on again with the ECHO ON subcommand. The ECHO subcommand acts as a toggle switch, toggling the echo feature off and on.

Once the ECHO OFF command has been executed, any REM entries will not be echoed to the screen. In order to display messages on the screen after issuing ECHO OFF, you can echo them by placing text after the ECHO subcommand. For example, to echo the phrase, "Happy computing!", you would include the subcommand:

ECHO Happy computing!

After a batch file has been executed, it is a good idea to reset any toggles to their default values. The default ECHO value is obviously ON, so any batch files that set ECHO OFF should reset ECHO ON at their conclusion. Using ECHO subcommands instead of REM entries, the FORMAT.BAT file would look like this:

FORMAT.BAT

ECHO OFF
CLS
ECHO This batch file only formats floppy diskettes.
ECHO To format the hard disk,
ECHO place the DOS System diskette in drive A
ECHO and follow the instructions in the DOS manual
ECHO for formatting the hard disk.
ECHO To abort this batch file
ECHO press Ctrl Break.
FORMAT A:
ECHO ON

In the preceding two examples, the messages included in the REM or ECHO entries will be displayed on the screen and will remain there because the next command, FORMAT A:, requires an action on the part of the user. This command causes the message:

Insert new diskette for drive A:
and strike ENTER when ready

to be displayed on the screen and pauses until the user complies. However, if the command following the REM or ECHO entries were to execute automatically, the messages contained in these entries would only appear briefly on the screen before disappearing with the execution of the subsequent command.

The PAUSE Option

It is possible to halt the execution of a batch file temporarily to allow the user to read the screen or perform some task. This is accomplished by including a special command in the batch file at the point where the file is to be temporarily interrupted. The PAUSE command halts the execution of the batch file and displays the message:

Strike any key when ready . . .

PAUSE may be used alone or with an accompanying prompt. For instance, suppose Linda wanted to have a batch file which would automatically back up her WordStar documents onto a floppy diskette. This special batch file, WSLINBU.BAT, could be run by Sue on a weekly basis to back up all the documents in Linda's WordStar work area. Linda wants to make sure that the files get stored on a special diskette reserved for this purpose.

One way to accomplish this would be to include a prompt instructing Sue to insert the diskette labeled "Linda's WordStar Backup" into the floppy drive. This could be accomplished with the PAUSE command in the following batch file:

```
WSLINBU.BAT

ECHO OFF
CLS
CD \ADMIN\WP\WS\LINDA
DEL *.BAK
PAUSE Place Linda's WordStar Backup diskette in drive A
COPY *.* A:
ECHO ON
```

When this batch file is executed, the screen will be cleared and the message:

```
Place Linda's WordStar Files diskette in drive A
Strike any key when ready . . .
```

will appear on the screen. The execution of the COPY command will be held up until Sue has had a chance to place the appropriate diskette in the proper drive. When Sue has performed this task, she indicates she is ready to continue by pressing any key. At this point, the batch file will resume and the COPY command will be executed.

REPLACEABLE PARAMETERS

The REM, ECHO, and PAUSE subcommands allow you to customize the execution of DOS commands by including your own messages and prompts. Still, all the commands contained in the batch files introduced so far have been pre-determined. This means that each batch file can only perform a specific function. Suppose you had several different but related tasks that you wanted to automate. Rather than creating a separate batch file for each of them, wouldn't it be nice if you could develop a general purpose batch file and then identify the specific task you wanted performed at the time of execution.

DOS gives you this flexibility by allowing you to include *replaceable* parameters in your batch files. Replaceable parameters serve as variables and are included with the individual commands in a batch file. Replaceable parameters can take the place of filenames, paths, and even DOS commands. The actual filename, path, or command is provided by the user at the time the batch file is executed. Replaceable parameters are indicated by the percent character, "%," followed by a digit, 0 through 9.

In a DOS command line, each word in the line is assigned to a replaceable parameter, beginning with the parameter %0. For instance, in the command line:

```
C>COPY LETTER.DOC \LINDA
```

the first command, COPY, is assigned to the variable %0, the filename, LETTER.DOC, is assigned to the variable %1, and the path name, \ LINDA, is assigned to the variable %2. DOS remembers these assignments until the next command line is entered. If the value %2 is referred to, it will stand for \ LINDA. Since batch file calls are a form of DOS commands, each of the words in the batch file call gets assigned to a replaceable parameter.

The following example will help you understand how replaceable parameters work in batch files. Consider the WSLINBU batch file. This file changes the directory to Linda's WordStar work area and then prompts the user to insert Linda's WordStar Files diskette in drive A. Once the user has acknowledged the completion of this task, the batch file copies all the files in this area onto the floppy diskette.

A similar backup batch file could be created for Bob and Jack's files as well. However, one batch file, WSBACKUP.BAT, could be made to serve all three users through the inclusion of a replaceable parameter as follows:

```
WSBACKUP.BAT

ECHO OFF
CLS
CD \ ADMIN \ WP \ WS \ %1
DEL *.BAK
PAUSE Place %1's WordStar Backup diskette in drive A
COPY *.* A:
ECHO ON
```

To execute this batch file, the user would supply the actual value for the replaceable parameter when entering the batch filename. For example, to backup Jack's files, the entry would be:

```
C > WSBACKUP JACK
```

At execution, every occurrence of the %1 parameter would be replaced with the entered value, JACK. The Change Directory command would change the directory to the \ ADMIN \ WP \ WS \ JACK subdirectory. The PAUSE command would instruct the user to:

```
Place JACK's WordStar Files diskette in drive A
Strike any key when ready . . .
```

You may include up to ten different replaceable parameters in a single batch file by using the variables %0 through %9. The use of multiple parameters is illustrated in the following example. Consider the useful but missing DOS command, MOVE. Such a command would move a file from one disk or diskette to another. The COPY command only transfers a copy of a file from one disk to another, leaving the original file on the source disk. You can create a batch file, MOVE.BAT, which will copy a file from the source disk to the target disk and then delete the file from the original disk. This batch file incorporates two replaceable parameters, one for the source filespec and one for the target filespec:

MOVE.BAT

ECHO OFF
COPY %1 %2
DEL %1
ECHO ON

To execute this batch file, you must supply both parameters. For example, to move the file, LETTER.DOC, from its current location on the hard disk to a floppy in drive A, you would enter:

C>MOVE LETTER.DOC A:

Upon entering the above command, LETTER.DOC would be substituted for %1 and A: would be substituted for %2 in the COPY and DEL commands. This would have the effect of copying the LETTER.DOC file from drive C to drive A and then deleting this file from drive C.

There is much more to batch files than simply stringing DOS commands together. In the next chapter, you will learn how to use the techniques of sequential execution, looping, conditional testing, and chaining to create fairly elaborate batch file programs.

While these techniques are powerful in their own right, the real power of batch file programming comes in allowing you to take control of your hard disk. You will learn how to combine batch file programming with your knowledge of DOS to create complete, menu-driven systems of batch files for accomplishing all the tasks of loading application programs, managing your system, and backing up your data files.

Chapter 7

Batch File Menus

While the batch file techniques learned in the preceding chapter extend the power of your system significantly, they are still rather limited in the range of applications to which they can be used. In order to gain further control over the operation of your hard disk, you will need batch files that can perform repetitive tasks, make decisions, and call other batch files.

In addition to the batch file subcommands covered so far, there are several other batch file subcommands which belong under the heading of Programming Techniques. These include GOTO, FOR and IF. Before discussing each of these subcommands in turn, it will be useful to consider the basic concepts involved in programming so you may better understand how each is used.

PROGRAMMING TECHNIQUES

Programming in any language is nothing more than the collection of individual commands into an executable file. While some commands included in a computer program can be executed directly, such as a command to print out the results of a computation, others are used to control the execution of the program itself.

There are four ways that commands in a program can be executed. The simplest of these is sequential execution. In sequential execution, program commands are executed one after the other from beginning to end. This is how all the batch files covered so far operate. Sequential execution of commands is the simplest programming technique.

Not all programming tasks can be accomplished sequentially, however. Certain repetitive processes are best handled by a technique known as *looping*. Looping applies a sequence of commands to a series of different values. Looping is accomplished through the use of variables, or, in the case of batch files, replaceable parameters. The variables are used in the commands within the loop and are replaced with actual values each time the loop is executed. Program loops must be properly controlled or they may continue indefinitely.

Sequential execution and looping are two important programming techniques. However, in each case, the specific execution of the commands involved is pre-determined and therefore limited. It is possible to select one command from a number of options through the use of *conditional* statements. Conditional statements typically begin with the word if. You deal with conditional situations every day: If the traffic light is green, you keep driving; if it's red, you stop. Similar conditional situations can occur in programming. If you have ever used a menu-driven program, you are familiar with the results of conditional programming: If you select "1," you get option one; if you select "2," you get option two; etc.

Another way to execute program commands is through *chaining*. Chaining is a technique that involves linking various groups of commands together. These individual groups of commands are each designed to perform some specific task and are sometimes called subroutines. A number of different subroutines may be chained together within a single batch file using IF and GOTO subcommands. In addition, separate batch files may be chained together to form a complex, sophisticated network of command files capable of monitoring and controlling your hard disk system. The goal of this book is to teach you how to develop just such a system of batch files specifically designed to meet the needs of your system.

Looping with the GOTO Subcommand

Certain tasks in computing are repetitive. Rather than reissue the same sequence of commands over and over again, they can be included in a loop. For example, consider the need to perform the same type of processing on all the records in a file. Suppose, for instance, that you wanted to print mailing labels for each of over 1000 names and addresses stored in a database file. Using a programming language such as BASIC or dBASE III, you could create the sequence of commands necessary to print a single label. These commands could then be placed into a loop. The loop commands would cause the computer to move to the next record in the data file, print out the mailing label, and proceed until all the records were completed.

Simple looping in batch files is accomplished through the use of the GOTO subcommand (available in DOS versions 2.0 and higher). This is similar to the way looping is performed in BASIC. The GOTO subcommand redirects the flow of commands in a batch file, skipping all subsequent commands until the specified point in the batch file is reached.

GOTO alone, however, is insufficient, because DOS won't know where to go to unless you tell it. Imagine responding to a lost traveler's request for directions with the single phrase, "Go to." Pretty uninformative.

In order for the GOTO subcommand to work, it must be used in conjunction with a *label*. Labels in batch files act like place markers or street signs. Just as you might say to the traveller, "Go to Maple Street and turn left," you can include a GOTO subcommand, such as GOTO DONE, in a batch file.

Labels are preceded by a colon and are placed on a line by themselves. Labels may be as long as you like, but only the first eight characters are recognized by DOS. Once labels have been inserted into a batch file at appropriate locations, they can be used in GOTO subcommands to alter the sequence of commands by changing the direction of the program.

To see how the GOTO subcommand can redirect the flow of statements in a batch file, consider the following nonsensical batch file:

```
NONSENSE.BAT

ECHO OFF
ECHO This batch file is
GOTO WORTHLESS
ECHO a wonderful batch file
ECHO full of useful commands.
:WORTHLESS
ECHO worthless!
PAUSE
ECHO ON
```

When executed, the above batch file will display the following on the screen:

```
This batch file is
worthless!
Strike any key when ready . . .
```

Do you see why the lines, "a wonderful batch file" and "full of useful commands" are not echoed to the screen? Instead of being executed, these two ECHO commands are skipped over by the GOTO WORTHLESS statement. The next line to be executed after the ECHO This batch file statement is the ECHO worthless! statement. Note that the :WORTHLESS label itself is ignored.

The preceding example illustrated the use of the GOTO subcommand to execute a forward jump in the batch file. You can also use GOTO to jump backward as well. However, once you go backward, you must proceed forward through commands already executed. This will continue until the backward GOTO command is encountered, when the process will repeat itself. For this reason, a backward GOTO can be used to create a circle of commands, or loops, within a batch file.

Consider the situation of an individual who must create multiple copies of a series of worksheet files for distribution within a large organization. Assume these files have already been placed into a special subdirectory on the hard disk. The path to this subdirectory is \ LOTUS \ DISTRIB. A batch file could be created which would repeatedly transfer all the files stored in this subdirectory onto separate floppy disks until the individual running the batch file aborted it with Ctrl C. A batch file to accomplish this task is shown below:

```
DISTRIB.BAT

ECHO OFF
CD \ LOTUS \ DISTRIB
```

```
:AGAIN
CLS
ECHO Place the target diskette in drive A.
PAUSE
COPY *.* A:
ECHO Copying completed.
ECHO To conclude this activity, enter Ctrl C.
ECHO To copy another diskette,
PAUSE
GOTO AGAIN
```

This batch file turns off the echo feature and moves into the \ LOTUS \ DISTRIB subdirectory. The AGAIN: label is ignored and the loop processing commences by clearing the screen. The user is then instructed to place a diskette into the A drive and strike any key when ready. Once this is done, the batch file transfers all files stored in the \ LOTUS \ DISTRIB subdirectory onto the diskette in drive A. When the copying is completed, a confirmation message is displayed, and the user is instructed to enter a Ctrl C to conclude the operation or proceed by striking any key. Unless a Ctrl C is entered at this point, the control of the batch file is transferred back to the :AGAIN label, and the batch file repeats itself.

The DISTRIB.BAT file is an example of an *infinite loop*. The file will repeat itself infinitely unless the user aborts its execution by entering a Ctrl C (or a Ctrl Break). Infinite loops are a quick-and-dirty programming technique for accomplishing repetitive tasks. Batch files employing infinite loops rely upon a certain competence on the part of the user. A rank beginner might respond to the prompt to enter a Ctrl C by literally typing in the letters CTRL C. (It's been known to happen!)

For this reason, two other looping strategies are often employed. They are FOR loops and conditional loops. FOR loops proceed through a specified sequence of parameters, performing the same processing on each of them in turn. Conditional loops involve the use of special *error codes*. An error code indicates a condition which can be used to control the looping process. These error codes are determined based upon user input. An entry of "Y" sets an error code to 0, and an entry of "N" sets an error code to 1. The error code can then be tested to determine whether the looping should continue or not.

FOR Loops

The DOS FOR subcommand allows you to specify a group of similar parameters which will be substituted into a command until each member of the group has been processed. Because the command does not have to be repeated for each element in the parameter list, the FOR subcommand can save you considerable typing. The general form of the FOR subcommand is:

FOR %%variable IN (parameter list) DO command

A *variable* is a generic code-word which can take on each of the specific words in the parameter list. You worked with variables back in your high school algebra days. In algebra, the variables, like X and Y, were used to represent unknown numbers. As such, they could be used to represent any number. The same is true with DOS variables. They can be used to represent any of the individual parameters within the parameter list. DOS variables are preceded by two percent symbols (%%) to distinguish them from replaceable parameters.

The use of variables and parameters in the FOR command can be clarified by the following example. Suppose you wanted to backup the dBASE III database files in a given subdirectory. In dBASE III, in addition to the database files themselves, which have a .DBF extension, there are memo files, which have .MEM extensions, and index files, which have .NDX extensions. Ordinarily, to copy all of the files with each of these extensions would require three separate COPY commands. However, by including these three extensions in a parameter list, you can use a single COPY command in a FOR loop as follows:

FOR %%FILE IN (*.DBF *.MEM *.DBF) DO COPY %%FILE A:

The above FOR loop uses the variable, %%FILE, as a dummy in the command COPY %%FILE A:. In fact, %%FILE itself never gets copied to A:. Instead, %%FILE is used to represent each of the parameters in the parameter list. In this case, the parameter list contains three parameters, *.DBF, *.MEM, and *.NDX. First, *.DBF is substituted for %%FILE, and the command COPY *.DBF A: is executed. Next, *.MEM is substituted for %%FILE, and the command COPY *.MEM A: is executed. Finally, the COPY command is executed with the *.NDX command.

Conditional Loops

FOR loops execute the command specified after the DO as many times as there are parameters in the parameter list. Conditional loops, on the other hand, continue until the user cancels them by entering the appropriate response to a prompt provided from within the loop. The correct response represents a *condition* which must be met before the looping can be discontinued. In order for conditional loops to be terminated, there must be some way to test for the correct condition.

This testing is done through the use of the DOS IF subcommand. Although the IF subcommand has other applications to batch file programming which will be discussed later in this chapter, its use is the key to creating conditional loops. For this reason, the IF subcommand will be described briefly in this section.

The general form of the IF subcommand is:

IF condition outcome

Statements involving the IF subcommand are called *conditional statements* because they involve testing for a given condition to see whether a specified outcome will result.

You are familiar with conditional statements—they are a part of our reasoning and vocabulary. For example, you might think to yourself, "If the sky is overcast this morning, I will take an umbrella with me to work." In this example, the condition to be tested is whether it is overcast or not. The outcome in this instance is taking an umbrella to work. Note that you will only take an umbrella to work with you if the sky is overcast, that is, if the condition is true.

The problem with this example is that it is hard to determine exactly what constitutes an overcast sky. Do scattered clouds qualify? Conditions in DOS, however, must be specific. Later in this chapter, the various conditional tests available with the IF subcommand will be described in detail. For conditional loops, the condition to be tested is the value in a special variable called ERRORLEVEL.

ERRORLEVEL is called an *exit code* in DOS terminology, and may be used to test a variety of conditions. In terms of conditional loops, ERRORLEVEL can be tested for the values 0 or 1. These values are established in response to a special ASK command, which displays a prompt message on the screen and then checks the user's answer. If the user enters a "Y," then ERRORLEVEL is set to 0; if the user enters a "N," ERRORLEVEL is set to 1.

ASK is not one of the DOS subcommands. Instead, it is a separate utility program which has been provided for you on the optional programs diskette. You will find it listed as ASK.COM. In order to use the ASK command in any of your batch files, this utility program must be in either the current subdirectory or in a subdirectory specified by the PATH command.

To see how a conditional loop using the ASK . . . IF ERRORLEVEL combination works, consider the modified DISTRIB.BAT file shown below:

```
DISTRIB.BAT

ECHO OFF
CD \LOTUS\DISTRIB
:AGAIN
CLS
ECHO Place the target diskette in drive A.
PAUSE
COPY *.* A:
ECHO Copying completed.
ASK Do you wish to copy another diskette (Y/N)?
IF ERRORLEVEL 0 GOTO AGAIN
```

In this version of the batch file, the loop is controlled by the IF ERRORLEVEL 0 GOTO AGAIN statement. As long as the value of ERRORLEVEL is 0, the loop will repeat another time. The value of ERRORLEVEL is determined by the user's response to the preceding ASK statement. This statement displays the message:

Do you wish to copy another diskette (Y/N)?

and then awaits the user's response. Once the user answers, the response is used to set the value of ERRORLEVEL.

Conditional loops involving ASK and IF ERRORLEVEL are much more user-friendly than infinite loops which must be aborted using Ctrl C. Remember to keep the skill level of the intended user in mind when designing batch files to automate repetitive processes. Also, if you're planning to ask the user to respond to a question, be sure to indicate the appropriate responses by including "(Y/N)" at the end of the prompt.

Your fellow computer users will appreciate these special touches. If nothing else, conditional loops are more professional looking than quick-and-dirty infinite loops.

Conditional Branching

The IF subcommand can do more than control conditional loops. It can also be used to allow your batch files to make decisions about what action to take based upon a given condition. This allows you to truly program your batch files to perform a variety of different tasks depending upon the specific conditions encountered when they are executed.

The three conditional tests that IF is able to perform are: EXIST, = =, and ERRORLEVEL. You've already seen how ERRORLEVEL is tested in the preceding discussion of conditional loops. In this section you will learn how to use the ERRORLEVEL test in other applications as well.

The EXIST Conditional Test

The EXIST conditional test is used to check for the presence on the disk of a given file in the specified subdirectory. (Note: in DOS versions 2.xx, you can only test for the existence of a file in the default subdirectory.) The EXIST condition follows the IF subcommand and precedes the filespec of the file being tested. The format of the IF subcommand when testing for the EXIST condition is:

IF EXIST filespec outcome

The following example shows how you would use the EXIST test in a simple batch file called WSLOAD.BAT. This file allows the user to specify a filename as part of the batch file call and have WordStar automatically open that file, placing the user directly into the Editing Menu upon execution. However, if the file is not present, the batch file will inform the user that the file is not available and will simply load WordStar and leave the user at the Opening Menu instead:

```
WSLOAD.BAT

ECHO OFF
IF EXIST %1 GOTO LOAD
ECHO %1 is not available.
PAUSE
WS
GOTO QUIT
LOAD:
WS %1
:QUIT
ECHO ON
```

This batch file is executed by entering the descriptive filename, WSLOAD, followed by the name of the file to be opened. For example, to open the file LETTER, you would enter:

C>WSLOAD LETTER

In this case, the filename, LETTER, would be substituted for the %1 replaceable parameter in the batch file.

If you follow the logic of this batch file, you will see that there are two possible outcomes, depending upon the result of the EXIST test. If the file specified by the %1 replaceable parameter is present on the disk, then the WS %1 command following the :LOAD label will be executed. Otherwise, the next command, WS, will be executed and the WS %1 command will be skipped over due to the GOTO QUIT statement.

The beauty of this batch file is that, if no filename is specified after WSLOAD, the batch file will default to the WS command, which is what you would want. This elementary example assumes that the file is located in the current subdirectory. You can improve on this simple batch file by including the commands to place the user into the correct subdirectory, transfer the necessary overlay files, load WordStar and open the desired document:

```
WSLOAD.BAT

CD \ ADMIN \ WP \ WS
IF EXIST %1 GOTO PROCEED
ECHO Subdirectory does not exist,
ECHO WordStar will not be loaded.
PAUSE
GOTO QUIT
:PROCEED
COPY *.OVR %1
CD \ %1
PATH \ ADMIN \ WP \ WS
IF EXIST %2 GOTO LOAD
ECHO %2 is not available.
PAUSE
WS
GOTO QUIT
LOAD:
WS %2
:QUIT
CD \
PATH \ DOS
ECHO ON
```

The execution of this batch file requires the user to enter two parameters after WSLOAD. The first of these is the user subdirectory in which the user expects to find the file. The second is the name of the file itself. For example, if Linda wanted to work in her \ ADMIN \ WP \ WS \ LINDA subdirectory on a file named LETTER, she would enter:

118

This fairly elaborate batch file breaks down into several simple logical components. The initial group of statements checks to see if the user subdirectory specified by the first replaceable parameter is available under the \ADMIN \ WP \ WS subdirectory. If this subdirectory is available, control is passed to the :PROCEED label and the program proceeds from there. If the subdirectory is not present, the user is informed of this fact, and program control is transferred to the :QUIT label, which concludes execution of the program. The remainder of the statements are from the previously explained WSLINDA.BAT and WSLOAD.BAT files.

The Equality Conditional Test

The IF subcommand can also be used to test for the equality of two items. This is the = = conditional test. Notice that DOS requires two equals symbols (= =) to represent equality. The = = conditional test allows you to create batch files which perform a variety of different tasks depending upon the parameter(s) supplied with the batch file call. Consider the simple batch file, LOAD.BAT, which loads either WordStar or Lotus 1-2-3 depending upon whether the user specifies WS or LOTUS after the initial LOAD:

```
LOAD.BAT

ECHO OFF
IF %1 = = WS GOTO WSLAND
IF %1 = = LOTUS GOTO LOTUSLAND
GOTO QUIT
:WSLAND
WS
GOTO QUIT
:LOTUSLAND
LOTUS
:QUIT
ECHO ON
```

If the user specifies **LOAD WS**, then the batch file will match up %1 with "WS," and control will be transferred to the :WSLAND label. If, on the other hand, the user enters **LOAD LOTUS**, control will be transferred to the :LOTUSLAND label instead.

There are several important points to note in the above batch file. For one thing, you should realize that there are really three outcomes possible. The batch file will either load WordStar, load Lotus, or terminate. In the first case, after the program has been loaded, the subsequent GOTO command transfers control of the batch file to the final :QUIT label. Can you see why this is necessary? If the GOTO QUIT command were omitted here, the batch file would proceed to load the Lotus 1-2-3 program after the user had exited from WordStar.

Another important point to note when using the = = conditional test is the case of the characters being tested. In this batch file, it is assumed that the user will enter the WordStar call letters in capitals. If the user were to enter the command in lower case, **load ws**, the test for "WS" would fail, and WordStar would not be loaded. Of course, you could circumvent this by including a separate test for lowercase "ws" as well:

IF %1 = = WS GOTO WSLAND
IF %1 = = ws GOTO WSLAND

The ERRORLEVEL Conditional Test

You have already seen one application of the ERRORLEVEL conditional test in controlling the exit from a conditional loop. The @ exist code was intended to allow programmers to check the way in which certain applications and utilities were exited. For example, if a utility for backing up the hard disk onto floppies successfully backed up all sectors in the FAT, ERRORLEVEL would be set to 0. The value of ERRORLEVEL could then be tested with an IF ERRORLEVEL 0 test.

For simple batch file programming, though, the value of the IF ERRORLEVEL test lies in its use with the ASK utility described previously. This utility has the capability of setting ERRORLEVEL in response to a user's response to a question. As you saw in the discussion on conditional loops, a "Y" response sets ERRORLEVEL to 0, while an "N" response sets it to 1.

The resulting ERRORLEVEL value can then be tested in an IF ERRORLEVEL conditional test to determine what action should be taken next. The outcome will usually be a GOTO subcommand redirecting the logic of the program to a set of statements elsewhere in the batch file. In conditional loops, this would be back to the beginning of the loop for another pass through the loop procedure.

There are other applications for the ASK statement besides controlling exiting from a loop. You can use an ASK statement to determine whether the user wishes to proceed with a course of action. For example, in the WSLINBU.BAT file, it is assumed that the diskette labeled Linda's WordStar Backup is available. Unless the user knows enough to press Ctrl C to abort, the batch file will remain in limbo until the user places a diskette in the drive.

It might be a good idea to ask the user if the required diskette is available before executing the rest of the batch file. This could be accomplished through the following set of statements:

ECHO This procedure transfers copies
ECHO of Linda's WordStar files onto the diskette
ECHO labeled "Linda's WordStar Backup"
ASK Is this diskette presently in drive A (Y/N)?

The user's response to the ASK statement can then be tested with an IF ERRORLEVEL statement. If the response is "N," a GOTO subcommand can be used to terminate the batch file.

The ASK . . . IF ERRORLEVEL combination can be used in batch files whenever you want to check with the user before proceeding with a sequence of commands. Prompts can take any of the following forms:

ASK Do you wish to proceed (Y/N)?

ASK Would you like to continue (Y/N)?
ASK Is this correct (Y/N)?
ASK Would you like to try again (Y/N)?

One last example will show how an ERRORLEVEL conditional test can be used to provide an *error trap* for an incorrectly entered filename. This involves a modification of the WSLOAD.BAT file. The modified version tests for the existence of the filename entered for the replaceable parameter %2. If the specified file is not present, the user is informed of this fact and asked if she wishes to view a directory listing. This version of WSLOAD.BAT employs several conditional branches. See if you can follow the logic of the various GOTO's:

WSLOAD.BAT

```
ECHO OFF
CD \ ADMIN \ WP \ WS/
COPY *.OVR %1
CD \ %1
PATH \ ADMIN \ WP \ WS
IF EXIST %2 GOTO OPEN
ECHO %2 not found.
ASK Do you wish to see a list of files available (Y/N)?
IF ERRORLEVEL 1 GOTO DONE
DIR /W
GOTO DONE
:OPEN
WS %2
:DONE
DEL *.OVR
CD \
PATH \ DOS
ECHO ON
```

The NOT Option

Sometimes you will be more interested in testing the opposite of a condition rather than the condition itself. For instance, in the previous example, the real purpose of the IF EXIST test was to determine if the file was unavailable. Otherwise the batch file would have caused WordStar to open a new file, which is not what the user intends. The absence of the file can be tested directly by including the word NOT before the EXIST conditional test:

IF NOT EXIST %2 GOTO . . .

Of course, NOTing the conditional test changes the logic of the batch file, and different labels would be required. Here's how the WSLOAD.BAT file would look using NOT:

```
ECHO OFF
CD \ADMIN\WP\WS/
COPY *.OVR %1
CD \%1
PATH \ADMIN\WP\WS
IF NOT EXIST %2 GOTO NOFIND
WS %2
GOTO DONE
:NOFIND
ECHO %2 not found.
ASK Do you wish to see a list of files available (Y/N)?
IF ERRORLEVEL 1 GOTO DONE
DIR /W
:DONE
DEL *.OVR
CD \
PATH \DOS
ECHO ON
```

You can also use NOT with the = = and ERRORLEVEL conditional tests. Note that the word NOT always precedes the conditional test. This may seem intuitively obvious for the EXIST and = = tests, but many beginners make the mistake of writing:

IF ERRORLEVEL NOT 0 . . .

which sounds better than:

IF NOT ERRORLEVEL 0 . . .

but which is incorrect.

Testing the opposite of a condition with NOT is called testing the *converse*. Using the converse of a conditional test often results in batch files that are easier to follow and understand.

Chaining

So far, you've seen how batch files can be used to issue a series of DOS commands and load applications. It is also possible to execute one batch file by calling it from another. To do so, you simply include the descriptive filename of the batch file you want to execute in the calling batch file. Using one batch file to call another is known as *chaining*. There is no limit to the number of batch files that can be chained together.

For example, suppose you had an AUTOEXEC.BAT file that set your system configuration at system startup. Suppose that at the conclusion of this batch file, you wanted to load WordStar. This could be accomplished by including the WSLOAD batch file call as the final line of the AUTOEXEC batch file. The resulting AUTOEXEC.BAT file would look like this:

122

```
AUTOEXEC.BAT
ECHO OFF
CLS
DATE
TIME
PATH \ DOS
PROMPT $P$G
WSLOAD
ECHO ON
```

While this version of AUTOEXEC.BAT saves the trouble of having to execute the WSLOAD.BAT file separately, it has a number of drawbacks. For one thing, the WSLOAD batch file will automatically be executed whenever the computer is restarted. This may not always be desirable. This problem can be overcome by including an ASK . . . IF ERRORLEVEL test in the AUTOEXEC file, such as the following:

```
AUTOEXEC.BAT

ECHO OFF
CLS
DATE
TIME
PATH \ DOS
PROMPT $P$G
ASK Do you want to load WordStar (Y/N)?
IF ERRORLEVEL 1 GOTO DONE:
WSLOAD
:DONE
ECHO ON
```

This revised version of the AUTOEXEC.BAT file permits the user to bypass the WSLOAD call by entering "N" at the prompt. However, this version still has several shortcomings. Remember that AUTOEXEC.BAT files load automatically at system startup. This means that there is no opportunity for the user to supply values for any replaceable parameters. The latest version of WSLOAD.BAT presented in this chapter employs two replaceable parameters, one for the work area and one for the file to be opened. Since AUTOEXEC.BAT can't accept user-supplied values, any batch file called from an AUTOEXEC batch file can't take advantage of this feature.

The only way to get around this limitation is to rename the AUTOEXEC.BAT file to some other name, such as STARTUP.BAT. This batch file can then be executed from the system prompt along with any user-supplied values. To open the LETTER document file in Linda's WordStar work area, she would enter:

```
C > STARTUP LINDA LETTER
```

Although the STARTUP batch file makes no reference to replaceable parameters, the WSLOAD.BAT file does. The two user-supplied values, LINDA and LETTER, will be transferred, or passed, to the WSLOAD batch file when it is executed from STARTUP.BAT.

Even with this difficulty overcome, there is one final limitation to the method of chaining batch files described so far. While application programs return control to the calling batch file when they terminate, called batch files do not. Once a new batch file is called from the original batch file, control passes to the new batch file. When that batch file concludes, the user is returned to the system prompt. In terms of the preceding example, what this means is that the final ECHO ON command in STARTUP.BAT will not be executed after the WSLOAD.BAT file terminates.

In this simple example, the consequences are rather minor. However, you may have batch files that need to reset certain system parameters or move back into the root directory at their conclusion. With the method of chaining described thus far, this could only be accomplished by chaining WSLOAD.BAT to a concluding batch file which tied up any loose ends. This is a clumsy solution at best.

The COMMAND/C Subcommand

Fortunately, DOS provides a solution to this problem through the use of the COMMAND/C subcommand. This subcommand is available in DOS versions 3.0 and higher. The COMMAND/C subcommand allows you to call a batch file, have that batch file executed, and return control to the calling batch file after the called batch file terminates. Batch files called using the # subcommand are sometimes referred to as *subroutines*.

The use of chained subroutines in batch file programming conveys several advantages. Obviously, it allows greater control over the execution of the calling batch file. Also, this technique permits a modular approach to batch file programming, a large programming task can be divided into a series of smaller tasks, each of which can be handled easily. Further, the same subroutine can be used, or called, by a number of different batch files. This reduces the amount of programming involved in large projects. For instance, in Chapter 10, you will find a batch file, SHUTDOWN.BAT, which performs special tasks at system shutdown. This batch file could be called from a number of different batch files, eliminating the need to include the same commands in each of these batch files separately.

The format of the COMMAND/C subcommand is:

COMMAND/C filespec [%#. . .%#]

The filespec following COMMAND/C refers to the batch file subroutine being called. This filespec may include paths and even drive designators. The optional replaceable parameters, %#. . .%#, represent any values you wish to send along to the subroutine. These values must have been entered when the original batch file was called.

In order for the called batch file to return control to the calling batch file, the called batch file must conclude with the special subcommand, EXIT. Consider the following illustration employing two batch files, STARTUP.BAT and LOAD.BAT:

STARTUP.BAT

```
ECHO OFF
CLS
DATE
TIME
PATH \DOS
PROMPT $P$G
COMMAND/C LOAD %1



LOAD.BAT

ECHO OFF
CLS
IF %1 = = WS GOTO WSLAND
IF %1 = = LOTUS GOTO LOTUSLAND
GOTO QUIT
:WSLAND
WS
GOTO QUIT
:LOTUSLAND
LOTUS
:QUIT
EXIT
```

The STARTUP batch file sets the system parameters and then calls the LOAD subroutine batch file with the COMMAND/C LOAD %1 statement. Any value entered with the STARTUP batch file call will be passed along to the LOAD.BAT file as %1. LOAD.BAT will determine if either WordStar or Lotus 1-2-3 are to be loaded and act accordingly. If neither of these programs were specified (as WS or LOTUS respectively), LOAD.BAT will do nothing. Whatever the outcome, at its conclusion, LOAD.BAT returns control to the STARTUP batch file due to the EXIT command.

You may have noticed that the LOAD.BAT file begins with the two subcommands, ECHO OFF and CLS. Why are these subcommands repeated in the subroutine batch file when they are already part of the calling batch file, STARTUP.BAT? The reason for this is that DOS automatically sets ECHO back on whenever a new batch file is initiated. DOS also sets ECHO on when returning to a calling batch file as the result of an EXIT subcommand. This means that, if a calling batch file calls more than one subroutine, ECHO will have to be set OFF after each subroutine call. Consider the sample batch file, SLAVDRVR.BAT, which calls three subroutines, DOTHIS.BAT, DOTHAT.BAT, and DOIT.BAT:

```
SLAVDRVR.BAT

ECHO OFF
CLS
COMMAND/C DOTHIS
ECHO OFF
```

```
CLS
COMMAND/C DOTHAT
ECHO OFF
CLS
DOIT
```

Notice that ECHO OFF and CLS appear after the COMMAND/C DOTHIS and the COMMAND/C DOTHAT subroutine calls. Why is there no ECHO ON statement at the conclusion of SLAVDRVR.BAT? Since DOS automatically turns ECHO ON at the conclusion of each subroutine, ECHO will be ON when DOIT.BAT returns control to SLAVDRVR.BAT. Thus, SLAVDRVR.BAT has no need of a final ECHO ON statement.

MENU SYSTEMS

If you have spent any time working with personal computers, you have probably been exposed to some form of menu-driven software. Any program that displays a list of choices or options and allows you to select from among them utilizes menus. When program commands or options are selected from a menu, the program is said to be *menu-driven.*

As with restaurant menus, software menus can take many forms, ranging from one-line menus to elaborate, full-screen menu systems. Some programs reserve a portion of the screen for displaying command options. These menus are called *screen menus*. With screen menus, you usually select the option you want by entering the code letter(s) or number corresponding to your choice in response to a prompt on the screen. The WordStar Editing Menu is an example of a screen menu.

Other programs place command options in a single line. Such one-line menus are often referred to as *menu bars*. To select a choice from a menu bar, you normally use the left and right cursor control keys (or the Tab key) to move back and forth across the menu bar. Command selection is accomplished by highlighting the desired command or option and pressing the Return key.

Some menu-driven programs provide brief descriptions for each of the choices included in the menu. Still others provide optional on-screen help which may be selected by pressing a special help key. Sometimes a single menu is insufficient for displaying all the command choices or program options. In these cases, the programs rely upon additional *submenus* for displaying additional commands. These commands are usually grouped together in some logical fashion.

The collection of menus, submenus, prompts, and attendant help screens that are used to guide a user through a program is called a *menu system*. You can create customized menu systems for controlling access to files and programs stored on your hard disk. Such menu systems may consist of simple, single-screen menus or elaborate systems complete with submenus and optional help screens.

Why Use Menus?

Menu-driven hard disk management systems have numerous advantages. The most obvious advantage is that a well-organized menu system makes using the hard disk computer easier for both the novice and the advanced user. Menus allow the user to enter short codes to load programs and locate files. This saves typing. Also, menus take the memory and guess-work out of working with complex, tree-structured subdirectory systems. Along these lines, menus and submenus that correspond to a hard disk's tree structure help users from inadvertently interfering with each other's work areas.

Another reason for using menu systems to control access to the hard disk is security. There are several security considerations which can be addressed through the use of menu-driven hard disk management systems. For one thing, DOS commands can be made part of a special DOS submenu. Within this submenu, one choice could be format a diskette. This choice would be tied to a batch file such as the one described in Chapter 6. By forcing the user to select DOS commands from a menu, you eliminate the possibility of incorrectly entered commands, such as the FORMAT command without a drive designator, which would result in formatting the hard drive and wiping out all the data stored there.

Other security considerations include limiting access to programs and data files. When access to programs and data is achieved through menu choices, password security can be added to ensure that only authorized individuals are allowed access. The techniques for including passwords as part of your menu system are covered in Chapter 12, Password Security.

Ease of use, convenience, and security are three reasons for developing a menu-driven hard disk management system. With only the techniques described so far in this book and a little help from your word processing program (or Edlin), you can develop your own customized menu-driven system for loading programs, accessing data files, and executing DOS commands. No prior programming experience is necessary.

Developing your own menu system is easy, creative, and fun. Most users get a kick out of designing and implementing their own menus. Also, customized menu systems are easily modified as your system requirements change. Whether your hard disk system is intended for a single user or several different users, and no matter what the skill level of the individuals using the computer, a set of customized menus will make your computer more efficient and easier to use, and will add a more polished and professional appearance to your hard disk system.

DEVELOPING A SIMPLE MENU SYSTEM

In this section, you will learn how to create a single-screen menu system. This simple menu system includes the menu screen itself, as well as the batch files which execute the various menu selections. Later in this chapter, you will see how you can add submenus and help screens to your menu system as well.

For this initial menu system, a simplified version of the CompuCard tree structure is assumed. The tree structure consists of one word processing subdirectory, \ WP, one spreadsheet subdirectory, \ LOTUS, one database subdirectory, \ DB, an accounting subdirectory, \ ACCT, and a subdirectory containing the DOS utilities, \ DOS. (See Fig. 7-1.) The root directory will be used to hold the system files, the AUTOEXEC.BAT file, the menu screen text file, and the various batch files needed to execute the menu choices. Later, this example will be expanded to accommodate the complete CompuCard tree structure described in Chapter 4.

Creating Menu Screens

Menu screens are nothing more than text files designed to display a series of commands or options. To create your menu screens, you can use any word processor capable of

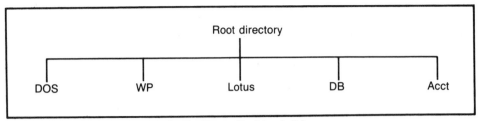

Fig. 7-1. Simplified tree structure for the CompuCard hard disk.

generating true ASCII text files. For example, you could use WordStar's non-document mode, or the DOS Edlin text processor.

Consider the simple menu screen shown in Fig. 7-2. This screen was created in WordStar using the non-document mode. Centering was accomplished with WordStar's Onscreen Center command. The menu was saved as a text file with the name MAINMENU.TXT. Assuming this file is located in the root directory of CompuCard's hard disk, it can be displayed on the screen with the command:

C>TYPE MAINMENU.TXT

Even better, this command can be included as part of the AUTOEXEC batch file as follows:

AUTOEXEC.BAT

```
ECHO OFF
CLS
DATE
TIME
CLS
TYPE MAINMENU.TXT
```

Once this AUTOEXEC batch file has been created, the menu screen will appear each time the computer is restarted. On the line following this menu, the regular DOS prompt will be displayed. (See Fig. 7-3.)

Adding User Prompts

While this menu may appear obvious to someone familiar with personal computers,

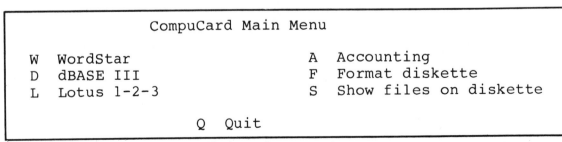

Fig. 7-2. Sample menu created using WordStar's non-document mode.

```
                          CompuCard Main Menu

        W    WordStar                    A    Accounting
        D    dBASE III                   F    Format diskette
        L    Lotus 1-2-3                 S    Show files on diskette


                           Q    Quit




   C>
```

Fig. 7-3. Menu displayed using the TYPE command. Note the DOS prompt which appears below the last line of the menu.

the use of the menu can be improved through the addition of a prompt, such as:

Enter the letter corresponding to your choice:

While your first inclination might be to include this prompt as part of the menu screen, the problem is that the DOS prompt would still appear on the next line. This intrusion of DOS into the menu screen can be distracting, especially to novice users.

A better approach would be to change the DOS prompt to include the text you wish to display on the screen. This can be accomplished by including a PROMPT command in the AUTOEXEC.BAT file as follows:

AUTOEXEC.BAT

ECHO OFF
CLS
DATE
TIME
CLS
TYPE MAINMENU.TXT
PROMPT Enter the letter corresponding to your choice:

Now, when the AUTOEXEC batch file is executed, the DOS prompt, which is the last line that appears on the screen, will read like a prompt to the user to enter one of the letters appearing on the menu (Fig. 7-4). Clever, isn't it?

Although this version of the AUTOEXEC.BAT file takes care of all the details needed to display the menu and user prompt on the screen, it is actually better to place the last two commands into a separate batch file, MAINMENU.BAT, and call this file from the AUTOEXEC.BAT file:

AUTOEXEC.BAT

```
                    CompuCard Main Menu

    W   WordStar                    A   Accounting
    D   dBASE III                   F   Format diskette
    L   Lotus 1-2-3                 S   Show files on diskette

                    Q   Quit




    Enter the letter corresponding to your choice
```

Fig. 7-4. Modifying the DOS prompt results in a more meaningful prompt.

```
    ECHO OFF
    CLS
    DATE
    TIME
    CLS
    MAINMENU


    MAINMENU.BAT

    ECHO OFF
    CLS
    TYPE MAINMENU.TXT
    PROMPT Enter the letter corresponding to your choice:
```

The reason for placing the TYPE and PROMPT commands in a separate batch file named MAINMENU.BAT is that this batch file can now be called from any batch file that needs it. This will become apparent in the following section.

Batch Files to Complete the System

Once the menu text file has been created and the AUTOEXEC.BAT and MAINMENU.BAT files have been established to display the menu on the screen, all that remains is to write the batch files needed to run the system. In this simple case, seven batch files are required. These batch files should be named: W.BAT, D.BAT, L.BAT, A.BAT, F.BAT, S.BAT, and Q.BAT respectively. Each of these batch files must be located in the root directory along with the AUTOEXEC.BAT and MAINMENU.TXT files.

Three of these files will be shown below to illustrate how the menu choices are used to load programs and execute DOS commands:

W.BAT

```
ECHO OFF
CLS
CD \ WP
WS
CD \
MAINMENU


F.BAT

ECHO OFF
CLS
CD \ DOS
FORMAT A:
CD \
MAINMENU


S.BAT

ECHO OFF
CLS
CD \ DOS
DIR A: | SORT | MORE
CD \
MAINMENU
```

Notice that each of these batch files causes DOS to move into the appropriate subdirectory before loading the application program or executing the DOS command. Also, each batch file concludes by returning to the root directory and redisplaying the menu and user prompt by calling the MAINMENU batch file. You can now see why it was necessary to have a separate MAINMENU.BAT file rather than including the commands to display the menu and prompt in the AUTOEXEC.BAT file.

The remaining batch files for loading dBASE, Lotus 1-2-3, and the accounting program are similar to W.BAT. The final batch file, Q.BAT, consists of special commands for backing up the hard disk and shutting down the system. This batch file can be patterned after the SHUTDOWN.BAT file described in Chapter 10. For now, you can have a simple file which parks the read/write heads and instructs the user to shut off the computer. The following batch file should suffice for now:

```
Q.BAT

ECHO OFF
CLS
ECHO Parking the heads . . .
PARK
ECHO Shut off the computer now.
```

SUBMENUS AND HELP SCREENS

The preceding example illustrated how you can create a menu screen with your word processor and use this screen in conjunction with the DOS prompt to instruct the user to run one of several batch files to load programs or execute DOS commands. For simple hard disk tree structures, a single-screen menu system such as this may be sufficient. However, many hard disk tree structures are much more complicated than this simple example. They may contain many different application programs or multiple work areas for each application program.

Such is the case with the complete tree structure for the CompuCard system. (You may want to refer back to Fig. 5-2 which provides a schematic diagram of the CompuCard tree structure.) In this tree structure, there are three different word processing programs, for example. The WordStar, Lotus 1-2-3, and dBASE application programs are shared by several users, each of whom has his or her own work area for storing data files.

In order to have a separate choice for each user's work area in each of the applications available on the CompuCard hard disk, a single-screen menu would have to contain at least twelve different options, not including options for DOS commands and the Quit option. The resulting screen would appear cluttered, presenting the user with too many options to choose from. Instead, a better approach would be to stick with a main menu containing fewer than eight options and use this menu to call for submenus containing specific options for each work area.

Submenu Systems

Consider the menu screen illustrated in Fig. 7-5. In this menu, the choices are indicated by multiple letters rather than single characters. This is because the overall system will contain numerous choices, and there are not enough single-letter choices to go around. For instance, both DOS and dBASE begin with the letter "D."

As your menu systems become more involved, you will find that single-letter options become unworkable. Of course, the prompt message will have to be changed slightly to indicate that the user should enter the complete option. A prompt such as the following should suffice:

Enter your choice (WP, DB, etc.):

Notice that the WP and DOS options are general in nature. They don't refer to a specific application program or command. Instead, they refer to categories. Selecting

```
         CompuCard Main Menu

    WP      WordStar           ACCT    Accounting
    DB      dBASE III          ART     Graphics
    LOTUS   Lotus 1-2-3        DOS     DOS Commands

                    Q   Quit
```

Fig. 7-5. Modified menu for CompuCard's hard disk.

```
                        Word Processing Menu

LIN     Linda's WordStar Files          MM   Multimate
JACK    Jack's WordStar Files           TT   ThinkTank

                     E  Exit to Main Menu
```

Fig. 7-6. The Word Processing submenu.

either of these options should cause a separate submenu to appear. For example, Fig. 7-6 shows the Word Processing Menu. This menu contains four choices for working with the various word processing programs available on the disk, plus an option for returning to the main menu.

As with the Main Menu, this menu screen could be created and saved as a text file with the filename WPMENU.TXT using your word processing program. This menu would be called from the Main Menu by the batch file, WP.BAT:

```
WP.BAT

ECHO OFF
CLS
TYPE WPMENU.TXT
PROMPT Enter your choice (LIN, JACK, etc.):
```

The various options from within the Word Processing Menu would be executed by batch files named LIN.BAT, JACK.BAT, MM.BAT, and TT.BAT respectively. These batch files are straightforward and need no explanation. The Exit option batch file, E.BAT, is shown below:

```
E.BAT

ECHO OFF
CLS
MAINMENU
```

The other options from CompuCard's Main Menu should produce similar submenu screens. For example, Fig. 7-7 shows the Lotus Menu. Does anything seem amiss to you? While on the surface this menu appears to present no problems, in fact it contains two options which will produce undesirable results. What will happen when the user selects the LIN or JACK options? Right, the LIN.BAT or JACK.BAT files will load the WordStar program, not Lotus 1-2-3.

There are two ways to avoid conflicts such as these. The easy way is to use different option codes, such as LINDA and JAC, for the Lotus Menu. This is a poor solution. You want to maintain a consistent look and feel to your menu screens. So how do you keep the codes LIN and JACK in each of your submenus?

```
┌─────────────────────────────────────────┐
│           Lotus 1-2-3 Menu               │
│                                          │
│   LIN     Linda´s Lotus Worksheets       │
│   JACK    Jack´s Lotus Worksheets        │
│   BOB     Bob´s Lotus Worksheets         │
│                                          │
│       E  Exit to Main Menu               │
│                                          │
└─────────────────────────────────────────┘
```

Fig. 7-7. The Lotus submenu.

The answer is by using subdirectories for each of your submenus. This solution results in a more orderly and systematic approach to developing a coordinated menu system. It also keeps the root directory from becoming cluttered up with submenu text files and little batch files to execute each of the submenu options.

While this solution may appear to require the creation of additional subdirectories for each of the submenus, this is not really the case. Remember, there are already subdirectories in the tree structure for each of the options in CompuCard's Main Menu. The submenu text files and batch files can be located in these subdirectories. For instance, the WPMENU.TXT file and attendant batch files, LIN.BAT, JACK.BAT, MM.BAT, TT.BAT, and E.BAT, can be placed in the \ADMIN\WP subdirectory.

This requires only two additional changes to implement. First, the WP.BAT file located in the root directory needs to be modified to reflect the new location of the WPMENU.TXT file:

WP.BAT

```
ECHO OFF
CLS
CD \ADMIN\WP
TYPE WPMENU.TXT
PROMPT Enter your choice (LIN, JACK, etc.):
```

Also, the E.BAT file, which is now located in the \ADMIN\WP subdirectory, must be altered to move back to the root directory before executing the MAINMENU batch file call:

E.BAT

```
ECHO OFF
CLS
CD \
MAINMENU
```

Adding Help Screens to Your Menu System

Submenus add to the overall user-friendly feel of a menu system. However, the use of a main menu and submenus requires the user to make certain generalizations. While the choices in the main menu may be obvious to the person creating the menu system, a new user may have some trouble figuring out how the menu system works.

One way to overcome this problem is to provide individualized training for each user sharing the system. Sometimes, however, this is not practical. In such cases, special help screens may have to be added to the system. Help screens provide extra information to explain how the menu system works and where specific applications or work areas are located within the menu system.

Often a single help screen, accessed from the main menu, is all that is required. The help feature may be included as an option within the main menu itself. See Fig. 7-8 for a modified version of CompuCard's Main Menu which includes a Help option. Another technique is to include instructions for obtaining help within the prompt itself, such as:

Enter your choice (WP, DB, etc.) or ? for Help:

Help screens are nothing more than text files describing the functions of the menu from which they are accessed. Figure 7-9 gives an example of a help screen to accompany CompuCard's Main Menu. This screen was created using WordStar's non-document mode and saved under the filename MAINHELP.TXT. Assume that this help screen is accessed through the batch file, H.BAT. This batch file contains the following statements:

```
H.BAT

ECHO OFF
CLS
TYPE MAINHELP.TXT
PAUSE
MAINMENU
```

As you can see, the H.BAT file displays the text of the file MAINHELP.TXT on the screen and then pauses until the user strikes any key. Note that the prompt, "Strike any key to continue . . ." will be displayed at the bottom of the help screen as a result of the PAUSE subcommand. After the user has had the opportunity to read the screen, pressing any key causes the MAINMENU batch file to be executed, returning the user to the Main Menu.

Help screens can be provided for each of the submenus as well. One point to keep

```
┌─────────────────────────────────────────────────────────────┐
│                    CompuCard Main Menu                       │
│                                                              │
│     WP      WordStar           ACCT    Accounting            │
│     DB      dBASE III          ART     Graphics              │
│     LOTUS   Lotus 1-2-3        DOS     DOS Commands          │
│                                                              │
│          H   Help                   Q   Quit                 │
└─────────────────────────────────────────────────────────────┘
```

Fig. 7-8. Modified Main Menu including Help option.

135

```
          Help for Main Menu

    The following options are available from
    the Main Menu:

    Word Processing - allows you to access
                      WordStar, Multimate
                      and ThinkTank

    dBASE III - allows you to access the
                customer database

    Lotus 1-2-3 - allows you to access worksheets

    Accounting - Accounts Receivable, Accounts
                 Payable, General Ledger, Payroll

    Art - allows you to access graphics designs

    DOS - allows you to perform DOS operations
          such as formatting diskettes, copying
          files, etc.
```

Fig. 7-9. A sample help screen.

in mind when creating help screens is to avoid overwhelming the user with too much help. Users feel intimidated by too much information on the screen. Keep your screens simple. If necessary, divide the information into several screens. A good rule of thumb is to limit your help screens to fifteen or so lines. Also, vertical and horizontal centering, indentation, and blank lines help draw the user's attention to the critical information you are trying to convey.

You have progressed from simple batch file programs to complete menu-driven systems. Congratulations! Did you ever think you would be a systems programmer? Actually, you've only just begun. Throughout the remainder of this book, you will continue to learn more DOS programming tricks and techniques for improving your menu-driven system.

While you may feel justifiably proud of the menus you have created in this chapter, the appearance of these menus is limited by the power of your word processor. Unless you have a word processing program capable of displaying the IBM graphics character set, such as WordPerfect or MicroSoft Word, you are probably limited to the simple character set displayed on your computer keyboard. As a result, your menus are pretty drab.

Have you ever worked with programs that have snazzy menu screens, complete with special borders and multiple colors? Wouldn't you like your menus to look like the ones you find in professional programs? In the next chapter, you will learn how to use DOS's EDLIN or a word processing program like WordPerfect to help you create slick, professional looking screen menus for your menu-driven hard disk management system.

136

Chapter 8

Fancy Menu

Now that you have a functioning, menu-driven system for accessing programs and data on your hard disk, you may feel your system is complete. In fact, there are a number of enhancements which you can add to your system. While the systems described in the previous chapter are functional, they are not very exciting. The screen displays consist of a simple list of options and a prompt telling the user to select from one of the choices.

You can use the full range of color, special graphics characters, and screen features like inverse video to really jazz up your screen displays. You can also perform some magic that will allow you to use the ten function keys to call up applications programs instead of entering in a batch filename. This will simplify your menu system significantly because you will be able to select options by pressing a single key. This chapter presents a variety of techniques for enhancing your screen displays and simplifying the use of your menu system.

IMPROVING YOUR MENU SCREENS

To take full advantage of the graphics capabilities of your computer, you will need to have access to the extended ASCII character set. In the last chapter you learned that ASCII files contain only printable characters. Most word processors add additional control characters which denote end of lines, end of paragraphs, special indentations, bold face, underscore, italics, etc. These control characters can produce unexpected results in a batch file, or when TYPEd to the screen.

Normally, we think of printable characters as those available on the standard keyboard; that is, the letters, digits, and characters like "*" and "#", etc. Actually, the ASCII character set includes a number of special characters such as greek letters, tiny hearts, smiling faces, arrowheads, and characters for producing single- and double-line borders.

Most word processors use these special characters to control the format, or appearance, of the documents they produce. This means that you can't have access to them to create special graphics effects. This is true of WordStar, for example. Some word processors, including WordPerfect and MicroSoft Word, do allow you to work with these extended ASCII characters. This means you can use these programs to create fancy screen displays. However, these screen displays can only be TYPED by DOS as long as you save them as ASCII files.

Just to give you a taste of things to come, consider the menu screen illustrated in Fig. 8-1. This screen was created with WordPerfect using the extended character set to draw the solid menu border and the double line border around the menu heading. The highlighting around the prompt message, "Enter your selection", was accomplished through the use of special screen controls. On a color system, screen controls for controlling foreground and background colors could be added as well. These screen controls are available in the PROMPT command. The techniques for drawing borders and controlling the screen will be described later in the chapter.

The Edlin Utility

In the preceding chapter you learned how to create simple menu screens using your

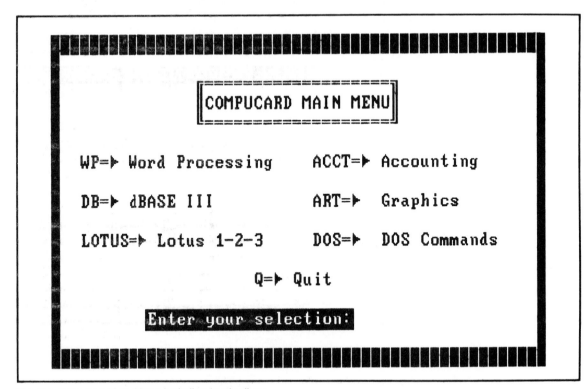

Fig. 8-1. Improved Main Menu including border lines.

word processor. It was assumed that your word processor could save text files in ASCII format. Even though your word processor may be able to save documents as ASCII files, it may not provide access to the extended ASCII character set. For either reason, you may find you need to use the DOS EDLIN utility to create your menu screens. While EDLIN offers only limited editing functions, it does provide access to the special graphics characters which you can use to enhance your menus.

The DOS EDLIN utility is a *text editor* which you can use to create text files. The main use for EDLIN is in the creation of batch files and menu screens. Normally, you would use either the COPY CON: technique or your word processor for creating batch files. Your word processor may also be used for creating menu screens according to the limitations mentioned above.

EDLIN is a utility program located on your DOS disk under the filename EDLIN.COM. In order to use EDLIN, this file must be available to you. If you have placed the DOS files into a special subdirectory on your hard disk, such as \DOS, you must either be in this subdirectory or initiate a path to it with the command:

<pre>
C>PATH \DOS
</pre>

Before electing to use EDLIN, you should weigh its advantages and disadvantages. EDLIN has three advantages: it produces ASCII text files, it can give you access to the IBM extended character set, and it is free. The disadvantages are: it is difficult to use and has only limited editing capabilities.

Advantages of EDLIN

First the advantages. As mentioned, you may be forced to use EDLIN if your word processor can't create ASCII text files. Even though your word processor is capable of producing ASCII files, it may require a conversion procedure that's more trouble than it's worth for short batch files. Also, to create a batch file with your word processor, you have to move into your word processing subdirectory, create the batch file, copy it to the root directory, and then move back to the root to execute it. On the other hand, if you have previously established a path to DOS as above, you can remain in the root directory and create the batch file from there.

For these reasons, you may find EDLIN to be a convenient way to create batch files. Of course, there's also the COPY CON: method. However, this method provides no editing capabilities. If you make a single mistake, you must delete the entire file and begin from scratch. The editing commands of EDLIN can be used both to edit text as you are entering it and to edit existing text files at some later time.

A second advantage is that EDLIN gives you access to the IBM extended character set. As mentioned earlier, this is a collection of special characters which can be displayed by the IBM family of personal computers and can be printed on IBM compatible graphics printers. You can use these special characters in your menu screens to enhance their appearance. At the end of this section, you will be shown how to create simple borders using EDLIN. You can experiment with other characters on your own.

The final advantage needs no elaboration. One thing you've got to agree with: you can't beat the price!

Disadvantages of EDLIN

The main disadvantage of EDLIN is that it is a text editor, not a word processor. EDLIN does not have many of the features found in word processors. In fact, you wouldn't want to write business correspondence, much less long manuscripts, with EDLIN. It does have simple text editing capabilities, including move and search-and-replace commands. These editing capabilities are sufficient for creating batch files and single-screen menus.

A second disadvantage of EDLIN is that it is only a line editor. With EDLIN, you can only work on one line at a time. You can't use the cursor control keys to move around the screen, editing at will. Instead, you must specify the line to be entered or edited in advance. This is done through the use of line numbers. Each line in a file is assigned a line number by EDLIN. These line numbers are used to reference the lines to be edited, moved, displayed, etc.

WORKING WITH EDLIN

Despite these disadvantages, you may find that the availability from the root directory or the access to the extended character set make EDLIN worth using for simple tasks such as batch file editing or screen generation. Again, before attempting to work with EDLIN, make sure you have established a path to it.

To access the EDLIN program, you enter the following:

C > EDLIN filespec [/B]

Note that the filespec is not optional. You must include a filespec with the EDLIN program call. The filespec may include a drive designator and path as well as the filename itself. The optional /B parameter will be explained later.

When you issue the command to load EDLIN, it looks on the specified drive and path to see if the specified file exists. If so, the file will be loaded into memory. (Actually, as much of the file as will fit into 75 percent of memory will be loaded, but for the purposes of batch file and menu editing, this is not a consideration.) If the specified file is not found, EDLIN assumes you intend to create the file, and the filename will be used when you save any entered text.

As a result of the above search and load procedure, one of two messages will be displayed on the screen. If the file exists and has been loaded into memory, the message will be:

End of input file
*

If, on the other hand, no file is found and a new file is assumed, the message will be:

New file
*

The asterisk following the displayed message is EDLIN's prompt. Note that, in the first instance, EDLIN does not display the contents of the input file. To view the file, you must issue the proper EDLIN command.

140

In order to do anything in EDLIN, you must first enter a command. You can't even begin entering text without first entering the Insert Lines command. In the following sections, the various EDLIN commands that you will need will be summarized.

Creating a New File

To create a new file, you simply call up EDLIN and include the proposed name of the file you wish to create. For instance, suppose you wanted to create a batch file named TEST.BAT. You would enter the following:

C>EDLIN TEST.BAT

EDLIN would respond with the message:

New file
*

With most word processors, all you have to do to enter text is begin typing. Not so with EDLIN. Remember, you must begin by entering a command. If you do start off typing, EDLIN will interpret your first keystroke as a command. This could be devastating, as many beginning EDLIN users have discovered. To begin entering text, you issue the EDLIN Insert Lines command (note: commands in EDLIN may be entered in either upper or lowercase):

*I

Since this is a new file, EDLIN will start inserting lines at line number 1. You will see line number 1 displayed on the screen waiting for you to enter text:

1:*

Note the asterisks to the right of the number 1. When the asterisk appears to the right of a line number, it indicates that the line is the *current* line. The meaning and use of the current line indicator will be explained later.

Once you are in the Insert Lines mode, you enter text by typing it in and pressing the Enter key at the conclusion of each line. Suppose you wanted the first line of TEST.BAT to include the command ECHO OFF. You would enter this after the 1* as follows:

1:*ECHO OFF

After pressing the Enter key, the next line would appear:

1:*ECHO OFF
2:*

The fact that the asterisk now appears in line 2 indicates that this is the new current line. (Line 1 is ancient history, which is why its asterisk still remains on the screen even though line 2 is now the current line.) To complete the text entry, you continue entering text until there are no more lines to enter. This is how the screen would look after entering the five lines of TEST.BAT:

```
1:*ECHO OFF
2:*CLS
3:*ECHO This is a test batch file
4:*PAUSE
5:*ECHO ON
6:*
```

Line 6 is awaiting additional input. However, in this instance, the file is complete. To conclude input, enter Ctrl Break (or Ctrl C) at the beginning of the next line. This will terminate the Insert Lines mode and take you back to the * prompt:

```
6:*^C
*
```

To save a file created with EDLIN, you enter the End Edit command. There is no need to specify a filename as this was entered when EDLIN was loaded. For example, to save the five lines you entered under the name TEST.BAT, you would merely enter:

```
*E
```

EDLIN would write the lines you entered to the TEST.BAT file and return you to the DOS prompt.

If you did not want to save the lines you entered, you could abort the EDLIN session without saving using the Quit Edit command:

```
*Q
```

This would cause EDLIN to ask you for confirmation:

```
Abort edit (Y/N)?
```

To abort the session, you must answer "Y."

Editing an Existing File

To edit a batch file located in the root directory of your hard drive and named TEST.BAT, you would enter the command:

```
C>EDLIN TEST.BAT
```

EDLIN would locate this file and load it into memory, responding with the message:

```
End of input file
*
```

As noted, the contents of the file would be stored in memory but not displayed on the screen. To view the file, you would have to enter the List Lines command:

*L

The contents of the file would then be displayed as follows:

```
1:*ECHO OFF
2: CLS
3: ECHO This is a test batch file
4: PAUSE
5: ECHO ON
```

The asterisk in front of line 1 indicates that this is the current line. The current line is the line EDLIN is looking at. As you will see, most EDLIN commands require you to provide a line number. You can refer to a line by its unique number, or, if you want to work with the current line, you can use a period, ".", to refer to the current line. The use of the period is a helpful shortcut when referring to the current line.

Up to 23 lines of a file can be displayed at one time. In this example, the entire batch file can be displayed in fewer than 23 lines. Later, you will learn how to work with text files that are longer than 23 lines.

Suppose you wanted to insert a line between lines 3 and 4. To do so, you would use the Insert Lines command. When used to insert an empty line between existing lines, this command requires a line number preceding it to indicate where the insertion is to take place. Lines are inserted immediately before the specified line. This means that, to insert a new line between lines 3 and 4, the command would be:

*4I

This would cause the following display to appear on the screen:

4:*

You would then type in the text of the new line and press the Enter key, causing the screen to look like this:

```
4:*ECHO That doesn't do anything useful
5:*
```

The number 5 on the next line indicates that you have another new line to work with if you want. Assuming that you didn't want to add any more lines at this time, you would terminate the Insert Lines command with a Ctrl Break (or Ctrl C). The Screen would then appear as follows:

```
4:*ECHO That doesn't do anything useful
5:*^C
```

*

Now suppose that you want to edit line 3. To edit a line, you simply enter that line number at the * prompt. This will cause the line to be displayed on the screen along with a second line displaying the same line number and the blinking cursor:

```
*3
        3: ECHO This is a test batch file
        3:
```

Editing is performed through the use of the function keys and the Ins and Del keys. For example, suppose you wanted to change the word test to read sample. You would need to delete the characters "t," "e," "s," and "t" and insert the characters "s," "a," "m," "p," "l," and "e". (What, no delete word key? How archaic!)

This change would be accomplished through the following sequence of steps. First, you would bring up the line as far as the "t" in "test." This much of the line you can reuse. To display a portion of the line up to a given character, you press the F2 key and then enter that character. In this case, you would see:

```
        3: ECHO This is a test batch file
        3: ECHO This is a
```

The cursor will be blinking under the "t" of the first line in the two-line display. You would then delete the four characters, "t," "e," "s," and "t" by pressing the Del key four times. Don't be concerned if you try this: nothing happens on the screen at this time. However, these four characters have been deleted from the computer's memory.

At this point, you want to insert the characters "s," "a," "m," "p," "l," and "e". Although you would like to simply type them in, this won't work. You must first press the Ins key to let EDLIN know you want to insert some characters. After pressing Ins and typing sample (don't press Enter yet), the screen would look like this:

```
        3: ECHO This is a test batch file
        3: ECHO This is a sample
```

Finally, you would ask EDLIN to complete the line by pressing the F3 function key. The remainder of the line would be added and your screen would look like the following:

```
        3: ECHO This is a test batch file
        3: ECHO This is a sample batch file
```

To save the changes to line 3, you would simply press the Enter key at this time. Note that, from the time you placed the cursor under the "t" of test using the F2 key until you completed the line with the F3 key, you did not press the Enter key. Pressing the Enter key accepts any changes made to that point and returns you to the * prompt.

If you had made a mistake and wanted to cancel the changes made, you could press Ctrl Break to return to the * prompt. You could then edit the line again by reentering the number 3 at the prompt.

To conclude your editing session and save all changes, including the added line and the alterations to line 3, you would enter the End Edit command:

*E

This would cause the changes stored in your computer's memory to be written to the disk, and you would be returned to the system prompt.

A SUMMARY OF EDLIN COMMANDS

There are a number of EDLIN commands. These are described in detail in your DOS manual. This is an instance of too much information being worse than too little. If you're like many computer users, you've probably avoided EDLIN because of the description in the DOS manual. It does seem intimidating.

Actually, you only need to know a limited number of commands in order to use EDLIN effectively. These commands are summarized in Appendix B. This appendix lists each command, any parameters, and its function.

Of these commands, the ones you will use most are: Insert Lines, Edit Line, List Lines, Replace Text, and End Edit. You've already seen how the Insert Lines, Edit Line, List Lines, End Edit and Quit Edit commands are used. However, for ease of reference, each of the commands in Appendix B will be described briefly in this section.

The Insert Lines Command

The Insert Lines command is used to add extra lines to a file. Lines may be added at the beginning, in the middle, or at the end of the file. The Insert Lines command may include an optional parameter. This may either be a line number, the period (.), or the number symbol (#). Once you enter the Insert Lines mode, you will continue to be provided with new lines until you terminate the command. The Insert Lines command is terminated by entering Ctrl Break at the beginning of a new line. All lines moved down by the Insert Lines command are automatically renumbered.

To add lines at the beginning of the file, you simply enter the command:

*I

To insert lines into the middle of a file, you enter the Insert Lines command preceded by the line number where you want the insertion to take place. Lines are inserted above the specified line number. For example, if you wanted to insert one or more lines before line 5, you would enter:

*5I

To insert lines above the current line, you would enter:

*.I

To insert lines at the end of the file, you use the number symbol (#):

*#I

The Edit Line Command

The Edit Line command is used to edit a single line in a file. This is by far the most difficult EDLIN command to master. It is clumsy and difficult to use. In fact, it is often easier to retype a short line than to edit it. Line editing is performed in memory rather than on the screen, so you can't always see what you are doing until after it's been done.

The general technique for editing a line is as follows: first, use the F2 key to bring up onto the screen all the text up to the point you want to edit; second, make the desired changes with the Del and Ins keys or by typing over existing text; finally, bring up the remainder of the text with the F3 key. This technique was illustrated in the example used to describe editing an existing file.

To edit a line, you merely enter the line number of the line to be edited. For example, to edit line 4, you would enter:

*4

The Edit Line command uses a two-line display. The first line shows the complete text of the line being edited. The second line is used as a work area. For example, suppose you entered the above command to edit line 4 of the revised file, TEST.BAT. You would see the following display:

```
4: ECHO That doesn't do anything useful
4:
```

You use the second line to make your changes. The F2 key is used to place text on this line up to the point where you want your changes to occur. This is done by pressing the F2 key (nothing will happen at this point) followed by the letter that indicates where the change is to occur. The text will be displayed up to the character you entered.

This process can be repeated as needed until the desired point is reached. For example, suppose you wanted to change the word anything. To move up to this word, you would enter:

```
4: ECHO That doesn't do anything useful
4: <F2>a
```

This would cause EDLIN to display the text of line 4 up to the "a" of "That":

```
4: ECHO That doesn't do anything useful
4: ECHO Th
```

Since this isn't where you want to be, you would repeat the F2 command followed by another "a". This time, the text up to anything would appear on the work line:

```
4: ECHO That doesn't do anything useful
4: ECHO That doesn't do
```

Once the cursor is positioned under the text to be edited, you can use the Del key to remove as many characters as you wish. Each time you press the Del key, another character will be removed. Unfortunately, EDLIN doesn't show the characters that have been removed at this point. To insert new characters, you press the Ins key once and then enter the required characters. You can also enter characters in the typeover mode by simply typing them without first pressing the Ins key.

One trap to avoid is pressing the Enter key after making the changes. This would cause the line to be concluded at that point. However, the line is not yet complete. Normally, the Enter key is only pressed after the editing process is completed.

To see how changes are made, suppose you wanted to change the word "anything" to "something." You might think that you could just type "something" in place of "anything." Actually, all you need to do is substitute some for any. This can be accomplished by pressing the Del key three times to remove any. The some could then be inserted by pressing the Ins key and entering some. You could also have just typed som in the typeover mode and then pressed the Ins key before entering the final e. Again, you would not press the Enter key at this time.

After making the desired changes, you complete the line by pressing the F3 key. This causes the remaining text to be brought up onto the screen. Once the complete, edited text is on the work line, you can accept it by pressing the Enter key. If further editorial changes are required, you can continue editing the line by pressing the F5 key.

You can also use the Edit Line command to retype a line from scratch. To do so, you enter the line number at the * prompt. However, instead of using the F2 and F3 function keys, you simply type the new line in place of the old one and press Enter when you're done.

The List Lines Command

The List Lines command is used to view one or more lines of a file. It may be used in conjunction with two optional parameters to view a single line, a group of lines, or the entire file (up to 23 lines).

To view a block of lines, you would use both parameters. For example, to view lines 4 through 10, the command would be:

*4,10L

To view the entire file (up to 23 lines worth), you simply enter the List Lines command with no parameters:

*L

The List Lines command is plural. That is, it is used to list *lines*. You might think that you could view a single line by merely including that line number before the List Lines command. However, this is not the case. If you enter the command:

*8L

for example, you will see the remainder of the file, beginning with line 8. To view a single line, you must enter the line number twice, separated by a comma. For example, to view line number 8, you would enter.

```
*8,8L
```

To view the current line, you would use the period (.):

```
*.,.L
```

The Delete Lines Command

The Delete Lines command is used to remove one or more unwanted lines from a file. It may include one or two optional parameters. To remove several lines at once, you enter the beginning line number, a comma, and the ending line number. For example, to delete lines 6 through 10, you would enter:

```
*6,10D
```

To delete a single line, you provide the line number of the line to be deleted. To delete only line 8, the command would be:

```
*6D
```

If no line number is specified for either the first or the second line number parameter, the current line is used by default. For example, to delete from the current line through line 10, the command would be:

```
*,10D
```

If no line numbers are specified, the current line will be deleted:

```
*D
```

After the lines are deleted, EDLIN renumbers the remaining lines to keep them in sequence.

The Replace Text Command

The Replace Text Command is used to replace one string of characters with another. The replacement can take place in a single line, a range of lines, or throughout the entire file. Optionally, the Replace Text command can be used to delete a specified character string by omitting the replacement string from the command.

The Replace Text command can be used for normal editing to correct errors or make changes to the text of a file. However, the real power of this command is that it provides a shortcut for text entry. For example, suppose you were creating a batch file which employed a number of ECHO statements. Instead of typing ECHO at the beginning of each statement, you could type some single character, such as DOS. When the text entry was complete, you could use the Replace Text command to replace all occurrences of DOS with ECHO. As you will see later in this chapter, this technique can also be used to facilitate the use of the extended character set.

The Replace Text command is usually used with both line parameters. These are used to specify the lines to be included in the text replacement process. Following the

148

two line parameters is the R of the Replace Text command. Next comes the two strings. These are separated by a Ctrl Z (you can use the F6 key to enter a Ctrl Z). The command is concluded by pressing the Enter key.

Suppose you had entered the TEST.BAT file as follows:

```
1:*# OFF
2:*CLS
3:*# This is a test batch file
4:*# That doesn't do anything useful
5:*PAUSE
6:*# ON
```

To replace every occurrence of "#" with ECHO, you would enter the following command:

```
*1,6R#<F6>ECHO
```

As EDLIN performs the replacements, it echos each line to the screen. Those lines which require no alteration are not echoed. In the above example, the following lines would be displayed:

```
1: ECHO OFF
3: ECHO This is a test batch file
4: ECHO That doesn't do anything useful
7: ECHO ON
```

Note that each occurrence of the string to be replaced constitutes a separate replacement action. This means that, if EDLIN performs several replacements in a single line, that line will be echoed each time the replacement takes place. As you will see, this can be rather time consuming when replacing keyboard characters with line drawing characters to produce borders for your menus.

As mentioned, the Replace Text command can also be used to delete character strings by omitting the second string from the command. To delete the string ECHO from the TEST.BAT file, the command would be:

```
*1,6RECHO<F6>
```

The End Edit and Quit Edit Commands

The End Edit command is used to save any changes to the file being edited. Once the changes are written to the disk, EDLIN is terminated and you are returned to the calling program (which is usually DOS). The End Edit command requires no parameters.

You may find times when you would rather not save your editing changes. This is especially true when you are first learning how to use EDLIN. To leave EDLIN without saving, you use the Quit Edit command. This will prevent the changes in memory from being written to the disk. EDLIN will display a confirming message:

Abort edit (Y/N)?

To confirm, enter "Y". The Quit Edit command can be a lifesaver. You can make mistakes in using the Edit Line or Delete Lines commands which would be time consuming to correct. The best strategy in these cases is to abort the editing session with the Quit Edit command. Although you will be returned to DOS and will have to reload EDLIN, this may be faster than trying to correct the mistake.

ADDING BORDERS TO YOUR MENUS WITH EDLIN

As mentioned earlier in this chapter, EDLIN gives you access to the extended character set available on the IBM family of computers. (Most clones provide this same set of characters as well.) The extended character set provides special drawing characters for producing single and double line borders. You may have seen such borders used in commercially available programs. Figure 8-2 shows a simple border added to the CompuCard Main Menu. This menu screen was created using EDLIN.

Working with the Extended ASCII Character Set

The border in Fig. 8-2 was created using six special characters from the extended character set. These are the four double line corner characters, the horizontal double line character, and the vertical double line character. These and other drawing characters are shown in Fig. 8-3. In Appendix C you will find a table displaying the complete extended ASCII character set. Note that, although these characters can be displayed on the screen, they can only be printed out on special, IBM compatible dot-matrix printers. Check your printer manual to determine if it is capable of printing the extended character set.

Notice that each drawing character is referenced by a number. These numbers are the ASCII decimal code values used to represent the characters. Every character in the ASCII character set has a corresponding decimal code value. For example, the character "A" has the decimal value 65. Fortunately, we don't have to enter code values for the normal characters. Instead, we simply type them from the keyboard.

The problem with the characters in the extended ASCII character set is that there

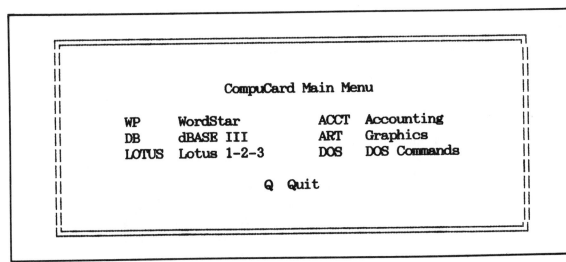

Fig. 8-2. Menu screen created using EDLIN.

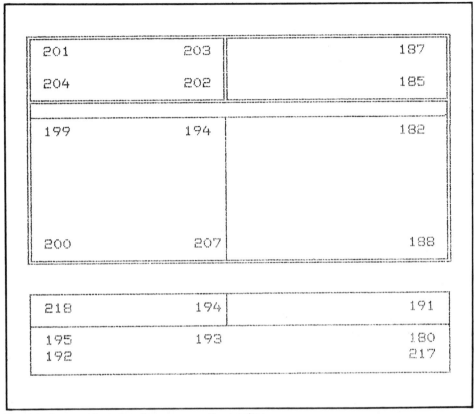

Fig. 8-3. A screen layout as it appears on the monitor.

are no symbols for them on the keyboard. Perhaps someday this will change, but for now the only way to get these special characters is to enter them as decimal codes. To enter the decimal code value for any ASCII character, you hold down the Alt key and simultaneously enter the decimal code. Note: you must use the numbers on the num keypad. The numbers across the top of the keyboard won't work.

Not all word processors are able to access the extended character set. If you try to enter any of these codes in WordStar, you won't get anything. MicroSoft Word and WordPerfect are two word processing programs which allow you to work with the drawing symbols and other special characters directly on the screen. Later in this chapter, you will see how WordPerfect can be used to draw some rather fancy borders and add other enhancements to your menu screens.

If your word processor does not allow you to work with the extended character set, you will need to use EDLIN to draw borders around your menu screens. EDLIN allows you to enter special characters by using the Alt key as described above. For example, to enter the upper left double line corner symbol, you would hold down the Alt key and enter the number 201 from the num keypad. This would produce the corner symbol on the screen. While entering numeric sequences from the num keypad is time consuming, you can at least get the characters on the screen. In the following section, you will see how to use the Replace Text command to shorten this process.

A Sample Menu Screen

Before actually entering the text and border characters for a given menu screen, it is a good idea to plan out the screen's appearance in advance. For example, notice that the border is centered in the middle of the screen. Also, notice the placement of the text within the borders. Finally, notice the margin between the top of the screen and the top border line. Keep these spacing factors in mind when creating your menu screens.

To create the menu screen in Fig. 8-2, you will create a file using EDLIN. Start off by calling this file MENU1. Later you can rename it to MAINMENU. You may not get this screen right the first time, and it would be a shame to overwrite the existing MAINMENU screen until you're satisfied with the new one. You create this file with the command:

C>EDLIN MENU1

At EDLIN's asterisk prompt, enter the Insert Lines command:

*I

Skip three lines by pressing Enter at line numbers 1, 2, and 3.

On line 4 you will enter the characters to produce the top border line. You will type this line as follows:

- First, enter 15 spaces.
- Next, hold down the Alt key and enter 201 from the num keypad—the upper left double line corner symbol will appear on the screen.
- Next enter 48 asterisks—these will be replaced by the horizontal double line symbol later.
- Finally, enter the upper right double line corner by holding down the Alt key and entering 187.

Your screen should look like Fig. 8-4 at this point.

For line 5, enter 15 spaces, Alt 186, 48 spaces, and Alt 186 again. On line 6, enter the 15 spaces, Alt 186, 14 spaces, the text CompuCard Main Menu, 15 more spaces, and another Alt 186. Continue on with this process until you come to line 14. This line is similar to line 4 except that you will use the lower left corner, Alt 200, and the lower right corner, Alt 188. At this point, your screen should resemble Fig. 8-5.

You are now ready to use the Replace Text command to substitute the horizontal double line symbol for the asterisks you entered in lines 4 and 14. The command to do this is:

4,14R<F6>Alt 205

Fig. 8-4. Graphics characters and their ASCII values.

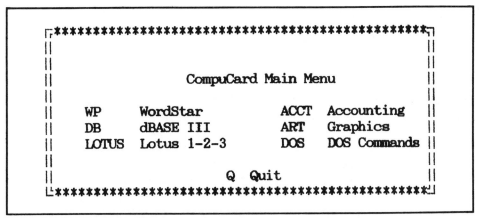

Fig. 8-5. CompuCard Main Menu.

EDLIN will proceed to make the necessary replacements. Each time EDLIN replaces an asterisk with a horizontal double line symbol, the line in which the replacement has taken place will be echoed to the screen. There are a total of 96 replacements in this operation, so you should be prepared to wait awhile for the process to be completed.

Once the file has been altered to include the horizontal double line symbols, you can view it with the List Lines command:

*L

If the screen is to your liking, you can save it with the End Edit command:

*E

To be sure you really like this screen, try it out using the TYPE command:

C>TYPE MENU1

This screen is now available for use in your MAINMENU batch file. Just make sure you rename it to MAINMENU first.

FANCY MENU SCREENS WITH WORDPERFECT

The CompuCard Main Menu screen created in the last section is a big improvement over the version developed in the preceding chapter. The addition of a border really enhances the menu, giving it an identity of its own. Unfortunately, using EDLIN to create such screens is tedious and time-consuming. If you have access to a contemporary word processing program, such as WordPerfect or MicroSoft Word, you can use these programs to create menu screens in a fraction of the time it takes with EDLIN

WordPerfect, for example, not only allows access to the extended character set, it also provides you with special commands for drawing on the screen. To draw a border in WordPerfect, all you need to do is select the drawing character you wish to use, say a solid block, and then use the cursor keys to draw with. Using WordPerfect to draw borders is somewhat like working with the old Etch-a-Sketch boards. (You were a kid once, weren't you?)

Using the Extended Character Set in WordPerfect

In addition to special commands for drawing borders, WordPerfect allows you to insert any of the extended characters directly into your text. For example, if you want to create a pointer, you could use a horizontal double line character followed by an arrowhead. Refer to Fig. 8-1 to see how these symbols have been combined.

To work with any of the special characters, all you do is hold down the Alt key and type in the decimal code for the character on the num key pad. The character will then appear wherever the cursor is located. For example, to create the pointer following the WP choice in the CompuCard Main Menu screen, the cursor was located after the "P". The horizontal double line character was produced by depressing the Alt key while the number 205 was entered. Then the arrowhead was added with the Alt-16 key sequence.

Rather than trying to remember the decimal codes for all the special characters, you can refer to WordPerfect's built in reference chart. To view this chart, you use the WordPerfect Screen Key (Ctrl-F3). This will produce a list of options at the bottom of the screen. From this list of options, select option 2, Ctrl/Alt keys. To read the chart, locate the character you are interested in. Find the row value of this character on the left. This will be a three digit number ranging from 0 to 250. To this number, add the column value of the character found at the top of the chart. These numbers range from 0 to 49.

To see how this works, try finding the code value for the solid block character. This character may be difficult to locate, because it is connected to two other solid characters to form a solid (though off-center) U shape in the next-to-the-last row. Got it? To determine this character's code value, take the row number, 200, and add to it the column number, 19. The resulting value is 219. To use this character, you would enter the Alt-219 key sequence.

Line Drawing in WordPerfect

WordPerfect provides a useful tool for creating borders. This is the Line Draw option, option number 2, which is accessed by pressing the Screen Key, (Ctrl-F3). When you select this option, you are presented with several choices for drawing, erasing, or moving lines. (See Fig. 8-6.) The first three choices let you draw lines using either the single or the double line character. The third choice displays an asterisk as the drawing character. However, you can change this to any other character you wish—including the entire range of extended characters.

To draw a border, you first place the cursor at one of the corners of the border rectangle. To use either the single or double line character, select the appropriate option (1 or 2). Then use the cursor keys to move left, right, up, or down as desired. As you press the cursor keys, a line is drawn in the direction you specify. If you change directions by 90 degrees, WordPerfect automatically inserts the correct corner character for you.

For example, to draw a double line border extending 40 characters across, 10 characters down, and centered on the screen, you would:

- Place your cursor on line 4, position 25.

```
    1 |;  2 ||;  3 *;  4 Change;  5 Erase;  6 Move: 1
```

Fig. 8-6. WordPerfect's graphics character reference chart.

- Next, you would press the Screen Key and select option 2, Line Draw.
- Then you would enter option 2 for the Line Draw command, which would activate the double line character.
- You would then use the right arrow key to extend the double line 40 characters to the right.
- At this point, you would use the down arrow key to draw a vertical line from line 4 to line 14. WordPerfect would automatically turn the corner for you.
- You would next use the left arrow key to move back to position 25, completing the third side of the border.
- Finally, you would use the up arrow key to draw the remaining side of the border.
- To get out of the Line Draw mode, you would enter the Exit Key (F1).

As you are drawing, you may find that your border lines do not meet up as you planned. It's sometimes difficult to determine exactly where to turn the corner (just like the Etch-a-Sketch). If you make a mistake when drawing lines in WordPerfect, just use option 5 to Erase. When this option is selected, any movement using the cursor keys will cause the line to be erased in the direction of the arrow key you are using.

To draw lines using any of the other extended characters, you will have to substitute this character for the asterisk in option 3. This is easily accomplished. You simply choose option 4, the Change option. This will display a list of eight drawing options consisting of various sizes and shades of drawing characters (Fig. 8-7).

You can either select from one of these, or choose option 9, Other. If you select this option, you will see a message:

Solid character:

displayed at the bottom of your screen. At this point, you can enter the Alt-number sequence for the character you want. (Remember, you can look up the code value using the Ctrl/Alt keys option of the Screen Key.) The character you select through this process becomes the new drawing character.

Once you've drawn your border, you can insert the text of your menu. Be careful to use the Typeover mode, though, or you will break up the vertical lines. Once they are drawn, borders are affected by any editorial changes you make. If you insert additional characters or lines, the borders will be broken up by the insertion, just as any other

```
    1 ░;  2 ▒;  3 ▓;  4 █;  5 ▄;  6 ▌;  7 ▐;  8 ▀;  9 Other: 0
```

Fig. 8-7. WordPerfect's line drawing menu.

characters would be. If you do inadvertently break up your borders, you can bring the border lines back into alignment by deleting empty spaces to the left of them or removing extra blank lines.

One way to avoid possible damage to your borders during screen editing is to enter the text of your menu before drawing your borders. Once the text is in place, you can use the Screen Key to draw borders around the menu text. Be careful here as well. Make sure you are in the Typeover mode, or your text will get moved around in strange and mysterious ways.

Screens that you generate with WordPerfect appear farther to the right than they will appear when TYPEd as ASCII files. This means that menu screen which appears centered in WordPerfect will in fact appear ten columns to the left when you TYPE it from DOS. To correct for this, use the Insert mode to move the entire menu, borders and all, to the right ten columns. While this will result in an off-center screen in WordPerfect, the resulting screen will be centered when displayed from DOS.

Saving WordPerfect Menu Screens as ASCII Files

After the menu screen is complete, you will want to save it in two forms. First, you will want to save the screen as a regular WordPerfect document. Just use the Save Key (F10) as usual. You will also want to save the menu screen as an ASCII file. Like many word processing programs, WordPerfect places hidden control characters into its files. While you don't normally see these characters when working in WordPerfect, they show up when TYPEd from DOS. Fortunately, WordPerfect provides a conversion command which can remove these control characters from the file and create a displayable ASCII file.

To save a document as an ASCII file, use the Text In/Out Key (Ctrl-F5). This key provides you with four choices. Option 1, Save current document as a DOS text file, will save the document in ASCII format as it appears on the screen. Be careful here, as WordPerfect will suggest the same name that you used to save the file as a WordPerfect document. If you accept this name, WordPerfect will replace the WordPerfect version with the ASCII version. You should use separate names for your WordPerfect and ASCII versions of your menu screens.

The reason for maintaining two versions of your menu screens is so you can make editorial changes to the menu easily. This is accomplished by bringing up the WordPerfect of the menu. This version can be edited using any of the WordPerfect commands. This includes moving or erasing border lines. The border lines in the ASCII version cannot be easily edited. After making any changes, be sure to resave the file as both a WordPerfect document and as an ASCII file.

CONTROLLING THE SCREEN CHARACTERISTICS

Using borders and other graphics characters is only one way to increase the impact of your menu screens. You can also employ a number of video tricks to draw attention to your menus and any special messages or prompts to the user. DOS provides access to a wide variety of video display features, including bold and inverse video, blinking, underscore, and color (providing you have a color display card and monitor—you can't get blood from a turnip).

The Power of ANSI.SYS

To take advantage of these special display modes, you must be able to manipulate the special DOS display driver, ANSI.SYS. ANSI.SYS is a file contained on your DOS diskette. It allows you to control the screen display in ways that you could not otherwise do from the DOS prompt or batch files. Through ANSI.SYS, you can control the location of the cursor, change video modes on monochrome systems and alter the foreground and background colors on color systems. ANSI.SYS also enables you to redefine the keyboard functions. This feature will be investigated in the final section of this chapter.

In order to work with ANSI.SYS, your system must be set up to recognize calls to this driver. This file should be in your root directory. If it is currently in the DOS subdirectory, either COPY or MOVE (see Chapter 6) it to the root directory.

DOS must be told that this file is available through a file called CONFIG.SYS. This file may already be in your root directory. The CONFIG.SYS file is a user-created file. You won't find it on your DOS diskette. If you find a file by this name in your root directory, it was placed there by the individual who set up your system. The CONFIG.SYS file can be created or modified using EDLIN.

If this file already exists in your root directory, all you need to do is add the following line:

DEVICE = ANSI.SYS

Don't worry if there are other lines saying DEVICE = something else. You may have more than one DEVICE = line in your CONFIG.SYS file.

If you don't already have a CONFIG.SYS file in your root directory, you will need to create one. Use EDLIN to create this file. It should consist of the single line:

DEVICE = ANSI.SYS

When DOS is booted, it checks to see if the file CONFIG.SYS is in the root directory. If it is, DOS reads this file to see if any special drivers are to be installed. In this case, the *device* driver, ANSI.SYS, is to be installed. This driver file will control the console device. Since the console consists of the screen and the keyboard, ANSI.SYS will control the way these two components of your system work. Of course, unless you alter ANSI.SYS, the screen and the keyboard will work the way they normally do.

That is to say, ANSI.SYS contains the default values for video output and keyboard input. These values can be altered, however, by making calls to ANSI.SYS. A *call* to ANSI.SYS is like saying, "Hey, yo, ANSI.SYS!" and then specifying what screen or keyboard attribute you want to alter. Calls to ANSI.SYS are made by sending DOS an *escape sequence*. An escape sequence is just an Escape character followed by one or more numbers or characters. Unfortunately, these escape sequences cannot be sent directly from the system prompt. Where there's a will, there's a way, though, and in this case the way is the PROMPT command itself.

Using PROMPT to Call ANSI.SYS

While you can't send escape sequences directly to DOS from the system prompt, the PROMPT command has a way of sending them. If you remember the discussion of the PROMPT command from Chapter 4, you will recall that PROMPT includes a number of optional parameters, such as $n, $p, $g, etc. One of these parameters is $e, which sends an Escape code to DOS. This Escape code can be teamed up with the ANSI.SYS control codes to make calls to this device driver.

The *DOS Technical Reference Manual* refers to ANSI.SYS escape sequences by categories: cursor functions, erasing, graphics modes, and keyboard reassignment. Each of these functions will be discussed in the following sections. The escape codes for each function are listed in Table 8-1.

To send an escape sequence to ANSI.SYS via the PROMPT command, you include the PROMPT Escape code ($e) followed by whatever ANSI.SYS control code you wish to transmit. For example, the escape sequence to clear the screen and home the cursor (the DOS subcommand, CLS) is Esc [2J. To send this escape sequence to ANSI.SYS, you would use the PROMPT command:

PROMPT $e[2J

Table 8-1. Escape Codes for ANSI.SYS Screen Functions.

```
ESC [ Pl ; Pc H     Moves cursor to line l; column c.
ESC [ l A           Moves cursor up l lines.
ESC [ l B           Moves cursor down l lines.
ESC [ c F           Moves cursor right c columns.
ESC [ c D           Moves cursor left d columns.
ESC [ s             Saves current cursor position.
ESC [ u             Restores cursor to previous position.
ESC [ 2 J           Clears screen and homes cursor.
ESC [ k             Erase from current position to end of line.
ESC [ 0 m           Normal text.
ESC [ l m           High-intensity.
ESC [ 4 m           Underscore.
ESC [ 5 m           Blinking.
ESC [ 7 m           Inverse video.
ESC [ 8 m           Invisible.
ESC [ 30 m          Black foreground.
ESC [ 34 m          Blue foreground.
ESC [ 32 m          Green foreground.
ESC [ 36 m          Cyan foreground.
ESC [ 31 m          Red foreground.
ESC [ 35 m          Magenta foreground.
ESC [ 33 m          Brown foreground.
ESC [ 37 m          White foreground.
ESC [ 40 m          Black background.
ESC [ 44 m          Blue background.
ESC [ 42 m          Green background.
ESC [ 46 m          Cyan background.
ESC [ 41 m          Red background.
ESC [ 45 m          Magenta background.
ESC [ 44 m          Brown background.
ESC [ 47 m          White background.
```

Escape sequences may be strung together and included with messages to the user. The above escape sequence could be combined with the inverse video escape sequence (Esc [7m) and the message "Enter your command:" as follows:

PROMPT $e[2J $e[7M Enter your command:

Cursor and Erase Function

ANSI.SYS allows you to position the cursor anywhere you want. You can move the cursor up a line, down a line, forward or backward across a line, or position the cursor by line and column number. ANSI.SYS also allows you to save the cursor position in memory, report on the cursor position, and restore the cursor to its former position. These latter functions are rather complex, and their applications are beyond this simple treatment.

The most useful of the cursor functions is the cursor position function (CUP). This function uses the escape sequence:

Esc[pl; pc H

The *pl* and *pc* values are the line and column parameters. For instance, to position the cursor on line 14, column 20, the sequence would be:

Esc[14; 20 H

You may be wondering how the prompt in the menu screen displayed in Fig. 8-1 was located within the menu itself. This was accomplished through the use of the CUP function in the PROMPT command:

PROMPT $e[14;20H Enter your selection

Note in this case that the line and column parameters, as well as the letter "H," are not separated by spaces in the interest of keeping the PROMPT command as compact as possible.

The ANSI.SYS erase functions, erase display and erase line, are rather limited. You are usually better off using the DOS CLS function within your batch files when you want to clear the screen.

Video Mode Functions

One of the most powerful capabilities of ANSI.SYS is the control it provides over the video display of your computer system. This control is similar to the control you can gain with the BASIC programming language. As in BASIC, you can use ANSI.SYS to set the foreground and background colors. However, you can also use ANSI.SYS to turn on and off bold and inverse video, underscore (in monochrome only), and blinking. These video modes can be used to produce exciting effects.

While most PROMPT attributes are canceled by subsequent PROMPT commands, the video modes will stick until canceled by another video change. This means that you can use one PROMPT command to set certain video attributes, such as foreground and background color, and another PROMPT command to display the prompt itself. The PROMPT command to set the screen color can be inserted into your MAINMENU batch file before the command to TYPE the MAINMENU text file, causing the screen to be displayed in the colors you choose. The PROMPT command to display the prompt can then be issued.

Suppose you wanted your menu screen to be displayed in blue, with a border and text in yellow. You would select a foreground color of yellow, with a background color of blue. This would be accomplished through modifying the MAINMENU.BAT file as follows:

```
PROMPT $e[44m $e[33m
TYPE MAINMENU
PROMPT $e[14;20H Enter the letters corresponding to your choice:
```

Besides setting the screen colors, you can use ANSI.SYS to control other video attributes, such as inverse video and blinking. Consider the following PROMPT command:

```
PROMPT $e[14;26H$e[5;7mW A R N I N G !$e[Om$e[15;26HEnter$e[1mQ$e[Om to Quit
```

This command will position the cursor on line 14, column 30 and display the word, "W A R N I N G!" in blinking, inverse video to grab the user's attention. The video attributes will then be returned to normal. Then, the cursor will be moved down to line 15, column 26 where the message, "Enter Q to Quit" will be displayed. Note the bold video attribute preceding the "Q". This attribute is turned back off before the remainder of the message is displayed. Also, be sure to include an extra space after the "t" in "Quit". Without this extra space, the user's response would appear immediately following the prompt message:

Enter Q to QuitQ

Instead, the user's response will appear as:

Enter Q to Quit Q

The above PROMPT command takes up more than one line in EDLIN, and would occupy more than one line in a command file. While this is no problem in DOS versions 3.xx, which allows command lines of up to 127 characters, it is a problem for earlier versions of DOS. These versions only allow command lines under 80 characters. You are likely to need longer PROMPT commands if you plan to work with ANSI.SYS. For this reason alone, you should consider upgrading your version of DOS if you are using version 1.xx or 2.xx.

Keyboard Reassignment Functions

Another feature of ANSI.SYS is its ability to reassign the function of any key on the keyboard. This includes the function keys (F1 through F10). While ANSI.SYS is limited in the number of reassignments it can accommodate at any one time, it is still a useful feature. On the other hand, if you have a full-featured keyboard macro processor, such as ProKey or SuperKey, you will be better off using that program to make keyboard reassignments.

Most computer users accept their keyboards at face value. Did you think that, when you entered an "A", the ASCII code for the letter "A" was actually sent to your computer? In fact, this is not the case. Instead, a special *scan code* is sent to the computer. In the case of the "A" key, the scan code is 30. There are even scan codes for the shift keys, so the computer can tell whether you are entering a lower- or uppercase "A".

The scan code for the letter you type is translated into the corresponding ASCII code by your computer's BIOS ROM chip. This ASCII value will then be sent on to the CPU for processing. However, the ANSI.SYS device driver can intercept the ASCII codes before they get to the CPU. ANSI.SYS will then send its own ASCII code on to the computer's processor. In fact, ANSI.SYS can send an entire sequence of characters. This means that a single key can be reassigned to represent a complete sentence.

The ability to reassign letter keys is not especially useful. After all, you ordinarily want an "A" to be an "A" and not a "B". (You might want to try some simple key reassignments on your friend's computer, though. This makes a great, if unappreciated, practical joke!) On the other hand, reassigning the values of the function keys can simplify the use of your menus. Consider the menu screen displayed in Fig. 8-8.

This menu refers the user to the function keys F1 through F8 to select the options displayed on the screen. The use of function keys to represent menu choices is often preferable to letter choices. There are several reasons for this. For one thing, pressing F1 is faster than typing "WS" and pressing the Enter key. Also, the function keys are easier for novice users to find.

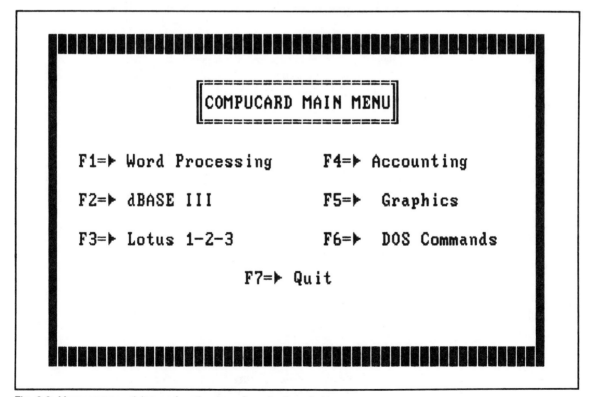

Fig. 8-8. Menu screen relying on function keys for selecting choices.

For these reasons, you may want to build your menus around function keys rather than letter choices. To do so, you will have to use ANSI.SYS to reassign the values of these function keys. Remember one thing. If you use ANSI.SYS to reassign the function keys, you won't be able to use these keys in their normal capacity as editing keys for EDLIN. Of course, if your system is fully menu-driven from power on to shutoff, you won't be using EDLIN anyway.

Keyboard reassignments are not returned to their default even if another PROMPT command is issued. The only way to get the default key assignments back is to reboot the computer. If the keyboard reassignments are part of a PROMPT command contained in the AUTOEXEC.BAT file, you will have to reboot off the floppy drive.

Keyboard reassignment using is accomplished by making calls to ANSI.SYS. The escape sequence consists of the Escape key, the ASCII code of the key being reassigned, and the new string value assigned to the key. For example, to reassign the function key F1 to assume the string "WS," you would use the following escape sequence:

Esc [0;59;"WS"p

The first two values, 0 and 59, are the extended ASCII code for the F1 function key. The final "p" is the ANSI.SYS keyboard reassignment function parameter.

To include this escape sequence in a PROMPT command, you would enter:

PROMPT $e[0;59;"WS"p

Once this reassignment is effected with the PROMPT command, pressing the F1 key will cause the letters "WS" to be sent to the processor and displayed on the screen. The only problem with this reassignment is that the user still has to press the Enter key. Even this task can be reassigned to the F1 key by including the ASCII code for a carriage return, 13, as part of the escape sequence:

Esc [0;59;"WS";13p

The corresponding PROMPT command would be:

PROMPT $e[0:59;"WS";13p

Now, whenever the user presses the F1 key, the WS batch file will be automatically called up. This simplifies the use of the menu system considerably.

The extended ASCII codes for the ten function keys are listed in Table 8-2.

One recommendation for reassigning function keys is to reassign each function key to its digit character and a return. For example, the key reassignment for the F1 key would be:

PROMPT $e[0:59;"1";13p

With this reassignment, whenever the F1 key is pressed, the "1" character will be sent. Of course, the WS.BAT file would have to be renamed 1.BAT.

F1	059
F2	060
F3	061
F4	062
F5	063
F6	064
F7	065
F8	066
F9	067
F10	068

Table 8-2. Scan Codes for the Ten Function Keys.

The reason for using digit characters is that you don't have to reassign to function keys every time you modify your menu. Instead, all you have to do is change the name of the batch file to match choice 1, 2, etc. on your modified menu. An even better approach is to keep a set of batch files labeled 1.BAT, 2.BAT, etc. in your root directory. Each of these batch files would contain a line which called the batch file for each of the choices in the menu. Using Fig. 8-9 as an example, the 1.BAT file would consist of the following lines:

```
1.BAT

ECHO OFF
CLS
WS
```

With this method, the only changes that need to be made when modifying the system are to edit the menu screen and change the batch file call in the numbered batch file. Suppose you wanted to change from Lotus 1-2-3 to SuperCalc4. You would edit your menu screen and substitute SuperCalc4 for Lotus. You would also substitute the batch call SC for LOTUS in the batch file labeled 3.BAT.

A Menu System Based on Function Keys

You can combine multiple key reassignments in a single PROMPT command. For example, the following PROMPT command will reassign the eight function keys, F1 through F8, to the batch calls, "1" through "8", respectively:

```
PROMPT $e[0;59;49;13p$e[0;60;50;13p$e[0;61;51;13p$e[0;62;52;13p
       $e[0;63;53;13p$e[0;64;54;13p$e[0;65;55;13p$e[0;66;56;13p
```

This PROMPT command could be included at the beginning of the AUTOEXEC.BAT file. Then, whenever the computer is started, the function keys will be reassigned automatically. These eight function keys can then be used to call up the eight menu choices displayed in Fig. 8-8. These choices relate to the batch files 1.BAT through 8.BAT. These batch files correspond to the batch files, WP.BAT, LOTUS,BAT, Q.BAT, etc.

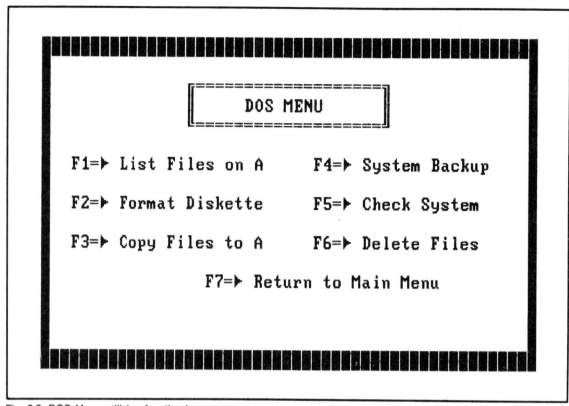

Fig. 8-9. DOS Menu utilizing function keys.

While some of these batch files execute commands or load programs directly, such as 4.BAT or 8.BAT, others cause submenus to be displayed. Consider the 6.BAT file, which is executed when the F6 function key is pressed:

```
6.BAT

ECHO OFF
CLS
CD DOS
TYPE DOSMENU
PROMPT $e[14,20H Press the function key corresponding
to your choice
```

The DOSMENU screen is shown in Fig. 8-9.

As you can see, the function keys are used to select choices from this menu as well. This poses no problem. The function keys retain their reassigned values. The only difference is that, in the DOS subdirectory, the batch files 1.BAT through 7.BAT contain different commands. For example, the 2.BAT file corresponds to the FORMAT.BAT file described in Chapter 6. Notice that pressing the F7 key returns the user to the Main Menu. The 7.BAT file would contain the necessary commands to return the user to the root directory and then call the MAINMENU batch file to redisplay the Main Menu.

Using this strategy, you can create a complete menu system including submenus, help screens, etc. all using function keys. When combined with borders, colors, and special video effects, your menus will rival those of professional programs. There is a special feeling that comes from creating your own, customized applications. If you have ever written a simple Lotus macro or dBASE command file, you have experienced this feeling. Just think how proud you'll be to show off your slick, integrated menu system. Will your computing buddies be impressed!

Chapter 9

DOS Shells

Now that you have learned how the disk structure of your computer is organized and have developed your own menu system, it's time to consider some really serious applications of these concepts. In other words, welcome to the big time. First, you'll learn about *menu generators,* which help you create fancy menu systems in a fraction of the time it would take on your own. Second, you'll discover how DOS shells can revolutionize your use of DOS.

MENU GENERATORS

In the last three chapters, you learned how to use the techniques of batch file programming to develop a professional looking menu system for accessing programs and executing DOS commands. As you can imagine, menu-driven hard disk systems, especially ones using function keys, are quick, efficient, and easy to use. Also, fully menu-driven systems which load automatically at system startup keep the user out of DOS. The system prompt can be a confusing and even hazardous place for the unwary computer novice. It is far better to protect such users from the rigorours and dangers of DOS. While this may sound a bit paternalistic to some, it makes good sense and is usually appreciated by the users whom you are protecting.

As you've seen, menu-driven hard disk management systems can range from the simple to the elaborate. A well-designed menu system includes attractive, eye-catching menu screens, submenus, and help screens which assist the user in working with the system. A menu system designed to be used by novice computer users should contain one or more DOS submenus which automate the DOS commands the user will need.

In addition, password security might be a consideration when several users will be sharing the system.

So far, the advantages of menu-driven systems have been highlighted without consideration for the disadvantages. Frankly, this is because there is only one real disadvantage to menu-driven systems: they are time-consuming to create. Unless you have a word processor capable of drawing graphics characters and saving text files in ASCII format, you need to create menus and borders with EDLIN. Also, reconfiguring the function keys with the PROMPT command is tedious. Wouldn't it be nice if there were a program designed to create menus for you?

In fact, there are several *menu generator* programs available. One of these, AUTOMENU, is a share-ware program described in more detail later in this chapter. AUTOMENU, and programs like it, help you draw menu screens, set up batch files for changing directories and loading programs, and have their own keyboard reconfiguration schemes. Many menu generator programs also include password security, which allows you to restrict access to programs or data.

Menu generator programs take much of the drudgery out of setting up menu-driven systems. AUTOMENU, for example, is so easy to use, you may wonder why you had to wade through the last three chapters on batch file programming. Actually, any menu generator assumes some understanding of DOS and batch files. While you don't have to write the batch file programs yourself, you are actually programming when you use any menu generator.

Closely related to menu generators are programs that simplify the use of DOS. These programs sit between you and DOS and provide menus or simplified versions of the DOS commands you need to manage your disks and files. Such programs are sometimes called DOS *front ends* or *shells*. The DOS-A-MATIC program, employs a user interface that is extremely easy to work with and is quite intuitive. It enables the user to load programs, delete and rename files, and move between subdirectories and disks by pointing at the file or subdirectory and then pointing at the desired function.

AUTOMENU

The AUTOMENU program, from Magee Enterprises, is a powerful, easy-to-use menu generator. Besides its menu generating capability, it includes several other features, including password security and data cryption. Discussion of these two features will be deferred until Chapters 12 and 13, which cover the subjects of password security and data cryption in detail.

AUTOMENU paints your menu screens for you. This makes menu-creation easy. However, you must adhere to AUTOMENU's menu format. AUTOMENU allows up to eight menu selections per menu. These menu selections are labeled 1 through 8 and are displayed vertically in a full-screen menu. When building menu screens with AUTOMENU, you can add a menu title and optional display information for each of your menu choices. In addition, AUTOMENU adds supplemental information to your menu screens, including the date, time, status of special keys (Caps Lock, Num Lock, etc.), and available memory. Finally, AUTOMENU provides on-line help which describes how to make selections from the menu. The various components of a sample menu screen are illustrated in Fig. 9-1.

Menu selections are made in one of several ways. The fastest is to type the number

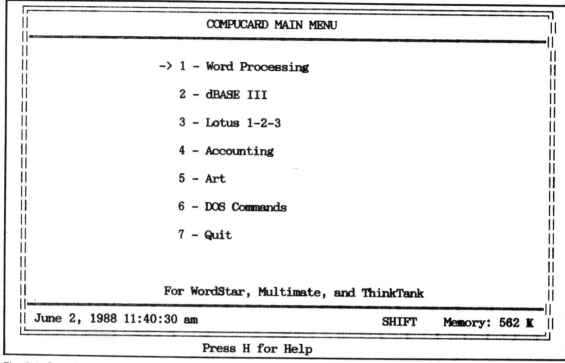

```
┌─────────────────────────────────────────────────────────────────┐
│ ║                                                               ║ │
│ ║                 COMPUCARD MAIN MENU                           ║ │
│ ║═══════════════════════════════════════════════════════════════║ │
│ ║                                                               ║ │
│ ║          -> 1 - Word Processing                               ║ │
│ ║                                                               ║ │
│ ║             2 - dBASE III                                     ║ │
│ ║                                                               ║ │
│ ║             3 - Lotus 1-2-3                                   ║ │
│ ║                                                               ║ │
│ ║             4 - Accounting                                    ║ │
│ ║                                                               ║ │
│ ║             5 - Art                                           ║ │
│ ║                                                               ║ │
│ ║             6 - DOS Commands                                  ║ │
│ ║                                                               ║ │
│ ║             7 - Quit                                          ║ │
│ ║                                                               ║ │
│ ║                                                               ║ │
│ ║          For WordStar, Multimate, and ThinkTank              ║ │
│ ║═══════════════════════════════════════════════════════════════║ │
│ ║ June 2, 1988  11:40:30 am             SHIFT    Memory: 562 K ║ │
│ └───────────────────────────────────────────────────────────────┘ │
│                    Press H for Help                                │
└───────────────────────────────────────────────────────────────────┘
```

Fig. 9-1. Sample menu created with AUTOMENU.

(not the function key) corresponding to the desired choice. Alternatively, the Up and Down arrow keys can be used to move the pointer to the desired selection. Pressing the Enter key causes that numbered choice to be selected. Finally, the space bar can be used to highlight individual selections. Each time the space bar is pressed the subsequent selection is highlighted. Highlighted options are selected by pressing Enter.

The full-screen, eight-selection, vertical format of AUTOMENU menu screens cannot be altered. However, you can customize the foreground and background colors and intensities. Also, you can create a series of menus, each containing up to eight individual selections. A menu series is not the same as submenus. Instead, it is a set of linked menus which can be accessed by using the Pg Up and Pg Dn keys to move from menu to menu. Each menu in the series is numbered, and this number is displayed in the upper right corner of the menu screen. Using a series of menus, you can provide the user with more than eight selections for a given application or work area.

AUTOMENU also supports submenus. Submenus are called as selections from a parent menu. For example, selecting option 1 from the CompuCard Main Menu shown in Fig. 9-1 causes the Word Processing Menu to be displayed (Fig. 9-2). Submenus are accessed from main or parent menus and are used to segregate the various programs and work areas on the disk. Submenus should always contain an option which returns the user to the main or parent menu. In a way, submenus help guide the user through the tree structure of the disk.

The AUTOMENU diskette includes a fairly large .DOC file which explains many of its features. However, certain important steps in using the program are unclear. For this reason, you will find the following discussion helpful if you plan to use AUTOMENU. The AUTOMENU diskette also provides you with a set of sample menus and submenus. These can be used to demonstrate the use of AUTOMENU. You can also use the files which produce these menus as guides for developing your own menu screens. The following sections describe the installation of AUTOMENU and the techniques for creating and using AUTOMENU menu screens.

Installing AUTOMENU

The instructions for installing AUTOMENU are quite simple. Installation is accomplished through the use of an installation batch file, INSTALL.BAT. There are a few questions to answer which are mostly self-explanatory. You will be asked to select a name for the subdirectory where the AUTOMENU files will be stored. You don't have to create this subdirectory; AUTOMENU will perform this task for you. You will also be asked to enter the name of the subdirectory where your DOS files are located. Next, you will be asked if your AUTOEXEC.BAT file creates a path to your DOS subdirectory. Finally, you will be asked if you want AUTOMENU loaded automatically at system startup. You should probably answer "No" to this question. Installation takes a few minutes, so be patient.

When you run INSTALL.BAT, AUTOMENU copies all the files on the AUTOMENU diskette onto your hard disk. Many of these are for illustrative purposes only. Once you have the AUTOMENU program up and running the way you want, you won't need

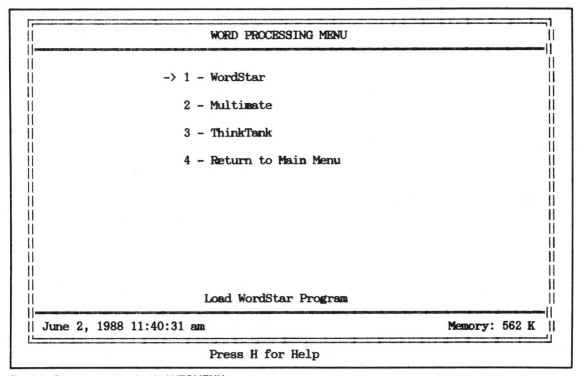

Fig. 9-2. Submenu created with AUTOMENU.

169

these files. Instead, you can use the following procedure to provide a more streamlined approach to using AUTOMENU. Place the AUTOMENU.COM and AUTOTEMP.BAT files into your root directory.

- Place your main menu file (say, MAINMENU.MDF) into the root directory as well.
- Modify your AUTOEXEC.BAT file (or whatever you call your main file) to include, as its last call, the command AUTOMENU MAINMENU.MDF.
- Place your other submenu files (files with .MDF extensions) in the subdirectories that they refer to.
- Finally, remove the original \ AUTOMENU subdirectory from your hard disk.

The above procedure will allow you to run AUTOMENU without taking up unnecessary disk space. If you need to modify existing menus later, you can run the AUTOMAKE.EXE or AUTOCUST.COM files from your floppy drive. Such modifications should only be necessary on an infrequent basis.

Running AUTOMENU

The AUTOMENU system uses a program, AUTOMENU.COM, to call up menu screens generated by the AUTOMAKE.EXE program. These menu screens are described in Menu Definition Files, indicated with an .MDF extension. The appearance of these screens is dictated by the AUTOMENU.COM program, but certain screen attributes can be altered through the use of the AUTOCUST.COM program. When you first install AUTOMENU, you are presented with a set of sample .MDF files, one of which is called AUTOMENU.MDF. You are also given an AUTO.BAT file which will automatically run AUTOMENU. All you have to do is enter:

C>AUTO

The AUTOMENU.MDF and other .MDF files provide you with a sample menu system to practice with. You can also view the contents of these files to learn how to create your own .MDF files. It is a good idea to play with the sample menus to get a feel for how AUTOMENU works. AUTOMENU lives up to the documentation claims for an intuitive interface. Selecting menu items is so simple it requires no explanation. Note, however, that the sample menus may contain choices which you won't be able to execute on your computer. The 4.0 version, for example, provides a word processing choice which calls up the IBM Personal Editor. Obviously this choice won't work if you don't have this program installed on your system.

Certain menu choices provide you with a text message at the bottom of the screen. These messages are used to clarify a menu selection. Still other menu choices will prompt you for additional information. For example, the Move choice in the DOS menu asks you for the name of the file to move and the location to which you want it moved. You will learn how these messages and prompts are implemented in the next section.

One thing to note when working with the sample menus is the menu number in the upper right corner of the screen. The first menu will appear as:

Menu 1 of #

where # is the number of menus in the series. Remember, a menu series does not refer to submenus. Instead, the series is really one large menu broken into a series of screens so no one screen overwhelms the user with too many choices. To move on to the next menu, you use either the F10, the PgDn, or the Right Arrow keys. To move backward through the menu series, use the F9, PgUp, or Left Arrow keys. Home selects the first menu in a series, and End selects the last menu.

AUTOMENU features a screen blackout feature that automatically blanks the screen after a specified period of disuse. Blacking out the screen can prevent your monitor from becoming permanently burned from the menu display. The delay before blackout can be customized to your specifications using AUTOCUST.COM. When the screen is blacked out, a message is displayed on the screen telling the user how to return to the menu. This message can also be customized or disabled entirely.

Designing Your Own AUTOMENU Screens

At the heart of the AUTOMENU program is a combination menu generator and batch file engine. The menu generator draws the menu screens, including the borders, menu tile, selections, and descriptions which have been specified by the user. The *batch file engine* creates the batch files necessary to execute the various menu choices. The menu selections and commands necessary to execute them are stored in a special .MDF file. .MDF files are created using the AUTOMAKE facility that comes with AUTOMENU.

AUTOMENU uses special symbols to indicate the various functions within an .MDF file. For example, an * is used to indicate a menu selection. Each entry in the .MDF file is preceded by one of the special symbols. Figure 9-3 shows a typical screen from the AUTOMAKE utility. This screen includes a portion of the MAINMENU.MDF file used to create the Main Menu illustrated in Fig. 9-2.

To create your own .MDF file, you use the AUTOMAKE facility. You can access this facility in one of two ways. If you have installed the complete AUTOMENU system on your hard disk, you can use the AUTOMAKE facility by selecting this option from the sample AUTOMENU menu that is installed on your hard disk. Just run the AUTO.BAT file to call up this menu and select option 2. AUTOMENU Building Facility. Alternatively, you can run AUTOMAKE directly from your hard disk or floppy drive. For example, you may not want to keep a copy of the AUTOMAKE.EXE file on your hard disk for reasons explained previously. In this case, you can insert the AUTOMENU diskette in drive A and call up AUTOMAKE as follows:

C > A:AUTOMAKE

AUTOMAKE offers three options: one to create or modify menus, one to print .MDF files, and one to exit from the program. To create a new .MDF file, choose option 1, Modify an old or start a new Menu Definition File. You will be prompted to enter the name of the file to work with. You may use any filename you want, but you must specify the .MDF extension. Path names and drive specifications are permitted. If the .MDF file you specify is already present on the disk, this file will be loaded for modification. If the file is not found, AUTOMAKE will assume that you want to create a new file.

You use the AUTOMAKE program like a word processor. It is extremely intuitive. The only feature which may not be obvious is the Insert function. To insert characters

MDF Information

Functions		
Comment	.	Set Up CompuCard Main Menu
Title	%	COMPUCARD MAIN MENU
Selection	*	Word Processing
Descript	?	For WordStar, Multimate, and ThinkTank
Load a MDF	@	WP.MDF
Selection	*	dBASE III
Password	<	dbase
Output Msg	>	Enter name of dbase program to execute
Input	<	
Batch-Res	!:	cd dbase
Batch-Res	!:	dbase %1
Selection	*	Lotus 1-2-3
Batch-Res	!:	cd lotus

```
=========================J MDF Functions L=========================
 . = Comment        ^ = Password      + = Batch-NRes    > = Output Msg
 % = Title          [ = Time Start    !: = Batch-Res    < = Input
 * = Selection      @ = Load a MDF    -- = Direct
 ? = Description                      == = Direct/P     # = End of MDF
===================================================================
```

F1 = Toggle Help ON/OFF   F3 = Insert line   F4 = Delete line   ESC = QUIT

Fig. 9-3. A screen from AUTOMAKE showing entries and special symbols used to create a menu display.

or new lines, you must have the Insert function turned on. As you might suspect this function is toggled on and off through the use of the Ins key. The various special symbols used by AUTOMENU are displayed in the bottom of the AUTOMAKE entry screen. As you enter one of these symbols at the beginning of each line, AUTOMAKE displays its function to the left. This helps you make sure that you are entering the correct symbol for the function you wish to accomplish with that entry.

Screen Functions

The special symbols are described in the AUTOMENU documentation that comes with the program; however, some additional explanations may serve to clarify certain symbols. The Title symbol (AUTOMENU) for example, is more complex than you might think. This symbol may be used more than once in a given .MDF file. Each time this symbol is used, it indicates a new menu screen within a series of menu screens.

Remember that you can only have eight menu selections in a single screen. This does not mean that you are limited to eight selections in a single .MDF file. Instead, you may define up to eight menu screens, each indicated by a new Title symbol, in an .MDF file. Each of these menu screens may include up to eight menu selections. This gives you up to 64 menu selections within a single .MDF file.

Each time you enter the Title symbol, AUTOMENU generates a new menu screen and assigns it a menu number. The menu number is displayed in the upper right as Menu X of Y, where X is the menu number and Y is the total number of menus in the series. As mentioned in the preceding section, the user can move between menu screens by using the PgUp or PgDn keys.

The Selection (*) and Description (?) symbols need little extra explanation. The text that you enter after a * is displayed as one of your menu selections. Again, you may have up to eight selections within a single menu screen. For each menu selection, you may include an optional description by including an entry preceded by a ?. Description entries are displayed at the bottom of the screen and serve to clarify the selection by providing additional explanatory information or instructions.

Command Functions

The commands to execute a particular menu choice follow directly after the Selection entry for that choice. There are five different ways to implement menu selections. These are: Direct (-), Direct/P (=), Batch-Res (!), Batch-NRes (+), and Load a MDF (DOS). Each of these implementations functions differently and has its advantages and disadvantages.

The Direct and Direct/P functions may only be used to implement a single DOS command, program call, or batch file call for the menu selection to which they are linked. At first, this seems extremely limiting, and you may wonder why AUTOMENU includes these two options. Actually, these two options are the fastest way to implement menu selections.

As you will see, the Batch options take time to create batch files from the commands included in the .MDF file. However, when you implement a menu option with either of the Direct options, the DOS command or program call is executed directly through the AUTOMENU command processor. This is useful for loading programs or performing a DOS function, such as deleting or copying a file. The Direct/P function includes a PAUSE command that asks the user to press a key before returning the menu which called the DOS command. This provides a way for information, such as a directory listing, to remain on the screen until the user has had an opportunity to read it.

The two batch options are used to implement a series of commands by placing them into a batch file. The batch symbols, ! and +, cannot be combined. To implement a given menu selection, you must use either !'s or +'s. The elegance of the AUTOMENU program is that it does not require a separate batch file for every menu selection. Instead, it creates the necessary batch file to implement a menu item only when that item is selected by the user.

Remember that every batch file takes up space on your hard disk (up to 8K depending upon your DOS and hard disk size). If you had a menu system with a total of 20 menu choices, this would require 20 batch files using the techniques described in Chapter 7. With AUTOMENU, you only need one. Of course, this means that AUTOMENU has to create a batch file each time one is needed. However, this takes almost no time at all. AUTOMENU always uses the same filename for its batch files to ensure that it doesn't clutter up your hard disk with lots of little batch files. AUTOMENU calls this file AUTOTEMP.BAT. This file needs to be available to AUTOMENU.COM, so be sure to include it in the same directory that you run AUTOMENU from.

The difference between the Batch-Res and the Batch-NRes implementations is that with the Batch-Res option, AUTOMENU remains resident in memory. This means that, when a menu selection is implemented using !'s, the user will be returned to the menu from which the item was selected. For example, if !'s are used to move into the LOTUS subdirectory and load Lotus 1-2-3, then, when the user exits from Lotus at the end of the work session, she will be returned to the AUTOMENU menu from which she selected the Lotus option. Menu selections implemented with +'s, on the other hand, return the user to DOS when they are concluded.

The Load a MDF symbol (DOS) is used to call another .MDF file. Load a MDF entries call up a submenu which is defined by the .MDF file named in the entry. This file is a Menu Definition File in its own right, and may employ up to eight menu screens each containing up to eight menu items. Through the use of Load a MDF options, you can create a virtually unlimited menu system. Note an important point: If you want to be able to return to the calling menu, be sure to include a Return to XXX menu selection in your submenu. This submenu selection should be followed by a Load a MDF call to the calling menu in your .MDF file.

Dialog Functions

It is possible to display a series of instructions to the user and accept user input through the use of the Output Msg and Input functions. Text following the Output Msg symbol (>) is displayed on a clear screen. You may have multiple lines of text, and you can skip lines by including >'s with no text after them.

User input may be captured in one of two ways. You can include a set of input options after the Input symbol (<). For example, suppose you wanted the user to select from one of three drive designators. You could include an Output Msg and an Input function as follows:

>Please enter the drive you want to use:
<A:,B:,C:

The three options would be displayed under the output message. The first option, A:, would be highlighted. To select a different option, the user would employ the left and right arrow keys to move the highlight onto the appropriate choice. Once the desired choice has been highlighted, the user presses Enter to conclude the selection process.

Alternately, the Input function can be used to record user input directly. This is accomplished by including a < symbol with no options. Then, whatever the user enters from the keyboard is treated as input. An example of this type of Input function is illustrated below:

```
>Please enter the name of the file to delete:
<
```

The Input function captures user input and places it into one of the replaceable parameters. For example, if the above two Output/Input implementations were combined with a Direct command, you would have the following sequence:

```
>Please enter the drive you want to use:
<A:,B:,C:
>Please enter the name of the file to delete:
<
-del %1%2
```

This command sequence would prompt the user for the drive to use and place the user's selection into AUTOMENU1. Next, the user would be prompted for the name of the file to be deleted. This would be placed into AUTOMENU2. Finally, the Direct function would execute the DOS command to delete the file from the specified drive.

A Sample .MDF With Explanations

Figure 9-4 is a listing of the complete MAINMENU.MDF file used to display and implement the CompuCard Main Menu shown in Fig. 9-2. While it is rather elementary, it serves to illustrate all the features of the AUTOMENU program. You may find this example helpful in designing your own .MDF files.

The first entry is a comment. Comments are used to describe what you are doing. The next entry is the title for the menu. AUTOMENU claims that the title will be centered automatically, but this was not the case in version 4.0. Instead, the title had to be centered manually.

The next three entries pertain to the first menu option. The entry, "*Word Processing* displays the selection *"Word Processing"* as option 1 in the menu and the entry, *"?For WordStar, MultiMate, and ThinkTank,"* displays the description *"For WordStar, MultiMate, and ThinkTank"* at the bottom of the menu screen when option 1 is highlighted. The entry, @ \ WP \ WPMENU.MDF causes the WPMENU.MDF file, located in the WP subdirectory, to be loaded and displayed if option 1 is selected from the CompuCard Main Menu.

The *"*dBASE III"* selection displays *"dBASE III"* as menu option 2. If this option is selected, the user will be prompted to enter a password. This password must match the password, dbase, in the Password entry indicated by the ^ symbol. If the user

```
A listing of MAINMENU.MDF printed on 03-18-1987.

.Set up CompuCard Main Menu
%                        COMPUCARD MAIN MENU
    *Word Processing
    ?For WordStar, Multimate, and ThinkTank
        @WP.MDF
    *dBASE III
    ^dbase
        >Enter name of dbase program to execute:
        <
        !cd dbase
        !dbase %1
    *Lotus 1-2-3
        !cd lotus
        !lotus
    *Accounting
    ?Run GL, AP, AR, Payroll
        >Enter module to use:
        <GL,AR,AP,PR
        !cd acct
        !bpi %1
    *Art
    ?To access graphics programs and games.
        @ARTMENU.MDF
    *DOS Commands
    ?Directory, Format, Check Disk, etc.
        @DOSMENU.MDF
    *Quit
    ?Backup all altered files and park hard disk.
        +q
#End of Main Menu
```

Fig. 9-4. Listing of the MAINMENU.MDF file.

passes this password check, he will be prompted to "Enter name of dbase program to execute:." The user's input will be captured and stored in %1. Then the dBASE subdirectory will be accessed. Finally, the dBASE III program will be loaded and an optional dBASE command file will be executed by the !dbase AUTOMENU1 entry. (Remember, the ! entries will first be assembled into a batch file.)

The "*Lotus 1-2-3" selection needs no explanation. The "*Accounting" selection includes an optional Descript function, "?Run GL, AP, AR, Payroll." This description will be displayed at the bottom of the screen whenever option 4 is highlighted. If option 4 is selected, the user will be prompted to select the module to use from GL, AR, AP, and PR. This selection will be stored in the replaceable parameter %1. The ACCT submenu will be accessed and the accounting program, BPI will be executed with the optional module indicator stored in %1. (Note: this is for illustrative purposes only—check your BPI manual if you plan to use this program for your accounting needs.)

The *"*Art"* and *"*DOS"* command selections function much like the *"*Word Processing"* selection in that they both load submenu .MDF files. The *"*Quit"* selection places the descriptive message, "Backup all altered files and park hard disk" and then runs the Q.BAT file. Note that this selection is implemented using the Batch-NRes function (+) rather than the Batch-Res function (!). This is because you don't want to return to the CompuCard Main Menu after executing this batch file.

The final entry in the MAINMENU.MDF file is the #End of Main Menu line. Make sure you conclude your menus with an End (#) entry.

PASSWORD SECURITY AND FILE ENCRYPTION

One useful feature of AUTOMENU is its password protection feature. Strategies and justifications for the use of password security will be discussed generally in Chapter 12, Password Security. For the present, the focus will be on the mechanics of password utilization in AUTOMENU. As you read in the preceding section, you can use the Password function (^) to program passwords into your menus. AUTOMENU also allows you to issue passwords to your .MDF files as well.

Password protection for your .MDF files serves two purposes. First, you may not want other individuals to be able to alter your menus once they have been created. Second, if you have included passwords as part of the .MDF file, they are not secure as long as anyone can view the .MDF file and read the passwords stored in it.

When you save a newly created .MDF file, AUTOMAKE asks you if you wish to protect it with a password. If you supply a password, you will be asked to reenter the password for verification. Note: be sure to write your passwords down! Otherwise, you will not be able to get back to your menus to modify them later. Once the .MDF file is saved with the password you supply, this password must be entered to edit or print the .MDF file. The password may be changed by viewing the file and then saving it again with a different password.

AUTOMENU menu uses the password you supply to *encrypt* the .MDF file as well as lock it. The topic of data cryption is covered in detail in Chapter 13, Hidden Files and Data Encryption. For now, think of encryption as converting the file to a secret code that only AUTOMENU can read. Once the file has been encrypted, you can't view it with the DOS TYPE command. In fact, the only way you can see the contents of a password protected file is through the use of the AUTOMAKE facility, which requires you to provide the password before decrypting the .MDF file.

Installing Your Own Menus

As mentioned earlier, AUTOMENU menu defaults to the AUTOMENU.MDF menu file whenever it is run. In order to use your own .MDF files, you will have to establish one of them as the parent menu. In the example used in this chapter, this has been the MAINMENU.MDF file. This .MDF file may contain entries to load other .MDF files. These child .MDF files provide you with access to submenus and may contain entries to load still other .MDF files. Be sure that each child .MDF file contains an entry to return the user to the preceding level, so that there is always a path back to the parent menu. The parent menu may or may not contain an option to return the user to DOS, depending upon the way you want your users to access the computer system.

Once your system of .MDF files has been established, you can move the children .MDF files to their appropriate subdirectories. Again, the only files you need to retain in your root directory are the AUTOMENU.COM file, the AUTOTEMP.BAT file, and your parent .MDF file. To run your parent .MDF file, you enter the call for AUTOMENU followed by the filename of the parent menu (be sure to include the .MDF extension). For example, to run the MAINMENU.MDF file, the command would be:

C>AUTOMENU MAINMENU.MDF

You can include this command as part of your AUTOEXEC batch file. This way, whenever the computer is turned on or rebooted, your menu will be loaded automatically. If you have not included menu options which return the user to DOS, loading the parent menu from system startup effectively locks the user into the menu system. This may be desirable, especially if password protection has been implemented to lock out users from certain applications or work areas.

The AUTOEXEC batch file can always be circumvented by booting off one of the computer's floppy drives. There are ways of hiding what's on the hard disk however, so that this trick does the unknowing user little if any good. More on this in Chapters 12 and 13.

DOS SHELLS AND FRONT ENDS

For many years, personal computer users had to deal with their computers' operating systems much the way users on large systems did. In many ways, personal computer operating systems mimicked the command structure of mini and mainframe computers. DOS is a descendant of an earlier microcomputer operating system, CP/M, which itself has antecedents in the large computer world.

Operating systems that rely on single character prompts, terse commands, and cryptic error messages couched in computerese may be fine for macho computing types (who read assembly language programs with their Cap'n Crunch at breakfast), but what about the rest of us? Apple Computer recognized that not everyone is as adventurous as those bold computer frontiersmen who strode forward to conquer the uncharted realms of DOS with nothing but their ten digits and a box of Ding Dongs to sustain them.

In fact, the Apple Macintosh revolutionized the way personal computer users looked at computing. The *user interface* took on an entirely different meaning. No longer did users have to struggle with DEL *.*'s, COPY PROG.BAS B:/V's, and "Invalid command or file not found"'s. Instead, users could look at cute little pictures on the screen, play with friendly mice, and point at what they wanted.

Actually, in fairness it should be noted that the *icon* based interface popularized by the Macintosh was developed as a large computer interface by a research team at XEROX. However, the prevailing reaction to such a cutesy interface was: "Real men don't use icons!". And so the project languished until it was revived by the developers of the Apple Lisa. DOS users were quick to jump on the user friendly bandwagon, and a host of products designed to simplify DOS were released. Most of these fell into one of two categories: shells and front ends.

DOS shells actually sit on top of DOS. They display their own, easy to use interface to the user. When the user indicates the command to be executed, the shell program performs the steps necessary to accomplish the command. Usually, this involves passing parameters down to DOS and having DOS do the actual work. The GEM program, by Digital Research, is an example of a DOS shell. This program represents files as little folders on the screen, and employs trash cans and other icons to represent operating system activities such as deleting files. With the addition of an optional mouse, this user friendly program converts your PC into something suspiciously resembling an Apple Macintosh.

DOS *front ends,* on the other hand, are little more than window dressing for the DOS operating system itself. User commands are handled directly by DOS; only the interface has been changed to protect the naive. Such programs make DOS easier to use without disguising the basic nature of the operating system itself. Files are still represented by their filenames, extensions and all, and commands retain their DOS nomenclature (COPY is still Copy, etc.).

DOS-A-MATIC

There are several popular DOS front ends currently available. One of these, DOS-A-MATIC, is an inexpensive shareware program from Marin Pacific Software (1001 Bridgeway, Suite 514, Sausalito, CA 94965), which includes most of the features found on front ends costing much more. One of the most convenient features of DOS-A-MATIC is the way it accesses files and directories. The files and subdirectories of the current directory are displayed on the screen (which may be scrolled if necessary). To select from the currently displayed files, you use the space bar to move a highlight bar onto the filename or subdirectory you wish to work with. Once this file or subdirectory is highlighted, you may execute a program, copy, delete, move, or rename a file (including paths and drive specifiers), and even create and delete subdirectories.

Moving from one drive or subdirectory to another is simple—just select the new drive or subdirectory you wish to access and press Enter. File listings may be viewed using either the Sort option or a *file mask.* Sorted files will appear in either alphabetical order, according to file size or date of creation.

A file mask is essentially a filter which is created through the use of DOS wildcards. For example, if you wanted to work only with .COM files, you would set the file mask to *.COM. One important feature of DOS-A-MATIC is its ability to search the entire hard disk for a specified file. The DOS directory command, DIR, can only search within the current subdirectory.

The DOS-A-MATIC interface is so easy to use it hardly requires explanation, although there is a fairly comprehensive manual that accompanies the program. DOS-A-MATIC also provides on-line, context sensitive help which can be accessed by pressing the F1 function key.

DOS-A-MATIC includes a number of other functions, such as the file *attributes* function. As you may recall, a file's attributes are stored in the directory along with its filename, length, and starting cluster number. A file's attribute byte determines whether the file may be altered, listed in a directory listing, and other characteristics. The topic of file attributes will be discussed in greater detail in Chapter 13, but suffice it to say that DOS-A-MATIC offers a simple utility for manipulating file attributes.

DOS front ends offer an alternative to more extensive menu-driven systems such as those described in Chapters 6 through 8 or ones developed using menu generators like AUTOMENU. Programs like DOS-A-MATIC make DOS convenient and easy to use without losing the flavor of the operating system itself. Some users, especially more experienced ones, would rather take this approach than be locked into menu systems with their predetermined set of selections.

In a way, a front end program such as DOS-A-MATIC combines the convenience of a menu system with the flexibility of the DOS command prompt. The convenience is based on the point and shoot interface—you merely highlight the disk, directory, or file you want to work with, rather than having to type in drive designator, directory path, and filename. On the other hand, you have a large degree of flexibility in terms of the variety and type of functions you can perform. In addition to those DOS functions included in the DOS-A-MATIC File Menu, you can run any DOS command directly.

Whether you decide to use a front end program like DOS-A-MATIC or opt for a more structured menu-driven system to manage your hard disk will depend upon the number and type of applications you plan to work with and the number and skill level of the individuals who will be using the computer system. Generally, the more complex the tree structure of your hard disk, the better off you will be using a menu-driven system. On the other hand, if you only plan to use three or four application programs on a regular basis, you may find a front end program to be entirely adequate.

Probably more important than the number of applications is the skill level of the intended users. While shells and front end programs like DOS-A-MATIC help the knowledgeable user find his way around a tree structured disk, less experienced users can still be overwhelmed by the sheer volume of files and the numerous file functions available. The very power of a program like DOS-A-MATIC may be overwhelming to such users. If your intended users are novice or occasional users, you are better off setting up a menu-driven system which limits the choices in any one screen to a reasonable number of well-documented options.

COMING UP

This concludes Part I of Hard Disk Management with MS-DOS and PC-DOS. By now, you should be comfortable with the terms and concepts of hard disks and file organization. You have learned a number of DOS commands related specifically to hard disk management, and you have seen how you can use the techniques of batch file programming to control access to your programs and data files. You have also been shown several methods for creating customized, professional-looking menu screens for guiding yourself and others through the intricacies of your hard disk tree structure. Finally, you have read about commercially available alternatives to DOS for managing your programs and files.

Unfortunately, there is more to hard disk management than the tasks of organizing and accessing programs and data. There are two other important issues of concern to owners. The first of these is hard disk security. This wide ranging subject includes data backup security, file access security, password protection, data cryption, and other topics related to the security of your data. Remember, the data on your hard disk system is typically far more valuable, in terms of time and information, than the hardware it is stored on. For this reason, it is important to provide adequate backup security so that, if your computer is damaged or stolen, the real value of your system is retained.

Part II of Hard Disk Management with MS-DOS and PC-DOS includes chapters on each of these topics. You will learn how to perform periodic backups using either the DOS BACKUP and RESTORE commands or one of several commercial programs designed to shortcut the backup process. You will also learn about hardware solutions to the problem of backup, including streaming tape drives and removable hard disk cartridges. You will also learn how to protect your files through the use of passwords, hidden and read-only attributes, and data cryption. Finally, you will discover a method for tracking individual usage through a time logging program. The advantages of such a program will be discussed in Chapter 14.

Part 2
Hard Disk Security

Chapter 10

Backing Up Data and Programs

By now you should have your hard disk set up just the way you want. You've learned about DOS commands, subdirectories, batch files, shells and the PC Menu program. You're probably enjoying the comfort, speed and efficiency of your hard drive every day. Everything works fine. You couldn't be more happy. Until . . .

It's that until you should worry about. Hard disks perform so flawlessly that most of the time you can just forget about them. And with the advances in technology, the hard drive has become much more reliable than it has in past years. Still problems might occasionally happen.

When a problem does pop up, it's important to be prepared for it. It's not recommended you fix your hard drive yourself. However, there are several things you can do in case something does go wrong.

In this chapter preventive maintenance is introduced; those things you can do to better prepare yourself for a potential mishap. DOS provides two programs for this, BACKUP and RESTORE. The RESTORE command is used in conjunction with BACKUP as part of that just in case. Also discussed in this chapter are two other DOS programs hard disk owners may find invaluable: XCOPY and REPLACE. Finally, numerous hard disk manufacturer's include with their hard disk a program called PARK or HEADPARK. This program adds a defensive level to hard disk protection, dealing with problems the other programs do not touch.

PREVENTIVE MAINTENANCE

There are several reasons for backing up important data: It's valuable to you. Whether your data consists of numbers in a spreadsheet, names and addresses in a mailing list or customer database, or important documents in a word processor time was spent to enter the data. Although some of that information could be re-entered into the computer at a tremendous loss of time and money, a greater amount of that information might be original and irreplaceable. Like most valuables you own, you should have an insurance policy to protect your data just in case. The BACKUP program is that insurance policy.

BACKUP provides a safety copy of your data by transferring the information on your hard disk to floppy diskettes. BACKUP makes efficient use of the floppies, filling each to capacity, not wasting one byte of space on the disk. Once the operation is completed, you have an extra copy—an exact duplicate—of your data already on the hard drive. If anything should happen to the hard drive now, say a hardware failure or disk crash, you would still have a copy of your valuable data.

To someone new to computers, backing up a hard disk may seem like a frivolous thing to do. After all, the data is already stored on the hard disk. Backing up takes time and requires someone to manually insert floppy disks (up to 60 of them for large volume hard disks) during the backup procedure. With all the benefits of having a duplicate copy of your data, you might think every hard disk owner would regularly perform backups. But that's not the case.

The importance of making backups cannot be over emphasized. If you don't backup your data, you are taking an unwise and unnecessary risk.

When to Backup

A general rule to follow when backing up your data is the following:

- Backup files used each day at the end of the day.
- At the end of the week, backup the entire hard disk.

As an example of the first rule, consider Jack at CompuCard. Each day he updates his customer database. At the end of the day, he'll backup all the customer files to diskette for safe keeping. Because these files are on disk in their own subdirectory, this operation is relatively easy to perform (yet another advantage of having subdirectories).

Friday afternoon, as CompuCard is wrapping up the week, the designated BACKUP employee (probably Sue) sits down and backs up the entire hard disk. This way, changes, additions, or modifications to any file on the hard disk are saved.

At CompuCard, each employee should be responsible for making backups of their work every day. At the end of the week, the entire hard disk is backed up. This same approach to backing up should be followed by anyone using a hard disk.

Now consider a hard disk crash. Recalling from Chapter 1, a hard disk crash is when something causes the disk's head to literally crash into the surface of the disk. The resulting collision scratches the surface of the disk, rendering it unusable.

If the hard disk up and dies early on Monday, the data backed up from Friday will provide a full replacement. Because the entire disk was backed up, nothing new was added and nothing needs to be replaced. After the problem is fixed, the backed up data is simply restored back to the hard disk. Only the time the computer is down is lost.

If a hard disk crash occurs on Wednesday, the problem still isn't that bad. First, there's the complete backup made on Friday. Second, there are the two backups of the work done on Monday and Tuesday. If this were the computer in the order entry department and backups of all orders taken the first two days of the week were made, chances are a full replacement of the information on hard disk would be available. (Combine the two daily backups with the full backup from Friday.) Only information other than that backed up Monday and Tuesday, say a memo or the high score of a game played during lunch break, would be lost.

THE BACKUP COMMAND

The purpose of the BACKUP command is to copy all information from the hard drive (or a large volume disk) onto floppy diskettes. Each file is copied one by one. When a diskette fills up, the BACKUP program asks you to insert another. If a data file or program can't fit on a single diskette, it's split between two diskettes.

Keep in mind BACKUP is *not* the same as COPY. BACKUP deals with *archiving* files—storing them just in case. The files on a BACKUP disk contain extra information readable only by DOS's RESTORE program. The backed up files are not the same as their originals.

The format of the BACKUP command is:

BACKUP d:path [filename] [.ext] d: [/S] [/M] [/A] [/D:]

The first item listed after the BACKUP command is the disk drive you're backing up, followed by a path designator. This drive is referred to as the *source* drive. The second item is the disk drive to which you're backing up, or the *target* drive. The source can be a single file, group of files, a subdirectory, or the entire tree structure of a disk drive. The target will always be one drive, which is normally a standard 360K drive but may be a large volume drive or another hard disk.

It's important the source drive not be write protected, otherwise the backup will fail. Also, if your computer is part of a networked system, BACKUP will not archive programs you do not have access to. Refer to your network guide for more information.

If you have two floppy drives in addition to your hard disk, you can sample the BACKUP procedure with the following. The two drives can be two 360K drives, or one 1.2M drive (which is assumed to be drive A:) and one 360K drive. Readers with only one floppy disk, follow closely:

C > BACKUP A: \ *.* B:

This tells the computer to backup all the files in the root directory of the source drive, A:, to the target drive,B:. After typing the above command, MS-DOS informs you:

Insert backup source diskette in drive A:
Strike any key when ready

Press the space bar.

Insert backup diskette 01 in drive B:

Warning! Files in the target drive

B: \ root directory will be erased
Strike any key when ready

The computer will beep, warning you that any information already on the target disk will be erased. Insert a freshly formatted or reusable diskette into drive B: and press the space bar.

DOS will now archive all the files from drive A: to drive B:

*** Backing up files to drive B: ***
Diskette Number: 01

The first thing BACKUP does is to erase every file from the root directory of the target drive. It then creates a new file named BACKUPID.@ @ @. This file contains the number of the disk (such as 01 in the above example), the date of the backup,and other information important to the BACKUP program. BACKUPID.@ @ @ is used primarily when restoring backed up programs to ensure each disk is used in sequence.

Next, as each file is archived from the source to the target disk, its name appears on the screen. For example:

\ MEMO1.TXT
\ MEMO2.TXT
\ FRED.DAT
\ JIM.DAT
\ LINDA.DAT

If another diskette is required to continue backing up, the following message appears:

Insert backup diskette 02 in drive B:
Warning! Files in the target drive
B: \ root directory will be erased
Strike any key when ready

The backup disks are numbered sequentially until all the information from the source disk is archived. A nice thing about the warning message is that it beeps at you. This way, you can be off doing something else and simply wait to hear the beep! Then return to the computer and insert the next diskette. When the entire BACKUP is completed, you'll be returned to DOS.

Before you do a backup, here are a few important tips to remember:

- All files in the target drive's root directory are erased by the BACKUP command.
- The disks you back up to should be formatted before you start the BACKUP procedure.
- If you don't specify a directory for the source drive, only the files in the current directory are backed up. BACKUP C: A: only backs up those files in the current directory on drive C.
- Backing up to 360K floppies requires a lot of diskettes. The multiplication factor

is 30 360K floppy diskettes per every 10 Megabytes of hard disk storage you have. That means 60 disks are required for a full 20 Megabyte hard disk backup. The 1.2M drives are more space efficient. You'll generally use only one 1.2M diskette per megabyte of hard disk storage.

- It's a good idea to number and date the diskettes you're using for the backup. Use them in order. When finished, bunch them up with a rubber band and store them in a safe place.

Backup an Entire Disk

The previous example had some limitations. The biggest one is that only files in the root directory of drive A: were backed up. When the following command is entered:

C>BACKUP C:\ *.* A:

only the files in the root directory of the hard drive C: are backed up. If you have quite an extensive tree structure this proves quite inefficient.

To backup all subdirectories as well as the directory listed, the /S switch is used:

C>BACKUP C:\ *.* A: /S

This reads, "Backup all the files from C in the root directory and all files in any subdirectories under the root directory to drive A." A complete backup of the hard drive would follow.

Suppose you have a subdirectory \WP containing your word processor. Under \WP you have several additional subdirectories, each containing various memos, letters, short stories, poems and essays. To backup \WP and all its subdirectories, use:

C>BACKUP C:\WP\ *.* A: /S

Say you have one, large subdirectory on your hard disk which contains all your Lotus 1-2-3 spreadsheets. To backup only the spreadsheets (using the .WKS file extension), use:

C>BACKUP C:\LOTUS\ *.WKS A:

Like the COPY command, wildcards can be used with BACKUP to archive only specific files. In this example, only the files with the .WKS extension are backed up. The /S switch is not needed in this case. If /S were included, all subdirectories under \LOTUS and all files in those subdirectories would have been archived as well.

Backup's Switches

The /S switch (mentioned above) is referred to as the subdirectory switch. It translates into "backup everything in the indicated directory, as well as any subdirectories in the directory—and everything in them as well."

BACKUP has several other switches which help simplify and tidy the backup process. These switches can be used in any combination to make for an efficient backup system:

/M

The /M switch is used to backup only those files modified, or changed, since the last backup. Every file on disk has a special bit associated with its directory entry called the Modify bit. (This information is not displayed by the standard DIR Command.) When a file is backed up, the BACKUP program sets this bit to 0. If the file is accessed or changed after the backup, DOS changes the modify bit to a 1.

When /M is specified, BACKUP archives only those files modified since the last backup:

```
C>BACKUP C:\ *.* A: /M
```

The backup proceeds as before, directing you to insert backup diskettes as required until the process is completed.

```
C>BACKUP \LOTUS\ *.WKS A: /M
```

The /M switch used above makes a backup of only those files with the extension .WKS that have been modified since the last backup. This is an example of a periodic or daily backup procedure. If a backup of the entire hard drive is made once a week, then the above example could be used daily to backup only the modified files.

/A

The /A switch adds files to the backup disk. BACKUP erases all files on the root directory of the target disk. When the /A switch is used, those files backed up are added to the files already on the target disk.

```
C>BACKUP C:\MYBOOK\CHAPT1?.* A: /A
```

This example backs up all files named CHAPT1?.* to the disk in drive A, adding those files to any already found there. The disk in drive A must be the last disk from any previous backup. If not, DOS prompts:

```
Insert last backup diskette in drive A:
Strike any key when ready
```

If the file is already on the disk, BACKUP changes the name of the file backed up. For example, suppose you're working on a novel and presently stuck on Chapter 7. After each day's work you run the following batch file:

```
ECHO OFF
ECHO Insert your backup disk into drive A:
BACKUP CHAPT10 A: /A
ECHO Done!
```

The first day, the following files would be on the disk:

```
BACKUPID.@ @ @
```

The second day, these files would be on that same backup disk:

BACKUPID.@@@
CHAPT10
CHAPT10.@01

The next day, CHAPT10.@02 would be added, and so on. BACKUP adds the filename extension .@*nn* to the file added to the backup disk, where *nn* increases by one with each additional backup.

It's important to note that similar files with different extensions will also be backed up in the same manner. If the backup command were:

C>BACKUP CHAPT10.* A: /A

and there were two files on disk, CHAPT10 and CHAPT10.BAK, these files would be copied (added) the backup diskette:

BACKUPID.@ @ @
CHAPT10
CHAPT10.@01
CHAPT10.BAK

The next day, after the backup, these files would be on diskette:

BACKUPID.@ @ @
CHAPT10
CHAPT10.@01
CHAPT10.BAK
CHAPT10.@02
CHAPT10.@03

Because the .BAK extension is already used, BACKUP renames that file CHAPT10.@03. This really doesn't present a problem. It only adds a sorting job of discovering which file is which if they ever need to be RESTOREd back to the hard disk. Keep in mind the files are backed up and archived for safe keeping. A good rule of thumb is that the files with the two highest @*nn* values are the most recent.

The .@*nn* numbering scheme only really presents a problem when you name your files CHAPT.1, CHAPT.2, CHAPT.3, and so on. This would be a nightmare as far as re-organizing a backup diskette full of CHAPT.@*nn* files. It's highly recommended you keep your file name's as descriptive as possible and use the extensions for describing what type of file it is, or just leave them blank.

/D

The /D switch backs up only those files created or modified *after* a certain date.

This is not the same as the /M switch. Even if a file might have been backed up since the date listed it will still be backed up when the /D switch is specified.

C>BACKUP C:\DATABASE\CUST*.DAT A: /D:10-19-88

Only the customer files (CUST*.DAT) created or modified after October 19th, 1988 are backed up to drive A. The /D switch looks at the date of the file (which is seen in the DIR listing). If that date is the same as or later than the date listed after /D, the file is backed up.

C>BACKUP C:*.* A: /S/D:2-12-88

BACKUP archives all files on the hard disk C: (because of the /S switch) dated on or after February 12th, 1988.

THE RESTORE COMMAND

Once you've done a daily or weekly backup, you should store your diskettes in a safe place. Normally, there's no need to use these diskettes—they're just there for insurance. Hard disks are fairly robust and perform flawlessly. However, if something does go wrong, or if you've accidentally deleted a file, you need to restore the archived file from your backup diskettes. This is done with the RESTORE command.

The format of the RESTORE command is:

RESTORE d: [d:] [path] filename [.ext] [/s] [/p]

The first item listed after RESTORE is the disk drive containing your backup diskettes. The second item tells RESTORE which files need to be restored. It can be a single file, group of files using a wildcard, a subdirectory, or the entire tree structure of a disk drive.

If your computer is part of a networked system, the RESTORE program will not restore programs you currently do not have access to. Refer to your network guide for more information.

After you start RESTORE, it asks:

Insert backup disk 01 in drive A
Strike any key to continue

RESTORE scans each backup diskette for the files to be restored. RESTORE asks you to insert each diskette sequentially until the indicated files are all found and restored. For example:

C>RESTORE A: NOVEMBER.WKS

RESTORE searches the backup diskette in drive A for the file NOVEMBER.WKS. Once found, RESTORE copies (un-archives) that file from the backup disk to the current disk drive/directory. If a file named NOVEMBER.WKS already exists it is replaced, otherwise the file is created.

C > RESTORE A: C: \ ACCTING \ MARTIN \ *.WKS

This command restores all the files *.WKS from the backup diskette in drive A to the subdirectory MARTIN in the subdirectory ACCTING on drive C.

C > RESTORE A: C: \ *.*

This command might not do what you suspect. RESTORE restores all backed up files from drive A to the root directory on drive C. Only those files originally in the root directory are restored. While this may seem odd, remember the BACKUP command BACKUP C: A: only backs up files from the root directory.

To restore the entire hard disk, the /S switch is used. This switch is the same for RESTORE as it is for BACKUP:

C > RESTORE A: C: \ *.* /S

This command restores the entire hard drive from the backup diskettes in drive A. RESTORE recreates the original tree structure (if necessary) to place every file back in its original subdirectory.

After restoring the entire hard disk, the following message might appear:

System files restored
The target disk may not be bootable

After a two hour restore operation, that can be a depressing message. Usually, it's nothing serious. What the message is telling you is that the system files, IBMBIO.COM and IBMDOS.COM were restored from the backup disk. These programs might be older versions of DOS in which case your disk will not boot. If you ever see this message, use the SYS command from your DOS master disk (the current version) to update the system files on your hard disk. Then copy COMMAND.COM from your DOS master diskette to the hard disk. (For more info on the SYS command, see Chapter 2, Preparing Hard Disks.)

The /S switch can also be used to reconstruct a smaller portion of the hard disk:

C > RESTORE A: C: \ ACCTING \ *.* /S

Only the files and the subdirectories of the \ ACCTING subdirectory are restored from the backup diskettes in drive A. If the files or subdirectories have been erased, RESTORE will recreate them. RESTORE will scan each backup diskette until it's found all files in all subdirectories under \ ACCTING.

RESTORE's /P Switch

When the /P switch is specified RESTORE checks each file on the backup diskette to see if it's read-only. (Read-only is discussed in Chapter 12.) If the file is read-only and the file already exists on the hard disk, RESTORE beeps and asks:

Warning! File *filename*

is a read only file
Replace the file (Y/N)?

To replace the version already on disk with the one on the backup disk, press Y. Pressing N leaves the file as it is—the previously backed up file is not restored.

The /P switch should always be specified when backing up an entire system disk. When RESTORE encounters the files IBMBIO.COM, IBMDOS.COM and COMMAND.COM, it will not restore them when the /P option is specified. (And, consequently, the "Target disk may not be bootable" message will not be displayed.)

SOME FINAL NOTES ON BACKUP & RESTORE

Backing up your hard disk is a must. Yet, RESTORE is a program rarely (and hopefully never) run. There's no real need to backup and then restore the hard disk unless something goes wrong with the hard drive. As a precautionary measure, it is suggested you do a complete backup, with the remote possibility of a necessary restore, before the following operations:

- When your computer is modified. Either by yourself or a professional. This includes adding a memory card or other expansion option, second hard disk or some other hardware modification.
- When you use a *new* hard disk controller card with the same hard disk you're presently using. Each controller card formats the drive differently, therefore when you use a new card, you'll need to backup, format and then restore your files to the hard disk now using the new controller.
- Before a major move involving the computer. This includes a move between offices, across town, or some long distance when the hard drive could be damaged.
- Always backup your hard disk before you take the computer into the shop (if possible). Even if they're fixing something unrelated, it's still a good idea.

THE XCOPY PROGRAM

Starting with DOS 3.2, the XCOPY program has provided a unique hybrid of the BACKUP and COPY programs. XCOPY made its debut with the IBM PC Convertible Laptop computer. This computer added 3 1/2" disk drives capable of storing 720K on a disk.

XCOPY has many of the advantages of BACKUP, but acts more like COPY in that the files are not stored in the special archived format. XCOPY can be directed to copy entire subdirectories, or part of a tree structure, from one place to another. And finally, XCOPY makes the best use of the memory in your computer. Rather than copy one file at a time, XCOPY loads as many files as it can into memory before actually copying them. This makes XCOPY much faster than a simple COPY.

One similarity XCOPY does not share with BACKUP is that XCOPY will not ask to insert a second floppy diskette if the first one runs out of room. If there isn't enough room on a diskette to copy all the indicated files, XCOPY displays an error message.

The format of the XCOPY command is:

XCOPY [d:] [path] [filename] [.ext] [d:] [path] [filename] [.ext]
[/A] [/D] [/E] [/M] [/P] [/S] [/V] [/W]

(Looks like it only needs the kitchen sink to be complete.)

XCOPY may look confusing at first, but it's really a powerful and flexible file copying program. The first item after XCOPY is the source, the second the target. Both items can be a single file, group of files (with the wildcard) or a subdirectory.

Where XCOPY differs from COPY is in its optional switches. Without any of the switches, XCOPY does a simple COPY.

C > XCOPY C:\ WP \ POEM*.* A:

XCOPY copies the files POEM*.* from the hard disk to drive A. After typing XCOPY, DOS displays:

Reading source file(s) . . .

Here XCOPY reads as many files as it can into memory. Then, it copies the files from memory to the target diskette A, displaying the name of each file as it's copied. As with COPY, the names of the files are not changed (unless specified).

XCOPY's Switches

Many of XCOPY's optional switches are similar to those used by BACKUP and RESTORE. Some of the switches can be used in conjunction with others to vary the extent of the files XCOPY copies.

/S

The /S switch directs XCOPY to copy all files in all subdirectories under the current subdirectory. If the subdirectories do not exist on the target disk, they are created. This is the same /S switch for BACKUP and RESTORE.

/E

The /E switch can be used with the /S switch. /E creates subdirectories on the target disk even if the subdirectory is empty on the source disk. The /S switch alone will not copy empty subdirectories.

C > XCOPY \ WP \ *.* A: /S/E

This command copies all files and subdirectories in and under the \ WP directory to drive A. The subdirectory structure under \ WP will be duplicated on drive A—even empty subdirectories will be copied by XCOPY.

/M

The /M switch directs XCOPY to copy only those files which have been modified or changed since the last backup (the same as BACKUP's /M switch). Once XCOPY /M is performed, those files are considered by DOS to be backed up (their modify bit is reset as is done by the BACKUP program).

/A

The /A switch works exactly like the /M switch with only one difference. /A does not reset the file's modify bit. According to DOS, the files copied have still been modified or changed since the last backup.

C>XCOPY \WP\BOOK1*.* A: /M

This command copies files from the \WP\BOOK1 subdirectory to drive A. Only those files which have been modified since the last backup are copied.

C>XCOPY \WP\BOOK1*.* A: /A

This command behaves the same as the previous example, copying only those files which have been modified since the last backup to drive A. However, those files' modify bit is left unchanged, meaning DOS still considers the files to be modified or changed since the last backup.

/D

The /D switch is followed by a date. When specified, XCOPY only copies those files which have been created or updated since that date. The date XCOPY checks is the same date which appears in the directory listing.

C>XCOPY \ADMIN\LOTUS*.* A: /S/D:5-6-88

XCOPY copies to drive A all files and subdirectories under \ADMIN\LOTUS which have a date of May 6th, 1988 or later.

/P

When the /P switch is specified, XCOPY prompts (Y/N)? for each file listed. Pressing Y directs XCOPY to copy the program. If N is pressed, the file is not copied.

C>XCOPY \WP\NOVEL*.* A: /P

Files in the directory \WP\NOVEL are copied to drive A. As XCOPY displays the name of each file, you're asked whether or not you want that file copied by pressing Y or N:

```
            CHAPT1 (Y/N)? y
            CHAPT1.BAK (Y/N)? n
            CHAPT2 (Y/N)? Y
            CHAPT2.BAK (Y/N)? n
            OUTLINE (Y/N)? y
                5 File(s) copied
```

/W

When the /W switch is specified, XCOPY displays the following message before it begins copying:

Press any key to begin copying file(s)

After any key is pressed, XCOPY proceeds with the copy operation.

/V

The /V switch turns on the verify option. This is the same for COPY /V and when DOS's VERIFY command is turned on. When specified, XCOPY verifies (double checks) that the information copied is the same as the original. Because of this extra checking, XCOPY with the /V switch operates slower than a normal XCOPY.

THE REPLACE PROGRAM

The REPLACE program was introduced with DOS 3.2. This utility is a clever and long overdue blessing to hard disk owners. What it does is to selectively replace files on the hard disk with newer versions of those files on floppy. It upgrades the files without you having to individually search and update each one. The REPLACE program can scan the entire hard disk for a matching file and then replace it with latest version. This greatly simplifies the task of updating software on a hard disk.

REPLACE is not a substitute for the RESTORE command, just as XCOPY is not a replacement for BACKUP. Instead, REPLACE is a very specific tool with a variety of interesting uses. For example, suppose you've just received an upgrade to your accounting system. To update the files on the hard disk, place your upgrade diskette into the floppy drive then use the REPLACE program. REPLACE will find any files on the hard disk which match those on the floppy. Depending upon which REPLACE options are specified, the old files will be replaced by the new ones, or the new files will be added to the hard disk.

The format of the REPLACE command is:

REPLACE [d:] [path]filename[.ext] [d:] [path]
[/A] [/P] [/R] [/S] [/W]

The first item after REPLACE is the source file name, directory or disk drive. The second item is the target drive or path specification. REPLACE searches the target drive or path for any filenames matching those found on the source. If a match is found, the file on the target is replaced.

C > REPLACE A:*.* C:

This command replaces any files in the current directory of drive C with matching files on drive A. If drive C is currently logged to the DOS subdirectory and drive A contained the latest upgrade of DOS, this command replaces all matching DOS files on drive C with the latest editions on drive A.

Many of REPLACE's switches are similar to those used by XCOPY. The /P, /S and /W behave exactly as described for XCOPY above.

REPLACE A: \ *.* C: \ /S

This command uses the /S (subdirectory) switch to replace all files on drive C with matching filenames on drive A. REPLACE searches the entire tree structure of drive C. Once a matching file is found it is replaced.

/A

The /A switch adds files not found on the destination. Not only will REPLACE update any matching files, but files not matching those on the destination are also copied. This switch cannot be used with the /S option.

C>REPLACE A: \ *.* C: \ DOS /A

This command copies all files from drive A to the DOS subdirectory on drive C. Any files in \ DOS matching those on drive A are replaced. Any files on drive A which are not already in \ DOS C are also copied.

/R

The /R switch is specified when the files on the destination disk are read only. (See Chapter 12 for information on read only files.) DOS sets the read only status on special files. DOS does not allow read only files to be changed, modified, or deleted.

When the /R switch is specified, REPLACE ignores the read only status and replaces the file anyway. This is under the assumption that the read only file is among those being updated and therefore the read only status can be ignored.

COMMERCIALLY AVAILABLE BACKUP PROGRAMS

Many private software developers have realized the limitations of DOS's BACKUP and RESTORE program—mainly that they are slow. Since computers are supposed to be time savers, any program which can do a job faster than another is worth looking into.

COREfast

COREfast high speed backup software from Core International (see Appendix D for an address) contains a variety of programs designed to assist you in a thorough and time saving backup.

There are seven programs on the COREfast diskette. COREFAST.EXE is a complete, easy to use, menu driven program. The other programs are command-line versions of the menu options in the COREFAST.EXE program. Advanced users will probably want to use the command-line programs. Yet, they're really missing an impressive show put on by the COREFAST.EXE program.

In a word COREfast is outstanding. Backup and restore options are chosen from a menu on the screen. Extensive help messages are always easily accessible from the program by pressing F1. One of the nicest things about COREfast is its well written, easy to understand manual.

COREfast can be used for a variety of backup operations. If you have a second hard disk (one just for backups), you can use the ultra fast image backup. Otherwise, a file-by-file backup is done. This second type of backup is similar to DOS's backup, though much quicker. By using a special diskette format, COREfast can cut the backup time down by two thirds. Where a typical 20 megabyte hard disk takes an hour and a half to backup using DOS, COREfast does the same operation in 32 minutes.

COREFAST.EXE calculates and displays the number diskettes needed for the backup. Then, while the backup is progressing, it displays the current diskette, number of bytes being backed up, percentage of space used on the current diskette, and percentage of the backup completed. A time ticker is also running, letting you know how much time has been spent backing up.

This program is smart. Rather than prompt you to remove and insert the next disk then press any key, COREfast knows when you've removed a backup diskette from the floppy drive and knows when you've inserted the next diskette. There's no need to wait.

The only drawback to COREfast is that it's fussy. You should remove all memory resident programs before using COREfast. Even your CONFIG.SYS file should be empty. It might be necessary to rename CONFIG.SYS and AUTOEXEC.BAT and reboot before doing a COREfast backup (then rename them back and reboot again after you're done). Also, a path should be set to the COREfast directory to make sure the backup doesn't stop in the middle. If the COREfast programs were in the /COREFAST directory, the path would be:

PATH = C: \ COREFAST

But other than that, COREfast is a real time saver and improvement over the standard DOS backup.

Fastback

Fastback is backup software which, as the name implies, is fast. It consists of three programs: FINSTALL installs the program in a special \ FASTBACK subdirectory on the hard drive (though from there the files can be copied elsewhere). FASTBACK is the backup program and FRESTORE is the file restoring program.

The nice thing about Fastback is it is completely selection driven. There are no command lines or menu choices. You simply answer a series of questions, or press RETURN to accept the choices offered. Once this is done the backup process starts. Like COREfast, Fastback knows when you've taken a disk from the drive and inserted another. It also uses a special format for the backup disks to make the backup processes faster. Fastback performs well and, as its name implies, is a very fast backup program.

EXTRA HARD DISK PRECAUTION: PARK

Most hard disks come with a special software disk. What's on this disk depends on the brand and model of your computer, the type of hard disk, or where you bought your hard disk. One program on this disk you should pay special attention to is called PARK. (It may also be called HEADPARK, HARDPARK, DISKPARK, SHIPDISK, or may incorporate the name of the computer.)

What PARK does and how you use it are crucial to the longevity of your hard disk. Yet, the PARK program is really quite simple. Its sole job is to instruct the hard disk drive to park the read/write heads on the far outside of the hard disk.

If you recall from the earlier discussion of hard disks, the read/write heads are responsible for storing and retrieving information from the hard disk. This device sits only microns above the hard disk itself. If the read/write head were to come into contact with the hard disk, irreparable damage could occur. With the hard disk spinning at 3,600 RPM, this contact is equivalent to a head-on collision at 60 MPH. Such hard disk collisions are known as *head crashes*.

The PARK program prevents a possible head crash. Because PARK moves the read/write head to the far outside of the disk (where no data is stored), any head crash would not interfere with your data.

It's recommended you PARK your hard disk just before turning the computer off, and especially before moving the computer. It might even be a good idea to PARK the hard disk when leaving the computer unattended for a period longer than, say, an hour.

Due to the variety of PARK and PARK-like programs, it is impossible to discuss how each is used here. However, it's important to note that for each brand of hard disk there is a unique PARK program. Your friend's PARK program might not work on your hard disk. (It may make your hard drive go nuts, but it won't mess up your data.) You should only use the PARK program which came with your hard disk, or one you know will work properly.

All PARK programs behave differently. Some merely move the read/write heads to the outside of the disk and then return you to DOS. Others park the read/write head then lock up in a loop, instructing you to turn off your computer. Still others may sit and continually beep at you until you turn the computer off. Unfortunately, this is something you have little choice over when you use your PARK program. But the most important thing to remember is PARK can prevent a possible head crash.

A DAILY BACKUP BATCH FILE

A special batch file can be written to ensure that a daily backup of important data files is done. This batch file should be run at the end of each working day. Just like the AUTOEXEC.BAT file is run when the computer is first booted, the SHUTDOWN.BAT file can be run just before the computer is turned off. However, unlike AUTOEXEC.BAT which is automatic, you'll have to get into the habit of typing SHUTDOWN at the end of each working day. One way to insure that the SHUTDOWN batch file is run at the conclusion of each session is to include it as part of the Q.BAT file in your menu system.

A typical SHUTDOWN batch file would be as follows:

```
ECHO OFF
CLS
CD \ ADMIN \ LOTUS
ECHO Insert today's LOTUS backup disk into drive A:
BACKUP C: \ ADMIN \ LOTUS \ *.* /S/M
CLS
ECHO Backup completed. Bye!
PARK
```

The line, BACKUP C: \ ADMIN \ LOTUS \ *.* /S/M, makes a backup of all the files in all subdirectories under \ ADMIN \ LOTUS which have been modified since the last backup. In other words, a backup of only the work done today. (When this is done, make sure a different set of disks are used everyday, with each day of the week's disks kept labeled and separate.)

Once the backup is completed, the computer waves goodbye and parks the recording heads on the hard drive with the PARK program. The computer can now safely be shut down.

The programs discussed in this chapter all help make using a hard disk easier. BACKUP provides an insurance policy by archiving files from the hard disk to diskette. RESTORE, if needed, brings the archived files back. XCOPY and REPLACE are two nearly invaluable utility programs provided with DOS. And PARK acts as preventive maintenance.

Though all these tools have been provided with DOS, other companies have seen their limitations. Because of this, you can choose a commercial BACKUP program, such as CORE*fast* and Fastback, to archive files on the hard disk more quickly than DOS's BACKUP. Beyond this lie hardware solutions; tape backup, removable hard disks, and fault tolerant systems. These hardware solutions are discussed in the next chapter.

Chapter 11

Tape, Removable Disk, and Fault Tolerant Systems

A computer's hard disk is not the final word in mass storage. For example, the last chapter pointed out that although backing up data is important, it's time consuming. A secondary form of mass storage is tape backup. Seeing the inefficiency of floppy diskette backup, several companies offer the convenience of backup onto tape.

Other alternative forms of mass storage consist of physically removable hard disks. Keeping all your valuable information on a single hard disk can be risky from a mechanical point of view, as well as from a security standpoint. Nothing could be more secure than taking the hard disk out of the computer and locking it up in a safe. And some users may want to remove their hard disks and treat them just like floppies—for example, taking them home or on a business trip.

This chapter describes the hardware alternatives for storing and backing up data. Tape drives are ideal for quickly backing up hard disks. And tape cassettes are more convenient to store than a stack of rubber-banded floppy disks. Some manufacturers, aware of the importance of valuable data, have implemented fault tolerant hard disk systems. These are two hard disks working in tandem, each containing a duplicate copy of information on the other. And finally, this chapter goes into the interesting subject of removable hard disks, including the amazing Bernoulli Box.

STREAMING TAPE SYSTEMS

The most popular alternative to backing up data on floppy disks is a streaming tape backup. The *streaming tape drive* is like a high quality cassette recorder. It copies all data from the hard disk in one, fell swoop, putting that information onto a cassette tape. Because the primary purpose of the tape drive is to backup a hard disk, it's very fast.

Streaming tape drives can be installed either internally or externally. Internal models occupy the same size as a 1/2 height disk drive and might require an expansion board. External models mount outside the computer. In most cases the external tape drives use the computer's own power supply. However, some do require an external power supply, or have one available as an option. The external models generally operate off the 37-pin external drive connector on the back of the floppy disk controller, in which case they won't take up valuable slot space, or they come with their own controller card.

Another advantage to external drives is that they can be shared by a number of computers. For example, an external tape backup system could be carted around to various computers in the office. Each user could connect their computer to the tape drive, perform the backup onto their own tape, and then roll the cart to the next user. As long as the external drive is one of the plug-in types, this would save the expense of buying a tape drive for each computer system.

The entire backup operation from hard disk to cassette takes about 10 minutes for a full 10 megabyte, and 20 minutes for a full 20 megabyte drive. The multiplication factor is about one minute per megabyte used on the hard disk. When the backup is done, the cassette cartridge should be put back into its box and stored away in a safe place.

Incidentally, tape drives were the original form of mass storage for computers, not hard disks. Information was recorded and retrieved from reel to reel tapes. However, because the tape is one long, continuous surface, this meant all data on the tape had to be accessed serially, one after another. The advantage disks had over tape was that they could use random access; any point on the disk could be read simply by moving the disk's read-write head to that spot. This saved time over searching through a serial reel to reel tape.

Information is stored on tape using two methods: Start-stop and Streaming. Start-stop refers to the way tapes were used in the old days for accessing data. Streaming is a continuous flow of tape, used primarily for backup. Some streaming drives are capable of start-stop data storage, but at a much slower speed than dedicated start-stop tape drives.

Streaming tapes are always moving. The information is written to the tape by a write head, and a few fractions of an inch away a read head reads back the data just written. This is how streaming tape drives detect a write error. When an error happens, the write head re-writes the bad information, all while the tape is still moving.

For example, suppose an error exists in a block numbered N. The read head catches the error while the write head is writing block N + 1. The write head then attempts to re-write block N, then N + 1 again. If all is okay, the following blocks are written (N + 2, N + 3, etc.) as the tape continues to move. So on the tape the block order would be:

$$N \quad N+1 \quad N \quad N+1 \quad N+2 \quad N+3 \quad N+4 \ldots$$

The first N contained the error. Block N + 1 was written before the error was detected, so the following block is a rewrite of block N again. Using this error detection scheme, data can be written to the tape in one continuous motion.

If an error occurs during a restore (when the tape is being read), the drive will backup and re-read the bad block. Read errors aren't corrected the same as write errors. Instead, special information is stored on the tape along with the data. This information tells about the data, such as the block number, and includes a CRC (Cyclic Redundancy Check) error check. When the information is read from tape, another CRC error check is performed and the two CRCs are compared. If they are not equal, the tape rewinds and the data is read again. If after a given number of attempts the data cannot be read, an error message is displayed, or depending on the type of tape software the block may be ignored.

Cost is about the most important item when looking for a tape drive. These devices are expensive, and they are an extremely specific item for the computer. As with anything you buy for the computer, the cost should be weighed against the alternatives—in this case, backing up using floppies. For large volume disks where backups are crucial, tape drives are worth the price. For other systems, tape drives are more convenient than diskette backups. But cost-wise you should ask yourself if they're really worth it.

Other than cost, the next most important items to look for in a tape backup system are the formatted capacity of the tape, the data transfer rate, and the speed of the drive.

The formatted capacity of the tape is important in relation to size of your hard disk. Unlike floppies, tape systems will not pause when the tape gets full and ask you to "Insert next tape." The tape backup must be smooth and contiguous. For a 20 megabyte hard drive you'll need a 20 megabyte capacity tape drive and 20 megabyte tapes. For specific tape systems, check to see the capacity of the drive and tape cartridge match that of your hard disk.

Tapes can also be used to backup one small portion of a hard disk, such as a group of files or subdirectory. Though the formatted capacity of the tape can be as large as your hard disk, you can put several backup sessions on a single tape. For example, if your company's order entry information takes only 1 meg, you could backup each day's information using a single tape. (The tape keeps a directory of its information just like a disk does.)

The data transfer rate, the speed at which information is read from or written to the tape, is measured in kilobytes per second, Kbytes/sec. The higher the number of Kbytes/sec, the faster information is transferred to and from the drive. Ninety to 100 Kbytes/sec is a good transfer rate for a tape drive.

The speed of the tape drive is measured in Inches Per Second (IPS). The larger the formatted capacity of the tape and the faster the tape speed (IPS), the less time a tape backup will take. For example, a tape capable of holding 20 megabytes and recording at 30 IPS will take approximately 12 minutes to do a full 20 megabyte backup. If the tape speed is tripled to 90 IPS, the backup takes only 4 minutes.

Final considerations might be the physical size of the drive and its interface. Some tape drives are fairly large and would tend to be external-only. Others can occupy the space of the typical half height disk drive. Still others are of the new, 3 1/2 inch size—the same size as disks used in small laptop computers and portables.

The interface on the drive should be IBM PC bus, or one that uses the 37-pin connector on the back of the floppy diskette controller. SCSI, Small Computer Serial Interface or "Scuzzy," tape drives can only be used if your computer is equipped with a SCSI controller card. These tape drives are high performance devices, often more efficient than PC bus tape drives. SCSI is rumored to be the wave of the future, but unless your computer sports a SCSI port you shouldn't mess with a SCSI tape drive.

One final note: Some tape drives are not considered a logical device. This means, you don't treat a tape drive as drive D: (or T:). You cannot load or execute programs from the tape drive, nor can you save directly to the tape drive using DOS. The tape drive is simply a device for storing backups. Only special software controls the action of the tape. As far as DOS is concerned, the tape drive does not exist.

For those interested, Archive Corporation of Costa Mesa, California offers a complete book on the subject of tape drives. The book is titled *Streaming,* and it retails for $14.95. It goes into detail about mass storage units, including the how's and why's of hard disks, floppy disks and tape drives. Contact Archive for more information:

Archive Corporation
1650 Sunflower Avenue
Costa Mesa, CA 92626

The IRWIN Tape Backup System

Irwin Magnetics is the leading manufacturer of tape backup systems for the IBM PC/XT, AT and compatibles. Irwin tape drives are not streamers, yet they provide a fast and space saving method of backing up hard disks. The design of the tape drive and the method information is recorded on the tape allows Irwin to guarantee that data recorded on one Irwin drive can be read by another Irwin drive.

One case mentioned in Irwin's literature tells of a man whose computer, hard disk and tape drive were stolen from his house. Fortunately, he made a backup of all his important information before the burglary. After purchasing another computer tape drive, the man was able to restore his entire system from his backup tape. This might not be possible with other tape backup systems.

Irwin tape drives come with everything you need, including the amazing EZTAPE backup software, on two disks. The INSTALL program copies all files to a directory on the hard disk you specify. It's very simple and straightforward. The only complications are if you have less than 512K RAM in your computer. EZTAPE needs at least that in order to run.

The manual which comes with the Irwin Tape drive (the 420-XT, 20 Megabyte External unit was tested for use with this book) is very well written. It contains an abundance of information on not only the product, but backup procedures as well. The manual is hefty, yet the reading is easy and well paced. No computerese.

Installing the tape backup hardware is relatively simple. If you're not used to messing with a naked computer, you should have a qualified technician install the tape drive unit. Otherwise, anyone handy with a screwdriver can install the tape unit in a matter of minutes.

For PC/XT and compatible computers, the external tape drives plug into the 37-pin connector on the back of the floppy disk controller. A power cable needs to be installed by using a Y-splitter between the floppy disk drive and the tape unit. Irwin provides the Y cable and a special backplate which attaches to the XT's rear panel.

On ATs and compatibles, the floppy disk controller is different than the XT's. A special expansion card is needed to operate the tape drive. This card plugs into a short slot on the motherboard. The Irwin drive then plugs into a 37-pin connector on the back of the card.

Internal tape drive units don't take up the desk space of the external units. The manual is very clear on internal (and external) installation, providing step by step procedures as well as photographs. However, if your technical skills are rusty you should have a qualified person install the internal drive.

The EZTAPE software is impressive. It goes above and beyond the call of duty. Besides being tape backup utility software, EZTAPE is capable of hard disk organization: copying files, moving files, deleting files, maintaining directories—an abundance of utilities. All that plus EZTAPE is easy to use and has extensive on-line help information.

Included on the EZTAPE disk is a special program for performing backups at specific dates and times. EZSTART is a unique memory-resident utility which directs the EZTAPE backup software to perform a backup at a given date and time. For example, using EZSTART, you could instruct the computer to backup one particular group of files at 5:30 p.m. on Monday, another group at 5:30 p.m. on Tuesday, and the whole hard disk at 3:00 a.m. Wednesday morning.

Before using a tape, it should be formatted or initialized. A tape should come with the unit ready for use. But eventually you will be purchasing other tapes (they're available at most computer dealers) or re-using old tapes. To initialize a tape, you choose the Initialize option from EZTAPE's Utility menu. If the tape already has any data, EZTAPE will let you know. The entire initialization process takes some time (31 minutes on the tape tested for this book), but fortunately it doesn't need to be done for each backup.

Once the tape is initialized, the backup can proceed. Again, this is as easy as choosing an item from a menu. EZTAPE lets you backup files by the entire disk, selected subdirectories, or individual files. Once everything is set and either the drive, subdirectories or individual files are selected, the backup begins.

The software writes information to the start of the tape drive, like creating a directory. Then it starts reading files from disk and saving them to tape. It happens quickly and automatically. There's no need to sit and watch (though it is interesting to watch if you have nothing else to do). And there are no disks to swap as with a floppy backup.

Once the information is on tape, EZTAPE resets the status bits of all the files it backed up, informing DOS that a backup was made (refer to the last chapter on the Modify attribute). Now a copy of those files, or the entire hard disk, is on one, compact tape the size of a deck of cards.

To restore the files from tape is as easy as backing them up. Because EZTAPE keeps a directory on each tape backup, individual files, subdirectories, or entire disk drives can be restored with ease. EZTAPE asks a series of yes/no questions. After answering each of them to determine what type of restore you'd like, the program goes out to tape, fetches the desired files, and places them back on the hard disk.

The nicest part of all this is the EZSTART program, combined with EZTAPE's backup and restore options, can make one heck of an automatic and efficient backup system. In an office where the workers forget to make proper backups, or for individual use where making backups automatic at a convenient time is better, the combination of EZTAPE, EZSTART and the Irwin tape backup system is hard to beat.

FAULT TOLERANT SYSTEMS

The most elegant hard disk and hard disk backup alternative is a fault tolerant system. While not exactly a replacement for the hard disk, a fault tolerant system involves using two hard disks in a mirror arrangement. Each disk contains a duplicate of information on the other. When one disk fails or contains a bad sector, the information is instantaneously read from the second disk.

Fault Tolerant technology is well established and highly reliable. Fault Tolerant systems are used by heavy computer users, banking industries, the defense department, and organizations where the integrity and timeliness of computer data is crucial.

Fault Tolerant systems involve two or more identical computers or devices (not necessarily disk drives), each updated at the same time. If one system fails, the second immediately takes over. It would be like having two computers, both with the identical data stored in them. When one fails, the second quickly moves in and continues a smooth, uninterrupted operation. While this system tends to be twice to three times as expensive as a single system, for industries relying upon critical data, it's worth the cost.

A Fault Tolerant disk system involves two hard disks hooked into one Fault Tolerant controller. Information stored on one hard disk is instantaneously updated on the second. Each hard disk is a mirror image of the other. And the updating of the second disk takes place so quickly it goes unnoticed to the computer operator.

With a Fault Tolerant system, backups would be done instantly. Errors are detected and recovered without any interruptions. The only drawback to Fault Tolerant systems is the price. Because the hardware contains two (or sometimes three) of everything, the price can be double or triple what individual devices cost. Also, Fault Tolerant systems are not for everyone. Only in critical situations do they come in handy. If the data is very sensitive and price is no object then a fault tolerant hard disk system should be considered.

REMOVABLE HARD DISKS

People who grew up as floppy drive users have an assortment of interesting questions regarding hard disks. For example, floppy-only users want to know why you can't take the disks out of a hard drive. The easily-paranoid find it hard to believe data will stick to the hard disk even when the computer is off. They want that data on a disk in their hands, not in some hermetically sealed black box at the mercy of the wicked machine.

The reasons why hard disks are rigid, fixed media were discussed earlier in this book. The disk must spin at an extremely fast rate. And the read/write head is only microns away from the disk surface. As an interesting aside, you might have heard the term "flying head" when referring to the read/write head of a hard disk. This is because with the read/write head so close to the spinning disk it creates a physical phenomena where it actually does fly over the surface of the disk.

The same performance could be obtained from a floppy diskette if it weren't for two problems. First, the diskette would have to spin at the same speed as the hard disk, upwards of 3,000 rpm or ten times faster than it spins in a floppy drive. At this speed, the flexible media flutters like a pinwheel. This does not make for good contact with the read/write head.

Secondly, the read/write head would need to be just as close to the surface of the disk as it would with a hard disk. It's the close distance that causes more information to be stored on a hard disk than a floppy. With the head so close and the speed of the drive so great, a head crash would be inevitable.

Because of these two reasons, hard disks are constructed the way they are. The rigid media provides stability at high spin rates. And the hermetically sealed black box provides a safe, air-tight environment to prevent disk crashing.

There are valid reasons for wanting a removable hard disk. Some of the oldest types of hard disks were called packs. The entire pack of disk platters was removable from the system. The packs could be removed, cleaned, taken to another site, stored away—all without damage to the media. Yet this form of removable hard disk would prove too costly for microcomputers.

The advantages to removing a hard disk are many, with security first among them. Nothing is safer than removing a hard disk from the computer and locking it up in a safe overnight. This avoids the potential problems of theft, vandalism, even fire. No password system, lock and key, or chain is as good as removing the hard disk from the computer.

Removable hard disks are also handy. Taking work home from the office, or from one branch to another is as easy as slipping out the hard disk. If many users all use the same computer, each of them can have their own hard disk. They simply sit down, plug the disk into the slot, then use the computer. When they're done, they remove the hard disk media and let others use the computer.

Backups are relatively easy with removable hard disks. Because they can be treated like floppies, copying a removable hard disk is conceivably as simple as typing DISKCOPY C: D:. And if the backed up disk is a system disk, then you have two working copies of your hard disk. Unlike other forms of backup (floppy and tape), with a second copy of a removable hard disk you simply slide it into the slot and you're ready to work.

Possibly the best advantage to removable hard disks is the potential limitless size of storage. Rather than buy yourself a second hard drive, you just buy a second removable disk—or a third or a fourth. Typically, the cost of the media is far less expensive than buying an entire hard disk.

Bernoulli Disk Drives

Daniel Bernoulli was an 18th century Swiss mathematician and inverter who discovered a number of interesting things, primarily dealing with the flow of fluids around certain, interesting objects (and air is considered a fluid). One of his theories states that "the pressure in a stream of fluid is reduced as the speed of the flow is increased." This is usually illustrated using an airplane wing; the pressures created by the airflow around the wing cause the wing to lift in the air. Because air takes longer to get around the top of the wing, the air pressure is greater than it is below the wing and the wing rises.

As Bernoulli was toying around with air pressure flow over certain objects, he discovered that if you spin a flexible disk fast enough, it will wobble like a pinwheel (not his words). He then discovered that if you spin that same flexible disk next to a flat, rigid surface, the disk stabilizes. The airflow causes the flexible disk to become as smooth as a solid disk. It's on this principle the Bernoulli Box operates.

In the early days of personal computing, the Bernoulli drive was an inexpensive alternative to a hard disk. For a comparative price, you got a faster (twice as fast as the original PC/XT's hard disk) disk drive. You also got removability. You could take the media out of the drive. Or, you could buy a lot of media and instead of only having a 10 megabyte drive, you could have as many megabytes of storage as you had removable disks.

The Bernoulli Box consists of an external or internal unit and the actual disk itself. The disk is a flexible floppy disk, contained in a hard plastic case. The disk spins next to a solid surface creating the Bernoulli Effect and enabling the Bernoulli Box to behave just like a hard disk.

The external Bernoulli Box comes in a variety of configurations. The most important thing to look for is whether or not the disk is bootable. A bootable Bernoulli disk means it's treated just like a hard disk; you start the computer and the computer looks at the Bernoulli drive just like a hard disk. Computers with non-bootable Bernoullis are booted from a floppy disk.

Like external hard disks or tape drives, the external Bernoulli Box needs to interface with the computer via an adapter card. The externals come in three sizes, 5, 10 and 20 megabytes. And one or two drives can fit into one unit. The Bernoulli Box Plus contains an 80 megabyte hard disk plus two 20 megabyte Bernoulli disks.

The internal Bernoulli drive is the same size as a half height disk drive. It uses the SCSI interface to connect to the computer (so your computer must have a SCSI card installed). It sports a smaller removable cartridge than the external Bernoulli Boxes, roughly 5 1/2 inches square.

The cartridges for the external Bernoulli Boxes are about the size of a sheet of paper, 8 by 11 inches and about half an inch thick. They contain the flexible media and the rigid surface it spins next to. The cartridge doesn't need to be hermetically sealed. Because of another interesting aspect of the Bernoulli Effect, any foreign material which comes into contact with the disk does not cause a disk crash. In fact, a dust particle on the spinning disk creates a dimple. The dimple temporarily wrecks the Bernoulli Effect, causing the disk to momentarily flutter. The flutter dislodges the dust and returns the disk back to normal. (It's incredible no one else ever thought of the Bernoulli Box before IOMEGA—pure genius.)

The speed of the Bernoulli drives is comparable to the best of hard disks. In terms of millisecond (ms) access time, Bernoulli drives average about 35 compared to 80 to 65 ms for XT drives and 40 ms for AT drives. The error rate is also impressively low when compared to traditional, fixed disks.

The only drawback to the Bernoulli Box is the price. Hard disk prices have literally gone through the floor in recent years. Yet, the Bernoulli Box is comparatively expensive. This makes it look a little odd to purchase a Bernoulli Box—even with its advantages of removable media, easy backups and speed—when hard disks are so cheap.

The pay off comes with volume of information. When fixed disk sizes climb into the 100 megabyte range, the prices really shoot up. For less than half the cost of a 100 megabyte hard disk you could purchase a single Bernoulli Box and a number of 10 megabyte cartridges. Not only will you have saved some money, but you have the added bonus of security and quick backup protection, with a reliable removable disk system.

Other Removable Hard Disks

The announcement of Tandon Computer's Personal Data Pac has changed the way people think about portable computing. The Data Pac is a totally removable, high speed hard disk. It's about the size of a fat little book, 7 by 5 by 3 inches. Inside this compact shape is a 30 megabyte hard disk. The unit contains its own shock mounts and is fairly durable. You simply slide the whole thing into a Data Pac subsystem on your computer and you're ready to compute.

The second half of the Data Pac removable hard disk is the thing you plug it into, the Ad-PAC 2. (Tandon also sells an AT-compatible computer system based around the Data Pac, called the PAC 286.) The Ad-PAC 2 contains the disk controllers and receptacles for Data Pac removable hard disks. The external unit plugs into an expansion slot on your PC/AT or compatible. At this time an internal unit is not available.

The Data Pac is truly a removable hard disk. You simply eject the drive and go with it. Unlike the Bernoulli Box, it's a true, fixed disk. But like the Bernoulli Box, it offers the same security and flexibility that any removable disk system has. The only drawback is that it's only AT-compatible. The unit does not work with the PC/XT and compatibles. Other than that, the Tandon Ad-PAC 2 is a truly unique device.

The most important point of this entire chapter is that you're not limited to a hard disk/floppy disk arrangement on your computer. Many hardware manufacturers offer interesting and productive options for hard disk storage. Some of these devices, for example, the Irwin Tape Backup System, provide a quick and easy alternative to BACKUP programs. Others, such as the Bernoulli Box and Tandon Ad-PAC 2, are complete removable disk systems. Each offers an alternative form of hard disk storage with its own advantages and disadvantages.

While this chapter concentrated on physical (hardware) solutions for hard disk security, the next few chapters deal with software solutions; programs you can use and certain tricks which allow you to further protect your hard disk investment and the security of your files.

Chapter 12

Password Security

If your computer is used by more than one person, you might want to look into a password security system. By adding password protection to your computer, you can selectively choose which users are allowed access to which areas of the computer. The password security system helps add this level of control.

Passwords are used on mainframe computers and public bulletin board systems (BBS's). Each user of the system is assigned his own unique password which only he knows. The password positively identifies the user as himself because only he knows what it is. Once the password is entered, it acts like a key only unlocking certain doors. The system can direct the user to the specific areas of the system they have access to. Not only will the password prevent the user from wandering around, but it prevents other users from getting into that user's area.

In this chapter adding password security to your hard disk is discussed. DOS has not built in methods or programs to establish any password security. Therefore password security must be done through either a commercial or public domain program, or by writing a batch file to check and verify passwords. Additional forms of security include an actual lock and key assembly on some computers, and special programs which further protect your machine.

A BATCH FILE TO TEST FOR PASSWORDS

If you're the only person using your computer, it really isn't necessary to have password protection. Nothing can be more frustrating than forgetting the password and being locked out of your own system. However, if more than one person uses a computer, a simple password system can be maintained by using DOS's Batch file commands.

The following batch file tests for the password "lucky." If lucky is not typed, the batch file displays "Invalid Password!"

Create this batch file and name it PASSWORD.BAT. Either use EDLIN by typing:

C>EDLIN PASSWORD.BAT

Or use DOS's COPY command:

C>COPY CON PASSWORD.BAT

Or use whichever text editor or method you're used to. (Remember if using DOS's COPY command to end the file by pressing F6 or typing Ctrl Z.)

```
ECHO OFF
CLS
IF %1NUL = = NUL GOTO NOPASS
IF %1 = = LUCKY GOTO OKAY
ECHO Invalid password!
GOTO END
:NOPASS
ECHO Try again, this time type your password after PASSWORD
GOTO END
:OKAY
ECHO Welcome aboard!
:END
```

This batch file is designed to check for the replaceable parameter, %1. After the batch file is run, and the screen is cleared (to prevent anyone else from seeing the password), the %1 parameter is compared with a possible password LUCKY (line 4). If the password matches, batch file execution branches to the :OKAY label and "Welcome aboard!" is displayed.

The third line of this is especially designed to verify that a replaceable parameter was written.

IF %1NUL = = NUL

tests to see if nothing was entered as the replaceable parameter. NUL is DOS's null, or empty, device. If the test is true, meaning no password was specified, batch file execution branches to the :NOPASS label where a warning message is displayed.

If an incorrect password was entered, a special message is displayed (in line 4). Because no matches were found, the ECHO command displays "Invalid Password!" Execution then branches to the :END label.

To use this batch file, type PASSWORD followed by your password:

C>PASSWORD LUCKY

The PASSWORD batch file runs and if lucky is the correct password, "Welcome aboard!" is displayed. If an improper password is typed, the following is displayed:

C> PASSWORD FRED
Invalid Password!

If no password is typed, the special NUL test in the second line of the batch file causes the following to be displayed:

C>PASSWORD
Try again, this time type your password after PASSWORD

To test for a number of passwords, they should be added to the batch file after line 4. Any number of passwords can be added simply by including them in lines with an IF %1 = = *test*. For example:

```
ECHO OFF
CLS
IF %1NUL = = NUL GOTO NOPASS
IF %1 = = LUCKY GOTO OKAY
IF %1 = = BOSCO GOTO OKAY
IF %1 = = ROMEO GOTO OKAY
IF %1 = = SNOOPY GOTO OKAY
ECHO Invalid password!
GOTO END
:NOPASS
ECHO Try again, this time type your password after PASSWORD
GOTO END
:OKAY
ECHO Welcome aboard!
:END
```

This modified version of the PASSWORD.BAT file checks for the passwords BOSCO, ROMEO, and SNOOPY, in addition to checking for LUCKY. Any number of passwords can be added in this manner, and any password can be as long as DOS will accept (though a good length for a password is 7 characters, plus or minus 2).

One thing to beware of when using a batch file such as this is that case is important.

C>PASSWORD lucky

According to DOS, lucky does not equal LUCKY. One is in lower case, the other in upper case. Therefore they are not equal. Of course, this can be to an advantage. Consider the following line in the batch file:

IF %1 = = lUcKy

While lUcKy may be a bit harder to type quickly, it will also be a bit harder for someone to figure out.

On the same train of thought, keep your passwords simple, yet not obvious! Too many people use their initials, their spouse's name, their children's name, etc., as their password. Be creative when it comes to passwords! NARCH, REEBO, MRONK and TORBIT are all interesting passwords which no one will guess.

One ideal use for the PASSWORD.BAT program would be in a department where more than one person uses the computer. For example, suppose Jack and Sue both need access to files in the DB3 subdirectory of CompuCard's computer. To add a level of password protection, the following batch file could be written:

```
ECHO OFF
CLS
REM test passwords:
IF %1 = = JACK GOTO JACK
IF %1 = = SUE GOTO SUE
REM wrong password entered
ECHO Wrong password!
GOTO END
:JACK
PATH = C:\ADMIN\DB3;C:\DOS
CD \ADMIN\DB3\JACK
DBASE TICKLER
GOTO EXIT
:SUE
PATH = C:\ADMIN\DB3;C:\DOS
CD \ADMIN\DB3\SUE
DBASE FILER
:EXIT
PATH = C:\DOS
:END
CLS
ECHO Type PASSWORD followed by your password below:
```

This batch file tests for two passwords, JACK and SUE. The first thing done is to clear the screen. Next the passwords are tested. If no match is found, the batch file echoes "Wrong Password!"

If a match is found, the batch file branches to the appropriate routine, either SUE or JACK. Both routines set the path to C:\ADMIN\DB3 and to C:\DOS. Next the CD command is used to change JACK and SUE to their respective private subdirectories under \ADMIN\DB3. Because the path has been preset to \ADMIN\DB3, there's no need for them to be logged to that directory.

Following that, the batch file runs the appropriate program for either SUE or JACK. Finally, the batch file branches to the :EXIT routine and the path is set to C:\DOS (where it was originally). The screen is cleared and the message "Type PASSWORD followed by your password below:" is displayed. This last line resets the entire process.

If other users of the same system had similar password protected routines set into the batch file, the final message would help them to use the PASSWORD program.

Limits of Batch File Passwords

The major drawback to using password batch files is it only requires a tiny knowledge of DOS and anyone can examine your PASSWORD.BAT file to check for passwords. A sneaky way around this might be to make the PASSWORD.BAT file *invisible*. This is discussed in detail in the next chapter. The only way around the limitation of batch files is to use an official programming language to test for passwords.

The following program can be used to prevent anyone from accessing your system. It's written in the BASIC programming language. What it does is prevent anyone from using your system who does not know the system's password.

This program can be typed in and saved using the BASIC programming language which is available on all versions of PC-DOS and most versions of MS-DOS. The BASIC program is used itself to write other programs, including the password program listed below.

To enter BASIC, type:

C>BASICA

The BASIC program's first screen is displayed. You are now in the BASIC program interpreter where other programs for your computer can be written.

Carefully type in the following program, including the line numbers. Double check your work to make certain you don't mistype anything (if you do, use the BACKSPACE key to erase). Once you've typed the file in be sure to SAVE it before running it. (Read the instructions at the end of the program listing.)

```
1000 '= = = == = = = = = = = = = = = = = = = = = = = = = = = = -
= = = = = = = = = = = = = = = = = = = = = = = = = = = = = = =
1010 'PASSWORD.BAS (From "Softalk", March, May & July, 1984)
1020 'minor mods and color added by P. Eskildsen, July 10, 1984
1030 'other mods and color removed by Dan Gookin, March 5th, 1987
1040 'Uses BASICA 2.0 key trapping to kill Ctrl-Alt-Del,
1050 'Ctrl-C, & Ctrl-Break—user cannot RESET
1060 '
1070 KEY OFF
1080 KEY 15,CHR$ (12) + CHR$ (83)                     'CTRL-ALT-DEL
1090 KEY 16,CHR$ (4) + CHR$ (46)                       'CTRL-C
1100 KEY 17,CHR$ (4) + CHR$ (70)                       'CTRL-BREAK
1110 ON KEY (15) GOSUB 1520 : KEY (15) ON
1120 ON KEY (16) GOSUB 1520 : KEY (16) ON
1130 ON KEY (17) GOSUB 1520 : KEY (17) ON
1140 '
1150 'Read in password
1160 '
1170 OPEN "password.dat" FOR INPUT AS 1
```

```
1180 LINE INPUT#1,PASSWORD$
1190 CLOSE
1200 ON ERROR GOTO 1620
1210 '
1220 'Check user's password entry one char at a time, as entered:
1230 '
1240 CLS
1250 LOCATE , ,1
1260 PRINT "Please enter your password:";
1270 TRY = 0
1280 I = 0
1290 A$ = IN KEY$: IF A$ = " " THEN 1290
1300    IF A$ = "~" THEN 1420
1310 I = I + 1
1320    IF A$ < > MID$ (PASSWORD$,I,1) THEN 1350
1330    IF I = LEN (PASSWORD$) THEN 1420
1340 GOTO 1290
1350    TRY = TRY + 1
1360    IF TRY > = 3 THEN 1480
1370    PRINT "Wrong! Try again from start of password."
1380 GOTO 1280
1390 '
1400 'Access granted
1410 '
1420 PRINT
1430 PRINT TAB(30);"Welcome!"
1440 SYSTEM
1450 '
1460 'Too many attempts, lock system
1470 '
1480 CLS
1490 LOCATE 12,20
1500 PRINT "* * System Locked * *"
1510 GOTO 1510
1520 '
1530 'Display ignore messages
1540 '
1550 BEEP
1560 READ AH$
1570 PRINT AH$
1580 RETURN
1590 DATA "So there!", "Think you're smart?"
1600 DATA "That won't work either.", "I'm sorry"
1610 DATA "Try harder . . .", "Okay. Give up now."
1620 RESTORE 1590
1630 RESUME 1560
```

Once this program is entered, type:

SAVE "C:\ PASSWORD"

This saves the BASIC program to disk in the root directory. This should be done before running the program to prevent you from being prematurely locked out of your system. (The program is very efficient about preventing anyone from accessing your system.) Incidentally, you can save PASSWORD.BAS in any directory on disk. Just remember to include its full path (see below).

Briefly, what the program does is to read a single password from a disk file called PASSWORD.DAT. In order to use your computer you must successfully type in the password. If you type in the wrong password, the BASIC program locks up your computer; the computer cannot be reset using Ctrl-Alt-Delete, nor can the program be stopped. To return to DOS from BASIC, type:

SYSTEM

The next step is to create the PASSWORD.DAT file in your system's root directory. This can be done with the copy command. For example:

```
C>COPY CON PASSWORD.DAT
BULLWINKLE
^Z
```

Remember to press F6 or Ctrl Z to complete the COPY command. The file PASSWORD.DAT now contains the single word BULLWINKLE. This is the password to your system. PASSWORD.DAT, like PASSWORD.BAS, need not be in your root directory. If you place PASSWORD.DAT in any other directory, modify line 1170 of the BASIC program to read:

1170 OPEN "\ PATH \ password.dat" FOR INPUT AS 1

where PATH is the path to the file PASSWORD.DAT.

To set the PASSWORD.BAS program into effect, it should be added to your AUTOEXEC.BAT file. This way, the first thing which comes up on the computer screen is a question asking for the system's password. If BULLWINKLE (or whatever password is in PASSWORD.DAT) is not entered, the user is denied access to your computer.

Modify AUTOEXEC.BAT with EDLIN, or create it if it doesn't already exist. Type:

C>EDLIN AUTOEXEC.BAT

As the first line in the batch file, or second line if the first is ECHO OFF, add:

C:\ DOS \ BASICA PASSWORD

(In EDLIN, the I command is used to insert text. Type 1I to insert the new line before line 1; type 2I to insert the new line before line 2. Press Ctrl C on the next line to stop inserting text.)

If the PASSWORD file is in another directory, include the full path:

C: \ DOS \ BASICA \ DOS \ PASSWORD

This assumes the PASSWORD.BAS file is in the \ DOS subdirectory. Likewise, line 1170 of the program should be modified to indicate the full pathname for the PASSWORD.DAT file.

Now the AUTOEXEC.BAT file will run the BASICA program PASSWORD when the computer is booted. Your screen will clear and the following is displayed:

Please enter your password:

The characters you type are not displayed on the screen. After typing BULLWINKLE, or whatever your password may be, the word "Welcome" is displayed and your AUTOEXEC.BAT file continues. If you make a mistake typing the password the program informs you:

Wrong! Try again from start of password.

Start over with the first letter of the password. If you make more than three mistakes, the PASSWORD program locks up your computer. You cannot press Ctrl Break, Ctrl Alt Del, or any other key to stop the computer. If the proper password is not entered after three tries, the computer displays:

* * System Locked * *

You must now turn it off, then on, to regain control. (If you attempt to press Ctrl Break, Ctrl C or any other key to stop the program it displays a smart-alecky message.)

The BASIC PASSWORD program provides an almost fool proof way to keep unauthorized people out of your system. It does, however, have a few drawbacks.

First, there is only one password for the entire computer. This program was originally used in a computer store where the salespeople used the computer to demonstrate software. They didn't want any kids or unauthorized people using the computer without their consent, so they added the PASSWORD program to their AUTOEXEC.BAT file. All the salespeople only needed to know one password to get into the system—a password which the customers did not know. Because PASSWORD only uses one password for the entire system, it might not provide enough protection in other circumstances.

Second, as with any BATCH file, AUTOEXEC.BAT can be halted by pressing Ctrl C. If it's halted *before* the PASSWORD program is run, anyone can gain access to your system. Likewise, anyone who understands BASIC and DOS could TYPE the PASSWORD.DAT file to see what the password was.

Last, and perhaps most important, is that no matter how sophisticated the hard disk PASSWORD program is, it doesn't prevent someone from booting the computer using a floppy disk. No matter how much protection you add to your system, it's still possible to put a DOS system disk in Drive A and start the computer.

To sum it up, no security system is entirely flawless. Even the PASSWORD program has a so-called back door to it. It's possible to enter a system which uses the PASSWORD protection program simply by pressing the ~ (tilde) key. As the old saying goes, this method of protection only helps keep the honest more honest.

Description of PASSWORD.BAS

The following explanation of the PASSWORD program is provided for those interested in BASIC programming. It is not required reading, nor necessary to understand if you plan on using PASSWORD in your AUTOEXEC.BAT file. If you are further interested in the BASIC programming language, refer to your library or book store for a complete selection of good, introductory BASIC programming texts.

- Lines 1000 through 1060 contain comments about the PASSWORD.BAS program.
- Line 1070 turns off the function key display on the screen.
- Lines 1070 through 1130 are responsible for shutting off the functions of Ctrl C, Ctrl Break, and Ctrl-Alt-Del. Whenever any of these keys are pressed, BASIC branches to the subroutine at line 1520.
- Lines 1170 through 1190 read in the password stored in the PASSWORD.DAT file on disk. This password is assigned to the variable PASSWORD$.
- Line 1200 turns on BASIC's error trapping. This is used in conjunction with the subroutine at line 1520 (which is called each time Ctrl C, Ctrl Break, or Ctrl-Alt-Del are pressed).
- Lines 1240 through 1280 prepare the program for entering the password.
- Lines 1290 through 1380 do the actual work of comparing characters typed at the keyboard with the characters in the PASSWORD.DAT file. Line 1290 reads one character at a time from the keyboard. Line 1300 is this program's back door. If at anytime the ~ (tilde) character is typed, the program automatically accepts it as the proper password.
- Line 1310 increments the character count in variable I. Line 1320 compares the character entered with the character in the same position of the password. If they don't match, program execution branches to line 1350. If they do match, line 1330 checks to see if all the characters are typed. If variable I, characters entered, matches the length of the password on disk, execution branches to line 1420. Line 1340 continues the input loop if all characters in the password have not been entered.
- Lines 1350 through 1380 are executed if an incorrect character was entered. Line 1350 keeps track of the attempts at entering the password. Line 1360 tests to see if more than 3 attempts have been made. If so, execution branches to line 1480. Otherwise, line 1370 displays a warning message and execution continues at line 1280.
- Lines 1420 through 1440 are executed once the proper password is entered. Line 1430 displays "Welcome!" and line 1440 exits BASIC and returns the user to DOS.
- Lines 1480 through 1510 are executed if the proper password has not been entered after three attempts. Line 1480 clears the screen. Line 1490 positions the cursor in roughly the center of the screen. Line 1500 displays "* * System Locked * *".

And line 1510 contains an *endless loop,* which locks up the computer.

- Lines 1550 through 1610 are executed any time Ctrl C, Ctrl Break, or Ctrl-Alt-Del are pressed. Line 1550 beeps. Line 1560 reads one of the six strings held in the DATA statements in lines 1590 through 1610. Line 1570 prints the rude comment and line 1580 returns from the subroutine.
- Lines 1620 and 1630 are this program's error trapping statements. The only error which can occur after the password is read from disk is if the user presses Ctrl C, Ctrl Break, or Ctrl-Alt-Del and all the rude messages have been displayed. Line 1620 restores the DATA statement pointer to line 1590 (so it rereads the same strings again), and line 1630 resumes program execution at line 1560.

To remove the program's back door, replace line 1300 with:

```
1300    REM
```

OTHER WAYS OF PROTECTING THE HARD DISK

Besides using a password, there are other ways of keeping unauthorized persons from your computer. In addition to a software password,some computers, such as the IBM PC/AT, come with a lock and key. Once the key is turned, the computer is locked and it sits tight until it is unlocked.

Depending on the make of the computer, the key can do a number of things. With most AT's and clones, turning off the key disables the keyboard and prevents the computer from being reset or booted. If you step out of the office for a moment, locking the computer ensures that no one else uses it while you're out. Because the keyboard is turned off, there's nothing they can do. If the computer is off and locked, turning the computer on will not cause it to boot. Your system is secure.

What the key does depends on the make of the computer. Some will boot up and run AUTOEXEC all with a disabled keyboard. Others will simply sit there until the key is turned. Still other AT compatibles use the key as a mere decoration. Internally, the key isn't connected to anything!

With some networked systems, the key might be used to lock your system out of the network. This would prevent other users on the network from accessing your system's hard disk. Again, this depends on the type of computer and networking software available.

A software form of the lock and key is the LOCK.COM program. It has the same effect as putting a giant write-protect tab on the hard disk. Once LOCK.COM is run, no file on the hard disk can be changed, renamed, modified, or deleted. It just won't work.

LOCK.COM is a memory resident program. What it does is to intercept all access to the hard disk. When the LOCK is on, it tests to see if the hard disk is being accessed to change information. If so, it immediately tells the operating system, "The hard disk is write protected." LOCK does allow the hard disk to be accessed to simply read information without any complications.

The best aspect of LOCK is that it will not allow the hard disk to be reformatted. With the LOCK on, a hard disk FORMAT only verifies information on the hard disk; nothing is erased.

To install LOCK, type LOCK at the DOS prompt:

```
C>LOCK
```

Your hard disk is not Write- & Format-protected
Run LOCK again to turn it OFF.

Any attempt to change anything on the hard disk will produce a write protect error. For example, an attempt to rename the file LETTER to LTTR results in:

C>REN LETTER LTTR

Write protect error writing drive C
Abort, Retry, Ignore?

Once LOCK is installed, it can be turned on or off again by typing LOCK at the DOS prompt. For example:

C>LOCK
LOCK is now OFF (no hard disk protection).
Run it again to turn it ON.

Now the disk is back to normal. Any attempt to change or modify a file on the hard disk will not be stopped. To turn lock on again, type:

C>LOCK

and the disk is once again write-protected.

A password protection scheme is a benefit to any computer system, especially in an area where security is important. Passwords can be implemented via a batch file, BASIC program, or other commercial program. However, because DOS offers no direct way to password protect the computer, the methods used are only half best—especially when given the fact any DOS computer can be booted from a DOS disk in drive A.

The public domain program LOCK can be used to secure the hard disk against possible change or reformatting. But this limits the power of the hard disk by making it a read-only device. In the next chapter, additional security measures are discussed. Included are making specified files read-only, hiding files, and data encryption.

Chapter 13

Hidden Files
and Data Encryption

If more than one person uses the computer and a password security system seems limited, or if you're the only one using your computer and you find a password system a bit much, you might look into individually protecting files. This can be done with DOS by changing the attributes by which DOS describes each file. It can also be done by data encryption.

This chapter discusses disk security measures. Some of these are built into DOS. DOS allows certain files to be made invisible; only DOS can see them. DOS can also mark files as read-only, which has the effect of putting a write protect tab on a single file. As a secondary line of defense, data files can be encrypted, or scrambled according to a specific key. Anyone who doesn't know the key would not be able to interpret information in the file.

HOW DOS HIDES FILES

PC-DOS has special ways of describing files on disk. Besides the information displayed by the DIR command, each file has other interesting information associated with it. Part of this information controls whether a file or directory is visible or invisible (hidden from a DIR listing). Anyone who's interested in data security will certainly see how hiding files can be very practical.

Every file in the directory has an attribute byte associated with it. Inside this byte are eight attribute bits which tell DOS a few things about the file. For example, one attribute bit, the modify bit, lets the BACKUP program know if a file has been changed or modified since the last backup. Each time the file is changed, or modified, DOS switches this bit's value to 1.

Altogether, the bits in the attribute byte are:

BIT if on (set to 1) means:
7   Nothing
6   Nothing
5   File has been modified since last backup
4   File is a subdirectory
3   File is a volume label entry
2   File is a System file
1   File is invisible
0   File is Read-Only

With regards to bits 4 and 3, every subdirectory and the volume label (name of the disk) take up space in the directory. They are considered files by MS-DOS even though they aren't used as such. Bit 5 is used during BACKUP and XCOPY operations (as described in Chapter 10). It is referred to as the modify, or archive, bit.

Bits 2, 1 and 0 are commonly used with system files. Bit 2 informs DOS that the file is a system file, either IBMBIO.COM or IBMDOS.COM. Bit 1 hides a file, making it invisible. And bit 0 puts a protective lock on the file, preventing it from any modification or deletion.

There's normally no reason to change any of these attribute bytes. DOS assigns them as needed, or to protect its own system files. However, you can manipulate them to add your own level of file security. This can be done with DOS's ATTRIB command, or the HIDE utility on the Supplemental Programs Diskette.

The ATTRIB Command

The ATTRIB, or attribute, command allows you to modify the attributes of any file on disk. ATTRIB will not modify subdirectories or other system files. However, all files in a particular subdirectory can be modified using wildcards.

The format of the ATTRIB command is:

ATTRIB [+ / − R] [+ / − A] [d:] [path]filename[.ext]

The R and A switches are used to set or reset the read-only and archive (modify) attributes of the filename listed. The filename can contain wildcards, or be a path to a file in another directory. If ATTRIB is used without the R or A switches, it displays the attributes of the file (or files) listed:

C > ATTRIB *.*

displays all files in the current directory and their read-only and archive attributes:

```
        C:\WP\LETTER
R       C:\WP\TEST1
R       C:\WP\TEST2
R    A  C:\WP\XMASCARD.TXT
```

```
A  C:\WP\CHAPT13
A  C:\WP\CHAPT13.BK!
A  C:\WP\KILL
```

Files with an R by them have a read-only status. Any attempt to delete, rename or modify that file results in an error.

Files with an A by them indicate they have been modified since the last backup. In the case of a file with both an R and A listed, it is assumed the file's read-only status was added after the last backup.

To change the attribute of any file, or a group of files, the R or A switch is specified. For example, to protect all files *.WKS with read-only status, use:

C>ATTRIB +R *.WKS

This command adds (+R) the read-only attribute of all files with the extension .WKS in the current directory. Those files can no longer be deleted, renamed, modified or changed. They can, however, be looked at (read only).

If you later discover you need to change or delete a file, switch its read-only status off with:

C>ATTRIB −R NOVEMBER.WKS

This normalizes the file NOVEMBER.WKS, removing its read-only protection. To do this for all files in the current subdirectory, use:

C>ATTRIB −R *.*

The A switch is a bit more unusual than the R switch. The A attribute is turned on only when a file has been modified. Once that file is backed up or XCOPYed, its A status is switched off. (Technically speaking, the bit in the file's attribute byte is set to 1 by BACKUP or XCOPY. When the A attribute is turned on, either by changing the file or by using the ATTRIB command, the bit in the attribute byte is reset to 0. If this sounds backwards, that's because it is.)

The only real advantage of changing the A attribute is when backing up or XCOPYing files. When the /M switch is used with BACKUP or XCOPY, those programs only look for files with the A attribute. Using ATTRIB, you can selectively turn on or off the A attribute and choose which files will be backed up or XCOPYed. Typing:

C>ATTRIB +A *.*

sets the A attribute on each file in the current directory. Now every file will appear to DOS as if it were modified since the last backup. To remove the A attribute, and make it seem as though all files have not been modified since the last backup, use:

C>ATTRIB −A *.*

Hiding Files

DOS is capable of hiding files, preventing them from being displayed in a DIR listing. Presently, there is no easy way of hiding files using DOS. The only way to hide a file is to modify its attribute byte directly by using DEBUG or some other disk utility.

Three programs HIDE, UNHIDE and FINDHIDE, all deal with hiding files and programs on disk. Once a file is hidden, it will not be displayed in a DIR listing, nor will it be changed by any command using *.*. You can still, however, use the file or program simply by typing in its name. The thinking behind hiding files is that others who might be using your system cannot access files and programs they can't see.

To hide a specific program or file, use the HIDE program. The format of HIDE is:

HIDE [d:] [path]filename[.ext]

HIDE renders the filename listed invisible. For example:

C>HIDE PASSWORD.DAT

This command hides the file PASSWORD.DAT. The file will no longer be listed in the directory, nor can it be accessed using a *.* wildcard search. It is invisible. Only by naming the file directly can it be used. For example:

C>TYPE PASSWORD.DAT

still displays the file's text data. Unfortunately, HIDE does not hide subdirectories, nor can it hide a group of files by using wildcards. To do this, it's necessary to use the DOS FOR-DO command as follows:

C>FOR %A IN (*.*) DO HIDE %A

This command searches the current directory for the files in the parenthesis (*.* or all files). Each file found is assigned the temporary variable %A. The HIDE command is then used on that file via the temporary variable A%. The above command has the same effect as HIDE *.*. (See Chapter 7 for more information on DOS's FOR command.)

Once a file is hidden it can become visible again by using the UNHIDE command. The format of UNHIDE is:

UNHIDE [d:] [path]filename[.ext]

Like the HIDE command, this command does not work with wildcards, nor can it UNHIDE any hidden directories. To UNHIDE the file PASSWORD.DAT, use:

C>UNHIDE PASSWORD.DAT

If the file was previously hidden, it will now be visible. If the file was not a hidden file, the UNHIDE utility would inform you so and not change the file in any way.

Because hidden files are invisible to DOS searches, using a FOR-DO loop will not work with UNHIDE as it does with HIDE. Hidden files should be individually named after the UNHIDE command, and only one file at a time can be made visible. To help locate hidden files in a specific directory, the FINDHIDE utility is used.

FINDHIDE works like the DIR command, except all files, even hidden files are listed. It was necessary to include this program simply because there's no easy way using DOS to locate hidden files. The format for FINDHIDE is:

FINDHIDE [d:] [path]filename[.ext]

Unlike HIDE and UNHIDE, this command accepts wildcards in the filename. For example:

C>FINDHIDE *.*

FINDHIDE displays all files in the current directory. Any hidden files are prefixed by an asterisk (*):

				*STIME	.ASM	STIME	.COM
.			..				
*ETIME	.ASM	ETIME	.COM	HIDE	.ASM	HIDE	.COM
*FINDHIDE	.ASM	FINDHIDE	.COM	*UNHIDE	.ASM	UNHIDE	.COM
*ASK	.ASM	ASK	.COM	*GREET	.ASM	GREET	.COM

16 Total File(s)

In the above FINDHIDE listing, all files in the directory which have the .ASM extension are hidden. The DIR command will not display them. To change those files back to a visible state, each file would need to be individually un-hidden with UNHIDE.

Using DEBUG to Hide Files

The HIDE and UNHIDE utilities cannot be used to hide and unhide subdirectories. To do this, you'll need a disk zapping utility, or a program like DOS's DEBUG.

Modifying a directory, especially on a hard disk, is not at all recommended. Instead, to illustrate this method of hiding files you should format a scratch disk in drive A. Copy a few files from your hard disk to the disk in drive A, then make a subdirectory and copy a few files there as well.

From drive C, use the DOS DEBUG program to load the first track from the disk in drive A into memory. Once in memory, the disk's root directory can be located. A file's attribute byte can then be modified, allowing you to make any file in the directory invisible. Finally, using DEBUG, the directory can be written back to disk, making the change permanent.

Enter DEBUG by typing:

C>DEBUG

Debug's L command can be used to load certain sectors from disk into memory. The format is:

226

L memory-address drive-number start-sector length

DOS numbers disk drives starting with 0 for drive A. Also, all numbers entered into DEBUG are assumed to be hexadecimal, or base 16. To load in the first 16 (10 hexadecimal) sectors from the disk in drive A to memory, type:

$$-L100\ 0\ 0\ 10$$

This command reads, "Load into memory location 100 from drive 0 (A) starting at sector 0 through the next 10 (16 decimal) sectors." Once DEBUG's prompt returns, sectors 0 through 10 (0 through 16 decimal) have been loaded into memory. To examine them, the D (display) command is used. To see the first 256 bytes (100 hexadecimal) on disk which are now in memory, type:

$$-D100\ L100$$

The root directory was loaded into memory with the first 16 sectors on disk. It is located at memory address B00 hexadecimal. To see the first few entries, type:

$$-Db00$$

Something like the following is displayed:

```
0B00   54 45 53 54 31 20 20 20-20 20 20 20 00 00 00 00    TEST1      ....
0B10   00 00 00 00 00 00 1B 72-4B 0B 02 00 54 00 00 00    .......rK...T...
0B20   54 45 53 54 32 20 20 20-20 20 20 20 00 00 00 00    TEST2      ....
0B30   00 00 00 00 00 00 33 73-4B 0B 03 00 55 00 00 00    ......3sK...U...
0B40   54 45 53 54 33 20 20 20-20 20 20 20 00 00 00 00    TEST3      ....
0B50   00 00 00 00 00 00 3A 73-4B 0B 04 00 55 00 00 00    ......:sK...U...
0B60   43 52 59 50 54 20 20 20-20 20 20 10 00 00 00 00    CRYPT      .....
0B70   00 00 00 00 00 00 47 5F-4D 0B 05 00 00 00 00 00    ......G_M.......
```

Fig. 13-1. Screen display showing root directory as displayed by the DEBUG command Db00.

All files listed in a DOS directory start with the filename and file extension. Following this is other information, including the date the file was last modified, the size of the file, the file's attribute byte and other important information. These are displayed as dots or miscellaneous characters after the file's name.

The attribute byte of each file is at an offset of 11 bytes from the start of the directory entry. For example, the file TEST1 above has an attribute of 20 hexadecimal. (Count over 12 bytes from the filename TEST1. The first byte, the letter T, is considered offset 0. So 12 bytes over is actually offset 11.)

The attribute byte for the file CRYPT is 10. (The 11th byte offset from the C in CRYPT is 10 hex.) This identifies this file as a subdirectory instead of a normal file. By using DEBUG, we can change this attribute byte to make the entire subdirectory invisible.

Without getting too complex with binary math, recall the chart describing the attribute byte at the beginning of this chapter:

BIT if on (set to 1) means:
7 Nothing
6 Nothing
5 File has been modified since last backup
4 File is a subdirectory
3 File is a volume label entry
2 File is a System file
1 File is invisible
0 File is Read-Only

The file CRYPT has bit 4 set to 1 (which is 10 hexadecimal), so it is identified as a subdirectory. To add invisibility to this file, bit 1 of the attribute byte needs to be set. In binary math, this works as follows:

```
                         BIT 7 6 5 4 3 2 1      hexadecimal
   The file's current attribute: 0 0 0 1 0 0 0           10
   Bit to change for invisibility: 0 0 0 0 0 1 0         + 2
                                                     = = = = = =
   File's new attribute should be:                    12 hex
```

(If you don't understand it, just nod your head so as not to confuse those who might be watching you read this.)

To change the attribute byte from 10 to 12, DEBUG's E command is used. The attribute byte for CRYPT is at memory location B6B. (If you're changing the attribute of a file on your scratch disk, enter another appropriate value in place of B6B.) Type:

– Eb6b
xxxx:0B6B 10.

The xxxx is replaced by a number value which varies from computer to computer, but make sure the number after the colon is 0B6B, or the byte you're modifying (it should end in the letter B). Also, make sure the byte before the period is 10, or the attribute byte of the file you are modifying.

To enter the new value, type 12 and press ENTER. This changes the attribute byte of the file CRYPT to invisible. Display the section of memory again to verify the change was made. Type:

– Db00

Note that the attribute byte for the file CRYPT is now 12 hexadecimal. This means the file is still a directory entry plus it is invisible.

```
0B00   54 45 53 54 31 20 20 20-20 20 20 20 00 00 00 00   TEST1       ....
0B10   00 00 00 00 00 00 1B 72-4B 0B 02 00 54 00 00 00   .......rK...T...
0B20   54 45 53 54 32 20 20 20-20 20 20 20 00 00 00 00   TEST2       ....
0B30   00 00 00 00 00 00 33 73-4B 0B 03 00 55 00 00 00   ......3sK...U...
0B40   54 45 53 54 33 20 20 20-20 20 20 20 00 00 00 00   TEST3       ....
0B50   00 00 00 00 00 00 3A 73-4B 0B 04 00 55 00 00 00   ......:sK...U..
0B60   43 52 59 50 54 20 20 20-20 20 20 12 00 00 00 00   CRYPT       ....
0B70   00 00 00 00 00 00 47 5F-4D 0B 05 00 00 00 00 00   ......G_M......
```

Fig. 13-2. Root directory showing hidden file attribute.

To write this information back to disk, making the change permanent, DEBUG's Write command is used. This command has the same options as the Load command, except a W is used:

$$-W100\ 0\ 0\ 10$$

DEBUG writes from memory starting at location 100 to drive A (0) and places that information in sectors 0 through 10 (all numbers are in hexadecimal). To quit DEBUG, type:

$$-Q$$

Now, pull a directory of drive A. The subdirectory CRYPT (or whichever file you changed) is not listed. You can still access the subdirectory with the CD command, or list the visible files in the subdirectory by typing:

$$C>DIR \setminus CRYPT \setminus *.*$$

Modifying a disk directly with DEBUG could be hazardous. This is why a scratch disk was used as an example. With a hard disk, or floppy diskette with many subdirectories, locating directory information with DEBUG can be incredibly inefficient. To modify directory information on a hard disk's subdirectory, it's strongly recommended you use a disk zapping utility to locate and modify files. But in all cases, be careful when you do this!

A Very Sneaky Way of Hiding Files

DOS allows certain special characters to be used when naming files. Though the DOS manual doesn't specifically state these characters can be used, they are accepted by DOS and serve as an excellent method of file security. It should be noted that because these characters are not specifically mentioned, this procedure may not work with future releases of DOS.

Normally, a file name can contain any ASCII character (letters, numbers, or punctuation symbols) except the following:

$$. \ " \ / \setminus [\ ] : | > < + = ; ,$$

Also, a file cannot contain any control character, ^C, ^A, etc., or a space. This leaves a wide variety of characters available on the keyboard for naming files. Additionally, it allows certain characters not available on the keyboard to be used for naming files. These are the *extended ASCII* characters. (See Appendix C.)

The extended ASCII characters can be typed at any time using the Alt key and your keyboard's numeric keypad. (Some utility programs, e.g. Borland's SuperKey, disable this feature.)

For example, the Extended ASCII character number 219 is a solid block. To type this character press and hold the Alt key and type 219 on the numeric keypad. When you release the Alt key, the solid block appears.

This can be done with regular ASCII characters as well. Try typing the following numbers. For each, press and hold the Alt key and type the number. Release the Alt key after the number is entered:

72, 101, 108, 108, 111, 33, 32, 1

Certain Extended ASCII characters display a variety of characters. However, character 255 is blank. If a file were renamed using this blank character it would appear as a blank in the directory listing. For example, suppose the file TEST1 is on disk. To rename this file as the Extended ASCII character 255 type:

C>REN TEST1 [255]

(Hold Alt and type 2, 5, 5 on the numeric pad for [255].)

TEST1, now [255], appears as follows in a DIR listing:

```
Volume in drive A has no label
Directory of A:\

                   84    2-11-88    2:16p ▐O
TEST2              85    2-11-88    2:25p
TEST3              85    2-11-88    2:25p
        3 File(s)        352256 bytes free
```

Unlike hiding a file, [255] is listed; Its name is blank, but the size and date show up. The other files in this directory could also be changed to blanks. Remember, no two files can share the same name. So TEST2 could be renamed [255] [255], TEST3 could be renamed [255] [255] [255]. Up to 11 files can be named in a single directory using the [255] (blank) character.

As long as no one else using your computer knows about the Extended ASCII names for files, other bizarre names can be created. Try renaming a file as 224, 225, 226. The new filename appears in the directory as alpha, beta, gamma, the first three letters of the Greek alphabet.

Along the same lines, it might be a good idea not to obviously name certain files on disk. For example, PAYROLL.WKS is one file any curious office employee might want to take a peek at. Renaming the file SAMPLE.WKS, or even MEMO.DOC, might be enough to keep potentially prying eyes away.

File Transfer Using Hidden Files

If hiding files and subdirectories is part of your file security system (along with or in addition to passwords), there needs to be a way of exchanging files between users who aren't aware of other user's hidden directories. Consider the CompuCard company. Both Jack and Linda have their own subdirectories under \LOTUS. Suppose both directories are invisible, or named using the blank character (see above). Further suppose that within each directory certain files are invisible. If Linda wanted Jack to examine a file she would have to either remove protection on the file or let Jack know what the protection scheme was.

Instead of jeopardizing security measures, a compromise can be reached in the form of a *public* directory. This would be a common place to which all users had access. If Linda wanted Jack to look at a file, she would simply copy it to the public directory. For example:

C>COPY SECRET \ADMIN\LOTUS\PUBLIC\FORJACK

This copies the file SECRET to the \PUBLIC directory and names the new file FORJACK. (SECRET might be a secret, or other hidden file.)

Another advantage to a PUBLIC directory would be to send messages to other users of the system. Large computers with several users have complete Mailing systems, complete with mailboxes for each individual user. A mail/message system can be set up under DOS using simple batch file commands.

The following batch file could be used to send a message to another user. It uses EDLIN to type and enter the message, so make sure EDLIN is on the path. Create this batch file using either EDLIN or the COPY command and name it SENDMAIL.BAT:

```
ECHO OFF
IF NUL%1 = = NUL GOTO CANCEL
EDLIN TEMPMAIL.@
ECHO = = = = Next Message = = = =  > >  \PUBLIC\%1
TYPE TEMPMAIL.@  > >  \PUBLIC\%1
DEL TEMPMAIL.@
ECHO Message sent
GOTO END
:CANCEL
ECHO No Mail message sent!
:END
```

To use this batch file, type SENDMAIL at the DOS prompt, followed by the name of the person you're sending to. For example, to send a message to Sue:

C>SENDMAIL SUE

The batch file then runs EDLIN and you can type and enter your message. As with the PASSWORD.BAT program in the last chapter, if nothing is typed after SENDMAIL, the program displays:

C>SENDMAIL
No Mail message sent!

This is done with the IF NUL%1 = = NUL test in line 2. If a name is entered, the batch file program runs EDLIN to edit a file called TEMPMAIL.@

Once editing is done, the line " = = = = Next Message = = = = " is appended to the person's mail file in the \PUBLIC directory. Next the TEMPMAIL.@ file is appended to the person's mail file. Finally, TEMPMAIL.@ is deleted and "Message Sent" is displayed.

SENDMAIL.BAT makes use of the double redirection symbol, > >. This way, if a mail file does not exist DOS creates it. And if the file does exist, the new message is appended.

The following batch file is used to read mail. It should be part of a password or similar batch file which can identify the user so no one reads anyone else's mail. Again it uses the %1 replaceable parameter as the person's name. Use either EDLIN or the COPY command to create this batch file as READMAIL.BAT:

```
ECHO OFF
IF NUL%1 = = NUL GOTO CANCEL
IF NOT EXIST \PUBLIC\%1 GOTO NONE
TYPE \PUBLIC\%1 ¦ MORE
DEL \PUBLIC\%1
GOTO END
:CANCEL
ECHO Enter a name after the READMAIL command
:NONE
ECHO No mail waiting
:END
```

To use this batch file, type READMAIL followed by your name. For example, if Sue wanted to read her mail, she'd type:

C>READMAIL SUE

The batch file first checks to see if any mail is waiting. If so, the mail file is TYPEd to the screen. The MORE filter is used to display the messages a screen at a time. As with SENDMAIL.BAT and PASSWORD.BAT, if nothing is typed after SENDMAIL, the program displays:

C>READMAIL
Enter a name after the READMAIL command!
No mail waiting

The test is done with the NUL%1 = = %1 in line 2. After this text, the batch file checks to see if the person has mail waiting. If a file with their name exists, then they have mail. Otherwise, the IF NOT EXIST text passes, the batch file branches to the :NONE label and "No mail waiting" is displayed.

If mail does exist, it's displayed using the TYPE command. The TYPE command's output is run through the MORE filter to display the messages one page at a time. Once the mail file is read, it's deleted.

WHAT IS DATA ENCRYPTION?

Data encryption is the systematic scrambling of information in a file, making that information unreadable. Because the information is scrambled systematically, or according to a specific pattern, it can be unscrambled and returned back to its original form. Scrambling information in this manner is often referred to as encryption. Unscrambling is referred to as decryption.

Encrypting a file typically involves the use of a key, or password. This key works like the secret decoder rings of old. These decoder rings had two moveable circles on them, one inside the other. On both circles were the alphabet. If the decoding pattern were A-P, the inner circle was turned so that its A matched the P on the outer circle. The relationship between the characters on both circles looked something like the following:

ABCDEFGHIJKLMNOPQRSTUVWXYZ
PQRSTUVWXYZABCDEFGHIJKLMNO

Kids could then use this relationship to translate strings such as:

TPI BPAID BTPA!

Into:

EAT MALTO MEAL!

Encrypting a computer file on disk works surprisingly similar to this. (Who'd have ever thought!) Every character of the file is translated using a special key. The key is also used to decrypt the file back to its original state.

Very simple data encryption routines operate like a secret decoder ring. Every character in the file is added or subtracted from a certain key value. However, these schemes usually prove too simple for most practical encryptions. (After all, knowing any kid with a secret decoder ring was capable of reading your encrypted files would prove distressing.) Because of this, more advanced methods of encrypting computer data are used.

Data Encryption Using BASIC

One such method works like the decoder ring, except the decoding key is not a single character but a string of up to 255 characters. This method is used in the file CRYPT.BAS (a BASIC language file). Encrypting files works by adding the key string of characters in sequence to each character in the file.

For example, suppose the key string is TESTING. The file to encrypt contains the following:

now is the time for all good men.

The CRYPT.BAS program works by adding the key string TESTING to each character in the file as follows:

TESTINGTESTINGTESTINGTESTINGTESTI
now is the time for all good men.

The result is a bunch of strange characters—not easy to read, nor understand. In fact, unless you know the exact string of characters and their length, decrypting the file would take quite a while. (Keep in mind, this is still an elementary form of data encryption and is not foolproof.)

To decrypt the file, the same key string of characters is subtracted from each character in the file. Only the exact key string of characters can properly decrypt the file. So, by adding the key string to the string of strange characters, the result is:

now it the time for all good men.

This method of encryption works on data and program files, as well as straight text, or ASCII, files. Just don't forget the key string!

The following program demonstrates the encryption routines discussed above. It is written in the BASIC programming language. You can type it in yourself using the BASIC program which came with DOS.

To enter BASIC, type:

C>BASIC

Carefully type in the following program, including the line numbers. Double check your work to make certain you don't mistype anything (if you do, use the BACKSPACE key to erase):

```
100 KEY OFF
110 COLOR 7,0
120 WIDTH 80
130 SCREEN 0,0,0
140 CLS
150 PRINT "A Simple File Encryption Program in BASIC"
160 PRINT "Written by Dan Gookin, Copyright (c) TAB Books"
170 PRINT
180 PRINT "Will you be <D>ecryting or <E>ncrypting? (D or E): ";
190 B$ = INPUT$ (1)
200 B$ = CHR$(ASC(B$) AND 95)
210 IF B$> <"E" AND B$> <"D" GOTO 190
230 PRINT B$
```

```
240 PRINT
250 LINE INPUT "Enter the INPUT file: ";FILEIN$
260 LINE INPUT "Enter the OUTPUT file: ";FILEOUT$
270 PRINT
280 LINE INPUT "Enter the keyword pattern: ";KEYWORD$
290 KEY.LEN = LEN (KEYWORD$)
300 IF KEY.LEN = 0 THEN 280
320 REM ************************
330 REM Encryption/Decryption routines
340 REM ************************
350 OPEN FILEIN$ FOR INPUT AS 1
360 OPEN FILEOUT$ FOR OUTPUT AS 2
370 FOR X=1 TO KEY.LEN
380     IF EOF(1) THEN 460
390     D$ = MID$(KEYWORD$,X,1)
400     A$=INPUT$(1,1)
410        ON INSTR("DE",B$) GOSUB 480,510
420     PRINT#2,C$;
430     PRINT C$;
440 NEXT X
450 GOTO 370
460 CLOSE
470 END
475 REM **************************
480 REM Decrypt it:
490 C$ = CHR$( (ASC(A$) – ASC(D$) ) MOD 255)
500 RETURN
510 REM Encrypt it:
520 C$ = CHR$( (ASC(A$) + ASC(D$) ) MOD 255)
530 RETURN
```

To save the Crypt file, type:

SAVE "CRYPT"

To run this BASIC program, type RUN, or from DOS type:

C>BASICA CRYPT

The Crypt program displays the following:

A Simple File Encryption Program in BASIC
Written by Dan Gookin, Copyright (c) TAB Books

Will you be <D>ecrypting or <E>ncrypting? (D or E):

Press D or E to decrypt or encrypt a file, respectively. Next the program asks:

Enter the INPUT file:

If you're encrypting, enter the name of the file you'll be encrypting. If decrypting, enter the name of the already encrypted file which you'll be decrypting.

Enter the OUTPUT file:

If you're encrypting a file, type the name of a new file on disk, one which will contain the encrypted data. If decrypting, enter the name of the file which will contain the decrypted output. In both cases, the OUTPUT file should be a new file on disk.

Next, you're asked to enter the key string:

Enter the keyword pattern:

Type up to 255 letters, characters or symbols. Press ENTER when done. Remember this string! It's the key by which information will be encrypted. Once this is done, the Crypt program reads information from the INPUT file and, depending on whether you selected D or E, it decrypts or encrypts that file's information and saves it to the OUTPUT file.

This simple, yet elegant, method for encrypting files is good as a general purpose security method for protecting your files. It can work on data, text and program files. Keep in mind that the CRYPT.BAS program and its methods of encrypting your data is not foolproof. Also, remember the key string! The authors and publisher take no responsibility for any information lost due to your forgetting your key string.

Description of CRYPT.BAS

The following explanation of the CRYPT.BAS program is provided for those interested in BASIC programming. It is not required reading, nor necessary to understand if you intend on using the Crypt program to protect your files. If you are further interested in the BASIC programming language, refer to your library or book store for a complete selection of good, introductory BASIC programming texts.

- Lines 100 through 170 set up the computer screen and display the title of the program. Lines 100 through 140 establish that the screen's function key display is off, the colors used are black and white, the computer is in the 80 column mode, the screen pages are all set to 0, and that the display is clear.

- Lines 180 through 240 determine whether the program is decrypting or encrypting. Line 180 displays the prompting message. Line 190 reads one character from the keyboard. Line 200 makes that character uppercase using a logical AND instruction. In line 210, the character entered is compared against E and D. If the input does not match E and D, execution branches back to the input statement in line 190. If the input does match, that letter is displayed.

236

- Lines 250 and 260 get the input and output file names and assign them to variables FILEIN$ and FILEOUT$.

- Line 280 gets the encryption keyword pattern and assigns it to the variable KEYWORD$. Line 290 assigns the variable KEY.LEN to the length of the encryption keyword string.

- The actual decryption/encryption is done in the FOR-NEXT loop between lines 370 and 450. First, each file is opened in lines 350 and 360. Then, the program incrementally reads a character from the key word (line 390) and from the file (line 400). Line 410 branches to the appropriate encrypting or decrypting routine depending on whether D or E was entered. Line 420 prints the resulting encrypted or decrypted character to the output file and line 430 prints the character to the screen.

- Line 440 completes the loop. Line 450 continues the program until the end of the input file is detected by line 380. Once the last character is read from the input file, the IF-THEN test in line 380 branches program execution to line 460 where the files are closed and the program ends.

- The actual crypting routines are in lines 480 through 530. The equation is the same for both, except for decryption addition ($+$) is used and for encrypting, subtraction ($-$) is used. The MOD 255 function keeps the resulting character within the values of a character to prevent BASIC from producing an error.

Commercially Available Data Encryption Programs

Most commercially available data encryption programs use schemes much more complex than discussed so far. The most popular and foolproof encryption scheme is referred to as the Data Encryption Standard, or DES, which is defined by the National Bureau of Standards. This encryption scheme is so powerful that the United States Government prohibits the export of programs which use it—even to friendly countries!

SuperKey

Borland's SuperKey memory resident keyboard macro program has two forms of encryption available. Both can use either the DES standard or a special encryption scheme developed by Borland. The two forms of encryption are non-text mode and text mode.

The non-text mode takes the information in a file and scrambles it according to a keyword. The keyword can be any combination of up to 30 characters, upper and lower case are considered the same. The resulting scrambled file is the same length and has the same name as the original. As with all encryption, only those knowing the keyword can unscramble the file. Borland makes a special note about attempting to unscramble the file with the improper keyword.

The nice part about the non-text mode is that it won't waste any disk space. Also, because the original file is overwritten by the encrypted file, there's no chance of someone stumbling across it and reading its contents.

When the text mode is used it places the encrypted information into a second file composed of only upper case letters of the alphabet. The original file is unchanged. Because the second, encrypted file only contains letters of the alphabet it's ideal for use when transmitting files via modem. Because of this translation, the encrypted file will be much larger than the original. Text (ASCII), data and program files can all be encrypted in the text mode.

Each file encrypted in the text mode has a special header and footer. Sandwiched between them is the actual encrypted file. For example:

```
***SUPERKEY TEXT-ENCRYPTION START***HFACNAOA
JHLHOEJLGEBHNGGBBCKIKIACPAHPJOFEEFCLNKMNMINKBFKBHKHEBFAG-
NOHMONMD
HNMEENFMMEHKHPLGHLHBKPNLJFIEOPHGAGEEIBKIAGCHHIKOMCDHOEG-
GMFMFODML
KJLGNFDPPHANIMHFJKFALGKCDKPKHPFNIINBPPM
KDPDPDEDAICHJHICJBHJHBOLGLIAMLGGDDKJKBL
***SUPERKEY TEXT-ENCRYPTION END***
```

The drawback to the text mode is that it leaves the original file unprotected on disk. If you're not sending the file to another computer, the non-text mode is the best choice for file security.

SuperKey can also use wildcards. This makes it possible, for example, to encrypt all the *.COM and *.EXE files in your \DOS subdirectory. This could be done in the AUTOEXEC.BAT file before a system password is entered, or by the SHUTDOWN.BAT file at the end of the day. Unless someone knew the proper password, your system would be useless.

This chapter covered two types of disk security measures. One is provided using the invisible attribute of files and directories on disk, as well as naming files using the special blank character. The second method involved scrambling, or encrypting, information inside files so that only those who know the proper key can unscramble the information. Both measures are reliable and proven methods of adding security to your hard disk.

Chapter 14

Tracking Computer Usage

Keeping track of things is one area computers are very good at. These things can range from the typical recipe file to the national debt. Though most computer users know this, it's amazing how many still rely on pencil and paper when it comes down to keeping track of simple things. For example, keeping track of your time on the computer.

There are a number of reasons to log computer usage. For example, if you're billing a client by the hour and need some form of record keeping a bit more convenient than writing the times down (computers are useful for these things after all). Or if a number of people from different departments are using the same machine, having the computer keep track of its usage is reliable and efficient—especially since it can be done automatically.

In this chapter methods of logging computer usage are covered. Though there really isn't a built in time manager for IBM Computers it is possible to keep track of computer usage by using batch files and by taking advantage of DOS's redirection commands, > and <.

A BATCH FILE PROGRAM FOR TRACKING USAGE

Because IBM computers have internal clocks, keeping track of computer time is as easy as looking at the computer's clock—trusting the clock is set properly every day or that the computer has a battery powered clock. To create a usage log, the current time from the computer's clock needs to be written, or redirected to, a disk file.

The best way to keep track of the time you use your computer would be by redirecting the clock's output into a file. For example, a file called LOG could be placed into a special \ USER directory. Recalling from Chapter 3, output is redirected from the screen (the standard output device) to a file by using the > symbol. To redirect the time to the LOG file, the > command is used. This sends all output to the LOG file instead of the screen.

To totally benefit from sending the time to a file, the double redirection symbols, > >, should be used. This way, the time is always appended to the LOG file. The only problem then is how to get the time out of the computer and into the file. DOS has no built-in display time functions. The time is only seen in a directory listing when a new file is created, or as part of the prompt when the TIME command is issued.

Three utility programs which display only the current time were written to assist in creating a usage log. They are STIME.COM, ETIME.COM, and TSTAMP.COM. The first two do roughly the same thing, display the current day, date and time. The only difference is STIME displays Start Time and ETIME displays End Time. TSTAMP.COM simply displays the time and date without the leading text.

Typing STIME at the command prompt displays something like the following (depending on the date and time):

Start Time = Thursday, February 18th, 1988 @ 11:14 am

ETIME displays:

End Time = Thursday, February 18th, 1988 @ 11:15 am

The program TSTAMP.COM is a little more simplistic. Typing TSTAMP at the command prompt displays the current time and date as follows:

11:16:32 02/18/88

All three of these programs read the computer's internal clock and display the current time to the screen. By themselves these programs are relatively pointless. Yet by redirecting their output to a LOG file, it's possible to track the time you use on your computer system.

C>TSTAMP > > \ USER \ LOG

This command redirects the output of the TSTAMP command, the current time and date, to the \ USER \ LOG file. If \ USER \ LOG does not exist, DOS creates it. If it does exists, the current time and date are appended to the file. Now the current time is stored in \ USER \ LOG. To view it, use the TYPE command:

C>TYPE \ USER \ LOG

Something like the following might be displayed:

12:16:07 02/18/88

If TSTAMP > > \ USER \ LOG is entered at the command prompt again, the current time is again appended to the end of the LOG file. Typing the \USER\LOG file a second time displays:

12:16:07 02/18/88
12:16:44 02/18/88

Of course, a file full of dates and times won't mean much unless you know what the times represent. This is why STIME and ETIME were written. Consider this batch file:

```
CD \ADMIN\WP\WS
ECHO Word processing . . . > > \USER>LOG
STIME > > \USER\LOG
WS
ETIME > > \USER\LOG
CD \
```

This batch file first changes to the word processing subdirectory, \ADMIN\WP\WS. The ECHO command is then used to append "Word processing .." to the \USER\LOG file. After that, the current time is appended to \USER\LOG by the STIME > > command. And finally, the word processing program WS is run.

Once the word processing is done, control returns to the batch file and the current time is appended to the \USER\LOG file via > > and the ETIME command. The \USER\LOG file now contains something akin to the following:

Word processing . . .
Start Time = Thursday, February 18th, 1988 @ 1:14 pm
 End Time = Thursday, February 18th, 1988 @ 2:45 pm

If a unique batch file were written for each of your programs, at the end of the day, the LOG file might contain something like this:

Word processing . . .
Start Time = Thursday, February 18th, 1988 @ 1:14 pm
 End Time = Thursday, February 18th, 1988 @ 2:45 pm
Updating Customer File . . .
Start Time = Thursday, February 18th, 1988 @ 2:51 pm
 End Time = Thursday, February 18th, 1988 @ 3:02 pm
Telecom to Seattle Branch . . .
Start Time = Thursday, February 18th, 1988 @ 3:05 pm
 End Time = Thursday, February 18th, 1988 @ 4:16 pm
Backing up files for today:
Start Time = Thursday, February 18th, 1988 @ 4:30 pm
 End Time = Thursday, February 18th, 1988 @ 4:52 pm
System Shutdown:
17:02:26 02/18/88

The TSTAMP program was used at the end of the day to log when the system was shut down. The last program run each day might be a SHUTDOWN batch file (see Chapter 10), in which case it's a good idea to save the shutdown time in the batch file. Also, if a BACKUP were performed, it should be logged to the/USER/LOG file. A couple of the last few lines of the SHUTDOWN.BAT file could be:

```
BACKUP C:\ADMIN\WP A: /S/M
ECHO "Backup completed" > > \USER\LOG
ECHO "System Shutdown:" > > \USER\LOG
TSTAMP >  \USER\LOG
```

The only disadvantage to indicating only the start and end time for each job is it still takes a bit of brainwork to figure out how much time was spent on each project. The \USER\LOG file helps to show when you started and then stopped work on each project, but does not show totals. This might not be that big of a problem seeing that most time cards show only a start and stop time. However, keep in mind this is a computer and it's capable of next to anything.

Commercially Available Programs

One commercially available which is capable of keeping track of computer usage is included with the Norton Utilities series of programs. Besides displaying the current time, Norton's TM program also keeps track of elapsed time—just like a stopwatch. By specifying certain parameters, TM can give you the exact number of minutes and seconds elapsed since you've started a particular job. Up to four of these stopwatches can be used to keep track of up to four different elapsed times.

TM is not a memory-resident program. However, it uses a secret portion of low memory at address 4FO hexadecimal called the Intra-application Communications Area, or ICA. There it stuffs the starting times for each of its four stopwatch functions. When you access TM to display the elapsed time, it looks at memory location 4FO for the start time, the displays the elapsed time.

The format of the TM command is:

TM [start|stop|comment] [/*cn*] [/1] [/log] [/n]

All parameters are optional with TM. When no parameters are specified, the current time is displayed, right justified on the screen:

11:08 am, Friday, February 26, 1988

The optional /L switch is specified to left justify the output:

11:10 am, Friday, February 26, 1988

When START is specified, a special stopwatch starts ticking away seconds. The /C switch is used to select one of four stopwatches:

C>TM START \C2

starts stopwatch number 2. If no /C number is specified, stopwatch number 1 one is used. To see the elapsed time, type TM STOP. The current date and time are displayed, followed by the elapsed time since TM START was entered:

C>TM STOP

11:12 am, Friday, February 27, 1987
15 seconds

If the TM START command is used again, the stopwatch starts all over. Specifying the /Cn with STOP displays the elapsed time for that particular stopwatch.

The COMMENT option displays a one word comment before the time string. COMMENT can only be a single word. Any extra words on the same line after COMMENT are ignored:

C>TM /L STARTING

displays:

STARTING 11:10 am, Friday, February 26, 1988

The /N switch suppresses the listing of the current date and time. TM STOP /N only displays the elapsed time since the last TM START command was issued:

TM STOP /N

33 minutes, 15 seconds

The /LOG switch is used to add a carriage return/line feed combination to the end of TM's output. As with the utilities STIME, ETIME, and TSTAMP, TM's output can be redirected to a log file. If this is the case, the /LOG switch should be specified to prevent TM's output to the log file from appearing all on one line.

TM STOP /L/LOG > \USER\LOG

Appends something similar to the following to the LOG file:

11:59 am, Friday, February 27, 1987
38 minutes, 9 seconds

By using combinations of TM's switches, it would be possible to add elapsed time comments to your /USER/LOG file. And because multiple stopwatches can be used, one timer for each user of the computer can be maintained. Consider the following additions to an earlier batch file:

CD \ADMIN\WP\WS
ECHO Word processing . . . > > \USER\LOG
STIME > > \USER\LOG

243

```
TM START /C1
WS
ETIME > > \USER\LOG
TM STOP /C1/N/L/LOG > > \USER\LOG
ECHO "—" > > \USER\LOG
CD \
```

TM START /C1 starts stopwatch one. When the job is done, the TM STOP /C1/N/L/LOG produces a left-justified string displaying only the elapsed time for stopwatch one. This string is then appended to the \USER\LOG file. (ECHO "—" has been added to clean up the \USER\LOG file a bit.) At the end of the day, the \USER\LOG file will probably look like this:

```
Word processing . . .
Start Time = Thursday, February 18th, 1988 @ 1:14 pm
  End Time = Thursday, February 18th, 1988 @ 2:45 pm
1 hour, 31 minutes, 5 seconds
—

Updating Customer File . . .
Start Time = Thursday, February 18th, 1988 @ 2:51 pm
  End Time = Thursday, February 18th, 1988 @ 3:02 pm
1 hour, 11 minutes, 52 seconds
—

Telecom to Seattle Branch . . .
Start Time = Thursday, February 18th, 1988 @ 3:05 pm
  End Time = Thursday, February 18th, 1988 @ 4:16 pm
1 hour, 11 minutes, 6 seconds
—

Backing up files for today:
Start Time = Thursday, February 18th, 1988 @ 4:30 pm
  End Time = Thursday, February 18th, 1988 @ 4:52 pm
22 minutes, 16 seconds
—

System Shutdown:
17:02:26 02/18/88
```

A special time could be set at the start of each day to keep track of the total time the system was on. For example, suppose stopwatch 3 were used for this purpose. The elapsed time could then be appended to the \USER\LOG file as part of the SHUTDOWN batch file program:

```
BACKUP C:\ADMIN\WP A: /S/M
ECHO "Backup completed" > > \USER\LOG
ECHO "System Shutdown:" > > \USER\LOG
TSTAMP > > \USER\LOG
ECHO "Total up-time today:" > > \USER\LOG
TM STOP /C3/N/L/LOG > > \USER\LOG
```

This works, assuming the following TM command exists in the AUTOEXEC file:

TM START /C3

Now the total time the system was on (up-time) can be tracked. This may come in extremely handy for maintenance records or repair work where the average amount of time you use your computer daily is important.

Keeping track of, or to sound more computer-ish, logging your time is something IBM computers are capable of after a fashion. Though DOS doesn't provide any direct means for logging the time, or for even easily retrieving the system time, there are numerous utility programs for that purpose. By combining these programs within a batch file and using redirected output, a simple time tracking system can be developed.

Part 3
Hard Disk Optimization

Chapter 15

Storage Optimization

The methods and procedures discussed so far will give you a firm grip on controlling your hard disk. You should be fairly proficient in operating, maintaining and organizing the hard disk by now. Yet, there are still many interesting things going on behind the scenes which are crucial to hard disk performance. Some of these are governed by DOS, others are controlled at the lowest hardware level of the hard disk. By tweaking these individual hardware and software controls, you can get the absolute most from your system.

There are dozens of special tricks for speeding operations on a hard disk, as well as methods for increasing hard disk storage. Surprisingly enough, many of these techniques are deceptively simple. Yet the results are astounding. By using all or a combination of these optimization strategies, you could improve your hard disk's performance by as much as 300 percent!

Storage optimization, or getting the most from your hard disk, is covered in this chapter. There are many techniques for squeezing more performance from a hard disk. Some are software solutions, such as squeezing and sorting a directory or entire disk drive, or storing files in a special, space-saving format. Other solutions are hardware which involve special disk formatting procedures. Not all of them are things you can do "with a screwdriver in your own spare time." In fact, because most of them mess with the actual structure of the hard disk, it's a good idea to have a current backup made just in case. However, once their job is done, you'll immediately notice the increased power, speed, and performance of your hard disk.

REVIEW OF DISK FORMATS AND RANDOM STORAGE

When DOS formats a disk, it lays down a series of concentric circles on which you store your files and programs. These circles are actually the magnetic tracks and sectors which make up the disk format. (Formatting is discussed in detail in Chapter 2.) The number of tracks and sectors are determined by the version of DOS you use, and the size of your disk drives.

Each disk contains a root directory and two FAT tables. If the disk is a boot disk, it also contains a boot record with various wake up information on it. System disks contain the DOS programs IBMDOS.COM and IBMBIO.COM (or for MS-DOS, MSDOS.SYS and IO.SYS) and the program COMMAND.COM.

The following DOS diskette formats are available from DOS versions 1.0 through 3.2. Hard disks vary, depending on the size of the drive.

The first six formats each use forty tracks on a diskette. When a diskette is double sided, it really has eighty tracks—forty to a side. Because the location of the tracks is one above the other, they are often referred to as cylinders. (The tracks occupy a cylinder in space.) A single sided disk contains forty tracks and forty cylinders. A double sided disk contains eighty tracks and forty cylinders.

The last two formats are for the IBM PC/AT's high density disk drive and the laptop PC convertible respectively. These two formats have eighty cylinders. (That's eighty tracks on each side of the disk, or 160 total tracks.) The formatting command FORMAT /4 is used to format a 360K disk in the AT's 1200K, or 1.2 megabyte, disk drive.

For hard disks, the size varies. There can be any number of physical disks inside a hard disk drive. For example, most 20 megabyte hard disk drives contain two physical disks. Each disk stores five megabytes on a side, and for each side there is a read/write head. This makes four surfaces for storing information 5 megabytes each, or 20 megs. (With all those surfaces and tracks you can see why the cylinder notation comes in handy.) Each track on each surface holds, on the average, 17 sectors. The number of tracks and surfaces varies depending on the drive. The 10 meg hard disks have about 310 cylinders (1,240 tracks, 21,080 sectors); 20 meg hard disks have about 620 cylinders (2,480 tracks, 42,160 sectors).

After the disk is formatted, programs are placed on the tracks in sequential order, filling the disk from the outside in. As the disk's manager, DOS's job is to fill the disk as efficiently as possible. DOS squeezes as much information as it can on the disk. When it can find no more room for programs, DOS reports the infamous "Disk is full" message.

Formatting command	Size	Comments	DOS
FORMAT /1/8	160K	1 side, 8 sector	1.0
FORMAT /8	320K	2 side, 8 sector	1.0
FORMAT /1/9	180K	1 side, 9 sector	1.1
FORMAT	360K	2 side, 9 sector	1.1
FORMAT /4 (AT drives)	360K	2 side, 9 sector	3.0
FORMAT (AT drives)	1200K	2 side, 15 sector	3.0
FORMAT	720K	2 side, 9 sector	3.2

Fig. 15-1. Disk formats for DOS 1.0 through 3.2.

Clusters and File Allocation

DOS allocates space for programs in chunks called clusters. The size of the cluster depends on the size of the disk. For 360K diskettes, the cluster size is 2 sectors or 1,024 bytes. This means DOS allocates 2 sectors (for 1K) each time you add a file to disk. Even if the file is less than 1,024 bytes in length, DOS allocates the full 1,024. This number is not reflected by the DIR command. DIR reports the actual, physical size of the program. However, the total bytes free at the end of the DIR command, shows the total space left on the disk has decreased by the size of one cluster.

If a program or file's size falls between a cluster size, the larger cluster size is allocated. A 20 megabyte hard disk formatted under DOS 3.1 allocates 8,192 bytes for each cluster. This means even a 27 byte batch file takes up 8K on the hard disk. IBM fixed this inefficient use of space by changing the cluster size down to a reasonable 2,048 bytes under DOS 3.2.

When a program is erased, the tracks and sectors it used (its clusters) become available. They don't actually get erased, like erasing a line with a pencil. Instead, DOS alters the file's directory entry and marks the tracks and sectors as open in the disk's FAT (File Allocation Table). The tracks still contain the program, only the directory and the FAT show the space as empty. This is the secret behind file recovery programs. Because the physical file is still on disk, these programs can look at the directory entry, examine the tracks and sectors, then repair the FAT table and directory to restore the file.

The file recovery programs are not fool proof. Because DOS is so efficient with the way it manages space on a disk, it will try to use the available tracks when you save or copy new files. Remember, the tracks are shown as free in the FAT table. When a new file actually overwrites the erased file's data on disk, file recovery is impossible. For this reason, you should be very careful when deleting files and even more careful (and prompt) when recovering them. (File recovery is discussed in detail later in this chapter.)

To make all this seem a bit clearer, consider a disk to be like a parking lot, for example, the parking lot at Disneyland. A formatted disk is like an empty parking lot. The yellow lines on the pavement marking the stalls are like tracks on a disk. The attendants who direct traffic are like DOS. As cars filter into the parking lot, the attendants direct them to the first available empty space. The cars fill up the parking spaces in sequence. When a caravan of six cars arrives, they all park side by side.

As people leave the parking lot, the space occupied by their cars is made available. New cars arriving fill up the empty spaces starting with the most convenient ones. If a caravan of six cars arrived now, they would fill in the empty spaces as best they could. This might mean that all six would not be next to one another.

DOS places programs on disk in the same manner. When a program cannot fit sequentially (all the pieces next to each other on disk, just like the caravan of cars), DOS splits it up according to the available space. DOS further keeps track of all the pieces so that the program can be properly accessed or loaded into memory. When a file is split up like this, it's said to be *fragmented*.

Disk Fragmentation

During the course of using your hard disk, you'll happen across a lot of fragmentation. Because the hard disk can store so many files, and because maintaining, deleting, updating, and creating new files is a big part of using DOS, after a good year of use your hard disk will suffer from fragmentation.

Fragmentation is the official word for what happens when a file does not sit on disk contiguously. For example, suppose that caravan of six cars which arrived late at Disneyland is a file. Three of the cars are parked in sequence close to the front gate. The remaining three had to park elsewhere. One of the cars found a spot a few rows over, and the last two cars found two side-by-side empty spaces further away. If the cars were a single file on disk, DOS would keep track of their locations in the directory and FAT table. When you want to load the file into memory, DOS would pick up the separate pieces and assemble them in sequence in memory.

To see which files are fragmented in a given directory, use the CHKDSK command. As one of its many features, CHKDSK displays fragmented files matching the filename specified after CHKDSK. The fragmented filenames are displayed as well as the number of non-contiguous chains (pieces) of the file.

C>CHKDSK *.*

This command displays all fragmented files in the current directory. If none are found, CHKDSK informs you "All files are contiguous." Otherwise, you might see something like the following:

> C:\WP\BOOK\CHAPT12
>   Contains 2 non-contiguous blocks.
> C:\WP\BOOK\CHAPT2
>   Contains 2 non-contiguous blocks.
> C:\WP\BOOK\CHAPT8
>   Contains 4 non-contiguous blocks.
> C:\WP\BOOK\CHAPT10
>   Contains 2 non-contiguous blocks.
> C:\WP\BOOK\INTRO
>   Contains 2 non-contiguous blocks.

All these files are fragmented. Some are split up into two, one (CHAPT8) is split into four separate pieces. Keep in mind, all these pieces are assembled into proper order by DOS as they are loaded into memory. Although CHKDSK does point out which files are non-contiguous, it does little to remedy the situation. (The DOS manual recommends you COPY the files to another disk, then copy them back. However, this does not guarantee they will become contiguous and will generally result in poorer performance from the hard disk.)

Files become fragmented as you use your hard disk. Naturally, as you first put files on the disk they will be in a nice, sequential order. But as you work on your file management, as you organize the disk, add and delete files, fragmentation will creep in. After a while, the disk may become seriously fragmented, with pieces of files scattered throughout the disk. Even directories might end up fragmented. Have you ever pulled a directory of a large subdirectory and noticed the last few files take forever to appear? Each file appears slowly at the end of the DIR listing, following a lot of disk activity.

That's fragmentation in action.

Disks which become severely fragmented lose performance. Obviously, it will take DOS longer to pick up and assemble the pieces of a fragmented file than it would for DOS to pick up an unfragmented file. To repair the disk, each file needs to be unfragmented. All the individual, fragmented pieces need to be picked up and reassembled into a nice, sequential order, like reassembling a jigsaw puzzle. Every file on disk is scanned. If the file is fragmented, its pieces are picked up and put back into sequential order.

PACKDISK

Since hard drives have dropped in price, and it's been a few years since folks first started using them, file fragmentation is now a problem most people have to deal with. Coincidentally, the number of file unfragmenting utilities are at an all-time high.

As with most hard disk optimization tricks, unfragmenting files is something DOS doesn't do. To iron the wrinkles out of a hard disk's file structure you need a special utility. One of those utilities is a shareware program called PACKDISK.

PACKDISK contains several interesting hard disk utilities. Two of them, LISTFRAG and PACKDISK deal directly with fragmented files on disk. The other programs, DELDIR, PARK, TRANSDIR, and NAMEDIR are interesting subdirectory manipulating utilities. (Each of these are discussed in detail in Chapter 17.)

LISTFRAG displays a list of all fragmented files and subdirectories on a disk drive. To see which files are fragmented, type LISTFRAG followed by an optional drive letter (no letter specifies the current drive):

C>LISTFRAG

The SoftPatch Utility LISTFRAG Version 1.2
(C) Copyright SoftPatch 1985
All Rights Reserved

Fragmented Files in Drive C:
\COMMAND.COM
    2 non-contiguous chains

\WP\CHAPT1
    2 non-contiguous chains

and so on . . .

This same information can be obtained using CHKDSK; however, LISTFRAG displays information for the entire drive, or the specified subdirectory and all directories under it. If no fragmented files are found, like CHKDSK, LISTFRAG informs you that all files are contiguous.

The PACKDISK program locates fragmented files and unfragments them. Depending on the severity of your fragmentation, this could take some time. To unfragment files, type PACKDISK followed by the drive letter, or no drive letter if you're unfragmenting the current disk:

C>PACKDISK

The first thing PACKDISK does is to warn you:

If you have a copy protected piece of software on your disk, press ESC! Certain programs rely on tricky copy protection schemes when they are installed on your hard disk. Some of these programs purposely fragment themselves as part of that protection. If you run PACKDISK, it will diligently reassemble the copy protected program into one piece. This might defeat the copy protection and render the program useless. Only if you are certain none of your programs on disk are copy protected should you use this utility.

If you have no copy protected software, running PACKDISK is a safe and reliable program. It unfragments each file on disk, putting it into sequential order. PACKDISK also squeezes any unnecessary space from the disk and from the directories.

After your disk is unfragmented (which could be quite a while depending on the size of the disk), you should immediately reboot. This is the most important caution regarding any unfragmenting utility. You should always reboot your computer after you've unfragmented the hard disk.

The unfragmenting utility goes about its job by rebuilding the entire disk. It moves files, then updates the file's location in the directory and in the FAT table. DOS uses the FAT table to locate files on disk. The FAT table is only loaded into memory once when the computer is started. Because the FAT table has been updated by the unfragmenting utility, if you do not reset the computer, you might see the following message:

Sector Not Found

This is a very bad message to read after messing with your hard disk. However, no real harm has been done. DOS merely needs to load the updated, unfragmented FAT just created. You should reset the computer with Ctrl-Alt-Del before proceeding.

With your new, unfragmented disk, you should first run the LISTFRAG utility. Don't be surprised when it informs you there are no fragmented files on the disk. You might not notice any improved performance immediately. However, after using the disk a while, and especially if the disk was severely fragmented before, you will notice little things: Directory listings will appear faster, data base files will operate quickly, spell-checks on word processing documents will proceed faster. And, above all, DOS will load programs into memory much faster than before. It may not be apparent immediately, but the improvements are there and for the better!

Commercially Available Programs

Paul Mace is one of the canonized saints of the Hard Disk Crusades. His Mace Utilities have blossomed into one of the most powerful software packages a hard disk owner needs. As an appetizer, the Mace Utilities claim to fame is that it will actually un-format a hard disk drive—the most hazardous thing which could happen to your data can actually be undone by the amazing Mace Utilities.

The Mace Utilities

There are many other saving graces included with the Mace Utilities, most of which are discussed in detail later in this chapter. One of the main features of Mace which pertains to this part of the chapter is file unfragmenting. Selecting option F7 from the main menu causes Mace to do two things: First, Mace performs a non-destructive read and verify of every sector on your hard disk. If any problems are detected, the program displays a diagnosis and possible treatment. (You can fix the problems by selecting option F5 from the main menu.)

Once the diagnosis is complete, the second operation of option F7 is to unfragment files on your disk. Mace displays a map of your disk (or diskette). You can visibly see the fragmentation and the empty, unused sectors. Each area of the disk is highlighted as Mace works at unfragmenting. Like a child's tile game, you can see the various pieces reassemble into a contiguous structure. While it's rather fun to watch, the entire process could take up to two hours (depending on how fragmented this disk is). After everything is done, you press a key and Mace automatically resets your computer.

One of the advantages of the Mace Utilities unfragment is that it does not alter any software copy protection schemes. Mace is aware of almost every copy protected program and scheme out there. The utility carefully skirts around any potential problem areas without risk to your copy protected software.

The entire unfragmenting event is documented by Mace in a file named REPORT.MU (or whichever name you specify). This file must be on a drive other than the one being unfragmented. This way, you can leave the computer unattended and review the proceedings at another time by simply TYPEing the report file. Mace, also, echoes any bad data to the report or to the printer. This way, if a bad area of the disk is stumbled upon, Mace can correct any problems and restore what it can to the report file.

Power Tools

Power Tools from MLI Microsystems is a complete hard utility package. It offers disk utilities, file recovery (un-erase), unfragmenting and disk packing, and it can be made memory resident. Power Tools can be told to stay in memory so you can access any of its numerous features from any other program you're using.

Power Tools is relatively straight forward and easy to use. Choosing DISK OPTIMIZE from the main menu allows you to optimize an entire disk or single files. You, next, have your choice of packing the files or unfragmenting them. Packing involves moving all the files toward the start of the disk; in effect, squeezing the empty space, or air, from between them. Unfragmenting brings the pieces of the files together, just as the Mace and PACKDISK utilities do. Unlike Mace, Power Tools does not check for any copy protection. If you have any copy protected files, choose the file-by-file optimizing options and avoid the protected files.

FORMATTING TECHNIQUES FOR INCREASING AND OPTIMIZING STORAGE

Aside from packing and unfragmenting files on disk, there are certain formatting techniques which optimize disk performance on a very low level. As technology races ahead, more and more of these techniques become available. They take standard, middle-of-the road hard disks and turn them into real storage monsters.

When DOS formats a disk, it lays down a series of tracks and sectors, as discussed earlier in this chapter. Because tracks can occur on both sides of a disk, or on the many sides or platters, of a hard disk, they are considered cylinders.

Cylinders are numbered starting at the outside of the disk with cylinder 0. These move in sequentially to the highest numbered cylinder. The sectors, however, are not numbered sequentially. Unlike numbers on the face of a clock, sectors are placed around the disk in a specific pattern according to the *interleave factor*.

For example, sectors on a 360K floppy diskette are numbered like this:

1 2 3 4 5 6 7 8 9

Their physical location on the disk, moving clockwise, is this:

1 3 5 7 9 2 4 6 8

This is referred to as a 1-6 interleave. The next sequentially numbered disk sector is actually 6 physical sectors away. The original hard disk in the PC/XT used a 1-6 interleave. The IBM PC/AT's disk drive uses a 1-3 interleave:

1 6 2 7 3 8 4 9 5

The reason for having an interleave is because the disk is spinning so fast. After each sector is read from disk, the disk controller performs an error-checking calculation on it called a Cyclic Redundancy Check, or CRC. This check assures that the information read from disk is identical to the information on disk. If there is a difference, a CRC error occurs and the controller makes another attempt to read the sector. If after a given number of attempts the sector cannot be read, the disk controller informs DOS and an error message is displayed.

While the disk controller is calculating the CRC, the disk continues to spin. By the time the CRC is calculated on sector 1, sector 2 has already passed and the read/write head is now over sector 3. For the drive controller to read in sector 2 it will have to wait almost one complete disk revolution. To prevent this waiting around, disk sectors are interleaved. While calculating the CRC on sector 1, the read/write head is over sector 3. When the CRC is done, the read/write head is already in position over sector 2, ready to read in data.

The interleave is invisible to DOS and to your programs. It is maintained by the disk's controller. So when DOS or your program reads information from disk, it's read sequentially, even though the sectors really don't sit that way on disk. As a matter of fact, many technical books leave out the subject of disk interleave because it's done automatically by the disk's controller.

A potential problem with some hard disk's interleave factor is that they are inefficient. The interleave may be too conservative for the disk controller, or the interleave may be too liberal, causing the controller to skip over sectors and wait a complete revolution for the next sector. Either way, an improper interleave slows the performance of a hard disk.

Several programs are available from Paul Mace Software, the same people who offer the fabled Mace Utilities, for optimizing your hard disk's interleave factor. The Advanced Hard Disk Diagnostics utilities contain two programs for optimum interleave performance: HOPTIMUM and HFORMAT.

HOPTIMUM analyses hard disk performance. It times the disk drive in a number of situations and determines which interleave factor is the most efficient. This information can be stored and used by a second program, HFORMAT. The HFORMAT program performs a thorough, low level format of your hard disk based on the optimization scheme provided by HOPTIMUM. Together, both of these programs could result in a more efficient interleave factor for the hard disk, and improve the hard disk's speed.

The only drawback to this brand of optimization is that it performs the dreaded, low level format of the hard disk. This will definitely erase anything on the disk. Even Mace's Un-Format program cannot recover from a low level format. You must first BACKUP all files from your hard disk, then perform the low level format and RESTORE your files. These extra steps are necessary, but the benefits of a higher performing hard disk are worth the time spent backing up and restoring.

CLEANING UP THE DIRECTORY

The order of files in a directory listing can be very important to the speed at which the programs are loaded. Each time you type the name of a program or file, DOS looks three places for it: First, DOS checks to see if it's an internal command. Second, DOS checks the current directory for the file or program. And finally, DOS searches any other directories or drives on the path.

When DOS is searching directories, it starts with the first directory entry and reads through the entire directory looking for a match. Files are listed in a directory in the order they were added. Therefore, a simple trick to speed up the time DOS takes to load a program is to put all the .COM, .EXE, and .BAT files at the start of the directory. Even more efficient would be to place the most often used programs first in the directory. Unfortunately, this is not easy to do after the programs are already on your disk. But it can be done with some interesting utility programs. (Some are discussed at the end of this section.)

Another interesting thing about directory searches has to deal with the way files are deleted. When a file is deleted, DOS places a special available tag in that file's directory entry. The file isn't actually erased from disk (which is why some special utility programs can un-delete deleted files). When DOS searches the directory, it still happens upon these available-tagged directory entries but instead of paying attention to them, it simply skips over them. This adds to the time it takes for DOS to search for and load a program. Not much time is added, granted, but consider if fifty files were deleted from one directory. That's fifty extra stops DOS has to make.

When DOS adds new files to a directory it puts them in one of two places: At the end of the current list of files, or in one of the holes left by deleted programs. For example, the following directory has three files:

CFS	4520	1-23-88	5:44p
JOBLOG 88	7516	2-17-88	4:44p
SCHED WCF	8404	11-11-89	8:08p

If a new file were added, the directory appears as follows:

CFS	4520	1-23-88	5:44p
JOBLOG 88	7516	2-17-88	4:44p
SCHED WCF	8404	11-11-89	8:08p
LOAN WKS	3680	11-17-89	11:34p

However, if the file JOBLOG.88 is deleted before the file LOAN.WKS was added, the directory would appear as:

CFS	4520	1-23-88	5:44p
LOAN WKS	3680	11-17-89	11:34p
SCHED WCF	8404	11-11-89	8:08p

DOS makes an attempt to fill in the tombstones left by deleted files only as new files are added to the directory. By getting rid of the empty directory entries as well as sorting the files in the directory, DOS could search through the entries much faster.

This is not something which can be done easily with DOS. You need a special piece of software designed to physically sort a directory on disk. Remember that sorting a directory as it is displayed is quite simple. Recalling from Chapter 3, the following command is used to sort a directory listing:

C>DIR | SORT

However, this does not touch the way the files are physically stored on the disk. It's only for show.

To actually sort the directory entries on disk, a special utility program is needed. Besides the file's name, each directory entry holds special information about the file used by DOS. This information includes the name of the file, it's size, the date, and time it was last updated, and other secret, DOS-only stuff. All these details fit in 32 bytes of space in one slot of the directory on disk. The position of the file's slot in the directory is not crucial to the file itself. The actual information which tells DOS where on disk the file is located is only referenced to by the directory entry. Because of this, directory entries can be moved from one slot to another without affecting the content of the files.

The utility programs which sort the directory entries carefully pick up all directory entries, then sort them in whichever order you specify: alphabetically, by extension, size, or date. Additionally, any tombstones left by dead programs are overwritten by the sorting processes.

As an example, suppose you sort a directory by file extension. The directory contained files with the following extensions:

.WKS   .BAT   .EXE   .ASM   .COM

After the sort, the directories entries would appear in alphabetical order:

.ASM   .BAT   .COM   .EXE   .WKS

This still won't put the .COM, .EXE, and .BAT files first, so a second technique is required.

Before sorting the directory, ensure that the .COM, .EXE, and .BAT files will come first by renaming them. This does not change the contents of the files. However, they will need to be renamed back after the sort. For example, the following commands could be performed before the sort:

```
C>RENAME *.COM *.000
C>RENAME *.EXE *.001
C>RENAME *.BAT *.002
```

In computer sorts, numbers take on a lower value than letters. The numbers 0 through 9 have a higher sort priority than the letter A. Just make certain there are no other files with the .000 extension in the directory.

After the sort is performed, files in the directory will be listed .000 first, .001 second, and .002 third. Other files will follow based on their extensions. And, of course, any tombstones in the directory will be removed. To rename the .COM, .EXE, and .BAT files back to their original names, use:

```
C>RENAME *.000 *.COM
C>RENAME *.001 *.EXE
C>RENAME *.002 *.BAT
```

Also note that files without extensions will appear before any files with extensions. (The character "space" is weighed as the first value by most sorting utilities.) Files without extensions would have to be given temporary extensions before the sort to ensure they wouldn't be placed before the .COM, .EXE, and .BAT files. The extensionless files would need to be renamed after the sort is completed.

Commercially Available Directory Sorting Software

Again, the Mace Utilities comes to the rescue with a directory sorting function. From the main menu, option F6 initiates a directory sort/squeeze. The sorting half deals with placing all the files on your hard disk in whichever order you specify. The squeezing half goes about removing the tombstones left by deleted files.

The Mace Utilities

The sort can take place on four options: filename, filename extension, date and time, or file size. After this, you are queried as to whether you want the read-only status of the .COM, .EXE, and .SYS files set. Since these files are not normally written to, modified, or deleted, setting the read-only status provides an extra level of protection against their accidental erasure. Also, because these files are read-only and are not modified, this helps to speed up other operations of the Mace Utilities and hard drive performance in general.

Once this is done, Mace displays each directory on disk as it is sorted. Depending on the size of your hard disk and number of directories and files, the entire operation could take anywhere from ten seconds to about a minute.

The Norton Utilities

Another directory sorting/squeezing program is called DS.EXE or DIRSORT.EXE. This program is part of a group of interesting utilities collectively called the Norton Utilities. The Norton Utilities collectively come from the father of PC disk utilities, Peter Norton.

DS sorts directory entries by either filename, filename extension, date, time or file size, or a combination of each. If the optional /S switch is specified, Norton's DS will sort all directories starting with the current directory on down.

To run Norton's DS, type DS on the command line, followed by either N, E, D, T, or S for fileName, filename Extension, Date, Time or Size, respectively. If the /S slash is included, DS continues to sort all files in any subdirectories under the current directory:

```
C > DS N
```

DS.EXE responds by telling you which directory it's sorting and exactly what it's doing:

```
DS-Directory Sort, Advanced Edition, (C) Copr 1987, Peter Norton
C: \ ADMIN \ LOTUS \ SUE . . . reading, sorting, writing, done.
```

After the entire operation (which happens rather quickly), you're returned to the DOS prompt. Now you have a nice, clean, sorted directory.

ARCHIVING PROGRAMS

Having a hard disk means you can put a lot of your stuff on it. But, because hard disks hold so much stuff at one time, you may notice some seldom used programs are taking up quite a bit of space. If you don't need the programs, you could copy or back them up to floppy disks, but is this really why you have a hard disk? Would organizing the floppy diskettes be more trouble than keeping the programs on hard disk?

The answer comes in two public domain programs called PKARC and PKXARC, whose ancestor, ARC, is one of the most popular utility programs for the PC and compatibles. These programs provide a cross between backing up seldom used programs to floppy, thereby releasing the disk space, and keeping excess programs on hard disk.

PKARC and PKXARC have their roots in the ARC program. This program started out as a convenient way for modem users to send and receive long programs using the phone lines. ARC compressed files on disk into a special archive-format file with the extension. ARC. It could compress all types of files, and continue to add files to the .ARC file. This way, a modem user could receive a group of files, say a program or series of programs, by only transmitting one file. This file would then be un-ARC'ed at his end, sort of like unpacking a box. The programs would be un-compressed and separated out into their original forms.

It didn't take long for folks to figure out that seldom used programs on the hard disk could be ARC'ed to save space. For example, suppose you've done your tax returns for the past few years on the computer. It's always wise to keep those records around, so rather than store them on floppy, you put them all into a single, space saving ARC file. You would have files titled 86.ARC, 87.ARC, 88.ARC, and so on. Because ARC compresses the files, they take up less space on the hard disk. And because files can be added to the .ARC file, meaning 86.ARC can contain all the tax information for the year 1986, this cuts back on the number of directory slots used. Now, all your tax information is still stored on hard disk. You can un-ARC your files and access the data faster and more efficiently than if they'd only been on floppy.

The latest versions of the ARC program are PKARC and PKXARC. These two programs have split the functions of the original ARC program: PKARC creates, adds, and squeezes files to an .ARC archive, and PKXARC eXtracts files from the archive. Both programs operate faster than the original ARC program.

PKARC and PKXARC come as a single file named PKXaaAbb.COM. The Xaa refers to the PKXARC version number and the Abb refers to the PKARC version number. The versions at this writing are PKXARC 34 and PKARC version 20, which translates into PKX34A20.COM. This was done so that by looking at the name of the file you can determine if you have the most recent version.

The reason the PKARC files are included in one PKXaaAbb.COM file is it makes them easier to transport. Newer versions of PKARC can be distributed more conveniently, and there's never any incompatibility because PKXaaAbb.COM un-ARCs itself when it's first run.

To release the files from the PKXaaAbb.COM file, type its name at the DOS prompt. For example:

```
C > PKX34A20
```

The PKARC program then proceeds to unfold itself:

```
PKARC 2.0/PKXARC 3.4   Creation Module   12-15-86
Copyright (c) 1986 PKWARE, Inc. All Rights Reserved.

Performing self-extraction . . .

unCrunching: PKARC.COM
unCrunching: PKARC.DOC
unCrunching: PKXARC.COM
unCrunching: PKXARC.DOC
unCrunching: PKXARCJR.COM
unCrunching: README.DOC
```

These programs are distributed as shareware. They are not public domain. Shareware refers to software distributed free of charge. Indeed, the distribution scheme expects you to make copies of the programs and give them to your friends. However, if you use the program and find it of value, a donation of $20 is expected.

The files PKX34A20.COM produces are used for the ARC'ing and un-ARC'ing of files. The files were originally stored in a "Crunched" format, saving space on disk. They are:

PKARC.COM   which creates and maintains .ARC archive files.

PKARC.DOC   the instruction manual for PKARC (a text file).

PKXARC.COM   which eXtracts files from .ARC archives.

PKXARC.DOC   the instruction manual for PKXARC (a text file).

PKXARCJR.COM   a special version of PKXARC designed to run on computers without much memory. It is, however, slower than PKXARC.COM.

README.DOC   a text file containing any last minute fixes and changes to the programs.

To archive a single file or a group of files, PKARC is used. The format is:

PKARC[old options] [acdflmuvx] filename[.ARC] [filename . . .]

The numerous options are all described in detail in the PKARC manual, PKARC.DOC. Refer there for details.

The PKARC program is used to create an archive. First you specify the "A" option for adding files to the archive. Next the ARC file (where the compressed files are stored) is specified. This is followed by the files you wish to place into the archive. For example, suppose last month's accounting data files all end with the extension .ACC. You wish to save them all into an ARC file called JUNE88.ARC:

C>PKARC A JUNE88 *.ACC

PKARC looks for the file JUNE88.ARC in the current directory. The .ARC extension is assumed unless another is specified. If JUNE88.ARC is not found, it's created. Next, it reads all files .ACC and determines which is the best way to store them. Depending on what information is in the file, it might be compressed according to one of the following methods: Stored, Packed, Squeezed, crunched, Crunched (with a capital C), or Squashed. PKARC analyses the file and determines which compacting method works best. As it creates the file and adds the filenames, something similar to the following is displayed:

Creating Archive: JUNE88.ARC
    Adding: PAYROLL.ACC   analyzing,   (49%)   squashing, done.
    Adding: AR.ACC   analyzing,   (40%)   crunching, done.
    Adding: AP.ACC   analyzing,   (41%)   crunching, done.
    Adding: OE.ACC   analyzing,   (35%)   Squashing, done.

The number in parenthesis refers to the size of the file in its compressed form compared to its original size. If the file AR.ACC were 10K long, it will take up only 4K in the .ARC file.

Once the files are archived, their originals can be deleted. This saves on disk space, and is more convenient and handy than backing up.

To retrieve a single file or all files from an archive, PKXARC is used. The format of the PKXARC command is:

PKXARC [/c/l/p/t/v] filename[.ARC] [d:\dir . . .] [files . . .]

PKXARC's options are all described in detail in the PKARC manual. Refer there for details.

PKXARC's primary function is to extract files from an archive. If no files are specified, all files are extracted. PKXARC can be used to look inside an .ARC file. An .ARC file could contain hundreds of files, yet appears as only one entry in a directory. To view the files in the archive, the /V switch is used:

C>PKXARC /V JUNE88

This command lists all files in the JUNE88.ARC archive. A single file could be extracted by specifying its name:

C>PKXARC JUNE88 PAYROLL.ACC

This command extracts (and unsquashes) the file PAYROLL.ACC from the JUNE88.ARC archive. This is done quickly and more efficiently than scanning backups on floppy diskettes.

The PKARC utilities are almost a must for your hard disk. Just by using them alone you could save a lot of space currently taken up by programs just along for the ride. For additional information on the PKARC utilities, write to:

PKWARE, Inc.
7032 Ardara Avenue
Glendale, WI 53209

Condensing "On the Fly"

CUBIT Optimization software from SoftLogic Solutions, does almost the same thing the PKARC programs do: compress data stored on hard disk. The difference is, CUBIT is a memory resident program. It compresses files as they are saved to disk and decompresses files as they are loaded from disk.

Initially, files need to be compressed before the "on the fly" part of CUBIT is used. The CUBIT program itself behaves a lot like PKARC—except there's only one program. CUBIT is smart enough to know when a program or file has been compressed. If the file has not already been compressed, CUBIT compresses it. If the file is compressed, CUBIT de-compresses it.

C>CUBIT JUNE.WKS

Suppose JUNE.WKS is a 17K spreadsheet file. CUBIT analyses the file, first detecting that it is not already compressed. It next proceeds to squeeze JUNE.WKS down by approximately 33 percent to 13K. The squeezing varies from file to file. Text files squeeze down quite a bit faster than other types of files. For example, a sample 10K word processing file could be crunched by 55 percent to 4K using CUBIT.

The CUBITR program is a memory resident part of CUBIT which intercepts all access to files on disk. The CUBIT manual depicts CUBITR as a traffic cop, directing and intercepting disk activity. CUBITR examines all files you access from disk. If it detects a compressed file, it decompresses it as it's loaded. Then, once the file has been updated (or whatever), CUBITR compresses it back as it's saved to disk.

Needless to say, this on the fly compressing and decompressing takes time. CUBITR ignores files not already compressed on disk. But for compressed files it takes about .6 seconds per 1K of file size to compress or decompress the file. Loading a 10K compressed file into a word processor took CUBITR an extra 12 seconds to do its job. (The file was originally 17K.) Another 12 seconds were tacked on by CUBIT when the file was saved back to disk.

But for saving space on the hard disk, CUBIT and CUBITR can cut down on disk space anywhere from 30 to 50 percent, depending on the type of file. The on the fly ability means you won't have to PKARC or PKXARC files which are saved in compressed format. On almost-full hard disks, CUBIT provides an excellent method of conserving disk space.

HARDWARE SOLUTIONS

The final trick to squeezing performance from a hard disk deals with the actual way information is stored on the disk. The way the bits, the 1's and 0's, sit on disk is important to the amount of information stored on the disk. While most reference manuals simply state that bytes are placed into sectors a bit at a time, it's much more complex.

There are several popular methods of recording information on disk. Recording 1's and 0's is done by leaving a magnetic flux reversal on the surface of the disk. (Don't go running away—this is not going to get overly technical!) The most common method of recording bits on disk is referred to as Modified Frequency Modulation, or MFM. It uses a special way of monitoring the flux reversals to mark the positions of the 1's and 0's. The MFM method makes it possible to store a lot of 1's and 0's on disk without too much overhead.

The next best step up from MFM coding is called Run Length Limited, or RLL coding. Briefly, RLL coding allows for an almost 50 percent increase in the amount of information stored on the same disk. The coding scheme squeezes more information onto disk because of the way it looks at the flux reversals. A drive which uses RLL coding can store much more information than an MFM drive—even if both contain the exact same physical components.

ERLL

Maynard Electronics of Casselberry, Florida, has taken RLL coding one step further. Using their new Enhanced Run Length Limited, ERLL, coding they are able to improve the storage capabilities of a hard disk by almost 100 percent, and the rate at which the controller accesses the disk by almost 200 percent.

ERLL coding changes the number of sectors on a hard disk from 17 to 33 per track. (This is the same physical disk—it's just the ERLL coding scheme which allows more sectors per track.) Because more information is on each track, the controller is able to read in that information twice as fast. Again, nothing is physically changed on the drive (e.g., it's not spinning twice as fast). And finally, ERLL coding offers unique, and fairly fool-proof error detection. Maynard's Advanced Error Correcting Code is considered twice as good as the error correcting procedures used on RLL and MFM disk drives.

264

The ERLL device is a controller card, a piece of hardware, available from Maynard Electronics. Upgrading to an ERLL system does not require that you buy a special disk drive system. Maynard even claims in its literature that you can start using the ERLL controller without reformatting your current hard disk. (With other controllers, you must re-low-level-format the drive to use the new controller.)

The Maynard ERLL controller is totally compatible with the IBM PC/XT and AT hard disk BIOS. It offers a superb way of improving hard disk storage and performance with only one piece of hardware, and is compatible with your existing hardware.

At this writing, the controller is not available on the retail market. Those desiring more information on obtaining a Maynard ERLL controller should contact a local dealer or Maynard Electronics directly. (Their address is in Appendix D.)

This chapter was packed with information about getting the most from your hard disk. A wide variety of hardware and software techniques were covered. These tricks included unfragmenting files; adjusting the hard disk's interleave factor; squeezing, sorting, and cleaning up the directory; archiving files to keep them handy, yet save on disk space; condensing files on-the-fly, and ERLL disk formatting.

These tricks are all more-or-less physical solutions to optimizing hard disk performance. In the next chapter you'll see how your computer's memory, or RAM, can be used to maximize disk access and overall computer performance.

Chapter 16

Disk Access Optimization

Computers typically store information in one of two places: internal memory, or on disk. The computer's RAM, or random access memory, is used for the temporary storage of information. Disks are used for permanent storage. In order to hold information in RAM, electrical current must constantly refresh the RAM circuitry. Once the power is turned off, any information in RAM is gone. Because of this, information needs to be saved to a more permanent site on disk. Disks retain information even when the power is off.

The computer's microprocessor runs programs and stores data in RAM. The microprocessor cannot directly access the information on disk, but it can load that information into RAM, work on it, then save it back to disk. The subject of this book is hard disks and this part of the book deals with optimizing hard disks. Amazingly enough, one interesting way of optimizing disk performance is by using RAM.

The previous chapter discussed boosting hard disk performance using various software and hardware tricks. This chapter concentrates on the interaction between the computer's random access memory and disk access. RAM can be used as a fast buffer between your programs and the hard disk. It can also replace some disk operations altogether. Again, the object of all this is to improve disk performance.

OVERLAY FILES

In the old, CP/M days of computing, memory was a scarce commodity. The computer's operating system, programs and data all had to fit inside a tiny 64K bank of memory.

It appears tiny today because PC-DOS computers are now capable of having ten times that much memory for storing the operating system, programs and data. Even more memory than that, called *Extended Memory*, can now be used by the computer in a variety of different ways.

The original IBM PC introduced in 1981 had only 64K of RAM out of a potential 640K. This made sense because all other computers at the time also had only 64K of RAM. Software houses developing for the PC were used to working in a 64K environment. To make the best use of that space, they divided the 64K RAM up into sections for their own program and for data. For example, the VisiCalc spreadsheet occupied about 30K of RAM and left the rest of memory for spreadsheet data.

If a program required more memory than the computer had, it would swap part of itself in memory with a new part from disk. The new part from disk was referred to as an *overlay file*. For example, suppose one program occupied 32K of RAM. Yet the program was actually 48K in size. The programmers would divide the program code into separate modules. The main part of the program would always be in memory. But the modules, those things in the program which weren't used that often, or were only used for special operations, they would be kept on disk. The program would then load the modules from disk as they were needed, replacing the modules in memory which weren't used. By juggling data from disk and memory, programs could be quite extensive, yet only use a moderate amount of memory.

As the price of RAM chips dropped, and greater numbers of people were putting more memory into their computers, programs took advantage of it. After a while, the IBM PC was sold off the shelf with 128K of memory standard. When the software houses realized computers were coming with more memory, they started abandoning the overlay file technique. Now, a program could all fit into memory at one time. By removing the overlay files, programs operated faster because they didn't need to access the disk as often.

The IBM PC/XT, which had a 10 megabyte hard disk, came with 256K of RAM. For the longest time in PC computing, this was the standard memory size. Amazingly enough, about the same time, most major software manufacturers needed that much memory to run their programs. This led to a belief that programs and programmers were becoming sloppy—After all, they had all that RAM. The belief was further proliferated when the programs requiring 256K had to resort to overlay files (again!) to fit into memory.

Currently, the standard memory size in IBM computers is the maximum, 640K. This is a limitation placed on the original PC in 1981. Remember, back then 64K was considered RAM heaven. The designers of the PC figured ten times that much RAM would be more than enough. They designed the computer and, more importantly, the operating system to only use 640K of RAM for running programs. Even at this size, several popular programs have to use overlay files to fit into memory.

It's not a negative thing for a program to use overlay files. For example, many programs provide their on-line help information through overlay files. The thinking is that later on, once the program is mastered, you won't need the help and can delete those files from your disk to save space. Also, some programs put lesser-used features on disk as overlay files. This way, if you need the features, they're there. If you don't want them, they won't take up any extra RAM.

EMS MEMORY

As the size of programs increased, the software houses began to see a real limitation on 640K of RAM. While the PC's microprocessor is capable of talking with up to 1 megabyte of RAM, the PC only allotted 640K for storing programs and data. Most standardized programs could get along fine in 640K. But graphics and computer assisted design, or CAD, programs needed more memory. Large spreadsheet users discovered that spreadsheets run out of memory quickly. Software designers were pushing the PC to the limit of its performance. They wanted more RAM.

When the PC AT was introduced, it sported the next generation microprocessor, the 80286. All by itself, this chip is capable of directly addressing 16 megabytes of RAM—16 times greater than the 8088 in the original PC. Yet, because computers with an 80286 are also running DOS, they are subject to the same memory limitations as the 8088: They can only run programs in 640K of their potential 16,000K of RAM.

To break beyond the 640K barrier, two software companies sat down and designed an Expanded Memory Specification, or EMS. Lotus, developer of the popular 1-2-3 spreadsheet, and Intel, makers of the 8088, 8086, 80286, and 80386 microprocessors, teamed up to create the EMS specification to allow IBM PC's to access memory above and beyond the 640K limit. Microsoft, makers of DOS, threw in their approval by announcing their support of the EMS standard. (In some circles, the EMS standard is also referred to as the Lotus/Intel/Microsoft Expanded Memory Specification.) EMS is not the same as Extended Memory used in the IBM PC AT. Extended memory refers to memory above 1 megabyte used by the 80286 microprocessor's "protected" mode.

By using EMS, a PC can have up to 8 megabytes of RAM (which includes the basic 640K). No matter how much EMS memory your computer has, it's used only 64K at a time. EMS memory is accessed in four 16K "pages". Each of these pages is a window to 16K of EMS memory. The page system works by swapping a particular 16K chunk of EMS memory with a 16K chunk of memory inside the PC. At any time, up to four pages of EMS memory can be accessed. While this may seem quite awkward, especially when dealing with 8 megs of memory, keep in mind information is read from the hard disk in only .5K chunks. The EMS standard is 128 times more efficient.

The only drawback to all this memory is that you cannot run programs there. Programs must still occupy and run in the first 640K of memory. However, this does not make EMS useless. There are a few programs which take direct advantage of EMS memory for storing their data. At this writing, Ashton-Tate's Framework II, Lotus' Symphony and 1-2-3 spreadsheet, and Microsoft's Windows all use EMS memory for storing data. Even more programs are on the way.

If you don't own any programs which take advantage of EMS memory, it can be put to use as a Print Spooler, RAM Disk, or as Cache memory. Most of these are configured via the CONFIG.SYS file when you start your computer. Each of them helps to speed up operations on the computer and, because they aren't in standard memory, they don't subtract space from running your programs.

Print Spoolers

Print Spoolers help speed up printer operations. The printer is the slowest part of any computer system. When a print spooler is installed, DOS sends characters to the spooler's memory rather than sending them directly to the printer. This way the computer doesn't have to sit and wait for the printer to finish. The characters stored in the spooler wait until the printer is ready to accept them.

DOS checks the spooler's memory every so often to see if any characters need to be printed. If so, it prints about a handful, then quickly returns to what it was doing before. These quick check-and-prints happen so fast you don't notice them. The printer continues to print and you continue to use the printer.

A RAM disk is a superfast electronic disk drive in memory. DOS offers its own RAM disk drive called VDISK.SYS. Quite a few RAM disk drivers come with the EMS hardware. RAM disks are discussed in the next section.

Disk caches are an excellent disk speed up technique using memory. Not the same as a RAM disk, caches are responsible for quick and efficient disk access. They are discussed later in this chapter.

RAM DISKS AND HOW THEY WORK

RAM Disks go by a number of names: MEMDISK, RAMDISK, VDISK, MEMBRAIN, and so on. Basically, a RAM disk is a superfast disk drive in memory. Because it's in memory, it's going to behave a lot faster than any physical disk drive. Disk access will be quicker and reads and writes will appear nearly instantaneous. The RAM disk will operate as fast as your computer's memory.

The disk drive is the most mechanical thing in your computer. As an interesting aside, chances are if some piece of hardware is going to fail, it's going to be a disk drive. Floppy drives are the most mechanical and the most susceptible to failure. Hard drives are less so because they're constantly moving. However, nothing moves in a RAM disk. It's all electronic.

Most RAM disks are created with device drivers in the CONFIG.SYS file. CONFIG.SYS is the first file read by DOS, even before AUTOEXEC.BAT. CONFIG.SYS's job is to CONFIGure your SYStem. It deals with hard disk partitions (as seen in Chapter 2), and controlling the way certain software behaves (as seen in Chapter 8). CONFIG.SYS configures and arranges every aspect of your system.

Basically, CONFIG.SYS contains a list of parameters for your system and device drivers. The parameters include information for DOS, such as how many files it can have open at one time, the number of file buffers to be used, even which country and language DOS should operate under. Device drivers are memory resident controller programs. Some device drivers, like ANSI.SYS, control the way DOS writes to the screen. Others control various devices. For example, the Microsoft Mouse peripheral uses a device driver called MOUSE.SYS. If you want a RAM drive in your computer, include the appropriate RAM disk driver in your CONFIG.SYS file.

To install a device, CONFIG.SYS should contain the word device followed by an equals " = " and the name of the driver software and the path if the driver is not located in the root directory. For example, suppose a RAM disk driver named RAMBO exists in the \DOS subdirectory. To install this device driver, and subsequently the RAM disk, the following should be in the CONFIG.SYS file:

DEVICE = \DOS\RAMBO

When DOS boots, it scans the root directory for the CONFIG.SYS file. If found, DOS reads CONFIG.SYS, sets any parameters and loads any device drivers. If a device driver is found, DOS loads it into memory and executes the instructions in the driver. In the above example, DOS would load the RAMBO driver into memory, then execute it. The RAMBO driver would then allocate a given amount of memory as a RAM disk. DOS then proceeds to read the rest of the CONFIG.SYS file, or if done, it looks for and executes AUTOEXEC.BAT.

The device driver is the key to running a RAM disk. It instructs DOS that it's operating memory as a disk drive. Depending on the driver, DOS assigns the drive a letter and allocates memory to the drive. Once space is assigned, the RAM disk allocates space in memory for a directory, FAT table, sectors, and clusters. Because DOS is informed the device is a disk drive, DOS will treat the RAM disk as if it were another disk. However, the driver also instructs DOS that the RAM disk cannot be formatted. The disk is formatted as it's installed. If the FORMAT command is used on the RAM disk, DOS returns the following:

Format not supported on drive D:

(or whichever letter is assigned the RAM disk.)

Other disk commands, including CHKDSK, XCOPY, SUBST, and ASSIGN, all treat the RAM disk just as if it were a real disk drive. The DISKCOPY and DISKCOMP commands might not work with some RAM disks, depending on the size of the RAM disk and the type of device driver used.

Installing a RAM disk in conventional (640K) RAM eats up quite a bit of space. A 360K RAM disk leaves a little over 256K with which to operate programs and store data. For most cases, this is very efficient. The majority of programs require only 256K of RAM to run. And 360K is exactly the size of one floppy diskette. Backing up the RAM disk would be as easy as COPY *.*.

Most RAM disks can also operate in EMS memory. Again, this depends on the type of the RAM disk and its device driver. Some RAM disks simply use an extra parameter in the CONFIG.SYS file to install in EMS memory. Other drivers may install only in EMS memory. The advantage is that a RAM disk in EMS memory won't hamper the tiny 640K of RAM you have to run your programs. In EMS memory, a RAM disk could conceivably be 8 megs in size.

The DOS VDISK

A RAM disk driver has been included with DOS, starting with DOS version 3.0. VDISK.SYS is the name of DOS's Virtual Disk driver. VDISK can create any number of RAM disks in either conventional memory, or the AT's Extended Memory. (EMS memory hardware for PC's and XT's usually comes with its own, customized RAM disk drivers.)

To install a VDISK, the name of the VDISK.SYS device driver must be specified in the CONFIG.SYS file. If VDISK.SYS is not in the root directory, its path should also be specified. VDISK installs itself as the next highest drive letter. If you have drives A through C, VDISK installs itself as drive D. If you're installing more than one VDISK (done by specifying VDISK more than once in the CONFIG.SYS file), each subsequent RAM disk takes on the next highest letter drive.

The format for installing VDISK is:

DEVICE = [path]VDISK.SYS [size] [sector] [dir] [/E:m]

Size is the size of the RAM disk. It can be anywhere from 1 (for a puny 1K RAM disk) to as much memory in your system, minus 64K. VDISK insists at least 64K of RAM be left in the system. If the size parameter is too large, VDISK adjusts itself to allow for that 64K. If a size value is not specified, VDISK installs as a 64K RAM disk.

Sector refers to the size of the sectors used in the RAM disk. DOS usually allocates 512 bytes to a sector, however smaller sizes can be specified to save space in the RAM disk. VDISK allows sizes of 128, 256, or 512. If none is specified, a sector size of 128 bytes is used.

Dir refers to the number of entries, or slots, allowed in the RAM disk's root directory. This can be any number from 2 to 512. VDISK uses 64 if none is specified. Directory slots take space on the RAM disk. Assigning more than you need means less space for program and data storage. If you know exactly what you're using the RAM disk for, liberally estimate the number of files and use that value for VDISK's [dir] option. Also, note that VDISK assigns the volume label VDISK to each RAM disk it creates. This volume label automatically takes up one directory slot.

The /E switch is used to install the RAM disk into the AT's Extended memory (this is not for EMS memory and will only work with IBM AT's or true compatibles). The M option specifies the number of sectors (see above) which will be read at a time. Unless specified, the value of M is 8, though it can be any value from 1 through 8. Lesser values increase the speed of some operations with certain types of "interrupt-driven" software. If your software behaves abnormally with a VDISK installed in Extended Memory, decrease the value of the M option.

Each of the options of VDISK, disk size, sector size, and directory entries, can be proceeded by an optional comment. For example:

DEVICE = \ DOS \ VDISK.SYS DISK SIZE = 360 SECTORS ARE = 256 62 /E

This assigns a 360K RAM disk with 256 byte sectors and 62 directory entries in Extended (/E) memory. The following command in the CONFIG.SYS file does the same thing:

DEVICE = \ DOS \ VDISK.SYS 603 256 62 /E

The following two lines of a CONFIG.SYS file install two RAM disks into conventional memory. The first disk is 64K in size, the second, 128K:

DEVICE = VDISK.SYS
DEVICE = VDISK.SYS SIZE = 128

When the computer is booted, and CONFIG.SYS is read, DOS installs the RAM disks into conventional memory. As each disk is installed, information about the disk is displayed:

VDISK Version 3.2 virtual disk D:
    Sector size adjusted
    Directory entries adjusted
    Buffer size: 64 KB

```
       Sector size:         128
       Directory entries:    64
VDISK Version 3.2 virtual disk E:
       Sector size adjusted
       Directory entries adjusted
       Buffer size:         128 KB
       Sector size:         128
       Directory entries:    64
```

There are now two Virtual Disks in memory. The first was assigned to drive D, the second to drive E. The first is 64K in size, the second 128K and all other options are at their predefined settings. Note that having these two RAM disks installed lowers the amount of conventional memory to 448K (assuming a full-blown 640K machine to start).

MEMBRAIN

MBRAIN12.EXE creates a RAM disk device driver named MEMBRAIN.SYS. By including this device driver in your CONFIG.SYS file you will have a 160K RAM disk installed.

The MEMBRAIN.SYS driver, unlike VDISK, sets its parameters as it's created by MBRAIN12. When creating the MEMBRAIN.SYS driver, the MBRAIN12 options are:

MBRAIN12 [size] [sector] [cluster] [dir] [path]

Size is the size of the MEMBRAIN RAM disk. It can be a minimum of 64K and a maximum of as much conventional memory as your system has. If a size value is not specified, MEMBRAIN installs a 160K RAM disk. If a value smaller than 64K is specified, MEMBRAIN installs a 64K RAM disk.

Sector refers to the size of the sectors used in the MEMBRAIN RAM disk. MEMBRAIN accepts any sector size as long as it's a multiple of 128. A size of 512 bytes is used if none is specified.

Cluster indicates the number of sectors per cluster. Each file on the RAM disk will be assigned a multiple of this many sectors no matter what its size. The values for cluster can range from 1 to as many sectors as will fit into a 2048 byte cluster. So, for a 512 byte sector size, a maximum of 4 can be used (4 × 512 = 2048). One sector per cluster is used if none are specified.

Dir refers to the number of directory entries allowed in the RAM disk. This can be any number, though if none is specified a value of 64 is used.

Path refers to the location of the MEMBRAIN disk drive. For example, to install a RAM disk as drive D, D:\ is used for the path.

To create the MEMBRAIN.SYS file, MBRAIN is typed at the command prompt, followed by any of the above options. MBRAIN alone creates a RAM disk drive using the following parameters:

C>MBRAIN12

< < < < M e m B r a i n > > > >

(C) 1984 Dennis Lee
160K MemBrain Created

512 bytes per sector
1 sectors per cluster
64 directory entries

1 reserved sector
1 FAT sector
4 directory sectors
314 data sectors

----

320 total sectors

The above command creates a MEMBRAIN.SYS driver. When included in the CONFIG.SYS file, this driver creates a 160K RAM disk with the above listed characteristics. To activate the driver, as with VDISK.SYS, include MEMBRAIN.SYS in your CONFIG.SYS file:

DEVICE = \ DOS \ MEMBRAIN.SYS

If you wish to change any of MEMBRAIN's options, you must recreate the MEMBRAIN.SYS file. For example, to create a MEMBRAIN.SYS driver for a 360K RAM disk, the following would be entered:

C > MBRAIN12 360

This command creates a new MEMBRAIN.SYS file, one which will create a 360K RAM disk.

Other RAM Disks

RAM disk drivers are usually available from the same manufacturer who provides your computer's RAM upgrade, or EMS expansion card. For example, when you buy the Intel Aboveboard, you get Intel's own EMS RAM disk driver. When you buy the AST Six Pack, you get AST's RAM disk driver. These RAM disks are tailored specifically to work with their own hardware. Often times they are easier to use, are faster, or they offer more power than DOS's VDISK. (Most of them use VDISK as their benchmark test, boasting their own software is anywhere from 20 to 80 percent faster.)

RAM Disk Techniques

There are many interesting things which can be done with a RAM disk. Keeping in mind the RAM disk's speed, it can do nothing but improve the time disk-intensive operations take. For example, a batch file could be written to copy all your word processing programs and files to the RAM disk for fast operation. As soon as you're done word processing, the updated files could be copied back to the hard disk.

The following batch file copies all the word processing files from the subdirectory

\ WP on the hard disk to the RAM disk, E:. The name of the word processor is WS. All files created with this word processor end in the .DOC file extension. Once the word processor is finished, any files created are copied to the directory \ WP \ DATA on the hard disk:

```
ECHO OFF
COPY C:\WP\*.* E:
E:
WS
IF NOT EXIST *.DOC GOTO DONE
COPY *.DOC C:\WP\DATA
:DONE
C:
ECHO Done!
```

The IF NOT EXIST statement tests to see if any .DOC files were created. If not (meaning writer's block had probably crept in), execution branches to the :DONE label. Otherwise, all files with the .DOC extension are copied safely back to the \ WP \ DATA directory.

With the increased size of conventional RAM and the popularity of hard disks, several word processing programs include spell checking and thesaurus software. Again, these are very disk-intensive activities. Copying the dictionaries and using them in RAM improves their performance.

RAM disks really shine when programs lean heavily on disk access. The most marked improvement has happened in the area of software development. Writing, editing, compiling and linking programs for the PC takes quite a bit of time. It involves a lot of reading and writing to disk. When all this activity is placed into a RAM disk, the time required to create a program is often cut in half.

Database operations are improved by placing programs and files on the RAM disk (as in the above batch file example). Each record on the database is accessed individually. During a search and sort, or an across the board update, there is a lot of disk activity. Placing database files on a RAM disk speeds up those operations greatly.

Generally, all activities are improved by using a RAM disk. Especially if your computer is equipped with EMS or Extended memory, having a RAM disk can come in quite handy. There's only one drawback.

Because the RAM disk is memory, when the power goes off or even if the computer is reset, any information stored on the RAM disk is gone. A few RAM disks offer a battery backup option. This saves any data left on the RAM disk while the computer's power is turned off. However, the best and only rule of thumb when dealing with a RAM disk is that when the power goes, the RAM disappears.

Because RAM can be so temporary, it should be checked before shutting down your computer. This could be another function of a possible SHUTDOWN batch file as introduced in Chapter 10. A good way to test for files in a RAM disk would be to include the following statements in a SHUTDOWN.BAT file:

```
REM RAM drive assumed to be drive D:
```

```
IF NOT EXIST D:\ *.* GOTO :EMPTY
DIR D: /W
ASK Backup the files in the RAM disk (Y/N)?
IF ERRORLEVEL = = 1 GOTO EMPTY
XCOPY D:\ *.* C:\ RAMDISK /S/E
:EMPTY
```

This batch file assumes the RAM disk is drive D. The IF NOT EXIST test determines if the RAM disk is empty. If no files exist (*.*), batch file execution jumps to the :EMPTY label and SHUTDOWN.BAT continues.

If files do exist, a directory is displayed. The ASK statement waits for keyboard input. Either Y or N must be typed before the batch file continues. If Y is typed an errorlevel of 0 is returned; N sets the errorlevel at 1. (The ASK.COM program is included on the supplemental programs diskette and was discussed in Chapter 7.)

If N is pressed, execution branches to the :EMPTY label and files in the RAM disk are not saved. If Y is pressed, the XCOPY program is used to copy all files and all subdirectories from the RAM disk to the subdirectory \RAMDISK on drive C. (This could be replaced with whichever directory you find most appropriate for the files in your own RAM disk.) Once the files have been saved, the batch file continues.

DISK CACHING

A *cache* (pronounced 'cash') is a secret storage place. Pirates often had a cache of jewels buried on some desert island. Modern day terrorists have caches of weapons hidden somewhere. And on a less-evil side, squirrels have caches of acorns stowed away for winter. Computers, not necessarily associated with pirates, terrorists, or squirrels, can also use caches. In this respect, a cache is a secret storage place in memory which speeds up disk operations.

A disk cache is not a RAM disk, though they are similar and easily confused. A disk cache monitors disk activity. It logs all reads and writes from disk, then keeps a copy of what was read or written in its own cache memory. If the computer makes a second request to read information from disk, and that information is already in the cache, rather than reload the information from disk it is read from cache memory. In computer jargon, "the read request was satisfied from cache memory." Because the cache is memory, it is much faster than reading the data from disk.

The disk cache always makes sure whatever it holds in memory is safely saved on disk. When you save a file to disk, a copy is sent to disk and physically stored there. A *second* copy is also saved in cache memory. This is what makes it different from a RAM disk where the information is only saved in RAM. If you wanted to access the same information again, the cache would intercept the call to disk and, instead of reloading the duplicate information, would simply copy it out of its own RAM. The disk access light will not glow and the information will be loaded much faster than without the cache.

Disk caches show the best performance with programs which use overlay files (as was discussed earlier in this chapter). Programs using overlays often load their various modules into memory as they're needed. If a disk cache were in operation, it would monitor the overlays loaded and keep a copy of each of them in its cache memory. When the program asks for an overlay from disk and that overlay is already in cache memory, the cache will intercept the disk call and automatically zap the overlay into memory. Because overlay files contain program code, they are not modified and there is really no need for a second disk access. This is an ideal and efficient use of cache memory.

Today, programs using overlays aren't that common. The best way to test a disk cache is with a database or accounting program which uses many modules. Databases are perhaps the most disk intensive programs. Each record is read from disk as it's individually called up. In the last section, you read how putting a database on a RAM disk speeds up certain operations (such as sorting). Using a cache, those operations would still be accelerated. However, unlike the volatile RAM disk, the cache is only a copy of what is already on disk. If a power failure occurred, nothing would be lost in the disk cache.

Disk caches are an excellent disk speed-up tool. They function simply based on the observation that most disk operations are repetitive. Like unfragmenting your hard disk, you may not notice the full effect of a disk cache until after you've used one a while. The only drawback to a disk cache is that it uses memory. Some can be installed into EMS memory. But if you lack EMS memory and if your standard memory is short on space, a disk cache might eat up too much RAM. However, as long as memory is not a problem, a disk cache is a quick and excellent RAM-based speed up tool.

COMMERCIALLY AVAILABLE DISK CACHES

Part of the superior Mace Utilities, besides the unfragmenting feature, un-formatting, and file recovering features, is a disk cache. Actually, the Mace Utilities comes with three versions of its VCACHE program: CACHE is for conventional memory; CACHE-EM is for EMS memory; and CACHE-AT is for the AT's Extended memory.

Cache

Only one program should be used at a time, depending on where you wish to place it in memory. CACHE can be installed at any time simply by typing the appropriate program name at the command prompt, or CACHE can be included as part of the AUTOEXEC.BAT file. And, unlike many similar programs, CACHE can be removed to free the memory it uses.

The format of the CACHE command varies with version. For most versions, the format is:

CACHE [size] [location] [/drive] [/W] [/T] [/Q]

CACHE can be either CACHE, CACHE-EM, or CACHE-AT.

Size refers to the amount of RAM used by the cache. The more RAM, the better the improvement. Mace's CACHE keeps as much information in cache memory as it can. The cache keeps track of which items are accessed the most and keeps them in memory with a high priority. Other, less accessed items stay in cache memory on a space available basis.

If size is not specified, CACHE assigns 128K to cache memory, CACHE-EM assigns all available (free) EMS memory to the cache, and CACHE-AT assigns any memory not being used by VDISK to cache memory.

Location is only specified with CACHE-AT. It assigns the starting location above the 1 megabyte mark in the AT where the cache is placed. If a location is not specified, the cache uses memory starting at the 1 meg mark.

The /drive switch is used with special, non-booting hard disks, for example, a Bernoulli drive. To install CACHE on any of these disks, use a slash followed by the drive's letter. For example, if drive C were a non-booting Bernoulli drive, the following installs a 128 cache in standard memory:

CACHE /C

The /W switch is used for AT compatibles (and with CACHE-AT) which handle Extended Memory differently than the PC/AT. Refer to the Mace manual for information on spotting the not-as-compatible differences.

/T displays the CACHE timer. A list of cache statistics are displayed on the screen. This gives a good gauge of how much work the cache is doing, and how much disk access it's saving:

```
C>CACHE /T

Vcache 1.15 version for the Mace+Utilities
Copyright (C) Golden Bow Systems 1985, 1986

Already loaded - Cache size 192 kb

Options: P
Statistics:      9 read requests -      55% satisfied from cache
                 1 write requests -     0% duplicates (ignored)
                 0 memory errors       0 disk errors
```

This indicates that 55% of the information read from disk was read instead from cache memory. This disk drive did not spin and the information was loaded as fast as the cache memory could go.

The /Q switch turns CACHE off. The memory used by CACHE is released and made available to other programs. If the memory cannot be released (which happens when you have another memory resident program installed after CACHE), a warning message is displayed and CACHE is not disabled.

Lightning

The Personal Computer Support Group's LIGHTNING program is one terribly efficient disk cache. Aside from doing all the wonderful things a cache is supposed to do, LIGHTNING is configurable. You can tell it which disk drives it's to cache and how much cache memory it can use. Up to 1.5 megabytes of expansion memory can be used for the cache.

LIGHTNING is memory resident and is typically loaded by your AUTOEXEC.BAT file. The only drawbacks to this program are that it does not function with the Mace Utilities (as pointed out in the Mace manual), and unlike Mace's CACHE, it cannot be removed from memory once installed. Two versions of the program are marketed, an inexpensive copy protected version and a more expensive unprotected version. As with all software, it's best to get the unprotected version. Other than these points, LIGHTNING is an excellent disk caching utility.

Though this is a hard disk book, this chapter dealt with RAM and the various ways RAM can be used to optimize hard disk performance. From the old tricks of using overlay files, to the new Expanded Memory Specification and its various uses, RAM Disks and RAM disk techniques, VDISK and MEMBRAIN, all up to the highly efficient disk caches, RAM can assist in making disk operations smoother, faster and more efficient.

Chapter 17

Shareware Programs

Mentioned throughout this book have been various utilities and hard disk tools. While most of these are commercial programs, available from software dealers, several of them are in the public domain or are so-called *shareware* programs. These programs are free to all who use them, or in the case of shareware, the author requests a modest donation if you enjoy and use the program.

PC SIG offers a disk that contains dozens of interesting programs, many of which have been mentioned in this book. Other programs have been included because they are invaluable to a hard disk owner. This chapter tells about the supplemental programs. It includes a description of each file on disk along with instructions on how to use the files and where to find more information.

The programs listed as Public Domain are free of charge. You may give them to your friends or use them yourself to your heart's content. Shareware programs, on the other hand, are only distributed free of charge. If you find the program useful, you are encouraged to send in the requested donation. This does a couple of things. Primarily, it supports the shareware concept: people writing and distributing helpful programs and asking only moderate charges for them. And it will also allow you to use the program free from guilt.

SUPPLEMENTAL PROGRAM CONTENTS

There are seven files offered by PC SIG on a supplemental program diskette. Four of the files are held in the special ARC format. These files actually contain dozens of other files, all neatly packed to make the most efficient use of disk space. (See the ARC description in Chapter 15.) To release these files you'll need to un-ARC them. This is done by running the INSTALL batch program.

The directory of the diskette is:

```
Volume in drive A has no label
Directory of A:\

ABOUT                 5475  4-15-87      4:59p
AUTOMENU ARC         86329  3-16-87      7:13p
DISKTOOL ARC         62052  3-16-87      7:06p
INSTALL BAT            450  4-17-87     10:45p
PACKDISK ARC         25554  3-16-87      7:03p
PKX34A20 COM         58368  3-13-87      1:57p
TOOLS1 ARC           53029  3-30-87      9:19a
                 8 File(s) 67584 bytes free
```

ABOUT is a text file describing the disk. To read this file, use the TYPE command. Press Ctrl S to pause the display; any other key to resume. Place the supplemental programs diskette into drive A and close the drive door. Type:

C > A:

to log to drive A. Then type:

A > TYPE ABOUT

If the MORE filter is on your path, try typing:

A > TYPE ABOUT ¦ MORE

This will page the listing a screen at a time as you read it.

ABOUT describes the disk and lists all the files on the disk in both their ARC and un-ARCed formats. Also listed are instructions about the INSTALL.BAT program and PKX34A20.COM. It's important to note that the files will not all fit on a floppy disk in their un-ARCed format. You must un-ARC the files to a hard disk.

INSTALLING THE PROGRAMS

After reading the ABOUT file, type:

A > INSTALL

This runs the INSTALL.BAT program which transfers the files from drive A to drive C and un-ARCs them. The following is a copy of INSTALL.BAT for your examination. If you think your batch file skills are up to par, try to determine what it does. (A description follows.)

```
ECHO off
cls
ECHO !This program will unpack your Supplemental Programs Diskette
ECHO !and put those programs in the directory \TOOLS on drive C.
ECHO !
ECHO !Make sure this diskette is in drive A.
ECHO !
ECHO !This will take approximately 3 minutes.
ECHO !Press Ctrl C to stop or
PAUSE
c:
cd \
md \tools
cd \tools
copy a:pkx34a20.com
pkx34a20
pkxarc a:automenu.arc
pkxarc a:disktool.arc
pkxarc a:packdisk.arc
pkxarc a:tools1.arc
```

Fig. 17-1. Listing of the INSTALL.BAT file.

What the INSTALL.BAT Program Does in Detail. First, INSTALL.BAT creates a directory named \TOOLS on drive C. All the files on drive A will be un-ARCed and placed in this directory. From there you can further copy the files to any subdirectory you wish. For example, you may want to copy all the Automenu files to their own subdirectory. Do this after the INSTALL.BAT program is run. After INSTALL creates the \TOOLS subdirectory, it copies the PKX34A20.COM file to drive C. When run, the PKX34A20.COM file unfolds itself into the files which do the actual unpacking: PKARC and PKXARC along with their appropriate .DOC files and a few other goodies. Once this is done every other .ARC file on drive A is un-ARCed to the \TOOLS subdirectory by the PKSARC program (the final lines of the batch file).

When the whole job is finished you'll be logged to the \TOOLS subdirectory on drive C. You'll also have a pretty ungainly subdirectory full of files. Each file on the PC SIG programs diskette is listed below in roughly the same order as it will appear in your \TOOLS subdirectory. Following each file name is a description of the name. Based on this description you can elect to move the file off elsewhere or perhaps keep it in the \TOOLS subdirectory for a while.

THE MANUAL AND .DOC FILES

Several of the programs on the supplemental programs disk contain companion .DOC files or files titled MANUAL. These contain the instructions, or documentation, for the programs which share their name. (MANUAL contains the documentation for the PACKDISK series of programs.) In the public domain-shareware world, this is how the instruction manuals are distributed.

There are two methods of reading the instructions. One is using the DOS TYPE command. A better way is to print the documentation. A majority of the .DOC files (and MANUAL) have been formatted perfectly for a dump to your printer. To get a hard copy of them, set your printer so that the print head is at the first line of a sheet of paper. Then, at the DOS prompt, type:

C>COPY filename.DOC PRN

This copies the documentation file, filename.DOC, to the printer (DOS's PRN device). Because most of these files are pre-formatted, they will come out rather nicely on the printer. Some even have headers, footers and page numbers.

Staple together the various documentation files you produce and put them with the rest of your computer documentation. It's much easier to refer to a hard copy list of instructions about a utility than it is to try to memorize commands as DOS TYPE's them—or get stuck in the middle of a utility and not know how to get out.

PKX34A20.COM

The PKS34A20.COM program is the latest version of the PKARC utility as this book goes to press. This file unpacks itself into the appropriate PKARC file utilities. PKARC is the latest version of the ARC program for the IBM PC and compatibles.

A $20 donation is requested for using this program. For $45 or more you will get the latest version of PKARC directly from PKWARE, Inc. For more information on this program, write to:

PKWARE, Inc.
7032 Ardara Avenue
Glendale, WI 53209

PKARC.COM

This program crunches, munches and scrunches programs, data and text files, then sticks them all into one ARC (archive) file. This makes it easy to transmit a group of files over a modem, or to pack a few dozen files into half the space.

PKARC.DOC

This is the documentation file for PKARC.COM.

PKXARC.COM

This program unpacks programs, data and text files from ARC files created by PKARC. Individual files, or groups of files can be extracted. The X in the file title stands for eXtract.

PKXARC.DOC

This is the documentation file for PKXARC.COM.

PKXARCJR.COM

This is a special version of the PKARC program for the PCjr. If you don't have a PCjr, this file can be erased.

README.DOC

This file contains a notice to people who distribute the PKX34A20.COM files and the PKARC files.

AUTOMENU.ARC

The files in the AUTOMENU.ARC file compose the entire Automenu system. They are the same programs you'd get if you ordered the Automenu package (version 4.0). The Automenu menu definition system was discussed in length in Chapter 9. For more information on Automenu write to:

Magee Enterprises
6577 Peachtree Industrial Blvd.
Norcross, Georgia 30092-3796

AUTO.BAT

A batch file which starts the AUTOMENU program, then runs an AUTOTEMP batch file.

AUTOCUST.COM

This is the AUTOMENU customization program.

AUTOEXEC.BAT

A sample batch file included on the Automenu disk. Basically, it contains a few typical AUTOEXEC.BAT statements (PROMPT, VER, etc.), then runs the AUTOMENU program.

AUTOMAKE.EXE

This program builds menus for use by AUTOMENU. It's a combination editor/outliner with a on-line help facility to assist in making .MDF (Menu Definition) files.

AUTOMENU.COM

This is the main AUTOMENU program.

AUTOMENU.MDF

A sample menu definition file. It contains some sample menus and can be used as an example for customizing your own .MDF files.

AUTOTEMP.BAT

A small batch file which changes to a directory /GAMES and runs a program BACK (for backgammon). It's used in conjunction with the included menu definition file AUTOMENU.MDF.

DOS.MDF

A sample .MDF file included with Automenu (and used in AUTOMENU.MDF) which contains a number of interesting DOS commands and utilities.

ENTER.MDF

A sample .MDF file which asks for a password (IBM is the password used). This file can be used for security purposes to limit or prevent access to the Automenu system.

INSTALL.BAT

A batch file which installs the AUTOMENU program. It executes the INSTAL.MDF file which actually does all the installation work.

INSTALL.MDF

A menu definition file which installs Automenu. Install asks you a number of questions, then proceeds to install Automenu on your hard disk.

PRINTER.MDF

A menu definition file which sets printer controls and options such as bold printing, wide printing, compressed, etc. This sample included with Automenu was tailored to Epson and Epson compatible printers.

READ.ME

A small text file which contains a plug from Automenu's Author, Marshall W. Magee, and an address where to write for additional information.

SW.COM

A screen swap program. If you have two monitors installed in your PC, one color and one monochrome, SW switches from the current monitor to the other. Or SW C is used to turn on the color monitor and SW M is used to turn on the monochrome. An interesting extra.

SW.DOC

This is a text file describing the SW.COM program.

TIME.MDF

A sample menu definition file which shows how a command or program can be executed at a specific time of day.

DISKTOOL.ARC

DISKTOOL is a remarkable collection of disk utilities all in one package. The hacker in you will really admire this program. With DISKTOOL you can change file attributes (make things invisible, etc.) examine the actual bytes on disk and optionally change them, erase files, search for files, rename files—a whole abundance of utilities, all in an easy-to-use package. The author is distributing DISKTOOL as shareware and would like a $20 donation for it. For information, write to:

R. P. Gage
1125 6th Street N., #43
Columbus, MS 39701

DISKTOOL.DOC

This is the documentation for the DISKTOOL program (DT below). If you intend on seriously using DISKTOOL, I'd advise you to print this out.

DT.COM

This is the actual DISKTOOL program—which is named DT for some reason. If you'd like, rename the file to DISKTOOL, or keep it at DT which is easier to type.

DT.PIF

This is one of those mysterious .PIF files which appeared about the same time Microsoft started to sell their Windows environment. PIF stands for Program Information File, and it's used by Windows to determine how the program is run. If you don't have Windows, this file may be deleted.

PACKDISK.ARC

PACKDISK contains unfragmenting and directory squeezing programs (PACKDISK and FINDFRAG) as discussed in Chapter 15. It also contains several other, interesting directory manipulation programs, as well as a PARK program for certain types of hard disks. The PACKDISK series of programs are shareware and the suggested donation if you use and enjoy the programs is $35.00. For additional information on PACKDISK, write to:

SoftPatch
P.O. Box 11455
San Francisco, CA 94101

DELDIR.COM

This powerful command deletes a subdirectory, all files in the subdirectory, and all subdirectories and files under those subdirectories. Or you could say, in the tree structure of a disk drive, DELDIR is a chainsaw: Needless to say, DELDIR should be used with extreme caution.

LISTFRAG.COM

Lists all fragmented files and non-contiguous chains in the specified directory or directories. Unlike CHKDSK, LISTFRAG also displays fragmented directory files and all files in any subdirectories under the one specified.

MANUAL

A text file which contains instructions and documentation for all the PACKDISK programs. It can be TYPED at the DOS command prompt, or sent to the printer as described earlier in this chapter.

NAMEDIR.COM

This program renames a subdirectory on disk. (Presently there's no way to do this using DOS.) Be careful of the format of this command; it uses a double backslash, \ \, to denote the new name of the subdirectory.

PACKDISK.COM

This file unfragments files and subdirectories, squeezes the tombstones from directories, and packs files toward the front of the disk.

PARK.COM

This program was included because it's part of the shareware distribution agreement (and as such, cannot be deleted). Considering the warning about all PARK programs not working with each hard disk it might be a wise decision not to use this program. It will not harm the hard disk, yet with some hard disks it might not work.

TRANSDIR.COM

This utility moves a directory, along with all its files and subdirectories, to another spot on disk. Unlike XCOPY, which does something similar, TRANSDIR also erases the original files and subdirectories. It's more like a move than a copy.

TOOLS1.ARC

These programs are taken from a variety of sources. Where indicated, the author requests money for the program. Otherwise, consider the program public domain and use it freely.

ASK.COM

This program can be used in a batch file to get a Yes or No response from the user. It works like ECHO, displaying whatever message is listed after ASK on the command line. Then ASK waits for either the Y or N key to be pressed. Pressing N returns an ERRORLEVEL code of 1, pressing Y returns a code of 0. ASK.COM is discussed in Chapter 7.

CRYPT.BAS

This is a demonstration program written in the BASIC programming language and saved as an ASCII file. CRYPT.BAS takes one file, encrypts its data according to a key string value, and then writes the encrypted data out to a second file. CRYPT.BAS is discussed and demonstrated in Chapter 13.

ETIME.COM

This program displays the words "End Time =" followed by the current date and time. It can be used in conjunction with STIME to log the time spent on your computer. ETIME is discussed in Chapter 14.

FINDHIDE.COM

This program works like the DIR command, except FINDHIDE displays all files in the current directory. Invisible files are prefixed by an asterisk (*). It is discussed in Chapter 13.

GREET.COM

This program is very friendly. It displays Good Morning, Good Evening, or Good Afternoon depending on the time of day. If a message is typed after GREET on the command line, that message is displayed after the time of day greeting.

HIDE.COM

This program hides selected programs on disk. Only single filenames can be listed after HIDE, no wildcards. Once a file is hidden it is excluded from all DOS searches and not listed by the DIR command. HIDE.COM is discussed in Chapter 13.

LOCK.COM

This utility program works like placing a write protect tab on the hard disk. LOCK.COM is a memory resident program which intercepts all writes, changes and modifications to the hard drive and returns a Write Protected error to DOS. It can be turned on or off at any time.

LOCK.DOC

This is the documentation file for LOCK.COM.

PASSWORD.BAS

This program is written in the BASIC programming language and saved as an ASCII file. PASSWORD.BAS is best used in the computer's AUTOEXEC file. It asks for a system password to be entered. If the proper password is not typed after three tries, the system is locked and cannot be reset or rebooted. PASSWORD.BAS is discussed and demonstrated in Chapter 13.

PASSWORD.DOC

This is the documentation file for PASSWORD.BAS.

SDIR5.COM

SDIR5 is Super-Directory version 5. This program contains all kinds of interesting directory and file manipulation utilities. You can sort a directory, change filenames and attributes, rename, TYPE, delete, copy—a whole variety of options all within this one program. SDIR5 is distributed as shareware and the author requests a donation of $10.00 if you use the program. For more information, contact:

W. Lawrence Hatt
76 Melville Drive
Nepean, Ontario
Canada, K2J 2E1

SDIR5.DOC

This is the documentation file for SDIR5.COM.

STIME.COM

This program displays "Start Time =" followed by the current date and time. It can be used in conjunction with ETIME to log time on your computer. STIME is discussed in Chapter 14.

TREED.COM

This program displays "Start Time =" followed by the current date and time. It can be used in conjunction with ETIME to log time on your computer. STIME is discussed in Chapter 14.

TREED.DOC

This is the documentation file for TREED.COM.

TSTAMP.COM

This program displays the current time and date as kept by your computer. It's part of the STIME and ETIME series of programs and is discussed in Chapter 14.

UNHIDE.COM

This program unhides hidden programs on disk. Only single filenames can be unhidden, and it does not accept wildcards. If a file is hidden it can be unhidden with UNHIDE. The FINDHIDE utility is used to display hidden files in the current directory. UNHIDE is discussed in Chapter 13.

WHEREIS.COM

This is a neat utility which locates any file or group of files on disk. Typing WHEREIS

*.BAT displays all batch files on disk and the subdirectory where they're located.

WHEREIS.DOC

This is the documentation file for WHEREIS.COM.

XWORD221.DOC

This is the documentation file for XWORD223.COM (below). Though the documentation is for version 2.21, it still applies to the version supplied on disk.

XWORD223.EXE

The XWORD utility (223 is the version number, 2.23) transfers text and word processing files between various formats, including: WordStar, MultiMate, XYWrite, WordPerfect and text formatted files. It also performs a basic data encryption using logical manipulations (NOT, ROL, AND, OR and XOR) on each character in the file. XWORD is distributed as shareware and the author requests $15.00 if you use the program. For information, contact:

Ronald Gans
350 West 55th Street
New York, NY 10019

Appendix A: Summary of DOS Commands

Command	Format

ASSIGN: External ASSIGN d1 = d2 [,d3 = d4], [etc.]

Reassigns logical devices, where d1 is the default and d2 is the new device. May be used with certain applications that automatically look to drive A for overlay or help files. To run such programs on a hard disk, the command would be: ASSIGN A = C.

BACKUP: External BACKUP d:[path] [filename] [.ext] d: [/S] [/M] [/A] [/D:mm-dd-yy]

Backs up files on the first specified drive onto floppy diskettes in the second drive specification. May be used to backup entire hard disks or only specified subdirectories or files. For example, to backup all .WKS files in the LOTUS subdirectory, the command would be: BACKUP C:\LOTUS*.WKS A:. /S option backs up all subdirectories in specified directory. /M option only backs up files modified since last backup. /A option prompts before overwriting existing backup files on diskette. /D backs up files modified after specified date.

BREAK: Internal BREAK [ON] [OFF]

Disables user termination of commands with ^C except for DOS requests for input. Default is OFF.

CHDIR: Internal CD [d:] [[path]

Changes current directory. Used to move from one directory to another. If moving from parent to child directory, preceding backslash (\ ) is omitted. May be used without optional path specifier to display current directory.

CHKDSK: External CHKDSK [d:] [filename] [.ext] [/F] [/V]

Displays file space remaining; memory remaining, directory of disk, hidden files, and volume label. If optional filename is provided, displays number of non-contiguous clusters occupied by file. /F option recovers data on unusable clusters. /V option displays messages indicating its progress at recovering lost clusters.

CLS: Internal CLS Clears the screen display.

COMP: External COMP [d:] [path] [filename] [.ext] [d:] [path] [filename] [.ext]

Compares two files and reports discrepancies.

COPY: Internal COPY [d:] [path] [filename] [.ext] [d:] [path] [filename] [.ext] [/V]

Copies file from one location to another. File may be renamed in process by specifying a new name for the destination. /V option verifies that file is copied correctly.

DATE: External DATE [mm-dd-yy]

Displays current date and prompts user to enter new date unless optional date is provided in command. Pressing Enter accepts current date as new date.

DEL: Internal DEL [d:] [path] [filename] [.ext]

Deletes specified file or files.

DIR: Internal DIR [d:] [path] [filename] [.ext] [/P] [/W]

Displays directory of specified drive and subdirectory. When used with optional filename(s), displays listing of specified files. Long directory listings are scrolled. /P option halts screen for viewing. /W option displays filenames in five columns across the screen.

DISKCOMP: External DISKCOMP [d:] [d:] [/1] [/8]

Compares two diskettes to see if they are identical. /1 option compares only one side of diskettes. /8 option checks 8 sectors per track.

DISKCOPY: External DISKCOPY [d:] [d:] [/1]

Copies contents of one floppy diskette onto another. May not be used with hard disks. /1 option copies only one side. Will format target diskette if it is not already formatted.

ERASE: Internal ERASE [d:] [path] [filename] [.ext]

Erases specified file(s). Same as DEL.

FDISK: External FDISK

Used to partition hard disk and select active partition.

FIND: External FIND[/V] [/C] [/N] *string* [d:] [path] [filename] [.ext] . . .

Finds all occurrences of *string* in specified file(s). Directory listings may be piped through FIND. For example, DIR | FIND "01/01/88" will find every file tagged with the specified date. /V option excludes lines containing *string*. /C option counts occurrences of *string*. /N option numbers each line as found.

FORMAT: External FORMAT [d:] [/S] [/1] [/8] [/B]

Formats disk. With floppy diskettes, includes both physical and logical formats; with hard disks only includes logical format. /S option places system files on disk. /V allows user to provide volume label for disk. /1 formats diskettes single-sided (DOS 1.0 format). /8 formats only 8 sectors per track. /B formats diskette and leaves room for system files to be transferred later (format is 8 sectors per track in this case).

GRAPHICS: External GRAPHICS

Enables graphics output to printer via PrtSc key. Printer must be capable of printing IBM graphics character set.

LABEL: Internal LABEL [d:] [*string*]

Used to add or change a volume label to a formatted disk. If optional *string* is omitted, displays current volume label.

MKDIR: Internal MD [d:] path

Creates a new subdirectory with the specified path name.

MODE: External MODE [d:] [= d:] [options]

Used to set system device specifications, including video display type, communications port configuration, and parallel printer options. Also used to redirect output from parallel to serial port.

MORE: External MORE

Filters output to screen a screenful at a time. Directory listings can be piped through MORE as follows: DIR | MORE.

PATH: Internal PATH [d:] path; etc.

Sets up one or more search paths for .COM, .EXE and .BAT files. Search path is followed if a specified file is not found in the default path.

PRINT: External PRINT [d:] [path] [filename] [.ext] [/P] [/T] [/C]

Used to set up a print queue of up to 10 files. /P option adds file to previously established queue. /T option terminates print queue. /C removes file from queue.

PROMPT: Internal PROMPT [*string*] [$option] [etc.]

Used to change system prompt. The command PROMPT without specified *string* or options resets system prompt.

$t displays time.
$d displays date.
$p displays current path.
$n displays current drive.
$g displays ">" symbol.
$l displays "<" symbol.
$_ inserts return and line feed.
$b displays "|" symbol.
$q displays " = " symbol.
$h destructive backspace.
$e escape character.

RECOVER: External RECOVER [d:] [path] filename [.ext]

Used to recover undamaged portions of a file when disk has developed one or more bad sectors.

RENAME: Internal REN [d:] [path] filename [.ext] filename [.ext]

Renames specified file to new filename.

RESTORE: External RESTORE d: [d:] [path] [filename] [.ext] [/S] [/P]

Restores onto hard disk files previously backed up onto floppies. /S option restores all subdirectories. /P option prompts user that file to be restored has been changed since it was last backed up.

RMDIR: Internal RD [d:] path

Removes an empty subdirectory. If subdirectory is not empty, it cannot be removed.

SORT: External SORT <[d:] [path] [filename] [.ext]>[/R]

Sorts contents from the input file into alphabetical or reverse (/R) order. Directory listings can be sorted by piping them through the SORT filter as follows: DIR | SORT.

SYS: External SYS d:

Transfers system files onto specified disk. This operation can only be performed if space has been left on the disk in advance as with the FORMAT /B option.

TIME: External TIME [hh:mm:ss:xx]

Displays current time and prompts user to enter new time. If optional time is included in command, this becomes the current time.

TREE: External TREE [d:] [/F]

Displays a list of all subdirectories excluding the root directory. /F option is used to display all files in each subdirectory.

TYPE: Internal TYPE [d:] [path] filename [.ext]

Sends contents of specified file to the output device. Output may be printed by first entering Ctrl PrtSc.

VERIFY: Internal VERIFY [ON/OFF]

Checks status of any file copied to disk. The default is OFF. Entering VERIFY without optional ON/OFF displays status of the switch.

VER: Internal VER

Displays DOS version number.

VOL: Internal VOL [d:]

Displays current volume label.

Appendix B:

Summary of

EDLIN Commands

Insert Line:

I   Inserts a new line at the default line number. When
                creating a new file, inserts at line number 1.

*n*I   Inserts a new line a line number *n*. The old line number
                n and all lines below are renumbered.

.I   Inserts a new line at the current line number. The current
                line and all lines below are renumbered.

#I   Inserts a new line at the end of the file.

+*n*I   Inserts a new line *n* lines forward from the current line.

−*n*I   Inserts a new line *n* lines back from the current line.

List:

L   List 23 lines: 11 before the current line, the current line,
                and 11 lines after the current line. With small files, will
                display the entire file.

*x,y*L	List lines beginning with *x* and ending with *y*. If more than 23 lines are specified, the screen will scroll.
*x*L	List 23 lines beginning with line *x*.
*,y*L	List 11 lines preceding *y*, line *y*, and 11 lines following *y*.

Search:

S *string*	Searches file for specified string.
*x,y*S*string*	Searches file for specified *string* within range specified by *x* and *y*.
x,y?S*string*	Searches file for specified *string* within specified range. Stops at each occurrence and displays "OK ?" prompt to stop. Answering "Y" stops; "N" advances to the next occurrence of the *string*.

Replace:

R*string1*^Z*string2*	Replaces all occurrences of *string1* with *string2* in file.
*x,y*R*string1*^Z*string2*	Replaces all occurrences of *string1* with *string2* within range specified by *x* and *y*.
x,y?R*string1*^Z*string2*	Replaces individual occurrences of *string1* with *string2* within specified range based upon user approval to "OK ?" prompt. Answering "Y" accepts change; "N" disallows change.

Delete:

D	Deletes current line. All subsequent lines are renumbered.
*x*D	Deletes line *x*. All subsequent lines are renumbered.
*x,y*D	Deletes lines beginning with *x* and ending with *y*. All subsequent lines are renumbered.
*,y*D	Deletes lines from current line to line *y*. All subsequent lines are renumbered.
*x,.*D	Deletes lines from *x* up to current line. All subsequent lines are renumbered.

Copy:

x,y,zC	Copies lines beginning with x and ending with y to line z. Leaves original lines in place. All lines following line z are renumbered.
x,x,zC	Copies line x to line z. All lines following z are renumbered.

Move:

x,y,zM	Moves lines beginning with x and ending with y to line z. Moved lines are renumbered as are lines following moved lines.
x,x,zM	Moves line x to line z.

Edit:

n	Selects line for editing.
$-n$	Selects n lines back for editing.
$+n$	Selects line n lines forward for editing.
.	Selects current line for editing.
F1	Calls up next character from line buffer.
F2x	Calls up all characters up to but not including x from line buffer.
F3	Calls up remaining characters from line buffer.
F4x	Deletes all characters up to but not including x.
Del	Deletes one character.
BkSpc	Destructive back space.
Ins	Toggles insert mode on for inserting characters.
Esc	Cancel current editing changes.

End:

E	Ends editing session and saves file to disk.

Quit:

Q	Quits editing session and leaves file unchanged. Used to abort editing session.

Appendix C:
Extended ASCII Chart

ASCII (pronounced ASK-ee) is an acronym for the American Standard Code for Information Interchange. The ASCII codes from 0 through 127 are assigned to letters, numbers, special characters, and other symbols. ASCII codes 128 through 255 vary from computer to computer. On IBM PC's and compatibles, these characters are referred to as the *Extended ASCII set*. The actual characters displayed on the screen are in Table 3-1.

Char	Dec	Hex	Binary	Code	Char	Dec	Hex	Binary	Code
^@	0	0h	00000000	NUL	SPC	32	20h	00100000	
^A	1	1h	00000001	SOH	!	33	21h	00100001	
^B	2	2h	00000010	STX	"	34	22h	00100010	
^C	3	3h	00000011	ETX	#	35	23h	00100011	
^D	4	4h	00000100	EOT	$	36	24h	00100100	
^E	5	5h	00000101	ENQ	%	37	25h	00100101	
^F	6	6h	00000110	ACK	&	38	26h	00100110	
^G	7	7h	00000111	BEL	'	39	27h	00100111	
^H	8	8h	00001000	BS	(	40	28h	00101000	
^I	9	9h	00001001	HT	)	41	29h	00101001	
^J	10	Ah	00001010	LF	*	42	2Ah	00101010	
^K	11	Bh	00001011	VT	+	43	2Bh	00101011	
^L	12	Ch	00001100	FF	,	44	2Ch	00101100	
^M	13	Dh	00001101	CR	–	45	2Dh	00101101	

Char	Dec	Hex	Binary	Code		Char	Dec	Hex	Binary	Code
^N	14	Eh	00001110	SO		.	46	2Eh	00101110	
^O	15	Fh	00001111	SI		/	47	2Fh	00101111	
^P	16	10h	00010000	DLE		0	48	30h	00110000	
^Q	17	11h	00010001	DC1		1	49	31h	00110001	
^R	18	12h	00010010	DC2		2	50	32h	00110010	
^S	19	13h	00010011	DC3		3	51	33h	00110011	
^T	20	14h	00010100	DC4		4	52	34h	00110100	
^U	21	15h	00010101	NAK		5	53	35h	00110101	
^V	22	16h	00010110	SYN		6	54	36h	00110110	
^W	23	17h	00010111	ETB		7	55	37h	00110111	
^X	24	18h	00011000	CAN		8	56	38h	00111000	
^Y	25	19h	00011001	EM		9	57	39h	00111001	
^Z	26	1Ah	00011010	SUB		:	58	3Ah	00111010	
^[	27	1Bh	00011011	ESC		;	59	3Bh	00111011	
^\	28	1Ch	00011100	FS		<	60	3Ch	00111100	
^]	29	1Dh	00011101	GS		=	61	3Dh	00111101	
^^	30	1Eh	00011110	RS		>	62	3Eh	00111110	
^_	31	1Fh	00011111	US		?	63	3Fh	00111111	
@	64	40h	01000000			`	96	60h	01100000	
A	65	41h	01000001			a	97	61h	01100001	
B	66	42h	01000010			b	98	62h	01100010	
C	67	43h	01000011			c	99	63h	01100011	
D	68	44h	01000100			d	100	64h	01100100	
E	69	45h	01000101			e	101	65h	01100101	
F	70	46h	01000110			f	102	66h	01100110	
G	71	47h	01000111			g	103	67h	01100111	
H	72	48h	01001000			h	104	68h	01101000	
I	73	49h	01001001			i	105	69h	01101001	
J	74	4Ah	01001010			j	106	6Ah	01101010	
K	75	4Bh	01001011			k	107	6Bh	01101011	
L	76	4Ch	01001100			l	108	6Ch	01101100	
M	77	4Dh	01001101			m	109	6Dh	01101101	
N	78	4Eh	01001110			n	110	6Eh	01101110	
O	79	4Fh	01001111			o	111	6Fh	01101111	
P	80	50h	01010000			p	112	70h	01110000	
Q	17	51h	01010001			q	113	71h	01110001	
R	18	52h	01010010			r	114	72h	01110010	
S	19	53h	01010011			s	115	73h	01110011	
T	20	54h	01010100			t	116	74h	01110100	
U	21	55h	01010101			u	117	75h	01110101	

Char	Dec	Hex	Binary	Code		Char	Dec	Hex	Binary	Code
V	22	56h	01010110			v	118	76h	01110110	
W	23	57h	01010111			w	119	77h	01110111	
X	24	58h	01011000			x	120	78h	01111000	
Y	25	59h	01011001			y	121	79h	01111001	
Z	26	5Ah	01011010			z	122	7Ah	01111010	
[	27	5Bh	01011011			{	123	7Bh	01111011	
\	28	5Ch	01011100			¦	124	7Ch	01111100	
]	29	5Dh	01011101			}	125	7Dh	01111101	
^	30	5Eh	01011110			~	126	7Eh	01111110	
_	31	5Fh	01011111			DEL	127	7Fh	01111111	

(See the chart for corresponding characters.)

	Dec	Hex	Binary			Dec	Hex	Binary
	128	80h	10000000			160	A0h	10100000
	129	81h	10000001			161	A1h	10100001
	130	82h	10000010			162	A2h	10100010
	131	83h	10000011			163	A3h	10100011
	132	84h	10000100			164	A4h	10100100
	133	85h	10000101			165	A5h	10100101
	134	86h	10000110			166	A6h	10100110
	135	87h	10000111			167	A7h	10100111
	136	88h	10001000			168	A8h	10101000
	137	89h	10001001			169	A9h	10101001
	138	8Ah	10001010			170	AAh	10101010
	139	8Bh	10001011			171	ABh	10101011
	140	8Ch	10001100			172	ACh	10101100
	141	8Dh	10001101			173	ADh	10101101
	142	8Eh	10001110			174	AEh	10101110
	143	8Fh	10001111			175	AFh	10101111
	144	90h	10010000			176	B0h	10110000
	145	91h	10010001			177	B1h	10110001
	146	92h	10010010			178	B2h	10110010
	147	93h	10010011			179	B3h	10110011
	148	94h	10010100			180	B4h	10110100
	149	95h	10010101			181	B5h	10110101
	150	96h	10010110			182	B6h	10110110
	151	97h	10010111			183	B7h	10110111
	152	98h	10011000			184	B8h	10111000
	153	99h	10011001			185	B9h	10111001
	154	9Ah	10011010			186	BAh	10111010
	155	9Bh	10011011			187	BBh	10111011
	156	9Ch	10011100			188	BCh	10111100
	157	9Dh	10011101			189	BDh	10111101

Char	Dec	Hex	Binary	Code		Char	Dec	Hex	Binary	Code
	158	9Eh	10011110				190	BEh	10111110	
	159	9Fh	10011111				191	BFh	10111111	
	192	C0h	11000000				224	E0h	11100000	
	193	C1h	11000001				225	E1h	11100001	
	194	C2h	11000010				226	E2h	11100010	
	195	C3h	11000011				227	E3h	11100011	
	196	C4h	11000100				228	E4h	11100100	
	197	C5h	11000101				229	E5h	11100101	
	198	C6h	11000110				230	E6h	11100110	
	199	C7h	11000111				231	E7h	11100111	
	200	C8h	11001000				232	E8h	11101000	
	201	C9h	11001001				233	E9h	11101001	
	202	CAh	11001010				234	EAh	11101010	
	203	CBh	11001011				235	EBh	11101011	
	204	CCh	11001100				236	ECh	11101100	
	205	CDh	11001101				237	EDh	11101101	
	206	CEh	11001110				238	EEh	11101110	
	207	CFh	11001111				239	EFh	11101111	
	208	D0h	11010000				240	F0h	11110000	
	209	D1h	11010001				241	F1h	11110001	
	210	D2h	11010010				242	F2h	11110010	
	211	D3h	11010011				243	F3h	11110011	
	212	D4h	11010100				244	F4h	11110100	
	213	D5h	11010101				245	F5h	11110101	
	214	D6h	11010110				246	F6h	11110110	
	215	D7h	11010111				247	F7h	11110111	
	216	D8h	11011000				248	F8h	11111000	
	217	D9h	11011001				249	F9h	11111001	
	218	DAh	11011010				250	FAh	11111010	
	219	DBh	11011011				251	FBh	11111011	
	220	DCh	11011100				252	FCh	11111100	
	221	DDh	11011101				253	FDh	11111101	
	222	DEh	11011110				254	FEh	11111110	
	223	DFh	11011111				255	FFh	11111111	

Control Character Codes:

NUL – Null
SOH – Start Of Heading
STX – Start of TeXt
ETX – End of TeXt

DC1 – Device Control 1 (XON)
DC2 – Device Control 2 (AUXON)
DC3 – Device Control 3 (XOFF)
DC4 – Device Control 4 (AUXOFF)

EOT - End Of Transmission	NAK - Negative AcKnowledgement
ENQ - ENQuiry	SYN - SYNchronus file
ACK - ACKnowledge	ETB - End of Tranmission Block
BEL - Bell	CAN - CANcel
BS - Back Space	EM - End of Medium
HT - Horizontal Tab	SUB - SUBstitute
LF - Line Feed	ESC - ESCape
VT - Vertical Tab	FS - File (or Form) Separator
FF - Form Feed	GS - Group Separator
CR - Carriage Return	RS - Record Separator
SO - Shift Out	US - Unit Separator
SI - Shift In	SPC - SPaCe
DLE - Data Link Escape	DEL - DELete, RUBout

	00	01	02	03	04	05	06	07	08	09	0A	0B	0C	0D	0E	0F
00	(Control Characters)
10
20		!	"	#	$	%	&	'	(	)	*	+	,	-	.	/
30	0	1	2	3	4	5	6	7	8	9	:	;	<	=	>	?
40	@	A	B	C	D	E	F	G	H	I	J	K	L	M	N	O
50	P	Q	R	S	T	U	V	W	X	Y	Z	[	\	]	^	_
60	`	a	b	c	d	e	f	g	h	i	j	k	l	m	n	o
70	p	q	r	s	t	u	v	w	x	y	z	{			}	~	△
80	Ç	ü	é	â	ä	à	å	ç	ê	ë	è	ï	î	ì	Ä	Å
90	É	æ	Æ	ô	ö	ò	û	ù	ÿ	Ö	Ü	¢	£	¥	₧	ƒ
A0	á	í	ó	ú	ñ	Ñ	ª	º	¿	⌐	¬	½	¼	¡	«	»
B0
C0
D0
E0	α	β	Γ	π	Σ	σ	µ	τ	Φ	θ	Ω	δ	∞	φ	ε	∩
F0	≡	±	≥	≤	⌠	⌡	÷	≈	°	∙	·	√	ⁿ	²	■	

Extended ASCII Chart

Appendix D: Product Names and Addresses

The following products are mentioned in this book. The manufacturer or distributor's name is included here for those desiring additional information:

	Product	*Category*
ARCHIVE Corp. 1650 Sunflower Ave. Costa Mesa, CA 92626	Streaming	Book
Borland International 4113 Scotts Valley Drive Scotts Valley, CA 95066	SuperKey	Security Software
Core International 7171 N. Federal Highway Boca Raton, FL 33431	CORE*fast*	Backup Software
Fifth Generation Systems 909 Electric Ave., Suite 308 Seal Beach, CA 90740	Fastback	Backup Software
IOMEGA 1281 Main Street Holly Pond Plaza Stamford, CT 06902	Bernoulli Box	Removable Disk

Irwin Magnetics 2101 Commonwealth Blvd. Ann Arbor, MI 48105	400XT Tape Backup System EZTAPE	Tape Backup
Maynard Electronics, Inc. 460 E. Semoran Blvd. Casselberry, FL 32707	ERLL	Disk Controller
MLI Microsystems P.O. Box 825 Framingham, MA 01701	POWER TOOLS	Disk Utility
Paul Mace Software 123 First Street Ashland, OR 97520	The Mace Utilities	Disk Utility
PC SIG 1030D East Duane Ave. Sunnyvale, CA 94086	Shareware	
Personal Computer Support Group 11035 Harry Hines Blvd., #206 Dallas, TX 75229	Lightning	Disk Cache
Peter Norton Computing 2210 Wilshire Blvd. #186 Santa Monica, CA 90403	The Norton Utilities	Disk Utility
SoftLogic Solutions 530 Chestnut Street Manchester, NH 03101	CUBIT	Disk Optimizer
Tandon Corporation 405 Science Drive Moorpark, CA 93021	Ad-PAC 2	Removable Disk

Index

A

access, 14
access arm, 15
active partition, 22
alphanumeric data, 4
ANSI.SYS, 157
appending, 54
application programs, 90, 100
archiving programs, 260
ASCII character set borders, 150
ASCII code, 4
ASSIGN command, 71
ATTRIB command, 223
auto menu, 137-165
automatic startup batch files, 103
AUTOMENU, 167
   command function in, 173
   designing screens for, 171
   dialog functions in, 174
   installation of, 169
   running, 170
   screen function in, 173

B

backing up data and programs,
   185-201
backup switches, 189
batch file engine, 171
batch file menus, 111-126
batch file programming, 97-110
batch files, 56

automatic date and time stamp-
   ing, 104
automatic startup of, 103
automatic system modification,
   104
backups for, 200
creating and running, 98
including messages in, 105
loading application programs
   with, 100
menu systems using, 130
passwords in, 211
simplifying DOS commands with,
   101
termination of, 103
tracking computer usage with,
   239
Bernoulli disk drives, 208
binary numbers, 5
boot disk, 25
boot record, 19
bubble memory, 7

C

CACHE program, 276
caching, 275
chaining, 112, 122
changing current drive, 40
CHDIR command, 78
CHKDSK command, 68, 85

CLS command, 60
clusters, 37, 251
CMOS memory, 6
combining files, 53
command processor, 49
COMMAND/C subcommand, 124
COMP utility, 65
conditional branching, 117
conditional loops, 115
conditional statements, 112, 115
console, 55
converse testing, 122
COPY command, 50
copying files between devices, 55
COREfast backup program, 198
CRYPT.BAS program, 236
CUBIT Optimization software, 263
cylinders, 14

D

data encryption, 222, 233
data representation. 4
data storage, magnetic vs. electronic, 6
DATE command, 59
dBASE, 90
DEBUG command, 226
destination file, 50
device name, 55
DIR command, 38

disk
  access to, 14
  ferric oxide molecules on, 8
  fixed vs. removable, 11
  formats of, 12
  hard vs. floppy, 9
  single-sided vs. double-sided, 14
disk access optimization, 266-278
disk directories, 36
  changing current drive in, 40
  cleaning up, 257
  DIR command for, 38
  entries for, 36
  partial, 42
  printing listings of, 42
  redirecting output of, 46
disk fragmentation, 251
disk storage, basics of, 3-16
DISKCOMP utility, 65
DISKCOPY utilities, 64
DOS, installing new versions of, 30
DOS commands, 48-71
  subdirectories and, 79
  summary of, 290-295
DOS macros, 98
DOS partition, formatting of, 25
DOS shells, 166-184
DOS VDISK, 270
DOS-A-MATIC, 179
drive designators, 20

E

ECHO subcommand, 106
EDLIN utility, 138
  adding borders with, 150
  command summary for, 145-150
  creating new files with, 141
  editing files with, 142
electronic storage, 6
EMS memory, 268
end-of-file, 54
equality conditional test, 119
ERASE command, 56
ERLL coding, 264
error codes, 114
error trap, 121
ERRORLEVEL conditional test, 120
escape codes, 158
escape sequence, 157
EXIST conditional test, 117
exit code, 116
extended ASCII characters, 296-303
extended memory, 267
extensions, 34
external commands, 63
external utilities, 45

F

Fastback backup program, 199
fault tolerant systems, 206
FDISK options menu, 22
file allocation, 251

file allocation tables, 36, 37
file encryption, 177
file mask, 179
file storage, random vs. sequential, 15
file transfer using hidden files, 231
filenames, 34
  rules for, 35
filespec, 76
FIND filter, 45
fixed disks, 11
fixed hard disks, 9
floppy diskette, 9
FOR loops, 114
format options, 26
formats, 12, 50
fragmentation, 251
function keys, 163

G

glossaries, 98
GOTO subcommand, looping with, 112

H

hard disk, 9, 12
  altering structure of, 28
  backup for, 199
  DOS 3.2 preparation of, 28
  floppy disk formatting vs., 19
  installing new DOS versions for, 30
  logical vs. physical formatting for, 17
  low-level format for, 31
  organization strategies for, 72
  partitioning of, 21
  preparation of, 17-33
  protection of, 220
  removable, 207
  repartitioning of, 28
  transferring system files in, 30
  using DEBUG for low-level format, 32
hard disk controller, 32
head crashes, 200
head tolerances, 11
help screens, 132, 134
hidden files, 30, 222
  DOS, 222
  extended ASCII characters for, 230
  file transfer with, 231
  using DEBUG to produce, 226
high-level format, 20

I

icon, 178
infinite loop, 114
initialization, 18
insufficient disk space message, 56
interleave factor, 256

IRWIN tape backup system, 205

L

label, 112
LABEL command, 26
latency, 15
LIGHTNING program, 277
LOCK.COM program, 220
logical device designator, 20
logical formatting, 17, 19
logical information, 18
looping, 111
Lotus 1-2-3, 92
low-level format, 19, 31
  DEBUG use for, 32

M

Mace Utilities, 254, 259
macros, 98
magnetic storage, 7
markers, 82
.MDF file, 175
MEMBRAIN, 272
menu generator, 166
menu screens, 127
  improvement of, 137
menu systems, 126
  batch files in, 130
  development of simple, 127
  function key-based, 163
  help screens in, 134
messages, 105
MKDIR command, 77
MORE filter, 44

N

Norton Utilities, 242, 260
NOT option, 121
numeric data, 4

O

overlay files, 266

P

PACKDISK program, 253
parameters, 50
  replaceable, 108
PARK program, 199
partial directories, 42
partition table, 21
partitions, 21
password security, 177, 211-221
PASSWORD.BAS program, 219
passwords, limits of batch file, 215
PATH command, 88
  application programs and, 90
paths, 76
pause option, 41, 107
physical formatting, 18
polarity, 8
Power Tools utility package, 255
pre-formatted, 21

preventive maintenance, 185
print spoolers, 268
product names and addresses, 304
programming techniques, 111
PROMPT command, 60, 157
prompts, 105

R

RAM disks and techniques, 269, 273
random access memory (RAM), 6
random storage, 16, 249
redirecting directory output, 46
REM subcommand, 106
removable hard disks, 11, 207
RENAME command, 57
repartitioning, 28
REPLACE program, 197
replaceable parameters, 108
resident commands, 49
RESTORE command, 192
RMDIR command, 78
root directory, 36

S

screen menus, 126
sectors, 12
seek time, 15
sequential access data file, 16
sequential storage, 15
shareware programs, 279-289
  installation of, 280
SORT filter, 43
sorting, 259

source file, 50
starting cluster address, 37
storage optimization, 249-265
  formatting techniques for, 255
  hardware for, 264
streaming tape drive, 202
string, 45
subdirectories, 72-96
  copying files between, 79
  DOS commands with, 79
  MKDIR creation of, 77
  moving between, 78
  removal of, 78
  system prompt inclusion of, 86
  transferring system utilities into, 83
  using CHKDSK with, 85
  using directory command with, 81
subdirectory commands, 76
submenu systems, 132
subroutines, 124
SuperKey data encryption program, 237
supplemental program contents, 279
supplemental programming, 281
surfaces, 14
sysgening, 21
system files, transferring of, 30
system modification, automatic, 104

T

text editor, 139

TIME command, 59
tracking computer usage, 239-242
tracks, 12
transferrring system files, 30
TREE command, 88, 92
trees, 76
TYPE command, 58

U

user interface, 178
user prompts, 128
utilities, 49, 281

V

variables, 105, 114
VER command, 62
verify option, 53
video display features, 156
volatile memory, 6
volume labels, 27

W

wide display option, 41
wild cards, 34, 35
  COPY command and, 52
WordPerfect, 92, 153-154
WordStar, 90
working directory, 40
word length, 4

X

XCOPY program, 194

Edited by David Gauthier